Paris Shopkeepers and the Politics of Resentment

. . .

PHILIP G. NORD

Princeton University Press

Princeton, New Jersey

Published by Princeton University Press, 41 William Street,
Princeton, New Jersey 08540
In the United Kingdom: Princeton University Press, Guildford, Surrey

Library of Congress Cataloging in Publication Data will be
found on the last printed page of this book

ISBN 0-691-05454-1

Publication of this book has been aided by the
Ira O. Wade Fund of Princeton University Press

This book has been composed in Linotron Garamond
by Vail-Ballou Press Inc.

Clothbound editions of Princeton University Press books are printed on acid-free
paper, and binding materials are chosen for strength and durability

Printed in the United States of America by Princeton University Press
Princeton, New Jersey

for Deborah and Joseph

Contents

List of Illustrations

Illustrations

List of Figures

List of Tables

Tables

Acknowledgments

TWO SCHOLARS have watched over the preparation of this project from its inception: Robert Paxton and Arno Mayer. Professor Paxton, as teacher and as exemplar, has offered steadfast and thoughtful support. The final design and structure of the project owe much to his probing and perceptive criticism. It was Professor Mayer who first suggested the subject to me. He has subsequently read and reread my work, offering guidance and encouragement when they were most needed.

I want to thank the Georges Lurcy Foundation and the French government for generous grants which financed my first year's research in France. The French-American Foundation provided timely support which permitted me to stay a second and crucial year abroad. I would like to thank not only the institutions that made possible my research in France but also the colleagues and friends who made my stay as pleasurable as it was fruitful. Philippe Vigier kindly welcomed me to join his seminar on small enterprise. There I met Alain Faure, Gerhard Haupt and Andrew Lincoln, friends who encouraged me, shared freely of their ideas and provided indispensable guidance through the archives. On this side of the Atlantic, the companionship—and criticism—of David Crew, Nicholas Papayanis, and Debora Silverman sustained me through the long period of writing up my findings.

Geoffrey Crossick, John Gillis, and Judith Walkowitz read various portions of the initial draft. The completed manuscript, in its various incarnations, was read by Maurice Agulhon, Lynn Hunt, Mark Kesselman, Edward Malefakis, and Allan Silver. I have profited greatly from their comments and suggestions. I owe a special debt to David Abraham and Robert

Acknowledgments

Moeller who worked through the manuscript with a painstaking thoroughness. Their detailed and telling criticisms have prompted me to revise and clarify my thinking on a variety of issues. Miriam Brokaw of Princeton University Press oversaw the final revisions of the manuscript, and I am grateful to her for her patience and intelligent advice.

My most profound debt, however, is to my wife Deborah whose warm and persevering confidence buoyed me through this project from beginning to end.

Bibliographical Abbreviations

AN	Archives Nationales, Paris
APP	Archives de la Préfecture de Police, Paris
AS	Archives de la Seine, Paris
BCC	Bibliothèque de la Chambre de Commerce, Paris
BHVP	Bibliothèque Historique de la Ville de Paris, Paris
BN NAF	Bibliothèque Nationale, Nouvelles Acquisitions Françaises
JOC	*Journal officiel de la République française:* débats parlementaires. Chambre des Députés

Paris Shopkeepers
and the Politics
of Resentment

Introduction

IN A SERIES of speeches—at Bordeaux in 1871, at Grenoble in 1872—Léon Gambetta, lawyer, deputy and ardent republican, announced "the birth of a new France." The future, he declared, belonged to "new social strata," to "that world of labor" which encompassed the manufacturer and the peasant, the professional and the small businessman. These new men were republicans, worthy scions of the Third Estate, but not for them the "misty sentimentality" of *quarante-huitard* republicanism. They embraced the principles of the Great Revolution, Gambetta claimed, in a spirit of sober practicality born of hard work and self-reliance. Their political maturity entitled them to a leading role in public life, but a parasitic oligarchy of notables, vestiges of the old regime, blocked the Third Estate's accession to power. Gambetta served notice on the oligarchy that the forces of democracy would no longer tolerate exclusion from public office.[1]

Historians have followed Gambetta's lead and interpreted the politics of the 1870s in France as a struggle between notables and a resurgent republican movement. And the republicans won the struggle. They outpoliticked their opponents, assembling a grand coalition of bourgeois and small owners. It was this "republican synthesis," in Stanley Hoffmann's phrase, which swept aside the old notability in the seventies and installed France's longest-lived regime since 1789—the Third Republic.[2]

---

[1] On Gambetta's lecture campaign, see Halévy, *The End of the Notables*, pp. 83–101.

[2] Hoffmann, "Paradoxes of the French Political Community," p. 5. See also Elwitt, *The Making of the Third Republic*, p. 1; Gouault, *Comment la*

No sooner had the Republic been established, however, than it was confronted with mass-based oppositional movements on the left and right that challenged its hard-won legitimacy. The collapse of the Union Générale bank in 1882 marked the onset of the Great Depression, a prolonged economic slowdown that placed an enormous strain on the republican synthesis. Hard times stirred working-class discontent and signaled a return to militancy after the quiescent seventies. A miners' strike at Decazeville in 1886 ended in a tense confrontation between labor militants and regular army units called in to maintain order. The new mood of militancy revitalized a socialist movement which had been decimated and dispersed in the wake of the Commune. But the socialism of the 1880s was different from the cooperative socialism of the sixties which had looked to mutualism and a restoration of communal liberties as the vehicle of working-class emancipation.[3] The militants of the last decades of the century stressed rather strike action, agitation for social reform and collectivist schemes that presupposed working-class control of the state. The new militants focused efforts on the formation of combat organizations, of trade unions and proletarian parties. An emergent labor left contested the republican synthesis in the name of the working class. Historians have pointed out that the working class did not constitute a major component of the synthesis.[4] The mobilization of labor then, while a challenge to the regime, did not represent an erosion of its social base.

The Republic, however, faced a threat from a second

France est devenue républicaine, pp. 192–193; and Thomson, *Democracy in France Since 1870*, pp. 40–41.

[3] On the shift from cooperative socialism to collectivism, see Moss, *The Origins of the French Labor Movement*.

[4] Hoffmann, "Paradoxes of the French Political Community," p. 7. Mayeur (*Les Débuts de la IIIe République*, p. 52) speaks of working-class support for the republican movement as "supplementary."

movement of protest which did indeed cut into its base of support. An appropriate label to characterize the phenomenon has not been agreed upon. Historians have referred to it variously as the new right, the revolutionary right or Nationalism.[5] But whatever the label, there is agreement on certain points. Firstly, the new right encompassed a range of submovements: anti-Semitism, Christian Democracy, and of most importance, anti-Dreyfusard Nationalism. These submovements, however diverse, shared a deep-seated antipathy to parliamentarism, an antipathy expressed with a powerful nationalist inflection. The Nationalist, like the socialist movement, experimented in new forms of political organization. The extraparliamentary league, long a mainstay of the radical left's organizational arsenal, was borrowed by the new right and adapted to a novel purpose, to the contestation of republican institutions through mass mobilization for street action.[6] And who constituted the constituency of the Nationalist leagues? They claimed to speak for the nation, for the people, but historians have identified the independent petite bourgeoisie as the new Nationalism's principal clientele.[7] There was then in the late nineteenth century a mobilization of petits bourgeois in opposition to the regime that paralleled the mobilization of labor.

It must be said straightaway that lower middle-class antiparliamentarism was confined to urban France and to Paris above all. In the pre-World War I era, the small-town petite bourgeoisie did not waver in its support of the Third Republic. It was in this rural and provincial milieu that the Radical party, a spin-off of the republican movement and France's largest party after 1900, recruited the bulk of its cadres. The

[5] Sternhell has used all three terms: *La Droite révolutionnaire, 1885–1914; Maurice Barrès et le nationalisme français*, note the title and p. 248.

[6] Rémond, *The Right-Wing in France from 1815 to de Gaulle*, pp. 227–232.

[7] See, for example, Rebérioux, *La République radicale?* p. 36.

Third Republic was indeed a regime rooted in the lower middle class, but at the same time it faced a movement of petit-bourgeois protest in urban areas that drew its strength from one-time participants in the republican synthesis. At the end of the century, the Third Republic confronted a double assault—from labor and from a segment of the petite bourgeoisie. The socialist revival and the origins of the new militancy that underlay it have been researched meticulously. The new Nationalism has also had its historians, but not the lower middle-class mobilization from which it drew its strength. Under what circumstances is the lower middle class moved to protest (I speak here of the independent lower middle class), and what political form does that protest take?

These questions have escaped empirical examination although a variety of hypotheses have been advanced. On the question of the origins of petit-bourgeois protest, the growth of large-scale enterprise and of the department store in particular has been cited time and again by way of explanation.[8] The political import of lower middle-class mobilization, on the other hand, has proven more difficult to pin down. Historians do not agree on the motives underlying petit-bourgeois Nationalism, and the disagreement is rooted in divergent interpretations of the new right. Insofar as the new right is seen as *bien-pensant* and reactionary, lower middle-class Nationalism is attributed to conservative fears of socialism. Interpretations that stress the *frondeur* and plebeian character of the Nationalist movement play up the fractious resentments of its petit-bourgeois constituency.[9] But such generalizations require testing, a task I propose to undertake in the ensuing pages.

Paris was the seat of lower middle-class militancy in late nineteenth-century France, and it was shopkeepers who took

[8] See Chapter II.
[9] See Chapter IX.

the lead. Numerous unsuccessful efforts were made in the 1880s to organize a shopkeeper movement. Retailers in the past had been represented as practitioners of a particular commerce or as members of the wider business community, but never as retailers. Efforts to organize shopkeepers at last bore fruit in 1888 with the formation of the *Ligue syndicale du travail, de l'industrie et du commerce,* the first such organization to attract a sizeable following—well over 140,000 members at its peak in the mid-nineties—as well as the first to last beyond a few years, surviving up to the outbreak of World War I. The Parisian shopkeeper movement represents a genuine and important manifestation of lower middle-class revolt and, as such, promises to shed light on the twin issues of mobilization and political significance raised above. These questions have determined the structure of the argument that follows, which accordingly falls into two parts, the first dealing with the *Ligue*'s origins, the second with its political evolution.

An investigation into the origins and politics of shopkeeper militancy in the 1880s and 1890s is not without wider interest, and for three reasons. Accounts of retailer protest have taken the rise of the *grand magasin* as a natural point of departure, but how is the success of the department store itself to be explained? The expansion of large-scale enterprise is too often taken as a given such that the conditions which shaped and favored commercial concentration have not received the attention they merit. A study of retailer mobilization inescapably poses the question of department store origins and more generally of the dynamics of commercial transformation in the late nineteeth century. The problem of the sources of retailer discontent then points beyond the *grand magasin* to the larger issue of the character and impact of economic change in late nineteenth-century Paris. As for politics, the right-wing inspiration of petit-bourgeois protest in France has often been assumed but remains to be documented. Were shopkeeper activists in fact sympathetic to turn-of-the-century Nationalism? I will answer yes, but such a reply raises as many questions as it puts to rest. Anti-Dreyfusard Nationalism, after all, is most familiar as a reflex of cultural *ressentiment*: anti-intellectual, anti-Semitic, and anticosmopolitan. The involvement of shopkeepers, presumably preoccupied with questions of commercial defense, in a movement of cultural reaction would at first glance seem to pose something of a puzzle. But on more careful inspection, two related points emerge. Retailer militants, too, harbored fears of a national cultural decline; and, *pari passu*, the cultural resentments that enflamed the new right were anchored in the identical socioeconomic context that engendered retailer revolt. The two movements, Nationalist and retailer, were drawn together by a common rhetoric of cultural reaction, born of a common origin. A close look at shopkeeper politics, then, will entail a reappraisal of the roots of the new right, of the etiology of the "politics of cultural despair."[10]

There is one final issue which a study of the Parisian shopkeeper movement can illuminate. Lower middle-class protest is neither unique to France nor chronologically limited to the end of the century. Other instances of the phenomenon have been recorded and studied, giving rise to a substantial corpus of historical and theoretical literature. I will naturally stress the peculiarities of the Parisian shopkeeper movement, but this is not to say that the Parisian case, however particular, has no relevance to the wider debate on the problem of the lower middle class. This debate has generated an abundance of hypotheses concerning the origins and consequences of lower middle-class mobilization, and the case of the *Ligue syndicale*, I would argue, provides a convenient vehicle to put such claims, often contradictory, to the test. A cursory review of the literature will show just how little agreement there is on these issues.

Explanations of petit-bourgeois mobilization fall into two

[10] For this phrase, see Stern, *The Politics of Cultural Despair*.

Introduction

major categories. One school of interpretation, favored in particular by social scientists, stresses "relative deprivation." The relative deprivation in question, some argue, is material. The development of capitalism profited most the owners and managers of large-scale enterprise, white-collar employees and organized labor. The independent proprietor, whether small businessman or farmer, found himself at a disadvantage in an economy increasingly dominated by agribusiness and corporations, by department stores and grocery chains. The independent did not experience a real economic decline, but was unable to turn to full account the opportunities created by market expansion. He developed in reaction a jealous resentment of all that was big—big business, big government, big labor.[11] A variation on this theme places more emphasis on the small owner's status anxiety in the new world of large-scale organization than on his material frustrations. Harold Lasswell is representative of this point of view:

> Materially speaking, it is not necessary to assume that the small shopkeepers, teachers, preachers, lawyers, doctors, farmers and craftsmen were worse off at the end than they had been at the beginning of the [nineteenth] century. Psychologically speaking, however, the lower middle class was increasingly overshadowed by the workers and the upper bourgeoisie, whose unions, cartels and parties took the center of the stage.[12]

The small owner had built a life on hard work, thrift and individual enterprise. He felt entitled to public recognition and for much of the nineteenth century had received it. Then,

[11] For a classic statement of the relative deprivation argument, see Lipset, *Political Man*, pp. 127–129. Also, Bechhofer and Elliot, "An Approach to a Study of Small Shopkeepers and the Class Structure"; and Gellately, *The Politics of Economic Despair*, pp. 12–57.

[12] Lasswell, "The Psychology of Hitlerism," p. 374. Bechhofer and Elliot ("An Approach," p. 190) and Gellately (p. 5) also make use of the concept of status anxiety.

suddenly, the world turned its back on the independent and showered its rewards instead on big business and organized labor. The little man, so the argument goes, raised his voice in protest and proclaimed himself the last bastion of the traditional values that had once made the nation (France, the United States, etc.) great. In one version of the relative deprivation argument, the principal stress is laid on status loss, in another on material frustrations; but in both versions, the question of whether or not the petite bourgeoisie experienced a real decline is treated as of secondary importance.

The second school of interpretation takes a contrary view. Historians of American Populism, for example, have linked the mobilization of farmers in the 1880s to the onset of a massive agricultural depression.[13] The collapse of grain and cotton prices erased profit margins and plunged desperate independents into indebtedness. The farmer faced debt bondage or expropriation. Once proud small owners emerged from the crisis as tenants or sharecroppers, as "white trash" condemned to dependence and a grinding poverty. Marxists, of course, have long maintained that the petite bourgeoisie was a "doomed class," a sacrificial lamb fated to be gobbled up by monopoly capital.[14] According to Daniel Guérin, writing in 1936:

> The middle classes have . . . suffered from competition and capitalist concentration. Their condition has grown worse; they have been impoverished. . . .[15]

If the petit bourgeois was moved to protest, if in Trotsky's phrase he was "ready to give himself over to the most extreme measures," it was because the specter of proletariani-

[13] Goodwyn, *Democratic Promise*; Hackney, *Populism to Progressivism in Alabama*, pp. 3–4; Hofstadter, *The Age of Reform*.

[14] Neumann, *The Democratic and the Authoritarian State*, pp. 251–253.

[15] Daniel Guérin, *Fascism and Big Business*, p. 42. Guérin, it should be noted, wrote not of the proletarianization of the petite bourgeoisie but of its pauperization.

zation haunted and poisoned his existence. [16] Marxists speak of capitalist concentration and of proletarianization; historians of small-owner movements focus on the adverse impact of economic depression, but these nuances of difference overlay a shared emphasis on real economic distress as the root cause of lower middle-class mobilization.

The political significance of lower middle-class protest, no less than the question of its origins, has divided historians and theorists. The overriding tendency is to view the petit bourgeois as predisposed to an authoritarian, if not fascist, politics. Theorists of the Frankfurt school—Adorno, Reich, Fromm—have cited petit-bourgeois personality structure in explanation. [17] The lower middle class, it is argued, contains a disproportionate number of authoritarian types, pseudo-conservatives who resent established authority, who feel impotent and crave compensation through punishment of so-called inferiors. Wilhelm Reich has blamed the caesarist proclivities of petits bourgeois on a repressive family structure. Children raised in the cramped quarters of a family enterprise, under the stern eye of a dominating father, learn to hate authority but also to repress their hatred. These "repressed impulses," Reich has written, "express themselves in sadism," and sadism directed at a group, like the Jews, who can be dominated as the hated father cannot. A pathological family structure, in Reich's scheme, breeds sick individuals with inherent and deep-seated fascist tendencies. [18]

American social scientists, while recognizing the psychological dimension of petit-bourgeois extremism, have on the

[16] *The Basic Writings of Trotsky*, pp. 267–268. See also Poulantzas, *Fascisme et dictature*, pp. 263ff. Marx himself in the *Communist Manifesto* predicted the eventual proletarianization of the petite bourgeoisie.

[17] Adorno et al., *The Authoritarian Personality*; Reich, *The Mass Psychology of Fascism*; Fromm, *Escape from Freedom*.

[18] Reich, pp. xiv-xv, 31–32, 59–63, 190. See also Ranulf, *Moral Indignation and Middle Class Psychology*.

Introduction

whole preferred explanations of a more socioeconomic cast. Seymour Martin Lipset may be taken as an example.[19] Lipset does not dispute the fascist proclivities exhibited by a segment of the twentieth-century petite bourgeoisie, but he does insist that such proclivities are of recent origin. In the not too distant past, the independent proprietor was a committed democrat, a liberal who sided with the people against the privileged. The experience of relative deprivation, however, broke the petite bourgeoisie's confidence. Status anxiety turned small owners inward and poisoned them with festering resentments. Dwarfed and impotent, lacking in organizational resources, independents sought redress in a radical politics characterized by scapegoating, a shrill moralism, and obsessive fears of conspiracy.[20] They sought, in David Saposs' words, "collectively to rise to a state of personal significance, by basking in the reflected greatness of institutions, organizations and notables—hence chauvinism, jingoism, provincialism, fraternalism, hero-worship, faddism, and styles."[21] Variations on this theme are possible. The phrases "economic decline" or "proletarianization" may be substituted for relative deprivation and status anxiety without changing the argument in its essentials: a once liberal petite bourgeoisie, psychologically scarred by socioeconomic dislocation, abandoned the left and embraced right-wing extremism.

Shulamit Volkov, historian of the master artisan movement in late nineteenth-century Germany, has advanced an interpretation similar to this one in many respects but with one critical difference.[22] Master artisans voted liberal at mid-century, but, Volkov argues, they were not genuine liberals. They embraced liberalism's promises of increased political

[19] Lipset, pp. 129–133.
[20] For a lucid critique of this position, see Rogin, *The Intellectuals and McCarthy*.
[21] Saposs, "The Role of the Middle Class in Social Development," p. 415.
[22] Volkov, *The Rise of Popular Anti-Modernism in Germany*.

participation, yet always harbored doubts about laissez-faire economics, doubts rooted in a traditionalist attachment to the preindustrial guild system. The Great Depression caused these doubts to surface and revealed the artisanate's fundamental hostility to the institutions and values of a modern, industrial economy. It is this underlying antimodernism, enflamed by economic hardship, that accounts for the master artisans' left/right volte-face in the late nineteenth century.

Volkov's interpretation accents the cultural variable, an approach much favored by sociologists of the German school, by Talcott Parsons, for example, or by Karl Mannheim. In the view of a Parsons or a Mannheim, industrialization involves a radical transvaluation of values, a leap from the traditional to the modern, from custom to rationality. Historical agents that oppose the process are irrational and tend to a politics of irrationality. The petite bourgeoisie is a case in point.[23] As no other, it celebrated the traditionalist credo of *famille, travail, patrie*. As no other, it lent itself to extremist movements of the right from Nationalism, to nazism, to McCarthyism.

The three interpretations I have outlined, however different in emphasis, do share one point in common: a tendency to assume that petit-bourgeois despair, whether psychological, economic or cultural in origin, translated automatically into right-wing extremism. A few of the theorists discussed have recognized that such an assumption obscures the role played by politics in channeling a mobilized petite bourgeoisie toward political reaction. There is some disagreement on this score, however, as to whether the choice for reaction was manipulated or spontaneous. Historians of Wilhelmine Germany, for example, and Hans-Ulrich Wehler above all, have laid the principal stress on manipulation. Entrenched landed

---

[23] Parsons, "Some Sociological Aspects of the Fascist Movements," pp. 135–138; Mannheim, *Man and Society in an Age of Reconstruction*, p. 105.

Introduction

and industrial elites, to counter a mounting socialist threat, orchestrated a popular right-wing mobilization through an insidious combination of demagoguery and pork-barrel politics. If the German petite bourgeoisie opted for reaction, it was motivated by fears and ambitions excited from above.[24] But perhaps, others have suggested, the lower middle class chose the course of political extremism, not in a fit of anxious irrationality stimulated from the outside, but because that was the best alternative available. The collectivist left threatened small owners with expropriation; the political establishment was indifferent, lukewarm or even hostile. The right alone made a serious and willful effort to cultivate lower middle-class support. Little wonder, it is argued, independents sought refuge in the camp of counterrevolution.[25] This line of argument has several important implications. It suggests that lower middle-class reaction was self-activated, that the petite bourgeoisie was capable of an autonomous politics.[26] It leaves open the possibility of tensions, if not outright conflict, erupting between a militant petite bourgeoisie and a more temperate conservative establishment. And finally, it implies that a different political configuration could have produced a different result. A responsive government, a more militant conservatism, or a sympathetic left might have bumped the petite bourgeoisie out of its radical-right trajectory. Unfortunately, the opportunity was missed.

[24] See, for example, Wehler, "Bismarck's Imperialism," pp. 144–146; "Industrial Growth and Early German Imperialism," pp. 87–89. For a critique of Wehler's position, see Eley, *Reshaping the German Right.*

[25] Poulantzas, p. 271; *The Basic Writings of Trotsky*, pp. 269–270. See also Lavau, "Classes moyennes et leur comportement politique," pp. 78ff.; Weber, "The Right in France: A Working Hypothesis," pp. 565–566; Hoffmann, *Le Mouvement Poujade*, from the introduction by Jean Meynaud, pp. xiv–xv.

[26] A point stressed by Eley, pp. 218, 335, 358.

Introduction

Historians and theorists have in the main refused to settle exclusively on one or the other of these modes of explanation—psychological, socioeconomic, cultural and political. The tendency is to combine modes, but the conclusion still remains the same: by one route or another, the independent petite bourgeoisie wound up firmly planted on the political far right. The equation of small owner and political reaction, however, has been the object of critical scrutiny in recent scholarship.

Lawrence Goodwyn, for example, historian of American Populism, has demolished interpretations current in the 1950s that dismissed farmer protest as irrationalist, if not out-and-out fascistic.[27] Goodwyn's farmers are family men, owners of family enterprises. They espouse the traditional values of family, labor and country. Hard times had plunged them into indebtedness; the mainstream parties had refused to respond. Here are candidates indeed for an outburst of small-owner reaction, and yet as Goodwyn has shown, Populists were fervent democrats, partisans of direct democracy who practiced a form of rural mutualism based on an extensive network of purchasing and marketing cooperatives. James Green's work on Oklahoma Populists indicates the potential of farmer protests to move beyond radical democracy and assume a socialist character.[28] The socialist farmers discussed by Green, of course, were for the most part not owners but tenants. Yet there are European examples that suggest the receptivity of even owner-farmers—viticulturalists in the Var and to a lesser extent peasants in Bavaria—to socialist appeals. What explains the left-wing leanings of strata consigned in most accounts to the right?

Two kinds of explanation have been advanced. Goodwyn

[27] Goodwyn, pp. 600–614.
[28] Green, *Grass-Roots Socialism*.

· 15 ·

has placed heavy emphasis on the democratic culture of rural America. The democratic commitment of Populist farmers was only intensified by economic distress. Tony Judt, in his study of peasant socialism in southern France, pursues a similar line of argument. Patterns of sociabililty in Provence (peasants lived in tightly knit village communities) and the cooperative practices which cultivation of the vine entailed predisposed local winegrowers to ideologies, like socialism, that stressed collective action.[29] Green, on the other hand, is inclined to emphasize politics more than culture. Oklahoma farmers backed socialism because local socialists made a sincere effort to attract farmer support. The official party position, in conformity with Second International doctrine, condemned small enterprise to expropriation in the event of a socialist victory. Oklahoma militants, however, revised the prevailing orthodoxy. The farmer, it was said, belonged to the producing classes, and local socialists proposed a genuine united front of all producers, small owners included, against an exploitative capitalism.[30]

Revisionist socialism in Europe had its origins, at least in part, in a similar desire to attract small-owner support. Bavaria was one of the principal strongholds of German revisionism, and the SPD leader in the region, Georg von Vollmar, among the first to challenge party doctrine on the question of small enterprise. The independent proprietor, Vollmar claimed, was not on the verge of extinction. If socialism failed to modify its program to appeal to the small owner, it was doomed to permanent minority status, a line of argument that would be more fully developed by Vollmar's colleague, Eduard Bernstein, and that in modified form was destined to crop up again in the 1930s in the neosocialism of the Belgian

[29] Judt, *Socialism in Provence, 1871–1914.*
[30] Green, pp. 72–86.

Henri de Man. Vollmar worked to establish a local SPD/peasant coalition in Bavaria, albeit with limited success.[31] The point implicit in Green's argument, and which the Bavarian example bears out in part, is that doctrinal flexibility can make a difference. Under favorable circumstances, skillful political maneuvering can convert disaffected petty entrepreneurs to the support of socialist demands.

A number of hypotheses emerge from this discussion of the literature on small-owner mobilization. No one disputes that the end of the century in Europe and North America witnessed a petit-bourgeois *prise de conscience*, a wave of protest undertaken in defense of the small owner by organized artisans, shopkeepers and farmers. The origins of lower middle-class militancy, however, remain a matter of some debate. Was it relative deprivation, status anxiety, economic decline or proletarianization that galvanized small owners to organize for their own protection? The question of political significance has generated an equal profusion of hypotheses: militant petits bourgeois are by nature reactionary; they are liberals (or is it pseudo-liberals?) turned fascists; they are the stuff of radical democratic, even socialist movements. And attached to each hypothesis is a mode of explanation—psychological, socioeconomic, cultural, political—that purports to account for the petite bourgeoisie's peculiar political choices. Where does the Parisian shopkeeper movement fit into this complicated structure of theories and possibilities?

A study of the *Ligue syndicale* then promises more than a detailed and particularized account of a local commercial revolt. Paris was the birthplace of the department store and of Nationalism, a focal point of commercial and political change

[31] On Bavarian revisionism, see Schorske, *German Social Democracy*, pp. 7–8. On Bernstein and de Man, see Gay, *The Dilemma of Democratic Socialism*; Sternhell, *Ni droite, ni gauche*, pp. 144–159.

in late nineteenth-century Europe. The *grand magasin* and the new right have been researched exhaustively, but it is my hope that they will appear in a fresh light when scrutinized through the optic of the Parisian shopkeeper movement. I would also like to think of the essay that follows as a case study, a particular instance of the larger phenomenon of petit-bourgeois protest. This investigation of retailer militancy in Paris, then, is intended not just as an exercise in local history, however interesting the locality, but also as a contribution to the continuing debate on the problem of the lower middle class.

I

. . .

THE ORIGINS
OF SHOPKEEPER
PROTEST

1

. . .

The Formation of
the *Ligue Syndicale*

T H E *Ligue syndicale* burst onto the Parisian scene with an astonishing suddenness. In July 1888, when it began publication of its own weekly newspaper, *La Revendication,* the organization counted a membership of not more than 6,000. An energetic recruitment drive, however, produced immediate and gratifying results. The *Ligue* sponsored formation of local committees throughout Paris and solicited the affiliation of sympathetic retailers' associations. Membership surged forward, peaking at upwards of 148,000 in 1894 (see Table 1).[1] Membership figures for the *Ligue* will appear less remarkable if one takes into account that the majority of members belonged only indirectly, as adherents of associated retailers' groups.[2] The *Ligue* also recruited heavily outside Paris, particularly in and around Versailles, Rouen, Dijon, Nancy and Tours. Just over half of the 140,000 members claimed in January 1894 were drawn from the provinces.[3] Still, the rap-

[1] 148,000 is a remarkable figure indeed. Compare it to CGT membership in 1902 which has been estimated at 100,000 (Dolléans, "Les temps héroiques du syndicalisme," p. 21).

[2] "Réunion extraordinaire de la Ligue," *La Revendication,* 15 December 1893.

[3] "La réunion à Troyes," *La Revendication,* 23 March 1890; "Partie officielle," *La Revendication,* 31 January 1894.

TABLE 1. Growth of the *Ligue syndicale*,
1888–1894

DATE		MEMBERSHIP CLAIMED
July	1888	6,000
April	1889	8,000
June	1889	10,000
March	1890	20,000
July	1891	50,000
November	1891	70,000
December	1893	120,000
January	1894	140,000
June	1894	148,000

SOURCE: *La Revendication*: "Programme de *La Revendication*," 5 July 1888; "Comptes-rendus," 25 April 1889; "Comptes-rendus," 6 June 1889; "La réunion à Troyes," 23 March 1890; "Conférence-concert," 26 July 1891; "Compte-rendu de la séance du 15 novembre 1891," 22 November 1891; "Réunion extraordinaire de la Ligue," 15 December 1893; "Partie officielle," 31 January 1894; L. Christophe, "A. Mme. Carnot," 30 June 1894

idity of the *Ligue*'s growth and the extent of Parisian dominance within the movement are unmistakable.

The *Ligue syndicale* advertised itself as a nonpartisan defense association of small shopkeepers (*petits commerçants*). The organization's rapid and impressive success attests to the formation of a distinctive small-shopkeeper interest, but how is such a *prise de conscience* to be accounted for? It is tempting to turn straightaway to a discussion of the social and economic context of retailer mobilization, but such an approach is based on two mistaken premises: firstly, that interests are the spontaneous outgrowth of objective circumstances, and secondly, that the conversion of interests into organization is an uncomplicated process, a matter of simple reflex. The constitution of *petit commerce* as a distinctive group endowed with a coherent set of interests owed as much to state policy, Radical ideology and pressure-group politics as to objective socioeconomic circumstances. Moreover, as labor historians have been at pains to point out, a shared sense of grievance does not suffice to mobilize a group to collective action. Collective protest is spun out of a network of preexisting ties, ties of occupation and neighbourhood that create solidarity and make organization possible.[4] And so it was with the *Ligue syndicale*. Social and economic circumstances generated an inchoate retailer discontent, but it was the political conjuncture of the 1880s and preexisting ties of solidarity that transformed discontent into a mass movement committed to the defense of *petit commerce*.

POLITICS AND THE FORMATION OF A SMALL SHOPKEEPING INTEREST

It was a change in state tax policy that occasioned the first stirrings of retailer revolt. In 1880, the Chamber of Deputies revamped existing legislation on the *patente*, a business tax levied on all commercial enterprises, large and small. Under the old law, businesses had been required to pay a *droit fixe*, a fixed sum that varied with the size of the city in which a shop was located, plus a *droit proportionnel* assessed at ten percent of the rental value of business premises. The legislation of 1880 altered the mode of assessment for clothing and department stores employing more than ten persons. These stores were obliged to pay, in addition to the old *droit fixe* and *droit*

---

[4]See, for example, Hanagan, *The Logic of Solidarity.*

proportionnel, a per capita tax on every employee above the number of five at a variable rate of 15 to 25 francs, depending on city size.[5] The reform did not substantially add to the tax burden of the businesses affected, but it did signal official recognition that the department store constituted a special case. The new law, moreover, alerted Parisian retailers to the potential use of *patente* legislation to single out and punish unwelcome competitors.

A handful of retailer militants, "about a dozen," organized a *Ligue du commerce et de l'industrie* to press for a sharp increase in the employee surtax on department stores.[6] The league invoked the principles of the French Revolution to legitimate its demands for fiscal discrimination. The Revolution had been fought to remove barriers to social mobility, to make it possible for every citizen to become his own master through accession to the ranks of the propertied. With the appearance of gigantic commercial emporia like the Bon Marché and the Grands Magasins du Louvre, a "new feudality" had begun to form that threatened to devour the little man and undo the Revolution's work. The league's efforts to agitate the shopkeeper question, however, evoked little response. It published a newspaper *Le Commerçant* which survived less than a year. Attendance at meetings was sparse at best, and the league faded out of existence in 1882.[7]

A second state initiative brought a sputtering shopkeeper movement momentarily back to life. In 1884, the Chamber of Deputies formed a special parliamentary committee, chaired by the Gambettist Eugène Spuller, to study reports of a

---

[5] Martin Saint-Léon, *Le Petit Commerce français*, pp. 119–120.

[6] For the origins of the *Ligue du commerce*, see du Maroussem, *Le Jouet parisien*, pp. 269–271.

[7] A.E.G., "1789 et 1882," *Le Commerçant*, 18 February 1882; Mucius Scaevola, "Les employés du commerce," *Le Commerçant*, 25 February 1882; Senente, "Les grandes entreprises commerciales," *Le Commerçant*, 25 February 1882.

deepening business recession in the wake of the Union Générale crash. Retailer militants patched together a *Chambre syndicale du commerce de détail et des spécialistes des industries diverses* and arranged a hearing before the Spuller Commission.[8] A *Chambre syndicale* spokesman, A. Girard, took the occasion to renew shopkeeper demands for antidepartment-store legislation, and he framed his case in language calculated to appeal to a man of Spuller's staunch republican convictions. Girard blamed the economic slump on department stores. The *grand magasin* undersold its competition by importing cheap foreign merchandise and with disastrous consequences. Native artisans lost orders to less highly paid foreign workers; the patriotic shopkeeper who shunned manufactures from abroad was driven into bankruptcy for want of customers. Girard detected a monarchist conspiracy in the sharp business practices of the big stores. The "old parties," in a determined effort to establish a "new feudalism," had invented the department store to effect the economic ruination of Paris, "the most resolute defender of French Liberties."[9] Girard's performance, however, did not persuade the Spuller Commission, which in fact concluded that the crisis it had been empaneled to investigate did not even exist. As for the *Chambre syndicale*, it disintegrated as rapidly as it had formed. It had never amounted to more than an ad hoc operation, exciting little grass-roots enthusiasm. Local meetings attracted paltry audiences of twenty to thirty persons, and total membership in the organization never exceeded an unimpressive two hundred.[10]

State initiatives had inspired the first manifestations of small-shopkeeper protest. The militants who organized the *Ligue du commerce* and the *Chambre syndicale du commerce de détail* char-

---

[8]L. Christophe, "Aux adversaires de la Ligue," *La Revendication*, 6 April 1890.

[9]The *Chambre syndicale*'s testimony to the Spuller Commission can be found in: Chambre des Députés, Spuller Commission, pp. 121–123.

[10]Du Maroussem, *Le Jouet parisien*, p. 270.

acterized themselves as *petits commerçants,* and it is clear from the political context what they meant. They were small shopkeepers not in terms of shop size or value of turnover but in relation to the *grands magasins* and clothing stores bracketed for special treatment under the business-tax law of 1880. But as the twin failures of the *Ligue du commerce* and the *Chambre syndicale du commerce de détail* make plain, few retailers were prepared as yet to lay claim to the ill-defined status of small shopkeeper. The intersection of the antidepartment-store struggle with Radical politics, however, refined the definition of a small-shopkeeper identity, investing it with a charged political content that galvanized retailer anger into a sustained and organized movement of protest.

The *Ligue syndicale du travail, de l'industrie et du commerce* sprang from the merger of two groups: the *Union républicaine du commerce et de l'industrie,* a retailer defense association founded in 1886, and the editorial board of *La Crise commerciale,* a shopkeeper newspaper that first appeared in 1887. The *Ligue syndicale* made a pretense of nonpartisanship, but the Radical political orientation of its antecendents belies this claim.

Little unfortunately is known of the *Union républicaine's* program and activities. In the 1886 Paris Tribunal of Commerce elections, the *Union* presented its own slate of candidates. The move provoked a clash with the city's business establishment, accustomed to dividing up seats on the Tribunal by agreement without contest from outsiders. The *Union* campaigned as a "democratic" organization challenging the establishment's "reactionary" monopoly on commercial politics.[11] And in keeping with its democratic posture, it demanded a simplification of bankruptcy procedures as well as direct shopkeeper access to the Tribunal of Commerce without intercession of approved counsel.[12] The *Union* in fact ex-

---

[11] APP B/a 1292, 18 December 1886; see also B/a 1420, 18 December 1886.
[12] APP B/a 1420, 4 December 1886; 18 December 1886.

hibited a particular dislike for the legal profession which it branded "a new aristocracy of the robe, vintage 1887."[13] The *Union républicaine*'s antioligarchical bias faithfully reflected the left republican sympathies of its organizers and supporters. Its secretary and vice-president, Alfred Prével and A. Girard, were veteran shopkeeper militants. They had both worked on *Le Commerçant* and been active in the *Chambre syndicale du commerce de détail*. And they were both Radicals. Prével, a jeweler, had at one time acted as secretary of the *Comité républicain radical-socialiste du XVIIe arrondissement*.[14] Girard's involvement in radical politics dated back to the Second Empire. He had fought the Prussians in the siege of Paris, remained in the city during the Commune and then turned in the 1880s to Radical committee work in the IInd arrondissement where he ran a boot-making business.[15] The political pedigree of the *Union républicaine*'s president, Léopold Christophe, was not dissimilar. Christophe had started out as a salesman for a silk firm on the rue Montmartre and then worked briefly at the Bon Marché department store before opening a commission business of his own on the rue Poissonnière in the IInd.[16] He was, moreover, a republican activist of long-standing. In the 1860s, he had taken part in a discussion group whose membership included Eugène Delattre, Charles Floquet, Pierre Tirard, Jules Méline, all luminaries of the left republican opposition.[17] Christophe served

---

[13] APP B/a 1292, 27 January 1887.

[14] A. Girard, "Appel," *L'Union démocratique*, 30 April 1887.

[15] For information on Girard, see A. Girard, "Le comité autonomiste, radical, socialiste et commercial du quartier Bonne-Nouvelle," *L'Union démocratique*, 16 July 1887; Girard's advertisement in *Le Commerçant*, 18 February 1882; and also "Séances des comités et groupes," *L'Union démocratique*, 3 March 1888.

[16] On Christophe's business career, see L. Christophe, "A Monsieur le vicomte d'Avenel," *La Revendication*, 15 March 1895; "Compte-rendu de la réception d'une délégation par une commission sénatoriale," *La Revendication*, 15 February 1896.

[17] "Christophe," *La Revendication*, 7 March 1889.

his political apprenticeship, according to one source "at the side of our best political strategists in the [Masonic] lodges of the late Empire."[18] The most radical of the *Union républicaine* group, however, was Louis Boeuf, a regular at *Union* meetings who pursued a double career as shopkeeper organizer and political militant. Boeuf ran a flower shop in the faubourg Saint-Martin and was active throughout the 1870s in the *Chambre syndicale* of flower sellers; but he was also a veteran of the Commune and an inveterate political agitator who had performed campaign services for a variety of left-wing politicians, from the Radical Henri Brisson to the ex-Communard Camélinat. A police report of 1886 identified Boeuf as a member of the Radical-Socialist committee of the Xth arrondissement.[19]

Union républicaine militants served the Radical cause not only as committeemen but also as publicists. The *Union's* officers turn up to a man in January 1887 as collaborators on the *Union démocratique*, a Radical weekly just beginning publication. Girard acted as the paper's editor-in-chief. His editorial secretary as well as two other members of the editorial board belonged to the Radical-Socialist committee of the Ist arrondissement. The rest of the staff consisted of three Radical-Socialist politicians (Maurice Vergoin, Gustave Mesureur and E. Robinet), Boeuf, Christophe, Prével and five others.[20] The paper from the very first made plain its intention to "support . . . democracy in commerce," to defend "the small and middle-sized retailer against the monopolistic practices [*l'ac-*

[18] Du Maroussem, *Le Jouet parisien*, p. 271.

[19] On Boeuf, see Louis Boeuf, "Concurrence professionnelle," *L'Union démocratique*, 10 January 1887; "Séances des comités et groupes," *L'Union démocratique*, 17 January 1887; APP B/a 1420, 27 January 1887; B/a 963, 27 December 1879; 13–14 June 1886; 13 August 1886; brochure dated 1890.

[20] "Séances des comités et groupes," *L'Union démocratique*, 17 January 1887; Rédaction, *L'Union démocratique*, 3 January 1887.

caparement] of *les gros.*"[21] But its principal raison d'être lay elsewhere. The *Union démocratique* proposed to coordinate the activities of the various Radical-Socialist and free-thinking groups and committees that dotted the Parisian political landscape.[22] Radical officialdom, of course, was not unappreciative of the *Union républicaine's* pro-Radical efforts. A trio of politicians, Mesureur, Vergoin and François Planteau, all Radical-Socialists, took out membership. Mesureur, a Freemason and pattern-drawer by trade, is best remembered as the initiator of municipal legislation establishing the Paris *Bourse du travail.* Vergoin, too, was a Freemason, who had been dismissed as advocate general of Grenoble for an imprudent speech recommending a purge of politically unreliable, antirepublican judges. As for Planteau, he was a known friend of the Commune and a founding member of the socialist worker's group in the Chamber of Deputies.[23]

The *Union républicaine* then was anything but apolitical. Its founders had long been active in republican politics. They belonged to Radical-Socialist committees or to Masonic lodges. They wrote for the Radical press and chose their political friends from the most radical wing of the republican movement.

The political complexion of the *Crise commerciale* by contrast is not so easy to define. The paper scrupulously refused to talk politics. Little more than name is known of the paper's editor-in-chief, a certain E. Berry. But the principles that informed the paper's programmatic pronouncements resonate with a left republican rhetoric that is difficult to mis-

[21] La Rédaction, "Notre programme," *L'Union démocratique*, 3 January 1887.

[22] La Rédaction, "Notre programme," *L'Union démocratique*, 3 January 1887.

[23] See APP B/a 1420, 27 November 1886; 27 January 1887; also APP B/a 1292, undated report, 16 December 1885, 25 November 1886, 30 August 1889, and a report dated simply 1889.

take. The *Crise commerciale* welcomed political support from whatever quarter it came, from any friend of the shopkeeper—provided he was a "true patriot."[24] But more than such patriotic flourishes, it was the paper's antimonopolism that most clearly betrayed its republican sympathies. The paper claimed to be the "organ of all who want to combat *les gros accapareurs*," and monopoly for the *Crise commerciale* was intimately associated with the feudal practices of the old regime. In an open letter to the owners of the Louvre department store, Berry asked: "Is there a distinction between those who once hoarded bread and drove up bread prices, and those who by their ambition deny a livelihood to millions in our own day? The first abuse led to the revolution of 1789. The second is preparing another revolution a hundred years later."[25] But how were the interests of the little man to be protected against the forces of monopoly?

In mid-January 1888, Berry organized a public meeting that attracted an encouraging turn-out. Shopkeepers debated measures to counter the department store threat. They vigorously rejected *ventes en commun*, the agglomeration of shops offering complementary lines of merchandise to form a *grand magasin du petit commerce*. The audience favored instead "specialization," a commercial equivalent of the one man, one vote principle. Every citizen was entitled to exercise a trade, but no citizen had a right to retail more than one line of merchandise. This was to encroach on a neighbor's territory.[26] The *Crise commerciale*'s advocacy of specialization represented an adaptation to commercial politics of the old republican com-

[24] E. Berry, "Ni politique, ni religion," *La Crise commerciale*, 15 April 1888; "Les vampires du commerce," *La Crise commerciale*, 15 November 1887.

[25] E. Berry, "Lettre adressée à M. Plassard directeur du Bon Marché et à M. Hériot propriétaire des grands magasins du Louvre," *La Crise commerciale*, 1 May 1888.

[26] For an account of the meeting, see A. Girard, "A la Salle de Rivoli," *L'Union démocratique*, 21 January 1888.

mitment to defend small property, to defend *morcellisme* against the forces of privilege and monopoly.

It was then from a conjuncture of the *Crise commerciale*'s patriotic antimonopolism and the *Union républicaine*'s Radical activism that the *Ligue syndicale* was born, and this double inheritance left its mark on the *Ligue*'s ideology and practice. The success of Berry's January '88 meeting prompted the *Crise commerciale* to organize a series of public debates to spread the message of specialization. The positive response elicited by the paper's campaign attracted the attention of *Union républicaine* militants, Christophe, Girard and Vergoin. In February, representatives of the two groups held private talks and agreed to join forces in a new organization, the *Ligue syndicale*.[27] The new *Ligue* made no secret of its patriotism. Foreigners were excluded by statute from membership.[28] At general assemblies, *ligueurs* inevitably came to their feet, heads bared, to thunder their approval as a military band invited specially for the occasion struck up the Marseillaise.[29] On the question of monopoly, the *Ligue* made an explicit commitment to *morcellisme*. It declared its intention "to block formation of the financial feudality constituted by the monopolistic practices of capitalist corporations, of which the Paris department stores are the most flagrant examples;" it expressed its desire "to protect small and medium-sized enterprises and thereby to assure wage earners the opportunity to join the ranks of the self-employed, to become independent and enjoy the fruits of their labor and industry."[30] "The people who made 1789,"

[27] Darmstadt, "Historique de la Ligue syndicale," *La Crise commerciale*, 15 December 1888; B. Montaigu, "Communication importante," *La Crise commerciale*, 15 October 1890; BHVP, Actualités, série 119, Commerce et Industrie, copy of the rules adopted at the Assemblée plénière provisoire.

[28] "Statuts," *La Revendication*, 25 October 1888.

[29] "Quatrième réunion générale," *La Revendication*, 1 June 1890.

[30] "Statuts de la Ligue," *La Revendication*," 23 February 1890.

the *Ligue* stated in its program,[31] would never allow the vision of small ownership for all to die, and to this end, it campaigned energetically to enshrine the specialization principle in law, to enforce the taxation of department stores on the basis of the number of specialties exercised. The *Ligue*, moreover, skillfully exploited its Radical connections to have the issue of *patente* revision raised in the Chamber. In July 1888, Delattre, deputy and *ligueur*, submitted a tax reform bill to parliament, and in 1890, Mesureur arranged formation of a special parliamentary committee to study the question with an eye to future legislation.[32]

The *Ligue's* republican convictions, expressed in its advocacy of specialization and manifest in its Radical associations, effectively recast the shopkeeper question in a new form. The economic conflict of *petit commerçant* vs. department store was transmuted into a vast political struggle between republican small owners and reactionary monopolists. *Petit commerce* was reworked into a political category with a potent symbolic appeal not only to republican retailers but to all citizens who celebrated the Revolution as the triumph of economic democracy over a privileged oligarchy. The *Ligue's* singular capacity to mobilize both popular and parliamentary support would be difficult to understand except against this background of a redefinition of small commerce as the social standard-bearer of the radical republican vision.

The emergence of a distinctive small shopkeeper identity was powerfully reinforced by the pattern of pressure-group

[31]"Programme de *La Revendication*," *La Revendication*, 5 July 1888.

[32]For the *Ligue syndicale's* plans for *patente* reform, see *La Revendication*: "Comité de centralisation," 2 August 1888; "Un document législatif," 25 October 1888; L. Christophe, "Aux adversaires de la Ligue," 7 November 1888; "Ligue syndicale pour la défense des intérêts du travail, de l'industrie et du commerce. Assemblée générale," 22 November 1888; for *L'Union démocratique's* views, see "Projet de loi," *L'Union démocratique*, 27 October 1888.

politics in fin-de-siècle Paris. At the moment of the *Ligue
syndicale*'s inception, an impressive array of interest-group associations representing businessmen, independents and shop
assistants was already in place. The *Ligue*'s difficult insertion
into this world brought home to its retailer constituency the
small shopkeeper's social and political separateness. He stood
apart, wedged uncomfortably between a conservative business
elite and a growing and increasingly militant mass of socialist
white-collar workers.

The most influential business orgainzation in Paris in the
1880s was the 8,000-member *Syndicat général du commerce et de
l'industrie*. While not large, the *Syndicat* represented powerful
exporting interests—the textile trade headquartered on the rue
du Sentier in the IInd arrondissement and the trade in *articles
de Paris* based in the IIIrd and Xth. The organization, moreover, enjoyed excellent relations with the republican political
establishment which had inherited power in the aftermath of
Marshall MacMahon's *seize mai* fiasco. Little wonder, as the
businessmen of the *Syndicat général* had since the 1860s rendered consistent and invaluable service to the moderate republican cause.[33]

The *Syndicat général* traced its ancestry back to the Second
Empire, to the *Union nationale du commerce et de l'industrie* formed
in 1858. The *Union nationale* was intended as an "office of
information and publicity," but its activities were never far
removed from politics.[34] At the time of the Commune, it
forcefully seconded the futile efforts of the *Ligue d'union républicaine des droits de Paris* to arbitrate a settlement between
Paris and Versailles.[35] *Union nationale* militants intervened once

[33] Sorlin, *Waldeck-Rousseau*, p. 278; APP B/a 40, clipping from *Le Journal universel*, 20 November 1886.

[34] Sorlin, *Waldeck-Rousseau*, pp. 98–99.

[35] For the relationship between the *Union nationale* and the *Ligue d'union
républicaine des droits de Paris*, see Greenberg, *Sisters of Liberty*, pp. 7, 117,
120.

again in the celebrated 1873 Seine by-election, pitting the republican Barodet against Thiers' candidate, the Orleanist Charles de Rémusat. The garment district, a *Union nationale* stronghold, was reported to have turned out for Barodet "as one man."[36] The same names that appeared on electoral materials circulated in the IInd arrondissement on Barodet's behalf, turn up once again on petitions signed by garment district businessmen protesting MacMahon's *seize mai* coup. The first petition, published in June 1877, carried twenty-one names, all from the Sentier area. The second, dated 24 November, called upon MacMahon to appoint a republican ministry in accordance with "the wishes expressed so clearly and loudly by our fellow citizens in the last elections [October 1877]."[37] The petition had been masterminded by Ernest Levallois, a founder of the *Chambre syndicale de la nouveauté* and L. Hiélard, president of the *Union nationale*.

The *Union nationale*'s political ardor cooled distinctly in the 1880s. Now that the Republic had been established on a firm footing, the organization evidently felt that the business of government ought to be business. While shopkeepers pursued a revision of the *patente*, the *Union nationale*, renamed the *Syndicat général* in 1883, advocated an increase in the number of commercial attachés assigned to embassies abroad, improved commercial education (with a heavier accent on languages and geography), an expanded consultative role for *chambres syndicales* in decision-making and reduced government expenditures.[38] The *Syndicat* blamed the commercial crisis, not on the department store, but on the high cost of labor inflated by excessive worker recourse to the strike.[39] Alexis Muzet, president of the *Syndicat général,* summed up the

[36] APP B/a 485, Pétitions, 30 November 1877.

[37] APP B/a 485, Pétitions, undated clipping from *Le Temps*; see also reports dated 2 June 1877, 30 November 1877 and 4 December 1877.

[38] APP B/a 40, 21 November 1886; 24 October 1896.

[39] APP B/a 1420, flier dated 13 December 1883.

organization's philosophy to an audience of Parisian business-men that included a sprinkling of politicians, most notably Jules Méline: "We want a genuine but pacific revolution that will persuade our [elected] representatives to set aside their differences, to devote less time to pure politics and more to questions that interest the agriculturalist, the merchant, the manufacturer, the worker, the employee."[40] Not that such strictures applied to the speaker himself. Muzet, a wig and hair wholesaler, also had an active political career. He was a moderate republican, an Opportunist, who sat continuously on the Paris municipal council from 1884 to 1898 represent-ing the Palais-Royal ward.[41]

Relations between the *Ligue syndicale* and the *Syndicat général* were not overtly hostile at first. Muzet put in occasional appearances at *Ligue* meetings and made friendly speeches on the necessity of tax-relief for the shopkeeper.[42] The *Syndicat général*, however, was strictly opposed to specialization. In May 1889, representatives of France's major business associations gathered in Paris for a national congress of *chambres syndicales*. Muzet chaired the proceedings, which were dominated by the *Syndicat général* delegation. Christophe attended the meeting, made a plea for the specialization principle, and was sum-marily rebuffed.[43] A second national congress, held in 1896, and once again presided by Muzet, produced an identical outcome. The defeat of the *Ligue syndicale* was all the more humiliating as it came after the intervention of M. Villain,

[40] APP B/a 1420, 29 March 1889.

[41] "A. Muzet, Candidat républicain-progressiste," *Le Premier Arrondisse-ment*, 22 September 1889.

[42] "Ligue syndicale pour la défense des intérêts du travail, de l'industrie et du commerce. Assemblée générale," *La Revendication*, 22 November 1888.

[43] "La Ligue syndicale," *La Revendication*, 27 June 1889; see also B. de L., "Les revendications du petit commerce parisien," *La Plaine Monceau*, 29 March 1890; Pierre Barberon, "Revue économique," *La Crise commerciale*, 1 August 1889.

director of one of Paris' better known *grands magasins*, the Petit Saint-Thomas. [44] The *Syndicat général* not only opposed specialization, but was in league—or so it seemed—with the shopkeeper's most hated opponent, the department store. The *Ligue syndicale*'s irritation with *Syndicat général* policies initially took the form of personal assaults on Muzet, variously caricatured as an "adversary," "a spoiled potentate," "a pretentious decoration chaser." [45] But contempt for Muzet easily spilled over into contempt for the *Syndicat général* as a body. Muzet's organization was sneeringly referred to as "the areopagus of big business. [46] As for the *chambres syndicales* affiliated with the *Syndicat*, they were disparaged in a fit of democratic pique as "coteries" of "notables" and "big shots." [47] Shopkeeper polemics had political overtones as well. The cozy relationship of the *Syndicat* with Opportunist politicans prompted Louis Boeuf to dismiss the entire organization as an "Opportunist front." [48]

The gulf separating the *Ligue* and the *Syndicat* was not in fact as profound as retailer militants of Boeuf's stamp liked to believe. Firstly, Muzet's organization was not that far removed politically from the *Ligue*. While Muzet himself traveled in Opportunist circles, many of his lieutenants did not. Alfred Mascuraud, for example, vice-president of the *Syndicat général* and a power in the costume jewelry trade, was deeply involved in Radical politics. In later years, he was to be elected

[44] APP B/a 40, 21 October 1896.

[45] "Elections du 3 septembre 1893," *La Revendication*, 31 August 1893; *La Crise commerciale*: Pierre Barberon, "Revue économique," 30 June 1889; Marc, "Palais-Royal," 30 June 1889.

[46] L. Boeuf, "Chronique du travail," *Les Droits du peuple*, 10 February 1890.

[47] Boeuf, "Chronique du travail," *Les Droits du peuple*, 10 February 1890; H. Meller, "Diffamation publique," *Les Droits du peuple*, 24 March 1890.

[48] L. Boeuf, "Chronique du travail," *Les Droits du peuple*, 10 February 1890.

senator from the Seine with Radical backing and gained notoriety as the Radical party's most lucrative contact in the business world. The *Ligue syndicale*, moreover, was tied indirectly into the larger business community through Alphonse Marguery, president of the *Comité de l'alimentation*. The Committee, the nation's largest association of food-and-drink retailers, had been formed in 1882 to protest the high price of gas lighting.[49] In the late 1880s, the organization shifted its attention to the question of *patente* reform. It entoned against consumer cooperatives and grocery chains in accents that echoed the *Ligue*'s antidepartment-store rhetoric. Marguery, himself a *ligueur*, proclaimed with some justification: "our aspirations are identical to those of the League."[50] And indeed, at Marguery's behest, the eleven *chambres syndicales* which comprised the *Comité* joined the *Ligue* en bloc in 1889.[51] Marguery's personal political preferences, moreover, conformed closely to the league's. He belonged to Henri Brisson's electoral committee as did Louis Boeuf, and he even married his daughter to a Radical deputy, Félix Gervais, son of a wealthy Swiss-cheese manufacturer.[52]

Marguery and the *Comité* too, however, were at the same time well connected in the business world. Marguery himself ran a successful and fashionable restaurant on the boulevard Poissonnière.[53] As one contemporary remarked, Marguery's

[49] Pierre Sylvain, "Pas de nouvelles taxes d'octroi," *L'Ami des petits commerçants*, 1 November 1902; du Maroussem, *Halles centrales de Paris* p. 246; L. Christophe, "A propos de la question du gaz à Paris," *La Revendication*, 18 September 1892.

[50] "Deuxième réunion extraordinaire de la Ligue," *La Revendication*, 15–31 March 1894; "La Ligue syndicale," *La Revendication*, 27 June 1889.

[51] "Comptes-rendus," *La Revendication*, 11 April 1889.

[52] APP B/a 1172, 17 November 1890 and 12 December 1890.

[53] For Marguery's early career, see "Société d'encouragement du bien," *Journal de la Chambre syndicale de la boucherie*, 3 June 1894; Sylvain, "Pas de nouvelles taxes d'octroi, *L'Ami des petits commerçants*, 1 November 1902.

"filets of sole . . . [had] made him a millionaire many times over."[54] As president of the 78,000-strong *Comité de l'alimentation*, Marguery shared the podium with Muzet at the national congresses of *chambres syndicales* held in 1889 and 1896. Active in charitable work, in the organization of public festivities, but above all in the *chambre syndicale* movement, Marguery was a minor power in Parisian public life. He was also careful, despite his Radical sympathies, to maintain friendly relations with the Opportunist political establishment. In the elections of 1898, the *Comité* endorsed Mesureur, Brisson and Edouard Lockroy, all Radicals, but also "our friend" Alexis Muzet.[55] Throughout the nineties, it searched in vain for a newspaper in which to publish the proceedings of its assemblies. One of its militants recommended one journal with the explanation: "'[The paper], being pro-government in every particular, is entitled to all our sympathies."[56] The Prime Minister at the time was the Opportunist Ribot. The *Comité* then straddled the two worlds represented by the *Ligue* and the *Syndicat général*.

Nevertheless, however fluid the frontier between the *Ligue syndicale* and the upper reaches of the Paris business community, the lines of battle were drawn with sufficient clarity to persuade the Radical shopkeeper that he held little in common with the Opportunist notables of the *Syndicat général*. In this context, the notion of *petit commerce* assumed a new layer of meaning. *Ligueurs* were indeed small shopkeepers, small by virtue of their exclusion from the city's business elite and the

[54] Edmond Benjamin and Paul Desachy, *Le Boulevard*, p. 119.

[55] "Comité de l'alimentation," *Journal de l'alimentation*, 21 June 1898. See also APP B/a 40, 10 November 1887; 24 October 1896; "La fête des récompenses du Comité de l'alimentation parisienne," *Journal de la Chambre syndicale de la boucherie*, 2 June 1895.

[56] "Comité de l'alimentation parisienne," *Journal de la Chambre syndicale de la boucherie*, 21 April 1895; also "Comité de l'alimentation parisienne," *Journal de la Chambre syndicale de la boucherie*, 1 April 1894.

Marguery's Restaurant on the Boulevard Poissonnière in 1910

easy access to political officialdom that membership in the establishment afforded.

The *Ligue syndicale*'s deteriorating relations with organized shop employees placed in yet sharper focus the political and institutional parameters of what it meant to be a *petit commerçant*. The most important white-collar union in the Paris of the 1880s was the *Chambre syndicale des employés* (CSE) founded in 1886. From the very first, according to police sources, the organization was controlled by "the Broussist party," by militants connected to the municipal socialist Paul Brousse. The CSE's president, Victor Dalle, worked on the Broussist organ, *Le Parti ouvrier*, and as of 1890, the *Chambre syndicale* had affiliated with the Broussist *Fédération du centre*.[57] But what did this Broussist commitment signify? The CSE contributed on a monthly basis to the Paris *Bourse du travail* strike fund, and members pointedly refused to come to work on May Day. But they also made a holiday of July 14 and firmly rejected strike violence.[58] Nor was the organization militantly proletarian, at least in its early years. As late as 1892, a Broussist municipal councillor closely connected to the *Chambre syndicale* could still say: ". . . the corporation of employees . . . is among the most interesting because its members, in terms of education and instruction, occupy a middle ground between the working class and the bourgeoisie."[59]

The moderate character of the CSE's socialism was nowhere more apparent than in its stance vis-à-vis the department store. In the 1880s, the union's stongest support came from department employees. The crowd of seven hundred in attendance at one of the CSE's first public rallies in July 1886 consisted for the most part of clerks from *magasins de nou-*

[57] APP B/a 153, 13 December 1890, 8 August 1891, and 7 September 1892.

[58] *Ibid.*, 12 July 1885; 3 July 1886; *Chambre syndicale des employés, Rapport annuel*, 31 December 1892.

[59] *Ibid.*, 8 August 1891; 16 June 1892.

veautès.[60] In 1894, of the twenty-four members of the union's central committee, thirteen had once or still worked as *employés de nouveautés* or *de draperies.*[61] Not surprisingly, the CSE directed its first polemics against the department store. When the union protested over working conditions for employees, it was invariably conditions in Paris' largest department stores that were at issue.[62] It was the Bon Marché, the Louvre or Au Printemps which worked employees fourteen hours a day, which refused to close up before eight in the evening or to give the staff a holiday on Bastille Day. Dalle declared to a CSE meeting in 1890: "The department stores are killing trade. They hog all the business; they bring ruin to small shopkeepers and force employees out of work who are then snapped up by the big stores at cut-rate wages."[63] In August, the Rouvier government published its budget for 1891. The *patente* for stores employing 200 to 1,000 employees was increased while the assessment on stores employing over 1,000 was lowered. The CSE responded with a poster:

> But this means the public will soon have no choice but to shop at the big Paris department stores, whose corporate organization represents a first step toward formation of a formidable monopoly.
>
> This means too that employees, forced to leave second-rank stores ruined by the *patente*, will be reduced to misery and made to pound the pavement in futile search of a new job.[64]

While socialist, the CSE did not attack the department store in the name of communal ownership. It was motivated rather

[60] *Ibid.*, 3 July 1886.
[61] *Ibid.*, 4 January 1894.
[62] See, for example, *ibid.*, handbill, "Aux employés des bazars," October 1890(?); *Chambre syndicale des employés, Rapport annuel*, 31 December 1892.
[63] *Ibid.*, 15 August 1890.
[64] *Ibid.*, clipping from *Le Prolétariat*, 10 August 1890.

by a hostility to monopoly that explicitly recognized a common bond between the salaried clerk and the petty proprietor. The CSE and *Ligue syndicale* then shared interests. Both espoused a radical left politics; both were adversaries of monopoly. And it was on this basis that relations between the two organizations developed. The league took enthusiastic notice of the CSE's antidepartment-store jeremiads. CSE militants were invited to make their case in the pages of *La Revendication*. The *Ligue* even made an offer of merger.[65] The 4,200-member employees' union shied away from the *Ligue*'s bearish embrace, but it did not reject shopkeeper overtures out of hand. As one employee militant put it: "Each one must work in his own way," but "in common accord because we seek the same goal."[66] The *Ligue* had found an ally in its campaign for *patente* revision, and as for the CSE, the police characterized its strategic interest in a shopkeeper alliance this way:

> The *Chambre syndicale des employés* has entered into negotiations with the *Ligue des petits commerçants*; it will use the league to woo small business support at election time. Dalle is the intermediary who will work out the agreement, which may prove advantageous to the *Parti ouvrier*.[67]

Relations between the two organizations, however, soured over the course of the nineties. The *Ligue*'s participation in the *Comité de l'alimentation*'s fight against cooperatives drew a reproach from Dalle. He warned the *Ligue* that it risked "alienating the sympathies of the organized proletariat."[68] The

---

[65] "Un document," *La Revendication*, 10 August 1890; "Comité de centralisation," *La Revendication*, 24 August 1890.

[66] APP B/a 153, *Chambre syndicale des employés, Rapport annuel*, 31 December 1891; "Comité de centralisation," *La Revendication*, 24 August 1890.

[67] APP B/a 153, 7 August 1890.

[68] "Comité de centralisation," *La Revendication*, 31 March 1895.

CSE at the same time was evolving toward a more militant socialism, hostile to the *patronat* as such, not excluding *les petits*. In the 1880s it came to embrace the orthodox Marxist position on the inevitability and progressive character of economic concentration. Department store growth, once viewed with dismay by the CSE, was now welcomed as a spur to the expansion of the employee class and to trade-union organization.[69] *Petit commerce*, of course, had no future in a world dominated by large-scale enterprise. As Brousse himself remarked in 1893: "small business is destined to disappear, crushed by the department store."[70] But this prospect no longer disturbed CSE militants as it had in the 1880s. The small shopkeeper, it was now claimed, had never been a reliable ally, and no class-conscious employee would mourn his passing. A CSE brochure published in 1899 concluded perfunctorily: "employees have no reason to take up the defense of any businessman, whether *petit* or *grand*."[71]

The constitution of small business as a group entailed a clarification of boundaries. The notion of *petit commerce* had no clear-cut meaning, and so the question was posed: what was *petit commerce*? The peculiar place assumed by the *Ligue syndicale* in the constellation of Paris pressure-group associations provided a partial answer, an answer with both a social and political dimension. The small shopkeeper was a man of middling social rank. In relation to the "big shots" of the business establishment, he was a *petit*. In relation to the salaried clerks of the CSE, he was a *commerçant*, no better or worse than any other. The partisan character of pressure-group politics sharpened the hazy social boundaries of *petit commerce*. The fragmentation of the republican movement in the 1880s into

---

[69] APP B/a 153, 7 June 1894.

[70] *Ibid.*, 3 August 1893.

[71] *Ibid.*, 3 February 1894; brochure distributed at meeting of 10 February 1899.

competing Opportunist, Radical and socialist factions reproduced itself in mediated form at the interest-group level. The *Ligue*, of Radical origins, occupied a middle position in a spectrum of partisan pressure groups that stretched from the socialist CSE to the Opportunist *Syndicat général*. The small shopkeeper was then a man in between, neither employee, nor notable, neither socialist nor Opportunist. *Petit commerce* was an amorphous category that derived a fragile coherence in social and political juxtaposition to the groups that flanked it on either side.

Politics then provided the medium through which a simmering retailer discontent was transmuted into a militant small shopkeeper consciousness. State tax policy, Radical ideology and the vicissitudes of pressure-group politics invested the uncertain status of *petit commerçant* with a potent sociopolitical content. The small shopkeeper was defined in opposition to an impressive complex of hostile forces: department stores, financial feudalism, well-connected business notables and socialist white-collar workers. The interests of *petit commerce* were perceived accordingly, in political as much as in economic terms. Institutionalization of the specialization principle was intended to confound not only the *petit commerçant*'s commercial enemies but also his political opponents—the parties of the old right, Opportunists, and collectivist socialists.

Ligue syndicale MEMBERSHIP

The *Ligue syndicale*'s articulation of a distinctive small shopkeeper consciousness, however, does not fully account for its remarkably rapid expansion. The simple enunciation of a cause, whatever its appeal, is no guarantee of instant success. The *Ligue* drew its initial impetus from a well-developed current of retailer activism which in turn was rooted in a particular and identifiable commercial milieu. It tapped preexisting loyalties born of common action and community solidarity. The men who joined the small shopkeeper movement were not strangers to one another, a dust of isolated individuals whipped into coordinated action by the pronouncements of an unknown leadership. They constituted rather a semiorganized mass, already in motion, whose energies the league focused and channeled into the service of small-shopkeeper defense.

The core of militants that oversaw the *Ligue*'s formation shared a common activist past. Almost without exception, they had done service as Radical committeemen or publicists, and most were graduates of the *chambre syndicale* movement. Louis Gazon, a *Ligue* vice-president, chaired the *Chambre syndicale* of herbalists.[72] Boeuf ran the *Chambre syndicale* of florists, and Marguery, the *Comité* of food-and-drink retailers. Louis Digard, president of the *Ligue*'s XVth arrondissement section, doubled as president of the *Chambre syndicale* of retail shoe-merchants.[73]

The activist strain that fed into the *Ligue* was a highly localized phenomenon, localized by neighborhood and by trade. Alfred Hamel and E. Bally, both jewelers and both *Ligue* vice-presidents, owned shops in the fashionable Palais-Royal, the center of Paris' jewelry trade. Girard and Christophe ran businesses in the IInd arrondissement, Gustave Mesureur's electoral district. The *Ligue*'s treasurer, a M. Bardet, came from the IXth, Boeuf from the Xth, and Gazon and Prével from the XVIIth. Between 1888 and 1896, the *Ligue* elected twenty-one officers. Of these, the professions of thirteen are known. Three were middlemen (*négociant, commissionnaire*, or *courtier*); two were jewelers or watchmakers; one was an engraver, one a dealer in porcelains, one a dealer in umbrellas, one a cloth-

---

[72] For information on Gazon, see APP B/a 1092.
[73] "Chambre syndicale des marchands de chaussures en détail du département de la Seine," *L'Union des syndicats de France*, 1 June 1899.

ier, one a tailor, one a herbalist and one a wineshopkeeper.[74] The *Ligue syndicale*'s leadership was recruited from a narrow spectrum of neighborhoods and professions. The *Ligue* did not appear *ex nihilo* but was anchored in a finite and already partially mobilized stratum of Paris' commercial community, center-city merchants concentrated in the commission business and the luxury and clothing trades.

A social and geographic breakdown of the *Ligue* rank and file affords a more detailed picture of the milieu that spawned the small shopkeeper movement. Membership fell into two categories: members who joined and paid dues as individuals and members who belonged indirectly as adherents of affiliated *chambres syndicales*. There were in all twenty-nine associated *chambres syndicales* in 1893, accounting as we have seen for over half of the *Ligue*'s total recruitment. The first seven *syndicats* to join belonged with two exceptions to the clothing and luxury trades: ceramics and glass retailers, herbalists, rug dealers, flower and feather retailers, jewelers, butchers and shoe merchants.[75] The eleven *chambres syndicales* of the *Comité de l'alimentation* took out membership en masse at this juncture, followed by associations, sometimes more than one to a profession, representing chandlers, cutlers, clothiers, firewood dealers, tailors, hatters, engravers, and hairdressers.[76] This breakdown points to two related conclusions. The *Ligue syndicale* was in large part an outgrowth of the *chambre syndicale* movement, but—and this is the second point—its capacity to draw on already existing retailer organizations for support was limited to certain trades and did not extend to others.

[74] *La Revendication*: "Comité de centralisation," 2 August 1888; 31 December 1894; 30 November 1896. Issues of *La Revendication* after 1896 have not been conserved, so adequate information on the *Ligue*'s leadership after that date is lacking.

[75] *La Revendication*, 11 April 1889; "Causerie hebdomadaire," *La Revendication*, 20 June 1889.

[76] *La Revendication*: 25 July 1889; 1 January 1893.

Food-and-drink men, retailers of luxury goods and clothing merchants proved most responsive to the appeal of small-shopkeeper defense.

The professional profile of the *Ligue*'s individual membership essentially confirms this last observation. Eighteen men gathered in April 1888 at one of the league's first public meetings.[77] They came from the following trades:

Clothing	7
Accessories (gloves, canes, fans, flowers, and feathers)	1
Middleman	5
Paper (stationery, printing)	1
Home Furnishings	2
Liberal Professions	1
Other	1
	18

In August, the *Ligue* published a petition "Aux Commerçants de Province," bearing eighteen signatures. Four were jewelers, eight middlemen, three clothiers, one a *marchand de nouveautés*, one an umbrella dealer and one a dealer in crystals and porcelains.[78] In February 1882, *Le Commerçant* published the names and addresses of 190 supporters.[79] The list casts an indirect light on the social composition of the *Ligue syndicale*, revealing the kind of businessman who became involved in the shopkeeper agitation out of which the *Ligue* grew. The list breaks down as follows:

Food	10
Watches and Jewelry	20
Textile Trade (*nouveautés*, linen, lace)	25

[77] "Ligue syndicale," *La Crise commerciale*, 15 April 1888.

[78] E. Berry, "Aux commerçants de province," *La Crise commerciale*, 15 August 1888.

[79] "Première liste d'adhérents," *Le Commerçant*, 25 February 1882.

Clothing—

Tailoring	5
Mercery	10
Hats	11
Shirts	7
Shoes	10
Other Clothing (lingerie, dresses)	8
Accessories	10
Articles de Paris (knick-knacks, fancy turnery)	5
Middleman	10
Paper (including photography)	11
Home Furnishings	7
Furniture	8
Building	2
Liberal Professions	7
Accountant	5
Employee	3
Retired or Unspecified	7
Other	7
Art	2
	190

A clear outline of the *Ligue*'s professional make-up emerges from these lists. From the very first, the *Ligue* elicited warm support from garment retailers, merchant tailors, drapers and clothiers. Purveyors of luxury goods and jewelers in particular responded with a similar enthusiasm. Organizations of intermediaries did not affiliate, but middlemen were quite active as individual members. It is interesting to note the relative absence of butchers, bakers and the like from the lists of individual adherents. But with the mass affiliation of the *Comité de l'alimentation* in 1889, the *Ligue* more than made up for its initial lack of popularity in the food-and-drink sector.

Ligue recruitment was no less selective with respect to ge-

T A B L E 2. *Ligue syndicale* Membership by Arrondissement

DATE	TOTAL LIGUE MEMBERSHIP	ARRON- DISSEMENT	NUMBER OF MEMBERS
1888	6,000	II	160
		II and IV	400–500
		IX	230
1889	8,000	I	570–600
		VIII	360–416
		XI	150
1890	20,000	XII	150
		XIX	63
1893	120,000	V	150

SOURCE: A. Girard, "La spécialisation," *L'Union démocratique*, 16 June 1888. *La Revendication*: "Comptes-rendus," 29 November 1888; "Comptes-rendus," 13 December 1888; "Comptes-rendus," 7 February 1889; "Comptes-rendus," 28 February 1889; "Comptes-rendus," 11 April 1889; "Assemblée générale de la Ligue," 29 December 1889; "Comité de centralisation," 9 March 1890: "Comité de centralisation," 12 January 1890; A. Fayet, "La discorde dans une section," 15 October 1893

ography. Individual members were organized into arrondissement committees. The first groups were formed in arrondissements I-IX, XV, XVI and XVIII. Next came X and XVII, and finally XI, XIII, XIV, XIX, XX with XII last of all.[80] Membership figures for these local organizations are hard to come by (see Table 2) and can provide only a shadowy glimpse of the *Ligue*'s pattern of implantation. Qualitative data, however, can be mustered to flesh out the picture. The *Ligue*

[80] *La Revendication*: "Comité de centralisation," 2 August 1888; "Comptes-rendus," 28 February 1889.

leadership singled out the recruitment efforts of two local committees for special mention. The Ist arrondissement section was praised as "one of the most organized . . . one of the most numerous," the VIth as "among the best organized."[81] The IIIrd was complimented for its success among the *commerçants* of the Temple, only to be rebuked some months later for functioning poorly.[82] The VIIth succeeded in publishing a booklet identifying local *ligueurs*, surely a sign of some organizational activity, yet Christophe deplored "that retailers are not more militant in the VIIth arrondissement. At local league meetings, it is always the same people who step forward; and yet, if there is a neighborhood hard hit by the crisis, it is surely the faubourg Saint-Germain and the Gros-Caillou, wedged as they are between the Louvre, the Bon Marché and the Petit Saint-Thomas [located on the rue du Bac]."[83] In February of 1890, the local committee failed even to muster a quorum to elect new officers.[84] Criticism was far more abundant than favorable comment. The Xth did not occupy the place it should in *Ligue* affairs; the XIIIth and the XIVth were among those with "the fewest adherents"; the XVth was apathetic, the XVIIIth and XIXth "very weak"; meetings of the XVIth were poorly attended.[85] And so on.

On the basis of this evidence, the *Ligue* appears to have been strongest in the Ist, IInd, IVth, VIth, VIIIth, and IXth and weakest in arrondissements X-XVI and XVIII-XX. The

[81] "Comptes-rendus," *La Revendication*, 13 December 1888; *La Revendication*, 15 May 1895.

[82] "Comptes-rendus," *La Revendication*, 7 February 1889; *La Revendication*, 2 May 1889.

[83] *La Revendication*: "Comptes-rendus," 7 November 1888; "Comptes-rendus," 7 March 1889.

[84] "Comité de centralisation," *La Revendication*, 6 April 1890.

[85] *La Revendication*: "Comptes-rendus," 21 February 1889; "Comptes-rendus," 29 November 1888; "Comptes-rendus," 11 April 1889; "La Ligue syndicale," 27 July 1890; "Comité de centralisation," 20 March 1892; Un Ligueur, "Un double lâchage," 1 December 1889.

situation in the IIIrd, Vth, VIIth and XVIIth arrondissements was more ambiguous. Clearly, the *Ligue* was geograph-
ically rooted in central Paris, although not so much in its artisan neighborhoods (III and X) as in its commercial districts
(I, II and IX). Reactions were mixed in Paris' wealthiest arrondissements: the parvenu XVIth and XVIIth and the older,
more established VIIth and VIIIth. The shopkeeper cause,
however, met with least enthusiasm in the city's working-class
neighborhoods on the periphery, a fact of which retailer militants were painfully conscious. The newly elected president
of the XXth arrondissement section promised to build up the
local committee "so as to rival those of the center."[86] If the
small shopkeeper movement lacked support in the XVIIIth,
a league officer explained, it was because "the *quartier* is too
far from the center, and the department store question has
little play here."[87] In the XIIIth, the weakness of the local
section was blamed on "the preponderance of the working-
class element."[88]

When addresses of shopkeeper militants are plotted by arrondissement, this pattern of recruitment emerges with greater
clarity (figures 1 and 2). These addresses have been culled from
two lists—one from *Le Commerçant* and the other published
by *La Revendication* in July 1888, enumerating the *Ligue syndicale*'s sixty-nine founding members. The two figures demonstrate the extent to which the center dominated in *Ligue*
recruitment. The Ist, IInd and IXth arrondissements alone
account for 45 percent of the names on the 1882 list and 32
percent on the 1888 list. The location of league strongholds
can be pinpointed with greater accuracy if the lists are broken
down further by ward (figures 3 and 4). The geographical
distribution of shopkeeper activism did not change apprecia-

[86] *La Revendication*, 15 May 1893.
[87] *La Revendication*, 30 April 1894.
[88] "Comptes-rendus," *La Revendication*, 29 November 1888.

FIGURE 1: The Recruitment of Shopkeeper Militants by Arrondissement, 1882

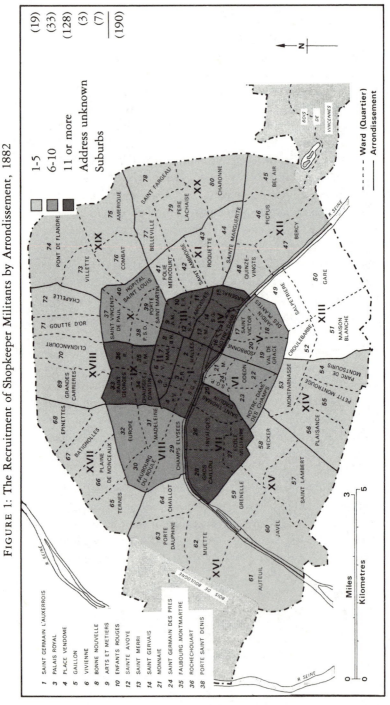

SOURCE: "Première liste d'adhérents," *Le Commerçant*, 25 February 1882.

FIGURE 2: The Recruitment of Shopkeeper Militants by Arrondissement, 1888

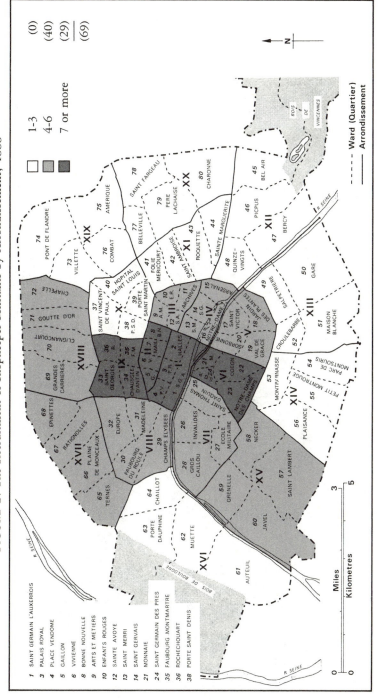

SOURCE: "Programme de la Ligue syndicale," *La Revendication*, 5 July 1888.

FIGURE 3: The Recruitment of Shopkeeper Militants by Ward, 1882

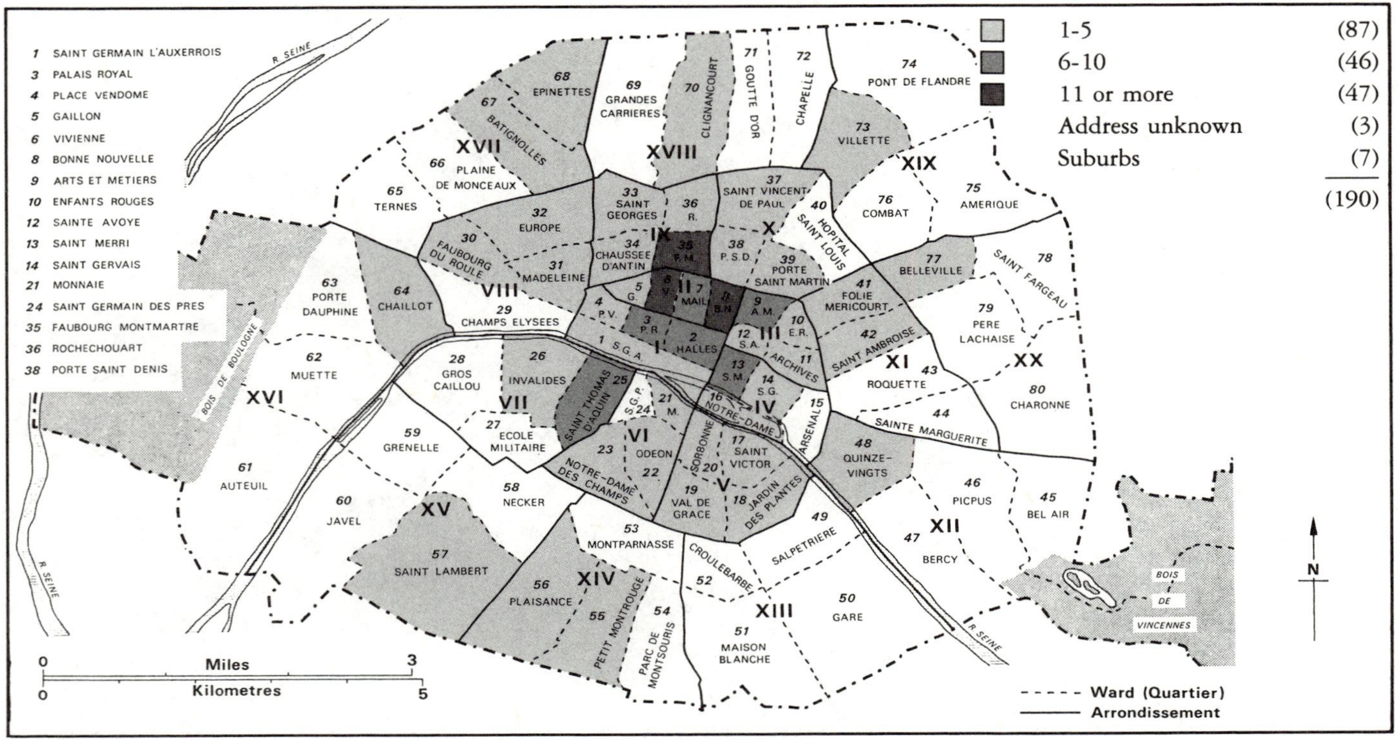

SOURCE: "Première liste d'adhérents," *Le Commerçant*, 25 February 1882.

FIGURE 4: The Recruitment of Shopkeeper Militants by Ward, 1888

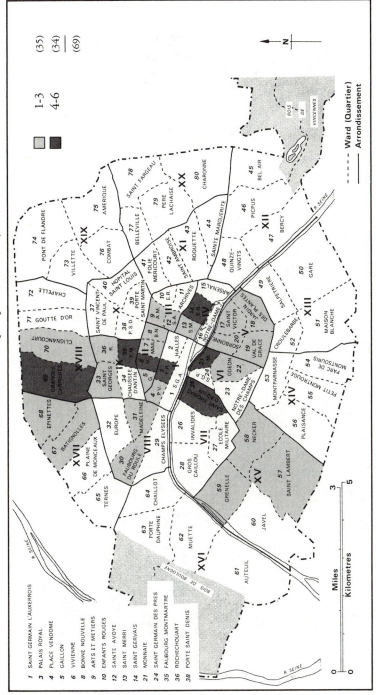

SOURCE: "Programme de la Ligue syndicale," *La Revendication*, 5 July 1888.

The Rue du Faubourg Montmartre in 1912

The Rue du Bac in 1905

bly over the course of the 1880s. New foci of retailer militancy had indeed begun to emerge by decade's end, around the carrefour de Buci in the VIth, along the rue Saint-Antoine in the IVth and on the slopes of Montmartre in the XVIIIth. But in 1888 as in 1882, the city's working-class neighborhoods displayed a consistent indifference to the shopkeeper appeal, and throughout, it was the city's commercial core that contributed the bulk of retailer activists. Four wards in particular stand out as centers of retailer agitation: Saint-Thomas d'Aquin, the Palais-Royal, the Vivienne and the Faubourg Montmartre. Together, they form a corridor running from north to south along the rue du faubourg Montmartre, down the rue de Richelieu past the Palais-Royal toward the rue du Bac. It was on this axis that the shopkeeper movement turned in the 1880s.

It was not then from the mass of street-corner retailers operating modest enterprises in out of the way neighborhoods that the *Ligue syndicale* drew its strength. The average *ligueur*, while not a member of Paris' commercial establishment, was by no means a marginal businessman. He was a Palais-Royal jeweler or rue de Richelieu tailor, a retailer of fancy home furnishings or of fine clothing who worked in the city's busiest commercial arrondissements. True, a *ligueur* might also sell herbs and spices on the avenue des Ternes in the XVIIth (as did Gazon) or used clothing at the Temple, but on the whole he was more likely to deal in quality goods than in junk, to serve a well-to-do rather than a working-class clientele. The *Ligue*'s base of operations was located in a particular sector of the commercial community of central Paris. This stratum, woven together out of interlocking strands of professional and local solidarity, had already begun to organize itself in the 1880s. The league, brandishing the standard of small-shopkeeper defense, brought the task of organization to completion, fusing a welter of trade associations and neighborhood committees into a mass movement of protest.

Interest-group formation is a complex process conditioned by politics and mediated through an array of preexisting loyalties. An appreciation of such complexity is crucial to an understanding of the social and economic origins of retailer protest. If the *Ligue*'s self-characterization as a nonpartisan defense association of small shopkeepers is taken at face value, the question of origins appears deceptively straightforward. Why do small shopkeepers protest? But the *Ligue*'s account of itself is doubly misleading. It conceals both the political connotations of the term *petit commerce* and the *Ligue*'s rootedness in a specific and restricted milieu. What is at issue is not a general uprising of *petits commerçants*, but the mobilization of a particular stratum of retail businessmen. The question of origins must be reformulated accordingly. Why did center-city retailers concentrated in the clothing and luxury trades turn to collective action in the name of small-shopkeeper defense?

2

. . .

Grands Magasins
and Small Shops

T H E *Ligue syndicale* identified the department store as its
principal enemy. *Ligue* ideology stressed the dangers of monopoly and the plight of the little man. Threatened with extinction by commercial juggernauts such as the Louvre, the
Bon Marché, the Printemps, small merchants had been obliged
to organize in self-defense. Historians have taken up this argument and interpreted shopkeeper revolt as a hopeless act of
defiance against larger and more dynamic rivals.[1] This line of
reasoning has the virtue of simplicity, and a strong case can
be made for it. It is worth rehearsing the department store
thesis at some length because it is so widely subscribed to,
but in the final analysis, I will argue, it fails as a satisfactory
explanation of shopkeeper mobilization.

THE DEPARTMENT STORE

Paris of the Second Empire was the birthplace of the department store. Aristide Boucicaut took over Au Bon Marché in
1852. Chauchard, Hériot and Faré formed the Grands Ma-

---

[1] Gellately, *The Politics of Economic Despair*, pp. 12–57. Miller; *The Bon Marché*, pp. 207–215.

gasins du Louvre in 1855. Au Printemps, property of Jules Jaluzot, went into business a decade later. Jacques Ruel's Bazar de l'Hôtel de Ville opened in 1860, Louise Jay and Ernest Cognacq's La Samaritaine in 1869. Observers, astonished by the heady expansion of the department store, cast about for an explanation. Economies of scale, rational bureaucratic organization, a symbiotic relationship with industry, and innovative merchandising—here was the formula that accounted for the success of the *grand magasin*.

Retailing a wide variety of merchandise under a single roof first and foremost permitted a drastic reduction in overhead. A storeowner who grossed 60,000 francs anually spent an estimated 2.5 percent of turnover, or 1,500F per annum, on rental costs. The *grand magasin*, with its large floor space (the Bon Marché in 1887 occupied a full city block), naturally paid a more substantial rent, perhaps as much as one million francs. But this figure represented less than one percent of yearly earnings which in the case of the larger stores, at the end of the century, averaged close to one hundred million francs. The problem, of course, was to sustain a high volume of sales.[2] The Bon Marché in the 1880s took in on average four to five hundred thousand francs a day, the Louvre three to four hundred thousand.[3] The department store, because it sold furs as well as straw hats, cotton goods as well as wool, did not suffer seasonal slumps as acutely as some more specialized retailers. Well-timed special sales—a white sale in January or a home furnishings sale in September—bolstered sagging volume in slack times.

Merchandise had to be moved not only as continuously but also as rapidly as possible. The aim was not to score a "coup"

[2] D'Avenel, "Le mécanisme de la vie moderne. Les grands magasins," p. 362.

[3] The fortnightly police reports in APP B/a 503 contain regular estimates of Au Bon Marché's turnover. For the Louvre, see BN NAF 10278, Zola, p. 74.

on any particular item but to sell in quantity.[4] What more effective measure to accelerate the flow of goods than slashing prices? The Louvre took a mark-up of only 15 to 25 percent while smaller competitors charged up to 50 percent over the wholesale price.[5] Haggling was an accepted feature of traditional retail practice. The *grands magasins* eliminated such time-consuming negotiations, charging fixed and clearly marked prices. And finally, the rational ordering of department store counters made it possible for shoppers to make all their purchases in one place and in the shortest time possible. Viewed from above, the lay-out of the shopping floor resembled "a French garden as designed by Le Nôtre."[6] The department store, a contemporary observed, was to the humble boutique what the Tuileries Gardens were to a pot of flowers.[7] But it was not so much baroque as industrial imagery that the *grands magasins* evoked. The efficiency and scale of the big stores called to mind a machine that functioned "with almost mathematical precision," "a great steam engine," "a mechanism of modern life."[8]

A well-organized and well-oiled bureaucratic hierarchy assured the efficient organization of the "machine." The Bon Marché, for example, was run by a fifteen-man administrative council. The council was divided into committees, each assisted by its own clerical staff, which handled a variety of specialized tasks: maintenance, publicity, personnel, accounting. Each administrator, in addition, supervised the operation of one or more sales departments. Within individual de-

---

[4]BN NAF 10278, Zola, p. 221; J. Angot des Rotours, "Les Grands Magasins du Louvre," p. 97.

[5]BN NAF 10278, Zola, pp. 74–75.

[6]Ambrière, *La Vie secrète des grands magasins*, p. 110.

[7]BN NAF 10278, Zola, contains a clipping from *Le Figaro* (23 March 1881) in which this analogy is made.

[8]Coffignon, *Les Coulisses de la mode*, pp. 179–180; BN NAF 10278, Zola, p. 69; d'Avenel, "Le mécanisme de la vie moderne. Les grands magasins."

partments, the chain of command flowed downward from the administrator through the department and counter chiefs to the sales clerks on the shopping floor.[9]

Contemporaries borrowed from military vocabulary to describe the hierarchical organization of the big stores. The department was a "combat unit," the employees "an army of salesclerks."[10] And the image of massed battalions and concentrated firepower which the military analogy conjured up was not an inappropriate one. In 1911, Paris' twelve largest *grands magasins* were staffed by a whopping total of eleven thousand employees, over nine hundred souls per store, and this at a time when nearly two-thirds of all retail establishments employed ten persons or less.[11] Most observers, however, preferred to elaborate on the machine metaphor. If the department store was a beautifully organized machine, then its employees were merely cogs. "The division of labor," one contemporary observed, "works on the employee as it acts on the worker; it makes of one as of the other a sort of animated motor, mechanically accomplishing a task always the same."[12] What a contrast with the small shop where, it was claimed, employer and employee shared the same table and often lived as one family in the same house.[13]

The big stores bent every effort to insure the loyalty of their "hired hands." An elaborate structure of material rewards— commissions, bonuses, pay raises, promotions—was designed to fire up the commercial zeal of the department store rank and file. *Grands magasins* leavened bureaucratic organization with heavy doses of paternalism. The larger stores offered free

[9] Miller, p. 114.

[10] Garrigues, *Les Grands Magasins de nouveautés*, pp. 23–25.

[11] Labrousse and Braudel, eds., *Histoire économique et sociale de la France*, vol. IV, pt. 1, p. 402.

[12] Garrigues, pp. 24, 72.

[13] A. Feyeux, "La question des grands et des petits magasins," pp. 358–364.

medical services, pension plans, accident insurance. The Bon Marché in particular earned a reputation for beneficence vis-à-vis its loyal employees. In 1880, three years after her husband's death, Madame Boucicaut turned the store into a joint stock company, taking special pains to encourage employee share-holding (store personnel provided 7.5 million of the company's forty-million-franc capital).[14] Where positive controls failed, an intense and pervasive discipline took over. Owners hired selectively giving preference to young provincials, under thirty years of age. Parisians and Jews, judged to be too independent-minded, were not taken on.[15] A handful of stores required clerks to wear uniforms, and all employed detachments of floorwalkers whose job was as much to police the staff as to arrest shoplifters and maintain public order.[16] Deductions in pay, demotion and summary dismissal awaited violators of the dress code, latecomers and back-talkers. During the day, no one as a rule was allowed to leave the store, and indeed, a substantial percentage of employees actually lived in. The larger establishments, such as the Bon Marché and the Louvre, provided communal staff housing, little better than "barracks" in the opinion of the *Chambre syndicale des employés*.[17] A high proportion of sales personnel was single, 58 percent at the Louvre in 1891, and many were women.[18] In the interest of discipline and morality, the lodgings offered were segregated by sex.

[14] Cucheval-Clarigny and Flavien, *Etude sur le Bon Marché*, pp. 19, 24.

[15] Du Maroussem, *Le Jouet parisien*, p. 244.

[16] D'Avenel, "Le mécanisme de la vie moderne. Les magasins de l'alimentation," p. 816; BN NAF 10278, Zola, p. 234; McBride, "A Woman's World," p. 673.

[17] *Chambre syndicale des employés*, "Réponse," *La Revendication*, 23 August 1891.

[18] Frédéric Honoré, "Les employés de commerce à Paris," p. 282. The importance of female personnel should not be exaggerated. At the turn of the century, only one in six of Au Bon Marché's employees was female. Miller, p. 193.

The department store's experiments in human engineering inevitably invited comparison with the utopian schemes of visionary socialists like Charles Fourier. Zola recognized in the *grand magasin* a "forerunner of the phalanstery."[19] Labelling a department store, indeed any institution, phalansterian usually implied an attack in the name of traditional values—the sanctity of the hearth, the simplicity of manners. "The principal vice of the big bazaars," noted a critical *Le Figaro*, "is their inherently phalansterian organization which is inimical to family life."[20] The boulevardier Gustave Claudin describes the Louvre Hotel, located in the same building as the Louvre department store and operated by the same management: "It's a phalanstery, it's a bee-hive all abuzz. You'll come upon an astonished face in a corner: it's that of some rustic fellow whisked by express train from the depths of the countryside to this ant-heap."[21] Whether as steam engine, fighting machine, or phalanstery, the *grand magasin* represented to the contemporary mind a triumph of rational, industrial organization. It was the commercial equivalent of a factory, indeed of a factory town with its company-provided services and company housing.

The very architecture of the department store testified to its links with the world of industry. In 1869, Au Bon Marché began construction of a new store, destined to occupy a full square block between the rue du Bac and the rue Velpeau, the rue de Sèvres and the rue Babylone. Boileau *fils*, whose father had designed the wrought-iron framework of the Eglise Saint-Eugène, and Gustave Eiffel, engineer and bridge builder extraordinaire, were appointed architects. The structure, completed in 1887, featured a cavernous inner courtyard roofed over with glass skylights. Store galleries rested on slender,

[19] BN NAF 10278, Zola, p. 244.

[20] *Le Figaro* clipping (23 March 1881) in BN NAF 12078, Zola; see also, Mataja, "Le grand magasin et le petit commerce," p. 471.

[21] Claudin, *Paris*, pp. 100–101.

iron columns which were ornamented with heavy plaster and copperwork.[22] Paul Sédille put up a new building for Au Printemps (1881–1889) constructed along similar lines—"a tall glass building with an iron frame."[23]

Department store design owed much to the architectural innovations of exposition halls, and contemporaries did not hesitate to draw the parallel. *Grands magasins* were, in a manner of speaking, "permanent expositions."[24] What could be more appropriate than that they imitate the form and structure of their more temporary counterparts. In 1887, Eiffel and Jaluzot sealed a deal that bore ironic witness to the bond between exposition and *grand magasin*. Eiffel agreed to sell all scrap from construction of his tower to Jaluzot and threw into the bargain the exclusive right to manufacture miniature reproductions.[25] The department store, like the Eiffel Tower and the exposition hall, was a wonder of modern engineering, a monument to the marvels of industrial progress.

The machine architecture of the big stores was, however, of more than symbolic significance. If *grands magasins* resembled "market halls, railroad stations and exhibitions," it was not only because all had been designed to signal the arrival of a new industrial age, but also because all shared a common function: "the rapid handling of business activities involving huge crowds of pedestrians."[26] Glass and iron structures were admirably suited to provide the space, well lit and adequately ventilated, which commercial operations on a grand scale required. Such operations, moreover, promised tangible benefits to industry. As the Le Playian sociologist Pierre du Maroussem observed: "Big commerce is the counterpart of big industry, of Oldham smelting works, Bochum mines and

[22] Giedion, *Space, Time and Architecture*, pp. 237–238; Cucheval-Clarigny, p. 16; Hautecoeur, "De l'échoppe aux grands magasins," p. 829.

[23] Valmy-Baisse, *Les Grands Magasins*, pp. 52–53.

[24] Gaillard, *Paris, la ville 1852–1870*, p. 529.

[25] Braibant, *Histoire de la Tour Eiffel*, pp. 96–97.

[26] Giedion, p. 232.

Manchester spinning factories."[27] The link between the department store and industry was functional as well as metaphorical.

The big stores were indeed favored customers of large-scale manufacturers—and for good reason. Small shops generally ordered in small quantities through the intermediary of a wholesaler, jobber or factory representative. Payment was not usually immediate but delayed for a three-month term. Department stores, on the other hand, placed bulk orders and paid in cash on delivery. A manufacturer could more easily estimate the size of his market. Instead of stopping and starting production as orders trickled in and were filled, he could budget production time over the entire year. The plant might not always work at full capacity but at least the machinery could be kept running, even through the off-season. Appreciative manufacturers, naturally, offered discounts. Merchandise sold to the shopkeeper at two francs per unit might cost the department store only 1,75 F.[28]

Grands magasins realized further savings through the elimination of intermediaries. Before the coming of the department store, a customer might enter a draper's shop, select an item from a sample-book and then place an order. The order was passed on to a commissionnaire who in turn relayed it to the manufacturer. The largest department stores, by contrast, purchased directly from the manufacturer, by-passing the commission agent entirely. Buyers traveled to Roubaix and Rheims for woolens, to Elbeuf and Sedan for cloth, to Calais for lace. "For silk," according to an employee at the Grands Magasins de Louvre, "someone goes almost every month to Lyon."[29]

The ties between big commerce and big industry could be

[27] Du Maroussem, *Halles centrales de Paris*, p. 100.

[28] BN NAF 10278, Zola, pp. 70, 193. See also Garrigues, pp. 28–29; and Daugan, *Histoire et législation des patentes*, pp. 29–30; Saint-Martin, *Les Grands Magasins*, pp. 103–104.

[29] BN NAF 10278, Zola, p. 193.

closer still. An ambitious storeowner might venture into production for himself. In 1859, Félix Potin opened up a food-
processing plant near La Villette, which, by the end of the
century, employed nearly two thousand people. From can-
ning and sugar refining, to the manufacture of preserves,
condiments, candles and chocolate, there was little that the
enterprise did not do. Potin also owned vineyards in Tuni-
sia—at Potinville—which supplied his grocery chain with over
twenty thousand hectoliters per annum.[30]

Grands magasins also engaged in production, particularly of
ready-to-wear clothing—but with a difference. While Potin
owned a factory, stores like the Bon Marché or the Louvre ran
elaborate putting-out systems or *fabriques collectives*. Cloth, cut
and prepared on the premises, would be farmed out to an entrepreneur who might manage a small atelier of his own as
well as employ a network of home workers. In the 1880s, for
example, the house workshops of the Bon Marché were manned
by a staff of two hundred, manufacturing "ladies gowns and
women's morning dresses"; seventy-eight independently run
ateliers under exclusive contract to the store undertook to finish the job, employing over fourteen hundred for the purpose.[31] The place of ready-made goods in the early department store's repertory of merchandise, however, must not be
exaggerated. The big stores carried dry goods, *articles de Paris*,
but above all fabric by the bolt (*nouveautés*). Au Printemps,
when it opened, had twelve departments, three of which specialized in the sale of cloth: silks, woolens and linens.[32] Silk
was by far the most popular item. As late as the 1880s, the
silk counter at the Louvre department store outsold the ready-
to-wear department by 50 percent, fifteen million francs to
ten million.[33]

[30] On Potin's commercial empire, see Saint-Martin, p. 126; d'Avenel,
"Le mécanisme de la vie moderne. Les magasins de l'alimentation," p. 816.

[31] Cucheval-Clarigny, p. 29.

[32] *Printania*, p. 22.

[33] BN NAF 10278, Zola, p. 76.

The department store was indeed a creature of industrialization. It participated in and coordinated a productive process that embraced the mill as well as the garret. No commercial institution could dispose of goods in such quantities, none functioned with such mechanical precision or bureaucratic efficiency. Industry, large and small, spurred on by bulk orders and a multitude of subcontracts, strained to meet department store demand. The whole operation collapsed, of course, if the big stores failed to turn over their inventory with sufficient velocity.

The *grand magasin*, whose success was premised on low markups and high turnover, could not afford a leisurely approach to merchandising. Customers had to be lured into the store and made to buy. ". . . [I]n old Paris," remarked the vicomte d'Avenel, "advertising never amounted to more . . . than the distribution of handbills at street corners, on the Pont Neuf in particular. . . ."[34] Such primitive advertising paled beside the elaborate and lengthy illustrated catalogues assembled by department stores. Most *grands magasins* organized separate publicity departments. The Louvre, Bon Marché and others regularly took out full-page ads in popular journals—the notorious "page four."[35] The *Figaro* journalist Pierre Giffard wrote in 1882: "It's the big bazaar that has spurred the growth of advertising in the last twenty years. . . . The daily press has grown in parallel; these two modern institutions, in view of their financial connection, are and will be for a long time, mutually reinforcing."[36]

Catalogues and advertisements alerted potential customers to bargains and sales—and to changes of fashion. Can it be coincidence that the department store and the fashion industry sprang up side by side? Until mid-century, women's clothing was tailored by seamstresses working on cloth pro-

[34] D'Avenel, "Le mécanisme de la vie moderne. Les grands magasins," p. 366.

[35] Garrigues, p. 31.

[36] Giffard, *Paris sous la Troisième République*, p. 230.

vided by the customer. The sale of fabric was handled by the draper, confection by working women. Urged on by an enterprising employee, Charles Worth, the Maison Gagelin (a draper's firm) was the first to combine in a single enterprise both operations, cloth sales and confection. The manufacture of a gown, from fabric selection to pattern and tailoring, even to the trimmings, could now be accomplished in a single, unified procedure.[37] Clothing, in short, could now be designed. Haute couture, of course, only catered to a wealthy and daring clientele (wearing a "creation" still requires boldness of a certain kind). But what could a woman do who wanted to imitate high society, without having to pay designer prices? This was the territory the department store staked our for itself in the emergent fashion industry. *Grands magasins* went to considerable effort to stock only the most up-to-date fabrics and trimmings. Shops which specialized in the sale of patterns and models occupied premises within close proximity.[38] A style-conscious woman had only to make the right purchases, hire an able couturiere, and she would have, at reasonable expense, an attractive imitation of the latest fashions. *Grands magasins* lured bargain-hunters with tales of giveaway prices, but nothing attracted customers more successfully than advertising campaigns that played on the emotions of fashion-worshipers.

The printed word, of course, was not the only means of drumming up business. An impressive store exterior caught the customer's eye and excited his curiosity. The monumental design of the *grand magasin* helped create the desired effect. The Louvre, Bon Marché and Printemps—each occupying a full city block—were isolated, as monuments, from surrounding buildings. Facades were uniformly rectilinear and symmetrical, large bay windows alternating with pilasters,

---

[37] On the emergence of fashions, see Zeldin, *France 1848–1945*, vol. II, pp. 434–436; see also Reboux, *La Rue de la Paix*, p. 80.

[38] Office du travail, *Le Vêtement à Paris*, p. 561.

cariatids or sculpted masonry. In place of the traditional hanging sign, department store fronts were adorned with grandiose decorative ensembles, *façades-enseignes* as one observer called them.[39] Expensive materials, statuary, wrought-iron grillwork, gilding and multichrome mosaics dazzled the stroller, the potential shopper, with an opulence and grandeur which the new Opera House itself could scarcely match. Emblazoned in bright colors or deep-carved in the masonwork, the store name—Au Printemps, F. Potin—occupied a commanding position amidst all the ornamentation. Big signs, lavish decoration, monumental architecture shouted the store's presence without modesty or shame to the unattentive passerby. One had only to approach to discover what the shouting was about.

Zola published *Au Bonheur des Dames* in 1883, a novel about a fictional department store by the same name. Newly arrived in Paris, the novel's heroine Denise and her younger brother Pépé are staggered by the department store's spectacular window dressing:

But the last window in particular held their attention. It was illuminated by a display of silks, satins, and velvets, piled in a supple and vibrant scale of delicate floral tones: at the top, the velvets, in deep-black or in the white of curdled milk; lower down, the satins, pink, blue, vividly shifting color at the folds to pale hues of an infinite tenderness; lower still, the silks in rainbow colors, folded like a scallop shell, wrapped as around an arching figure, given life by the knowing fingers of the clerks; and between each motif, between each colored phrase of the display played a discreet accompaniment, a light, flounced band of cream foulard.[40]

[39] Fegdal, *Les Vieilles Enseignes de Paris*, p. 216.
[40] Zola, *Au Bonheur des Dames*, p. 8.

In the eighteenth century, technological limitations restricted the possibilities of store display. Silvering impaired the transparency of glass, and panes exceeding two meters square could not be manufactured. To exhibit their wares, to overcome the barrier between interior and exterior, stores were obliged to open out onto the street much as newsstands and greengrocers do to this day. More elegant establishments, disdaining such direct and promiscuous contact with the public, turned in on themselves. The introduction of clear plate glass allowed a more complicated relationship between street and shop. A store could display, yet maintain its distance, attract customers while excluding street people. *Grands magasins* exploited the possibilities to the limit. Ringing the ground floor, a glass belt of enormous windows allowed a virtually unobstructed view of store activity from the outside.[41] Shopping could begin before entry. The trick was to transform the idle spectator into a customer.

This task fell to the window-dresser, an artist or, more precisely, a *metteur en scène* who specialized "in the combination of effects of light and color, in the fascination exercised on lady shoppers by the profusion of fabrics, by the enchantment of a thousand and one shimmering and glittering objects, provoking the coquette, astounding even the serious woman with the evocation of a sort of bargain-basement poetry [*poésie de pacotille*]."[42] How different from the boutiques of yesteryear, "those holes of old Paris where in former times a piece of fabric was all the sign there was."[43] The front of Au Vieil Elbeuf, a draper's shop unluckily located just across the street from Zola's Au Bonheur des Dames, consisted of two darkened windows through which bolts of cloth could

[41] On the changing character of shop design, see Richardson, "Visage du magasin de détail à travers les âges," pp. 25–27; Janneau, "De l'échoppe au 'shopping center,' " pp. 8–15.

[42] Martin Saint-Léon, *Le Petit Commerce français*, p. 16.

[43] Zola, *Pot-Bouille*, pp. 23–24.

barely be distinguished and a door that seemed to open onto "the humid darkness of a cave."[44] The department store by contrast spilled itself out into the street, boldly displaying its "parvenu face to the noisy and sunlit streets of new Paris."[45] The commodity was no longer hidden, as though shameful, but celebrated. Via advertising and display, indeed, via architecture itself, the commodity made its presence known, appropriating the street for trade.

Commercialization of the street helped to create the mass clientele that the department store needed to survive. But it was not enough simply to draw customers into the store; once there, they had to be persuaded to open their pocket-books. Traditional merchandising practice barred passers-by from entering a store unless they intended to make a purchase. And once a purchase was made, no returns were permitted. There was little room for wandering in and out of stores, for buying on fancy, in a word, for "shopping." The design of shop interiors reflected this state of affairs. Goods were not attractively displayed, but often piled up in corners or stored behind counters out of the customer's reach. Poor lighting hampered visibility, and cramped quarters inhibited circulation.[46] Department stores, under constraint to maximize turnover, could not wait for merchandise to sell itself. This meant, first of all, permitting free entry into the store. A liberal policy on returns turned an irrevocable business transaction into an experiment that could be entered into tentatively, even frivolously. An "informal sales situation," artfully created through innovative display, removed some of the stiffness and ceremony surrounding the act of exchange.[47] Goods were not stacked in out-of-the-way corners accessible

[44] Zola, *Au Bonheur des Dames*, pp. 10–11.

[45] *Ibid.* p. 456.

[46] See, for example, Zola's description of the interior of Au Vieil Elbeuf in *Au Bonheur des Dames*, pp. 13–14.

[47] Artley, *The Golden Age of Shop Design*, p. 7.

only through the intermediary of a salesclerk, but placed where they could be touched and arranged so as to play on the consumer's senses.

Zola compared the department store interior to that of a cathedral where, under vaulting metallic naves, celebrants practiced the rites of commodity worship. But there was little of sober piety or quiet prayer in the noise and movement of department store crowds. Little wonder as interiors were designed to inspire delight not awe, pleasure not humility. Department stores, as we have seen, keenly appreciated the advantages of brilliant lighting, hence their extensive use of glass skylights. They were also among the first to install electric lamps in place of gas. Au Printemps made the transition in 1883. The first experiment with electric lighting in France had been attempted only five years earlier, during the Exposition of 1878, to illuminate the Place de l'Opéra. A well-lit store made good, practical sense; business could not be carried on in the dark. But bright lights also had a dazzling effect on the customer. "It's fairy-like," exclaimed a woman on entering the Palais-Royal Hall of the Grands Magasins du Louvre.[48] Zola describes the impact of switching on the lights in the late afternoon at Au Bonheur des Dames: ". . . there was an enraptured murmur from the crowd. Under the new lighting, the great white sale took on the fairy-like splendor of an apotheosis."[49]

Marvel, fairyland, enchanted palace—these were the images the department store projected.[50] The Bon Marché billed itself as the Eighth Wonder of the World.[51] The department store was indeed a sight to be seen, a tourist attraction as much as an iron shed for the conduct of business. Counters

[48] BN NAF 10278, Zola, p. 97.

[49] Zola, *Au Bonheur des Dames*, p. 497.

[50] See the Louvre's house publication, *Le Louvre. Grand hôtel et grands magasins*, pp. 10–11, 40.

[51] Miller, p. 166.

were laid out to simplify circulation—and at the same time to overpower customers with the variety and quantity of goods:

> *Magasins de nouveautés*, aren't they a play of a thousand divers acts—each department a scene unto itself—, where set design is all important, where *metteurs en scène* rival one another in ingenuity, an immense theater where the shoppers themselves take part in the show and become the stars of some gigantic music-hall fantasy [*féerie*]?[52]

Contemporaries recognized that this commercial fairyland was not to be had without a price. Parisians committed to a leisured pace, to strolling and witty conversation, bemoaned the department store's shattering impact on the character and design of their beloved old city. Transformation of the street into a commercial corridor had quickened the rhythms of urban life, addicting city-dwellers to movement, to stimulation. The advertising revolution—with its passion for the monumental, the loud and the prosaic—had swept aside the picturesque signs of yesteryear whose poetry and rich symbolism had once been the delight of strollers.[53] "In former times," wrote John Grand-Carteret, "stores looked for charming names to grace signs of a high-flown romanticism. Today, what counts is a name that can be read from afar, thanks to its extraordinary size and the éclat of its gilt-lettering."[54] Where picturesque streets and quaint shops had once prospered stood the *grand magasin*, a massive stone and iron construction that seemed to devour entire neighborhoods whole.

Indeed, it was said, the department store had built its success on the cadaver of the *quartier*. Zola's fictional Au Bonheur des Dames, much like the real Au Bon Marché, expanded gradually, swallowing up its smaller competitors one

---

[52] Jarry, *Les Magasins de nouveautés*, p. 139.
[53] Baudin, *L'Enseigne et l'affiche*, pp. 54–55.
[54] Grand-Carteret, *L'Enseigne*, p. 119.

at a time. The unhappy Baudin, proprietor of the ill-fated Au Vieil Elbeuf, prophesied with fear and trembling the demise of his neighborhood: "One day, the Bonheur all by itself will cover the *quartier* with its roof."[55] The Louvre, by contrast, came into existence full-blown on a site cleared by Haussmann to make way for the rue de Rivoli. A store publication described the change: "When the old *quartier* was razed, out of the ocean of debris emerged an edifice almost as vast as its illustrious neighbor [the Louvre Palace]."[56]

But had the *quartier* been utterly obliterated? The department store, like the *quartier* it displaced, had streets (aisles) and shops (counters), arranged and juxtaposed to create effects that real life could not rival. "Isn't all of life to be found there in miniature," asked Baudelaire, "and so much more colorful, polished and sparkling than real life. . . . ?"[57] Indeed, the department store interior called to mind something grander than a mere *quartier*; it was itself a cityscape "with its monuments, its streets, its squares."[58] Like the real city in which it was set, this city in microcosm, "this city of fabrics and knick-knacks," as Martin Saint-Léon called it, contained streets, houses, "*quartiers* unknown to one another. . . ."[59] The *grands magasins* were, just as much as Paris herself, "great agglomerations"[60]—but with this difference: the city was never quite able to disguise the human misery of its slums and bidonvilles. The department store, with its spectacular atmospherics and special effects, banished troublesome second thoughts about how and why the commodity had come into being. What, after all, was visible to the eye of

[55] Zola, *Au Bonheur des Dames*, p. 258.

[56] *Le Louvre. Grand hôtel et grands magasins*, p. 9.

[57] Cited in Jarry, p. 29.

[58] Zola, *Au Bonheur des Dames*, p. 60.

[59] Martin Saint-Léon, p. 106; Ambrière, p. 38.

[60] Bernard, *Du Mouvement d'organisation et de défense du petit commerce français*, p. 52.

the casual observer? Neatly dressed personnel busily serving customers in an impressive glass and iron setting? Bureaucracy and the machine appeared to bend to the customer's service, neither crushing nor awesome, but considerate and delightful. Even the spectator himself was the object of the big store's transforming powers. The merchandising revolution worked by *grands magasins* extended the marketplace into the street, onto buildings, into the newspapers. Everyone became a potential customer. For the harsh realities of an industrial, urban world, the department store substituted a utopian vision of the modern metropolis populated by shoppers awash in commodities, where machines and bureaucracy labored not to deny but to satisfy needs. To participate in this world, one had only to yield to the pleasant and pervasive temptations of consumerism. Who could resist? Commercial utopianism drummed up the necessary custom which alone could sustain an enterprise of the scale and complexity of a department store.

Economies of scale, bureaucratic management, close ties to industry, and innovative merchandising enabled department stores to mobilize for the commercial struggle with an awesome efficiency. And department-store growth *was* spectacular. The Bon Marché's gross earnings, seven million francs in 1863, had shot up to sixty-seven million by 1877. The Louvre, in 1875, after only twenty years of business, was taking in forty million per annum.[61] By the end of the century, department-store turnover amounted to nearly half a billion francs.[62] *Grands magasins* apparently got the mass clientele they needed to survive. But where did all these shoppers come from? Who were they?

Information on the actual clienteles of department stores is

[61] For figures on the growth of department store turnover, see Martin Saint-Léon, p. 15.

[62] D'Avenel, "Le mécanisme de la vie moderne. Les grands magasins," p. 367.

scarce indeed, and what there is of it precludes an uncomplicated answer. Certain kinds of *grands magasins* definitely catered to a working-class public. La Belle Jardinière, from 1867 located on the rue Pont-Neuf, specialized in the sale of ready-made workclothes, drawing its custom primarily from "the laboring class: stall-keepers and workers from les Halles, market-gardeners, butchers, *charcutiers*, cheese-dealers, porters, etc."[63] La Samaritaine's first customers were *dames de la Halle* in search of cheap apron material.[64] But these were not, by any means, Paris' biggest stores. La Samaritaine grossed two million francs in 1877. La Belle Jardinière as late as 1909, when the Louvre was turning over in the neighborhood of 150 million francs, did only twenty-nine million francs worth of business in Paris.[65]

The larger establishments—the Bon Marché, the Louvre and Au Printemps—served a much different class of buyer. With their impressive facades and expensive interiors, these stores made a bid for the patronage of the city's affluent market. Wealthy fashion-setters naturally preferred to buy their own gowns at Doucet's or Worth's, deigning to shop at *grands magasins* only for underwear or household items.[66] The department store's clientele began just one notch below with the well-to-do who cared for fashion but also liked a bargain, who wore costly fabrics but bought by the bolt. There might be variations in clientele from one store to the next. The Bon Marché, more staid than some of its competitors, was patronized primarily by solid bourgeois.[67] The store, it was remarked, "smelled a little of the provinces."[68] The Louvre appealed to a faster crowd that was also somewhat less careful

[63] *La Vie d'une grande industrie moderne*, p. 14.
[64] Laudet, *La Samaritaine*, p. 5.
[65] *Ibid.*, p. 8; Martin Saint-Léon, p. 15.
[66] Ambrière, p. 50; BN NAF 12078, Zola, p. 209.
[67] Valmy-Baisse, pp. 37, 40.
[68] BN NAF 10278, Zola, p. 209.

with its money ("The Louvre is more coquette and costlier," noted Zola), while Jaluzot's Printemps placed the accent on youth.[69] In Zola's *Au Bonheur des Dames*, one of the peripheral characters, Madame Desforges, holds a weekly four-o'clock tea where ladies, often fresh from a shopping expedition, gathered to gossip and discuss the afternoon's purchases. They are all loyal boosters of Au Bonheur des Dames. Their social profile pinpoints with some precision the milieu from which the early department store attracted its first clientele. The hostess was a daughter of a councillor of state and widow of a stock speculator; her guests included—apart from the owner of Au Bohneur des Dames himself, Octave Mouret—the wives of a deputy head clerk at the Ministry of Finance, of a lawyer "known at the Palace," of a professor at the Lycée Bonaparte, and of a "former *viveur*" down on his luck "who was spending his retirement in the civil service . . . as inspector general of breeding-studs."[70] The *grands magasins* recruited their most ardent patrons among the moneyed bourgeoisie: among the financial, professional and administrative middle class. The department store was indeed, as du Maroussem dubbed it, a "palace for parvenus."[71]

The early department store's relative neglect of confectioned goods is explained in large part by the social cut of its clientele. At mid-century, ateliers and not factories manufactured ready-to-wear items.[72] Handwork, not steam power, was the rule. What kinds of goods could be mass produced by hand? Primarily low-quality items such as workclothes and articles of clothing (undergarments, great coats, nightwear) which did not have to be well tailored to fit. Department stores that catered to well-to-do patrons could market successfully

[69] *Ibid.*, p. 209; Valmy-Baisse, p. 52.

[70] Zola, *Au Bonheur des Dames*, pp. 71–82.

[71] Du Maroussem, "Les grands magasins tels qu'ils sont," p. 923.

[72] Worth, *La Courture et la confection des vêtements de femme*, p. 96.

only goods of the latter sort. When the Empress Eugénie made a purchase at the *confection* counter of the Louvre, it was for a bathrobe.[73] There were of course big stores—the Belle Jardinière for example—that specialized in ready-to-wear goods, but they served, as we have seen, a primarily working-class clientele. From the point of view of most *grands magasins*, ready-to-wear production was as yet too primitive to meet the demands of a newly rich buying public.

The greatest parvenus of all, of course, were the department store owners themselves, men of modest social origins who, by dint of hard work, cunning, imagination and good luck, managed to build vast commercial empires virtually from scratch, amassing enormous personal fortunes along the way. Many were provincials, young Rastignacs who had come to the capital city to make their mark. Boucicaut was born in Normandy, Potin in the department of the Seine-et-Oise, Cognacq on the Ile de Ré. They did not begin life in poverty, but neither did they enjoy substantial material advantages. The father might be a farmer, as was Potin's, a hatter, as was Boucicaut's, a registrar, as was Cognacq's, a wineshopkeeper, as was Hériot's—in short, a man of some means but of not enough to set up an ambitious young son in business for himself. The first generation of department store owners, as a rule, began their careers at the bottom, as lowly employees, as clerks or buyers in one of mid-century Paris' numerous *magasins de nouveautés*. Boucicaut worked at the Petit Saint-Thomas, Chauchard at the Pauvre Diable, Hériot at the Ville de Paris, Jaluzot at the Bon Marché. Department store founders were not atypical in this respect. Most petty entrepreneurs got their start without benefit of an inheritance either in the form of cash or of an already established, ongoing business.[74]

[73] Vanier, *La Mode et ses metiérs*, p. 208.

[74] For details on Boucicaut, Potin, etc., see: Cognacq, "Causerie sur les grands magasins," pp. 30–31; Cucheval-Clarigny, pp. 7–8; d'Avenel, "Le mécanisme de la vie moderne. Les magasins de l'alimentation," pp. 812–

Given their pinched circumstances, how did a Boucicaut or a Ruel manage to scrape together the necessary capital to launch an enterprise of their own and finance its expansion? Matrimony on advantageous terms offered the easiest solution to the problem. Jaluzot married a woman with a three-hundred-thousand-franc dowry. Cognacq's wife, Louise Jay, brought seventy thousand francs to their marriage.[75] Access to capital might also be secured through partnership with well-heeled backers. Faré, an established *marchand de nouveautés* in the faubourg Montmartre, put the Louvre on its feet with an initial investment of one hundred thousand francs. Between them, Chauchard and Hériot, whose energy and ambition made the store's success, contributed only forty thousand francs to the enterprise. The Bon Marché was already a going concern run by a man named Videau when Boucicaut bought into it. Videau sold his share of the business in 1863 for one and a half million francs put up on Boucicaut's behalf by a wealthy New York restaurateur.[76]

It took hard maneuvering, a timely marriage or profitable partnership, to escape the credit bind that cramped most commercial enterprises. A department store owner had to be able to cajole investors, as well as customers, into parting with their money. He was a "self-made man" who built gigantic commercial fairylands for a clientele of *nouveaux riches* much like himself.

Frenchmen who witnessed the rise of the department store sensed a major transformation in the world of commerce. They summed up the change in terms of an emerging conflict between large and small commerce, between the *grand magasin* and *petit commerçant*. The department store, of course, had all the advantages in the struggle, and few doubted its ultimate

---

818; d'Ydewalle, *Au Bon Marché*, pp. 12–15; Jarry, p. 74; Valmy-Baisse, pp. 11–12.

[75] On Jaluzot's and Cognacq's marriages, see Saint-Martin, pp. 34–35.

[76] D'Ydewalle, p. 32.

triumph over the inefficient and frumpy shops of yesteryear. The old-fashioned boutique, mired in routine and hopelessly traditionalist in its methods, was no match for its larger rivals. From this perspective, the emergence of a protest movement like the *Ligue syndicale* appears as a reaction in the name of tradition against the encroachment of modernity. The explanation of shopkeeper mobilization is seen to lie in an unequal competition between *petits boutiquiers* and department stores. But the department store thesis—in one or another version advanced by *ligueurs*, historians and contemporaries alike—has serious weaknesses. It assumes firstly, that the small shop and *grand magasin* were locked in a mortal combat from which only one could emerge victorious; and secondly, that *petit commerce*, barring radical state intervention, was bound to lose out in this Darwinian struggle for commercial survival because it was almost by definition a traditional structure, a vestigial organ of an outworn past.

THE ADAPTATION AND SURVIVAL OF RETAIL COMMERCE

Shopkeepers liked to compare the *grand magasin* to a manchineel, a tropical tree whose toxic fruit poisoned the ground, destroying the unfortunate plants (shops) that grew in its vicinity. The octopus was another favorite metaphor: "Each counter is a tentacle of the octopus that has grasped, sucked and drained all within its reach. Death and silence lay all about it."[77] A stroll today on the blocks neighboring the Bon Marché, along the rue du Bac or the rue de Sèvres, belies this claim. Was it any different a hundred years ago? Jeanne Gaillard has shown that in 1862, a half dozen *marchands de nouveautés* carried on business along the rue du Bac in the very shadow of

[77] Beurdeley and Drucker, "Les grands magasins et la liberté commerciale," p. 572.

the Bon Marché.[78] Of course, 1862 is an early date, perhaps too early to register the ruinous effects of the store on its hapless neighbors. Yet, at the end of the century, the picture had not changed dramatically. The rue du Bac and the rue de Sèvres are filled with food stores but also "tailors, stationers, a piano-dealer, a retailer of artificial flowers, a watchmaker, an optician, a pet-store, a framer, a merchant in porcelains and faiences. . . ." And if one proceeded up the rue de Sèvres toward the boulevard Montparnasse, one encountered "numerous displays of shoes, bedding and even '*nouveautés*.' "[79] In an interview recorded in 1911, M. Duru, president of the *Chambre syndicale de la mercerie*, advanced a simple explanation for the phenomenon: "In *quartiers* where department stores are located, one can find petty mercers in number. That's because *grands magasins generate a current of business*; many customers, not finding exactly what they want in the department store, turn to the nearby small shop as an alternative."[80] In the first years of this century, department stores were under considerable pressure to close on Sundays. Shopkeepers working in the neighborhood of La Samaritaine allegedly petitioned the Cognacq family to remain open, arguing that the "animation" generated by the store was vital to their own prosperity.[81] Department stores staked a claim to a substantial market share but did not monopolize all commercial activity. According to one estimate, *grands magasins* handled only about ten percent of the four to five billion francs of business turned over by all commercial enterprises in Paris at the turn of the century.[82]

Large-scale enterprise was not necessarily fatal to the small

[78]Gaillard, p. 540.

[79]D'Azambuja, "Les grands magasins doivent-ils tuer les petits?," pp. 290–291.

[80]Cited in Martin Saint-Léon, pp. 72–73.

[81]Joseph Bernard and Louis Hoffman, "Le petit commerce et les grands magasins," p. 301.

[82]Daugan, p. 33.

shop. A trip to the downtown area of any major Western city will show that the clothing boutique and jewelry store can flourish even in the corporate world of the twentieth century. Many retailers, of course, survived because they traded in goods not susceptible to large-scale merchandising. Fruits and vegetables, meat and poultry, bread and dairy products, did not preserve well; maintaining a large inventory, however rapid the turnover, involved substantial losses to spoilage.[83] For small inexpensive articles—paper goods, tobacco, or for articles of daily consumption—comestibles, newspapers, a trip downtown to the department store was an inconvenience not worth the minimal savings.[84] And finally, where new products were involved—bicycles, incandescent lamps, photographic equipment, department stores were often slow or, given the uncertainty of the future, reluctant to act, leaving the market uncontested to the small entrepreneur.[85]

Not every commerce, of course, was immune to department store competition. For trade in products such as dry goods (sugar, spices, coffee) whose quality did not vary substantially from one item to the next, large-scale merchandisers enjoyed powerful advantages. *Grands magasins* could virtually monopolize the sale of underwear, men's shirts (save for de luxe items) and gloves.[86] But smaller establishments could take measures to defend themselves.

No law bound small retailers to traditional business methods. A shirt-seller might add ties, socks, canes and umbrellas to his inventory.[87] The *chemisier* of yesteryear vanished only to reemerge as a men's clothing store. Customers who appreciated the convenience but not the impersonality and bustle of the department store could find at a modestly sized hab-

[83] D'Azambuja, pp. 282–283.

[84] Mataja, "Le grand magasin et le petit commerce," p. 459.

[85] Bernard, pp. 37–38.

[86] Martin Saint-Léon, pp. 64, 69; BN NAF 10278, Zola, p. 199.

[87] Martin Saint-Léon, p. 65.

erdashery the range of items they sought without having to sacrifice the personal attention and intimate atmosphere of the boutique. If, in addition, a clothing store could claim the cachet of fashion for its merchandise, its fortune was made.[88] A boutique that specialized in a particular style or cut of clothes, that set fashion trends or purveyed a particular look, offered the shopper a kind of product he might not be able to find elsewhere, even at Au Bon Marché or Au Printemps. In fact, where cloth was not concerned, department stores were at some disadvantage in fashion retailing. They bought in bulk and dealt in items that were produced in quantity or by unskilled labor. Department store merchandise was cheaper but not highly individualized. A woman who bought a hat at the Bon Marché ran the risk of bumping into another Boucicaut customer wearing the identical article.

Trade in high-quality luxury goods posed similar problems for department stores.[89] Discounts received on large factory orders and high sales turnover allowed *grands magasins* to slash prices, but luxury goods did not lend themselves to this approach. Valued at least in part for their original, unique character, they could not be churned out *en masse.* While a *grand magasin* might sell jewelry or furs, it could never hope to outdistance a Boucheron or a Révillon.

Differences in taste also moderated the impact of massmarketing techniques on service businesses: restaurants, hotels, photographers, hair dressers.[90] The Grand Hôtel might offer the most spectacular luxury accommodations in town; a *bouillon* on the model of Chartier's or Duval's might supply the cheapest fare. But fortunately for the small businessman, where services were involved, spectacle and cheapness were not the sole or even the most important criteria in customer de-

---

[88] D'Azambuja, p. 285.
[89] Duclos, *La Transformation du commerce de détail*, p. 141.
[90] D'Azambuja, p. 283.

cision-making. Some travelers preferred quarters at more elegant and subdued, albeit smaller, hotels; some diners were content with the home-cooked meals and healthy portions served up at their local bistro. A clientele that valued discreet elegance, high quality or service more than bargain prices might well prefer a boutique to a *grand magasin*.

Retailers with imagination and energy could compensate for the advantages of scale enjoyed by department stores. Much depended on the product or service a shopkeeper offered, but he was not entirely helpless. He might multiply the lines of merchandise he retailed or improve his services; he could introduce new products or update and upgrade his inventory. Smallness even had some virtues. A *grand magasin* lacked the exclusivity of a small shop; it could not build a loyal clientele the way its smaller rivals did. Personal attention and friendly chat were not to be found at busy department store counters. And small shops were always close at hand, just down the street or around the corner.

As for the organizational advantages of the department store—an extensive division of labor, a clearly articulated chain of command, these could be and were imitated by smaller retailers. Enterprising *boutiquiers* scrambled to streamline their businesses, a scramble that affected the structure of work within the shop. In the interest of efficiency, industrial and commercial activities were separated, a separation consummated by division of the business premises into a back room and a selling area up front. The shopkeeper and his wife busied themselves serving customers while in the back of the store "workers . . . were hunched over their tools producing what the boss sold over the counter. . . ."[91] This division of labor freed the store owner from manual tasks and allowed him to concentrate on managerial activities: bookkeeping, merchandising, supervision of personnel. Under such an arrangement,

[91] Frantz Funck-Brentano, *Grandeur et décadence des classes moyennes*, p. 33.

what skills did a *patron* have to have to succeed? Did he require intimate knowledge of productive processes, or was it enough that he be able to recognize a good product and know how to market it? Du Maroussem, writing at the end of the century, identified a variety of small businesses, from high-fashion houses to pastry shops, which were owned and operated by men who were themselves strangers to their profession. They were not couturiers or pastry chefs by training, but businessmen versed in the techniques of management and marketing.[92]

The division of labor within a small enterprise, of course, could be pushed yet further. The *patron* might choose to parcel out his responsibilities, hiring a bookkeeper, a cashier, clerks, delivery boys, an entire mini-bureaucracy. A prosperous tailor, for example, who ran a shop on the *grands boulevards*, did not himself wield scissors or shears, nor did he even necessarily wait on customers. He purchased materials and supervised the store personnel. Commercial operations were handled by a small staff of clerks and other white-collar workers. Taking measurements and cutting the cloth to pattern were the work of *coupeurs* while basting and sewing were performed by *pompiers* who never saw the front of the shop. Additional personnel, some shop employees, others garret workers paid by the piece, put on the finishing touches: linings, buttonholes, etc.[93]

Bureaucratic organization, naturally, transformed the character of labor relations within a small enterprise.[94] The businessman was not likely to dine with his employees let alone

[92] Office du travail, *Le Vêtement à Paris*, p. 679; Office du travail, *L'Alimentation à Paris*, p. 180. Du Maroussem directed the latter inquiry and acted as chief researcher for the former. Armand Audiganne cites the example of a baker who "had never touched dough in his life. . . ." See, Audiganne, *Mémoires d'un ouvrier*, p. 86.

[93] Office du travail, *Le Vêtement à Paris*, pp. 26–29.

[94] Office du travail, *L'Alimentation à Paris*, pp. 19, 49.

share lodgings with them. A wage earner could not realistically aspire to succeed an employer whom he hardly knew. The hiring process was no less impersonal. In the bakery business, store owners hired personnel through placement bureaux, which kept lists of available workmen. To find a job, young bakers were obliged to join the reserve army of labor commanded by the *placeurs*. Worker resentment against employment offices was intense, particularly in the food trades where they were quite common. The *Chambre syndicale de l'alimentation*, formed in 1894, threatened a general strike to secure abolition of the bureaux.[95] With CGT support, this threat was executed successfully in 1904, prompting the government to submit legislation suppressing privately run bureaux.

Commentators who celebrated the family character of *petit commerce* failed to observe that a small shop could become a mini-bureaucracy and, for that matter, a locus of class conflict. The store owner himself was transformed in the process. He had once been and been looked upon as "a worker, master of his trade" risen from the ranks. He had now become a professional businessman, "the head of a staff of cashiers, secretaries and clerks" and, in the eyes of his workers, "a representative of the so-called 'bourgeoisie.' "[96]

However hard the small shop strove to adapt to the presence of a department store or to imitate its methods, there were limits to what could be done. *Grands magasins*, as purchasers of cloth and as coordinators of a vast, urban putting-out system, were in a position to exert some control over the productive process. Their buying power decided what kinds of items were manufactured; their command over a network of finishing industries allowed them to determine the final

[95] APP B/a 1408 bis, 14 September 1896; 19 May 1893.
[96] Funck-Brentano, *op. cit.*, p. 34; Office du travail, *L'Alimentation à Paris*, p. 94.

appearance of the goods they sold. Smaller enterprises could not influence to the same degree the selection and appearance of the articles that passed over their counters.

Many small businesses, of course, still produced what they sold and were able to assert some control over the commodity in this way. Du Maroussem, however, argues strenuously that the mixed-function enterprise which both manufactured and retailed was increasingly a relic of the past.[97] At mid-century, for example, it was not unusual for a milk dealer to own his own stable and cow. The improvement of the Paris transport system made possible the emergence of large suburban dairies which rapidly won a monopoly on the production of milk, reducing the milkman to the status of a simple retailer.[98] *Charcutiers* and *tripiers* experienced a similar transformation. Curing factories, which could mass-produce smoked hams, salt pork and sausage at minimum expense turned pork butchering into a large-scale industrial enterprise. In the city of Paris at the end of the century, a single firm, Artus, had a virtual corner on the manufacture of tripes. *Charcutiers* and *tripiers* continued to perform certain "industrial" tasks—meat-cutting, the preparation of *pâtés*—but to an increasing extent, they were becoming simple food shops, commercial outlets for items processed by separately owned food factories.[99] In 1856, according to Louis Chevalier, "Industry was very close to commerce and intermingled with it, commerce and industry alike being characterized by direct relations with the clientele."[100] As the century wore on, commerce and industry parted ways.

Petit commerce could never, as did the big stores, master the

[97] Du Maroussem, *Les Enquêtes, pratique et théorie*, p. 83.

[98] Office du travail, *L'Alimentation à Paris*, pp. 289ff.; du Maroussem, *Halles centrales de Paris*, p. 93.

[99] Office du travail, *L'Alimentation à Paris*, pp. 255ff.

[100] Chevalier, *La Formation de la population parisienne*, p. 75.

forces of industry, but it was more than a match for its larger rivals in the field of innovative merchandising. Nothing prevented small businesses from rationalizing store lay-out, organizing seasonal sales or instituting marked prices. And the department store held no monopoly on the rites of commodity utopianism. It was not, after all, the *grands magasins* that had invented the concept of the consumer fairyland. The arcades of central Paris—passage des Panoramas, passage des Princes, passage Ste.-Anne, passage Choiseul, passage Vivienne, etc.—are today peaceful, sometimes gloomy commercial backwaters, but they were not always so.[101]

Most of the city's arcades were built in a fifty-year span, stretching from Napoleon's Consulate through the July Monarchy. The passage des Panoramas appeared in 1800, the passage Jouffroy in 1845.[102] At the time of their construction, the arcades represented a daring innovation in commercial architecture. Rows of elegant shops flanking a paved promenade were sheltered from the elements by glass and iron skylights. In the daytime, natural lighting was adequate; nighttime posed problems eventually resolved with the installation of gas jets. Au Printemps, as we have seen, was among the first to experiment with electric lighting. The Panoramas was among the first to experiment with gas, installing the necessary equipment as early as 1817. The combination of fancy shops, marble pavements, iron, glass and gaslight produced a spectacular effect: "One seemed to be transported into some fairy country on entering them of an evening, so brilliantly illuminated were they by light reflected endlessly off window panes and mirrors."[103] The arcades, a network of sheltered streets, constituted a parallel, enchanted city—"a city, indeed, a world in miniature"[104]—

[101] See Walter Benjamin's brilliant discussion in Benjamin, *Charles Baudelaire*, pp. 157–160.

[102] Ginisty, *Les Anciens Boulevards*, pp. 41, 62.

[103] Cited in Malet, *Le Baron Haussmann*, p. 129.

[104] Cited in Benjamin, p. 158.

which existed within the muddy, conflicted reality of Restoration Paris.

The shops of the *passages* were not equipped with vast, interior halls or with enormous, baroque facades, yet in their way they strove to impress, to create a monumental effect. An ambitious and well-to-do *boutiquier* might hire an architect to design his shopfront. Classical forms were preferred: pilasters, columns, cornices, friezes, frescoes, etc. The aim was to transform "the perfumer's boutique into a temple of the Graces, the wineshop into a sanctuary of Bacchus."[105] Where, because of expense, the building materials of classical architecture could not actually be used, *trompe l'oeil* was employed. A skillful artist could imitate lapis, bronze, gold, marble of any hue. An ably applied coat of paint imparted a classical magnificence to an otherwise uninteresting exterior.

Elegance and *bon ton* were as much themes of shop design as grandeur. A facade was not complete without a painted, hanging sign that played on literary or theatrical motifs. Interiors were decorated to resemble fashionably appointed sitting rooms. A genteel shop owner made every effort to conceal that his store was a place of business where cash changed hands. A veil of salon elegance was draped over the premises. The commodity, of course, was not treated with such tasteful reticence. Counter display, window-dressing, the prospectus, all predate the department store.[106]

Grands magasins, for all their innovations, were heirs to a merchandising tradition pioneered in the *passage*. Nor were they the only heirs. The *grands boulevards* threaded their way between the IInd and IXth arrondissements. Tree-lined malls where dandies, lions and fashionables had promenaded in the days of the July Monarchy, these spacious avenues emerged as the leading shopping district of Paris under the Second

[105] Hautecoeur, p. 817.

[106] For shop interiors of the Restoration period, see Hautecoeur, pp. 821–824; and also Cahen, "L'enrichissement de la France sous la Restoration," p. 192.

Empire. An "uninterrupted file of boutiques" extended from the rue Drouot to the Madeleine, "all lit-up until midnight."[107] Cafés, restaurants and luxury shops monopolized the ground floors of the buildings along the boulevards while linen drapers, modistes and tailors occupied the apartments above.[108]

The boulevard, it was said, aspired to outbid the *grands magasins*, "caravansaries of fashion," to become the principal "furnisher of *tout Paris*."[109] Stores spared no expense to rival their larger competitors in sumptuousness and grandiosity. Charles Garnier, architect of the Opéra, was commissioned by the Café de Paris to design a spectacular entrance. The classical lines of the Restoration boutique dissolved into the florid arabesques of the Second Empire shop. The shops of the late nineteenth century lavishly used the materials which stores of an earlier epoch had only imitated. "A vermouth," we are told, "can't be had but under a gilded ceiling. Fresh pork calls for porphyry. Sauerkraut is complemented with Carrara marble and *museau de boeuf* displayed against a backdrop of authentic Gobelins."[110] Less luxurious establishments off the boulevards could not afford the rococo ornamentation of a Café de Paris, but even these more modest boutiques found ways to spruce up their appearance. Filigree and gilt were beyond their means, but painted paneling was not. A bakery might sport harvest scenes, sheaves of wheat or the tools of farming; *charcutiers* preferred depictions of the hunt and wild game. The

[107] Reboux, *Histoire et les dessous de Paris*, p. 62.

[108] *Les Boulevards de Paris*, p. 96. The BHVP contains a book of illustrated fold-outs, which probably dates from the late 1870s or early 1880s, depicting the double line of storefronts facing out onto the boulevards and important neighboring streets. See *Les Boulevards. L'Avenue de l'Opéra et la rue de la Paix*. This source shows clearly the prevalence of small and medium retailers on the city's major shopping streets.

[109] Montorgueil, *La Vie des boulevards*, p. 19.

[110] *Ibid.*, p. viii.

second half of the nineteenth century witnessed a renaissance of shop design.[111]

Nowhere was the spectacle of commercial renewal more evident than on the boulevards. The terms invoked to describe the scene should by now be familiar. In Zola's *La Curée*, the incestuous lovers Renée and Maxime contemplate the boulevards at the stroke of midnight from a private cabinet on the first floor of the Café Riche (rue Le Peletier):

> And the parade passed back and forth without end, with a tiring regularity, a strangely mixed world but ever the same. . . . A fairyland riot of a million dancing flames, pouring from the boutiques, coloring windows and kiosks, running along the shop-fronts, in shafts, in letters, in fiery designs, piercing the darkness beneath the stars, and shooting endlessly down the street.[112]

And the shops whose dazzling lights were the joy of the noctambule, they resembled "beneath a finery always fresh . . . palaces in miniature irradiated by diamonds and lustrous cloths, where the art of the haberdasher competed in elegance with that of the bootmaker."[113]

The boulevards were a fanciful land of enchanted palaces, a characterization that was, as we have seen, also applied to the *grands magasins*. The lavish and sometimes loud boulevard boutique was as much a part of the new parvenu culture as the department store. To be sure, aristocrats and dandies continued to haunt the boulevards under the Second Empire. Tortoni's remained their headquarters as in the days of the July Monarchy, but a new element had begun to creep in. Xavier Aubryet, mid-century littérateur and man about town describes the boulevard des Italiens in 1877: "There it is that

---

[111] Reinharez and Chamarat, *Boutiques du temps passé*, pp. 9–11.

[112] Zola, *La Curée*, p. 205.

[113] De Lannoy, *Les Plaisirs et la vie de Paris*, p. 24.

finance and literature cross paths, that inspiration and speculation march hand in hand, that men of business rub shoulders with men of pleasure."[114] The neighboring boulevard des
Capucines offered to view a similar social landscape. Jules Vallès
wrote in the seventies: "But the current that washes over the
thoroughfare carries with it a world of new-made bourgeois.
. . . This boulevard, because so near to the avenue de l'Opéra,
has become the rendezvous of wheeler-dealers, of newspaper
and company promoters, of idea-men and all the inventors of
bold, new projects,"[115] Boulevard shops flourished in a milieu populated by *arrivistes*, *nouveaux riches* and parvenus. The
store owners themselves were very much a part of this new
world. "It's hard to imagine," wrote Georges Montorgueil,
"the boldness of one-time waiters now become café-owners:
one hundred thousand francs to decorate a door is nothing to
them. They'll spend a million to make their customers feel
welcome."[116] For every venerable firm of long-standing and
good name, there was a new enterprise run by an ambitious
young man on the make. In the seventies, for every Dusautoy
(a men's tailor whose business was renowned in the days of
the July Monarchy), there was a Marguery. Shopkeepers could
be parvenus as much as department store owners. The Second
Empire was a period of ascension for new men, for financiers,
department store owners, but also for shopkeepers. Maxime
du Camp, writing in 1875, captures the change:

> Not so long ago a boutique was a boutique, now it's an
> establishment; the tradesman has become a merchant, the
> counter an office, the *garçon* a clerk, customers a clien-

[114]*Les Boulevards de Paris*, p. 70.

[115]Vallès, *Le Tableau de Paris*, p. 52. This volume, edited by Lucien
Scheler, contains a series of newspaper articles written by Vallès on his return from exile. The articles appeared in *Gil Blas* and *La France* from 1882
to 1883.

[116]Montorgueil, *op. cit.*, p. viii.

tele; all apothecaries are pharmacists today, and while a single caretaker's lodge (*conciergerie*) is nowhere to be found, everyone's a concierge. . . .[117]

The small shop did not wilt in the face of competition from department stores. *Grands magasins* did not sell everything nor did they sell everything well. Certain trades—butchers, bakers—were never severely tested by department stores. Businesses in the rapidly expanding service sector, from hairdressers to maintenance and repairmen, had little to fear from mass-marketing techniques. Even in the clothing and luxury trades, where department store competition was most formidable, an enterprising *boutiquier* could stake out a market share. Efficient marketing machinery and rational, bureaucratic organization, of course, were essential to survival in the new world of commerce. One could not count on the patronage of a loyal clientele; shoppers had to be rounded up. Small businessmen with an eye to the future adopted the new merchandising techniques, from cash-and-carry and free entry to flashy facades and newspaper advertising. The commercial struggle for life took a fresh turn under the Second Empire, obliging small shops to abandon established, familiar ways of conducting business in favor of new methods better suited to attract and process an expanding clientele. The *Ligue syndicale*'s complaints against the *grands magasins* were to be sure not entirely unwarranted. Certain lines of business—shirt sellers, linen drapers, etc.—knew real difficulties on account of department-store competition. The transition from the old to the new world of commerce, moreover, increased small-business dependence on industry. The manufacturer was coming to replace the wholesaler as ultimate arbiter of the shopkeeper's fate. Just the same, it was not as though the small retailer could not survive and prosper if he swallowed his pride and adapted to the new conditions.

[117] Du Camp, *Paris et ses organes*, vol. VI, p. 323.

Two false assumptions then underlie the department store thesis. First of all, the antagonism between department store and small shop was not necessarily fatal to *petit commerce* as is so often claimed. Scores of small businesses managed to thrive in the very shadow of *grands magasins*. It is, moreover, mistaken to dismiss the small shop as a traditional structure, inefficient and outmoded. The boulevard boutique, for one, was hardly the relic of a premodern past. Three additional arguments can be adduced to round out the case against the department store thesis.

The *quartiers* in which the *Ligue* recruited with greatest success did indeed contain some of the city's largest department stores. The now-defunct Louvre was located virtually across the street from the Palais-Royal on the rue de Rivoli. The Gagne-Petit occupied premises not far away, on the corner of the rue des Pyramides and the avenue de l'Opéra. The Bon Marché stood, and still stands, at the southern end of the rue du Bac, on the border between the VIth and VIIth arrondissements. Department stores, however, were also to be found in neighborhoods where the *Ligue* enjoyed less support: around the Hôtel de Ville and the Place de la République and just north of the Opéra. The presence or absence of a department store cannot account fully for the variations in the geographical pattern of *Ligue* recruitment. Why, for that matter, did the *Ligue* recruit so successfully among merchants in the jewelry trade if its origins are to be traced to a confrontation between big store owners and humble *boutiquiers*? *Grand magasins* as a rule did not retail fine jewelry but concentrated above all on the sale of textiles, clothing and clothing accessories, and to a lesser extent home furnishings. Finally, there is the question of timing. Why did the shopkeeper movement only take shape in the 1880s, over a quarter of a century after the founding of the first department store? For these reasons, the department store thesis will have to be set aside, and the roots of shopkeeper mobilization looked for elsewhere.

The rhetoric employed by contemporaries to describe the department store offers a clue as to where to look. One metaphor in particular recurs with a suggestive frequency. The *grand magasin* was a city, a microcosmic edition of a Paris that was half industrial town, half consumer's utopia. The urban metaphor betrays an implicit recognition that the rise of the department store and the emergence of a new metropolitan Paris were linked phenomena. Consciousness of this connection, it should be added, did not always remain unarticulated.

A handful of observers made a stab at explaining the relationship between urban and commercial change. The first half of the nineteenth century, it was agreed, had been the "golden age" of the small shop. Parisians rarely left their neighborhoods, living and working within a small radius. People did not shop but, more or less automatically, made their purchases at local stores. "It was a happy era . . . when each *boutiquier* could exploit at leisure the clientele delivered up to him by the neighborhood. . . ."[118] Paris was not a unified market but an amalgam of neighborhoods, each isolated from the next, autarkic as nations separated by high tariff barriers. The coming of cheap and rapid transportation, however, broke down the frontiers that fragmented the city into a mosaic of autonomous *quartiers*. People now moved about with greater facility; they no longer had to satisfy themselves with the goods offered at the corner store but could dash off to another part of the city in search of the merchandise they desired. The unification of the retail market, it was claimed, made it possible for a store, particularly if centrally located, to draw custom from the various districts of the city. It was this opportunity that department stores capitalized upon, and the consequences were momentous. With virtually the whole of Paris at their disposal, there were apparently no limits to their potential for expansion. Centralization of the market,

[118] Demolins, *La Question des grands magasins*.

on this view, was the essential precondition of commercial concentration.[119]

As for the local markets of yesteryear, suddenly exposed to the harsh competition of larger, more efficient retailing units, they withered and with them the small shops and neighborhood communities they had once sustained. Zola's *Au Bonheur des Dames* concludes with a rash of bankruptcies, deaths and near suicides as the small businesses—perfumers, shoemakers, modistes, florists—that had struggled to survive in the shadow of the department store finally go under. At the funeral of his daughter, the draper Baudu, himself near ruin, laments: "The little one, it's the *quartier* we are burying. . . . Oh! I make no mistake, old commerce might as well be thrown in along with the white roses we have strewn on the grave."[120] Having mangled himself beneath the wheels of a passing coach in an unsuccessful suicide attempt, the bankrupt silk merchant Robineau gasps: "it's the end of a world."[121] The department store, like some enormous suction pump, drained the *quartier* of trade, merging the *"petites clientèles"* of Paris' myriad neighborhoods to form a single city-wide shopping public.[122] The small shop was crushed in the process, a victim of a profound recasting of urban market structures attendant upon Paris' metamorphosis from a city of autonomous and picturesque *quartiers* into a centralized metropolis.

The implications of this interpretation of events for a study of retailer protest are evident. It suggests that the *causa causans* of shopkeeper discontent is to be looked for not in the

[119] For various expressions of the perspective discussed in this paragraph, see: Ambrière, pp. 68–69; Bernard, p. 23; L. Dausset, "Paris et les transports en commun," p. 184; Demolins, *op. cit.*, pp. 4–7; Jules Domergue, *Comment et pourquoi les affaires vont mal en France*, pp. 11–12; Duclos, pp. 15–19; Garrigues, pp. 12–14.

[120] Zola, *Au Bonheur des Dames*, p. 435.

[121] *Ibid.* p. 446.

[122] Zola, *Pot-Bouille*, p. 195.

department store but in the process of urban transformation that made department store growth possible. Simple mention of urban change in connection with nineteenth-century Paris inevitably brings to mind the name of Georges Haussmann, Louis-Napoléon's prefect of the Seine. It is then to an account of Haussmann's program of public works and of its commercial consequences that I will turn in the next chapter. Does this shift in emphasis mean that the *grand magasin* is to drop out of the discussion altogether? Not entirely, for the rise of the department store and urban transformation were intimately associated in the public imagination. Contemporaries borrowed from the same stock of images to characterize both processes. Haussmannic Paris, like the department store, conjured up visions of phalansteries, barracks, machines, fairgrounds, wonderlands, and the theater. The department store remains as a potent symbol of the larger phenomenon of Haussmannization, a convenient scapegoat for embittered retailers victimized by urban change.

3

. . .

Haussmannization

THE ROOTS of the shopkeeper movement are to be traced, not to the department store, but to changes in Paris' commercial geography under the impact of Haussmannization. I use the term Haussmannization as shorthand for a complex of urban transformations largely, although not exclusively, the achievement of the baron Haussmann. The process of urban renewal, with which Haussmann's name is so intimately linked, transcended the limits of his public career, extending back in time to the comte de Rambuteau's tenure as prefect of the Seine under the July Monarchy and forward into the infant years of the Third Republic.

The renovation of Paris gave shape to a distinctive center-city environment, mercantile and middle class in character. The heart of the old city became commercialized, shed much of its working-class population and underwent a definite embourgeoisement. Haussmannization created the milieu, the conditions favorable to commercial interest-group formation. Haussmannization, moreover, created a network of boulevards and avenues, a new downtown that eclipsed the city's old shopping districts. The department store emerged as a symbol of the new downtown, its most successful representative, and as such, focused upon itself the resentments of merchants and middlemen who had lost out because of changes in the shape of the retail market consequent upon Haussmannization. On this account, the *Ligue syndicale* appears a last-ditch effort, not to preserve the small shop, but a dying commercial world threatened by department stores but above all by urban change. The Haussmannization thesis, however, is not without weaknesses and can provide only a partial explanation for the shopkeeper mobilization of the 1880s and 1890s.

HAUSSMANN'S PARIS

Haussmann's program of public works was devised to create a more salubrious and from the point of the view of the Imperial government a more secure urban environment. But hygiene and social control were not Haussmann's sole preoccupations. The Paris that emerged from the traumas of urban renewal was a city reborn: a business capital, a showpiece of Imperial grandeur, and a congenial playground for a rising bourgeoisie. Economic, political and social prestige concerns informed every aspect of Haussmann's grand design. He made of Paris "the metropolis of the industrial era,"[1] par excellence, "the capital of the nineteenth century."[2]

Paris in the 1850s was rapidly becoming a major exporter of goods and services. According to one contemporary observer, ". . . the tendency for trade to concentrate in Paris is today one of the most remarkable features of commercial organization in France."[3] From the end of the July Monarchy to the mid-1860s, Paris' share of total French exports rose from 11 to 12 percent to 16 to 17 percent. In 1861 nearly

[1] Giedion, *Space, Time and Architecture*, p. 642.
[2] The phrase is Walter Benjamin's. See the fragment, "Paris—the Captial of the Nineteenth Century," in Benjamin, *Charles Baudelaire*, pp. 155–176.
[3] Audiganne, "Industrie et commerce," p. 3.

one-quarter of the 1.5 billion francs in goods and services produced by the city was destined for markets outside the capital.[4]

The city, in large part, owed its growing importance as an export center to its strategic location at the hub of the national railway system. The railroad boom of the 1840s had endowed Paris with a ring of railroad termini, located "on the fringes of the city center," from which radiated trunk lines linking the capital with the rest of France.[5] The new streets of Haussmann's Paris were admirably designed to ease the flow of passengers and merchandise to and from the new railway stations. Haussmann's "plan of public works accorded the rail termini the place they deserved as Paris' new doors, as entrance-ways for France, indeed for the entire world into the capital city."[6]

The nodal point of old Paris' street system had been the crossroads where the rue Saint-Honoré met the rue Saint-Denis. Haussmann shifted the axis of city traffic to the Châtelet, thereby greatly improving the internal communications of the city. The rue de Rivoli and the boulevard Sébastopol which intersected at the Châtelet were broad, straight thoroughfares that provided direct access to the two rings of boulevards—interior and exterior—that girdled the city center. Indeed, the rings themselves were in no small part Haussmann's achievement. From the Châtelet, via a network of avenues and boulevards, almost all either constructed or planned by Haussmann, the hurried businessman could reach with relative ease the major economic institutions scattered across the Parisian cityscape. The Tribunal of Commerce was located just across

[4] Gaillard, *Paris, la ville 1852–1870*, p. 380; Cochin, *Paris, sa population, son industrie*, p. 68. The 1.5 billion figure cited by Cochin excludes the food and building industries.

[5] Sutcliffe, *The Autumn of Central Paris*, p. 28.

[6] Préfecture du département de la Seine, *Commission d'extension de Paris, Aperçu historique*, vol. I, p. 114.

the Pont au Change on the Ile de la Cité. A westward turn off the boulevard Sébastopol onto the rue Rambuteau brought one to the Bourse. If one continued straight on the boulevard Sébastopol, one arrived directly in front of the Gare de l'Est; a left onto the boulevard Magenta led to the Gare du Nord. One took the rue de Rivoli, the avenue de l'Opéra, the rue Auber and the rue de Rome to the Gare Saint-Lazare; after crossing the river, the boulevard Saint-Michel, the boulevard Saint-Germain and the rue de Rennes to the Gare Montparnasse. Haussmann spun a web of streets and railways "in the middle of which sat Paris like some gigantic spider."[7] With Haussmannization was born *la ville tentaculaire*.[8]

With Haussmannization was also born a new urban architecture. Les Halles, the Gare Saint-Lazare, the Galérie des Machines—feats of engineering that boldly and without disguise employed the construction materials of the industrial age, glass and iron—proclaimed Paris' rebirth as the economic linchpin of a great economic power. The development of glass and iron architecture was intimately connected not only with the railroad[9] but also with what was perhaps the century's most potent form of economic advertising: the World's Fair. Les Halles, designed by Baltard and Horeau, were built on the model of the Crystal Palace.[10] The Galérie des Machines, a museum for the exhibit of the mechanical wonders of the modern age, was constructed specifically for the Paris Exposition of 1855. And, of course, the Exposition of 1889 occasioned the construction of Paris' best known iron

[7] Claudin, *Paris*, p. 67.

[8] For the origins of this metaphor, see Emile Verhaeren's collection of poems, *Les Villes tentaculaires*; also, Abercrombie, "The Many-Tentacled Town," pp. 133–149. Lewis Mumford has a predilection for predatory images of octopi and spiderwebs (*The Culture of Cities*, pp. 226–233).

[9] De Foville makes this point in *La Transformation des moyens de transport*, p. 412.

[10] Du Maroussem, *Halles centrales de Paris*, p. 5.

monument, the Eiffel Tower, "symbol of machinism,"[11] "the aggressive embodiment of calculation."[12] Industrial architecture exalted in symbol what Haussmannization consummated in fact: the emergence of Paris as the business capital of the nation.

Haussmann's efforts to link "key points" within the city had distinct political as well as economic motives. Not just institutions of economic power, but also institutions of administrative and police power were integrated into the impressive structure of boulevards and avenues Haussmann imposed on the chaos of old Paris. Like the Bourse or the Gare du Nord, the Prefecture of Police and the Hôtel de Ville were massive edifices, located on or at the end of an imposing boulevard and isolated from the buildings around them. Haussmann designed a city whose spatial arrangement symbolized, whose awesome monumentality affirmed, the unity and power of the nation's ruling institutions.[13] A recent commentator has observed: "The formal concept of linking major architectural units by grand avenues, of superimposing a simplex of monumental proportions over a complex of smaller units, has baroque precedents."[14] Just as the baroque of the seventeenth century celebrated the power of the absolutist state, so the pseudo-baroque of Imperial France enshrined the neoabsolutism of the Bonapartist state. The common citizen felt out of place, dwarfed and intimidated in a "magnified Paris" that had "lost all human proportion."[15]

Baroque precedents can be detected not only in Hauss-

[11] Poète, "Les idées bergsonniennes et l'urbanisme," p. 584.

[12] The phrase is Le Corbusier's. Cited in Braibant, *Histoire de la Tour Eiffel*, p. 174.

[13] On Haussmannized Paris as a power landscape, see Saarinen, *The City*, pp. 107ff.

[14] Saalman, *Haussmann*, p. 16. The preceding discussion owes much to Saalman's work.

[15] Cornu, *La Conquête de Paris*, p. 36; Claudin, *op. cit.*, p. 52.

mann's predilection for "raising symbols of wealth and power to monumentality,"[16] but also in his passion for rectilinear and symmetrical street design. The straight tree-lined boulevard with a spectacular vista culminating in a *place rayonnante*—think of the Place de l'Etoile—recalled "the sylvan geometry" of the royal forests at Versailles.[17] The street plan of an emergent new Paris, to the critical eye of a Victor Hugo, had all the romance, all the *"je ne sais quoi* of grandeur, simplicity and surprise . . . that is to be found in a checkerboard."[18]

The Haussmannic building itself bespoke the power of the new order. The state decided on construction materials—freestone—and set specifications regulating facade design. Standardization extended to building interiors as well. The Haussmannic apartment house typically consisted of five stories, each laid out according to the same floor plan. Alphonse Daudet invoked the image of the phalanstery to describe the monotonous regularity of the Second Empire *immeuble de rapport*.[19] Proudhon was reminded of a barracks. A third critic complained: "The city is becoming monotonous; all the *quartiers* look the same; everywhere the same big streets, straight, cold, bordered by immense edifices constructed after the same plan."[20]

Zola's *Pot-Bouille* suggests a third interpretation of the Haussmannic cityscape. The architect Compardon, resident of a new apartment building on the rue de Choiseul, shows a friend and future fellow tenant, Octave Mouret, around: "Water and gas on every floor," Compardon repeats. "You see, these

---

[16] Saarinen, pp. 107–108.

[17] Cornu, pp. 34–35.

[18] Hugo, *Notre-Dame de Paris*, p. 128.

[19] Cited from Daudet's *Le Nabob* in *Le Parisien chez lui au XIXe siècle, 1814–1914*, exposition catalogue (Paris, November–February, 1977), p. 79.

[20] Vachon, *La Crise industrielle et artistique*, p. 76.

buildings are made for effect . . . and they impress people, they inspire confidence. . . . Oh! they're solid enough, they'll last as long as we do!"[21] The "violent luxury" of the vestibule and the staircase, the well-appointed apartment interiors, were constructed to insure the comfort of the tenant, but also to gratify his self-esteem and establish his self-worth. Haussmannic exteriors, eclectic, often exotic, with their "Corinthian pilasters, mouldings, fillets, masks of women and garlands, and sumptuous ironwork balconies," testified to the cultural respectability of the inhabitants.[22] Who were these inhabitants, the ambiguous "we" referred to by Compardon? According to Arnold Hauser, the grandiose, "unreliable" architecture of Haussmann's Paris "corresponded to the ambitions with which the risen bourgeoisie was trying to fill out these proportions."[23] It confirmed the social aspirations of the "financial *arriviste*," of a "rising upper middle class."[24] Not only buildings but entire streets could be characterized as *nouveau riche*. Xavier Aubryet appropriately classed the boulevard Haussmann as "parvenu."[25] Following on construction of the boulevard Malesherbes, real-estate speculators raced to develop the soon to be fashionable Parc Monceau area. It was here that Zola fixed the residences, and lavish residences at that, of the entrepreneur Saccard and of the courtesan Nana. Houses, streets, indeed whole *quartiers* announced the arrival of an upwardly mobile bourgeoisie. From the speculative rush generated by Haussmannization emerged a new Paris, a "parvenu cityscape."[26]

Paris nouveau testified to the dynamism and power of the new world of industrial capitalism, a world of glass and iron,

[21] Zola, *Pot-Bouille*, pp. 10–13.
[22] Cornu, p. 54.
[23] Hauser, *The Social History of Art*, vol. IV, pp. 63, 103.
[24] Mumford, *The Culture of Cities*, p. 273; Saalman, p. 47.
[25] See the snide comments in *Les Boulevards de Paris*, p. 84.
[26] Silverman, "The 1889 Exhibition," p. 71.

of Imperial might and parvenu wealth. Haussmann had rede-
signed the city to accommodate it to its new role as business
hub of the nation, to enhance state power and to flatter a newly
rich middle class. In the process, the distribution of economic functions within the city was reordered and existing
patterns of residence overturned. Haussmannization shifted the
balance of forces in Paris in favor of commerce as against industry, in favor of the bourgeoisie as against the proletariat.

COMMERCIALIZATION AND EMBOURGEOISEMENT

The transformation of Paris created an urban environment inhospitable to large-scale industry.[27] In 1859, the city limits
were extended to their present boundaries. Merchandise entering the newly annexed territories was now subject to payment of the city excise tax (*octroi*), inflating fuel and raw material costs to the detriment of the numerous industries located
in the former *banlieue*. Urban renewal and real-estate speculation, moreover, jacked up land values. Soaring rents obliged
firms with large floor-space requirements to vacate in search
of cheaper premises. The changing tax structure and mounting overhead costs, not to mention the traditionally high price
of Parisian labor, drove industry to abandon the city. According to the Chamber of Commerce inquiry of 1848, 10.98
percent of industrial firms in Paris employed eleven or more
workers, 38.75 percent employed two to ten, and 50.27 percent employed one or none at all. A second survey undertaken twelve years later showed an actual decrease in the
number of large and medium-sized establishments. The percentages broke down as follows:[28]

[27] Gaillard, p. 62. See also Bastié, *La Croissance de la banlieue parisienne*,
p. 138.
[28] For the 1848 and 1860 statistics, see Cochin, p. 63.

11 or more	7.38%
2–10	30.99%
1 or none	61.63%

In a third report, dated 1872, the Chamber of Commerce concluded: "In Paris, small industry has grown year by year, while large-scale industry has shown a marked tendency to move out."[29]

Other influences, however, acted to counterbalance the decentralizing thrust of Haussmannization. Paris was equipped with first-rate and centrally located shipping facilities. Factories forced out of the city did not wander far but relocated in the new *banlieue*. The manufacture of heavy metals migrated to the north along the canals and railroads that crisscrossed the Saint-Denis plain. The chemical industry settled along the banks of the Seine in the south. Poulenc opened a factory at Ivry in 1864.

Industries, moreover, that marketed a substantial portion of their product in the capital could not afford to move out. The Maison Cail, a manufacturer of heavy construction equipment, did a brisk business in Paris, profiting from the city's building boom. The Cail workshops were situated in the industrializing Grenelle ward of the XVth arrondissement. Food industries in particular were tied into the Parisian market. The Say sugar refinery, the La Villette slaughterhouses, the Potin food-processing plant, all operated from premises located in the XIXth arrondissement.

The centrifugal impact of Haussmannization altered the distribution of heavy industry in the Paris region. Firms that remained within the city limits concentrated on the periphery, creating de facto industrial zones as in the XVth (Javel and Grenelle) and in the XIXth (La Villette and Pont de Flandre). Factories established beyond the fortifications clus-

[29] Chambre de Commerce de Paris, *Enquête sur les conditions du travail en France pendant l'année 1872*, p. 54.

TABLE 3. Percentage of Paris Working Population
Employed in Commerce and Industry, 1856–1886

YEAR	COMMERCE	INDUSTRY
1856	11.80	60.00
1866	13.06	58.00
1872	21.72	44.07
1886	29.17	44.46

SOURCE: Louis Chevalier, *La Formation de la population parisienne au XIXe siècle* (Paris, 1965), pp. 74–78

tered along transportation routes, forming the first industrial suburbs: Saint-Denis, Saint-Ouen, Aubervilliers, Ivry.

As large-scale industry shifted to the Paris outskirts, commerce assumed an expanding role in the city, and above all the center-city, economy. From the middle decades of the century, the commercial sector began to approach industry, without ever surpassing it, in percentage employed of the Paris working population (see Table 3). Expansion of the commercial sector was most dramatic in the city's core arrondissements. Exporters and commission firms had colonized the rues de Paradis and d'Hauteville in the IXth since the days of the Restoration.[30] The startling growth of the Parisian export trade under the Second Empire spurred on the commercialization of the *quartier*. The *Paris-Guide* of 1867 observed: "The boulevard Montmartre is the equator. . . . In adjacent streets, silent and still at eight in the evening, are lodged a host of exporters, purchasing agents, commissionnaires, factory and commercial representatives. Knock at random on any door, and you will summon up some middleman or broker."[31] Ac-

[30] Daumard, *Maisons de Paris*, p. 99.
[31] Cited in Gaillard, p. 555.

cording to one estimate, fully nine-tenths of the city's export firms were housed in the narrow block of streets bounded by the boulevard Poissonnière, the rue du faubourg Montmartre, the rue Lafayette, and rue du faubourg Saint-Denis (roughly corresponding to the Faubourg Montmartre ward of the IXth and the Porte Saint-Denis ward of the Xth).[32]

The Vivienne and Mail wards of the IInd underwent a parallel evolution. At the beginning of the century, the wholesale textile trade had concentrated north of les Halles, along the rue Saint-Denis. The *monarchie censitaire* and the Second Empire witnessed a mass migration of wholesalers to the Sentier neighborhood. The rue du Sentier, the Place des Victoires, and adjoining streets offered more spacious business accommodations and a convenient location not far from the city's major financial institutions, the Bourse and the banks of the Chaussée d'Antin.[33]

As noted earlier, Haussmannization transformed the *grands boulevards*, at the border between the IInd and IXth, into the city's premier shopping parade. The fancy boutiques that lined the boulevard retailed over the counter the goods traded on the Sentier or in the faubourg Montmartre. The completion in 1877 of the avenue de l'Opéra, "Haussmann's masterwork of town planning,"[34] linked the booming quartier de l'Opéra, fast becoming the focal point of the city's luxury trade, to the rue de Rivoli and the Left Bank. The new avenue "became almost immediately the main shopping street of the interior of the right-bank center, and rivalled the *grands boulevards*."[35] Although originally intended for residential use, the apartment buildings on the new avenue were quickly occupied by

[32] Vibert, *Mon Berceau*, p. 305.
[33] Daumard, *op. cit.*, p. 86; Sutcliffe, p. 152.
[34] Giedion, p. 656.
[35] Sutcliffe, p. 164.

shops and offices, banks and insurance companies.[36] The construction of the avenue de l'Opéra consummated the commercialization of central Paris.

Commercialization was most pronounced in the Ist, IInd and IXth arrondissements. The statistics presented in Table 4, though taken from sources that post-date the Second Empire, give an indication of the long-term trend determining central Paris' vocation as a business center. From 1889 to 1911, twenty-three *quartiers* in the city registered growth in the percentage of rentable value given over to commercial and industrial purposes. Ten of these were located in the Ist, IInd and IXth arrondissements. Business was still concentrating in the city's center at the turn of the century. New areas of concentration had begun to emerge—the VIIIth in particular stands out—but were in no position as yet to challenge the supremacy of the Ist, IInd and IXth. Commerce reigned supreme in the heart of the capital, and this indeed had been Haussmann's intention. By driving "streets right through the city from one side to the other, by tearing open the central districts," Haussmann insured that Paris' renovated core would "retain and even expand its existing functions as a commercial, service and administrative center, and abandon part of its residential function."[37]

The metamorphosis of old Paris into a thriving business district involved major changes in the size and composition of its residential population. While the total population of the city grew over the period 1861–1896 from 1,667,841 to 2,536,834, the number of persons residing in the sixteen *quartiers* that make up the Ist–IVth arrondissements actually decreased. Only nine other wards suffered a population loss: Saint-Victor and the Sorbonne in the Vth, Monnaie and Saint-

[36] Daumard, "L'avenue de l'Opéra," p. 194.
[37] Haussmann, *Mémoires*, vol. II, p. 33; Sutcliffe, p. 33.

TABLE 4. Wards in Which Commercial and Industrial Premises Account for over 50 Percent of Total Rentable Value for All Buildings, 1889 and 1911

1889		1911	
Ward (in rank order)	% of Rentable value given over to commercial or industrial use	Ward (in rank order)	% of Rentabl value given over to commercial o industrial us
Mail (II)	77.21	Gaillon (II)	85.26
Bercy(XII)	74.93	Vivienne(II)	80.32
Vivienne(II)	72.59	Mail(II)	79.43
Gaillon(II)	66.10	Chausée d'Antin(IX)	72.34
Palais-Royal(I)	63.75	Place Vendôme(I)	70.56
Bonne-Nouvelle(II)	63.67	Palais-Royal(I)	70.45
Les Halles(I)	63.67	St.-Germain l'Auxerrois(I)	69.50
Ste.-Avoie(III)	62.70	Bercy(XII)	67.54
Arts-et-Métiers(III)	58.63	Faubourg Montmartre(IX)	67.19
Saint-Merri(IV)	57.89	Les Halles(I)	65.42
St.-Germain l'Auxerrois(I)	57.83	Porte St.-Denis(X)	64.98
Quinze-Vingts(XII)	56.01	Bonne-Nouvelle(II)	63.09
Faubourg Montmartre(IX)	55.88	Sainte-Avoie(III)	58.89
La Villette(XIX)	53.12	Arts-et-Métiers(III)	58.70
Chaussée d'Antin(IX)	52.81	Saint-Merri(IV)	55.01
Enfants-Rouges(III)	51.71	Archives(III)	50.62
Archives(III)	51.26	Pont de Flandre(XIX)	50.58
Pont de Flandre(XIX)	51.05		

SOURCE: Statistics drawn from Préfecture du département de la Seine, *Direction des finance. Commission des contributions directes de la Ville de Paris, Les Propriétés bâties de la Ville de Paris 1889 et en 1890* (Paris, 1890), pp. 2–9; and from Préfecture du département de la Seine, *D. rection municipale des travaux du cadastre de Paris (Albert Fontaine, directeur), Commission des contr butions directes, Ville de Paris, Le Livre foncier de 1911* (Paris, 1911), pp. 2–9

Germain des Prés in the VIth, Madeleine in the VIIIth, Chaussée d'Antin and Faubourg Montmartre in the IXth, Porte Saint-Denis in the Xth and Bercy in the XIIth.[38]

There is little argument as to who abandoned the city center for residence elsewhere. Over 50,000 working men and women, according to one estimate, were forced out by Haussmannization. Louis Lazare recounts the example of a journeyman cabinet-maker who had once lived on the rue Tixeranderie not far from les Halles. Uprooted by demolitions, the cabinet-maker, his wife and children resettled temporarily in Ménilmontant. Unable, because of high rents, to return to their old neighborhood or even to remain where they were, the family made its way to Belleville and then finally to Charonne.[39] High rents and demolitions spurred the working-class exodus from the center, but people also moved out in search of employment. During the Second Empire, working-class neighborhoods crystalized behind the Gare Montparnasse, around the Gares de Lyon, du Nord and de l'Est and along the Canal Saint-Martin. Emigration from the center contributed as well to the explosive growth of the industrial suburbs. In 1861, 33,000 lived in the suburbs of Saint-Denis, Aubervilliers and Pantin; by 1896, the total population had leapt to 80,000.[40]

Paris' population then was deconcentrated, sprawling outward on beyond the old city limits, the fortifications and into the new *banlieue*. The capital outgrew its administrative boundaries. It was no longer just a city but an agglomeration,[41] something monstrous and inorganic. Louis Veuillot execrated Paris as a "city of deracinated multitudes," a "mo-

---

[38] For population statistics, see Meuriot, *Les Agglomérations urbaines*, pp. 261–263.

[39] Lazare, *Les Quartiers pauvres de Paris*, pp. 51, 84–85.

[40] Meuriot, p. 340.

[41] The term agglomeration is used in *ibid.*, p. 42; and Forestier, *Grandes villes et système de parcs*, p. 6.

bile mass of human dust."[42] To a Catholic conservative like Veuillot, Haussmannization loomed as the very antithesis of rootedness, of integrated community life. But did everyone abandon "their father's house?" Did no one stay behind to pray "in the church where he was baptized?"

The population of central Paris was indeed aging in the last half of the century. An increasing proportion of inhabitants were female. But was it only women and the elderly who remained loyal to their roots in old Paris? What was the social profile of the center-city residential population? The very design of the Haussmannic apartment house suggests the beginnings of an answer. With an apartment layout essentially the same on every floor, the new buildings that lined the streets of downtown Paris discouraged vertical stratification; tenants were not likely to differ widely in social background. Neither villas nor *hôtels*, yet well-appointed and fitted with the latest conveniences, Second Empire *immeubles de rapport* were admirably designed for middle-class occupancy.[43] Their bourgeois demeanor might be ruffled by the presence of a skilled artisan on the top floor, under the eaves, but by little else.

The residents of the *maison neuve* in Zola's *Pot-Bouille* suggest a more precise rendering of the social profile of central Paris. Located in the rue de Choiseul in the IInd, the building was inhabited by its owner, a retired notary, his two sons—the one a silk merchant, the other a "little old man of 28" who had dabbled unsuccessfully at a dozen métiers, a counselor at the Court of Appeals, a writer, an architect, "a small household of employees," a cashier in a large crystal business, and the hero of the novel, Mouret, future owner of the Au Bonheur des Dames department store.[44] Businessmen, employees and liberal professionals took possession of the apart-

[42] Veuillot, *Les Odeurs de Paris*, p. x.

[43] Daumard, *Maisons de Paris*, p. 207; Raymond, *La Politique pavillonnaire*, p. 84.

[44] Zola, *Pot-Bouille*, pp. 10–11, 57.

ment houses erected along the new avenues that traversed old Paris. Edouard Fournier, *flâneur* and devotee of old Paris, reflected on the construction of the rue Turbigo in the following terms:

> We will have a beautiful new street which will attract a new class of resident for, I repeat, small-scale industry will find these spanking new buildings too fine and too costly to inhabit. Who will take its place? I'm not certain, but persons who have made money in trade and local banking will have their share. They'll move here as they have already moved to the rue de Rivoli and boulevard Sébastopol.[45]

The center, abandoned by the working class and the very poor, was rapidly becoming the province of the middle classes, of *"les commerçants."*[46]

Statistics from the 1872 census bear out the qualitative evidence. Only five arrondissements—the Ist, IInd, VIth, VIIIth, and IXth—exceed both citywide averages for persons classified as *patrons* and employees while falling short of averages for persons employed as workers and day laborers (Table 5). The geographical distribution of population by sector (commerce, industry, etc.) provides a similar if somewhat more nuanced picture. Table 6 indicates that the residential population of the VIIIth, if bourgeois, was not concentrated in the commercial professions. The IXth indeed housed a heavier concentration of persons employed in commerce than the outer arrondissements, but it lagged distinctly behind other central districts in this respect. In the 1880s, however, it caught up with and began to surpass its neighbors. According to the industrial census of 1881, the IXth ranked only

[45] Fournier, "Promenade dans Paris," p. 55.

[46] Lazare, pp. 25, 53.

[47] Préfecture de la Seine, *Secrétariat général, Service de la statistique municipale* (1884), pp. 117–156.

TABLE 5. Distribution of Working Population in Paris
by Social Position, 1872

Arron- disse- ment	Patrons, chefs, etc. (% of total)	Employees (% of total)	Workers (% of total)	Day laborers (% of total)	TOTAL
I	35,491(49.50)	14,416(20.16)	15,028(20.96)	6,765(9.43)	71,700
II	29,275(40.97)	16,606(23.24)	17,998(25.19)	7,574(10.60)	71,453
III	36,432(41.85)	12,959(14.79)	33,308(38.01)	4,923(5.62)	87,622
IV	31,212(35.97)	13,327(15.36)	22,263(25.69)	19,964(23.01)	86,766
V	29,525(33.77)	11,396(13.03)	27,573(31.53)	18,946(21.67)	87,440
VI	42,686(52.49)	12,885(15.83)	20,892(25.67)	4,923(6.05)	81,386
VII	29,894(47.58)	9,203(14.65)	19,518(31.06)	4,271(6.71)	62,832
VIII	44,641(64.30)	10,903(15.71)	8,130(11.71)	5,746(8.28)	69,420
IX	57,818(57.61)	21,514(21.44)	15,011(14.96)	6,022(6.02)	100,365
X	44,001(34.32)	23,420(18.27)	44,340(34.59)	16,440(12.82)	128,201
XI	35,156(21.85)	14,367(8.92)	97,167(60.38)	14,235(8.85)	160,925
XII	22,342(27.81)	11,332(14.11)	36,998(46.05)	9,670(12.03)	80,334
XIII	24,709(43.54)	7,966(14.04)	11,979(21.11)	12,093(21.31)	56,747
XIV	22,220(34.51)	7,537(11.86)	20,706(32.15)	13,928(21.63)	64,391
XV	20,777(29.04)	7,429(10.38)	34,209(47.81)	9,137(12.77)	71,552
XVI	18,965(48.08)	5,228(13.25)	11,977(30.36)	3,275(8.30)	39,445
XVII	34,492(35.28)	18,859(19.29)	32,024(32.75)	12,397(12.68)	97,772
XVIII	25,435(19.07)	24,865(18.64)	67,462(50.59)	15,607(11.70)	133,363
XIX	19,398(21.87)	8,287(9.34)	34,503(38.89)	26,527(29.90)	88,715
XX	19,003(21.33)	4,543(5.10)	53,192(59.69)	12,370(13.88)	89,108
Paris	623,472(36.05)	257,042(14.86)	624,270(36.09)	224,753(12.99)	1,729,537

SOURCE: Toussaint Loua, *Atlas statistique de la population de Paris* (Paris, 1873), p. 68

behind the IInd, IIIrd and Xth in percentage of residents engaged in commerce.[47] Even without this addendum, Table 6
identifies with reasonable clarity the arrondissements contain-
ing the highest proportion of persons in commercial professions: the Ist–VIth, the IXth and Xth. The mix of professions within these arrondissements, however, was by no means
uniform. Relatively high percentages of liberal professionals
and property owners lived in the Ist, IInd, Vth, VIth and
IXth. The IIIrd and Xth, traditional centers of artisanal production, and the Vth, with its concentrations of chemical and

T A B L E 6. Distribution of Working Population in Paris
by Profession, 1872

Arron-dissement	Industry (% of total)	Commerce (% of total)	Liberal profs. (% of total)	Proprietors, rentiers, etc. (% of total)	Other (% of total)	TOTAL
I	17,517(24.01)	35,040(48.02)	4,468(6.12)	9,238(12.66)	6,702(9.19)	72,965
II	24,367(33.43)	30,072(41.26)	4,278(5.83)	8,732(12.06)	4,943(6.78)	72,892
III	49,986(56.57)	24,428(28.62)	2,662(3.01)	7,398(8.37)	3,885(4.40)	88,359
IV	38,949(42.15)	30,875(33.41)	3,548(3.84)	6,724(7.28)	12,311(13.32)	92,407
V	41,100(45.11)	21,197(23.26)	4,926(5.41)	9,232(10.13)	14,663(16.09)	91,118
VI	25,731(30.45)	20,592(24.37)	8,275(9.79)	16,230(19.21)	13,662(16.17)	84,490
VII	24,757(32.02)	8,516(11.01)	5,057(6.54)	16,378(21.18)	22,604(29.24)	77,312
VIII	13,653(18.49)	12,161(16.46)	5,357(7.25)	29,955(40.56)	12,919(17.49)	73,845
IX	24,210(23.93)	21,638(21.39)	9,505(9.39)	29,308(28.97)	16,511(16.32)	101,172
X	61,425(46.23)	35,490(26.71)	5,883(4.43)	12,938(9.74)	17,120(12.89)	132,856
XI	110,918(67.89)	31,187(19.08)	2,986(1.83)	9,522(5.83)	8,565(5.24)	163,378
XII	46,289(54.31)	15,003(17.60)	1,557(1.83)	3,766(4.42)	18,621(21.85)	85,236
XIII	19,245(32.02)	11,522(19.17)	2,997(4.99)	14,505(24.13)	11,842(19.70)	60,111
XIV	34,661(52.24)	13,855(20.88)	3,453(5.20)	5,309(8.00)	9,069(13.67)	66,345
XV	36,739(49.79)	14,196(19.24)	1,799(2.44)	5,015(6.80)	16,042(21.73)	73,791
XVI	13,917(33.52)	6,003(14.46)	2,787(6.71)	10,472(25.22)	8,345(20.10)	41,524
XVII	35,633(35.29)	18,888(18.70)	6,301(6.24)	21,278(21.07)	18,682(18.50)	100,982
XVIII	76,354(56.10)	22,982(16.89)	5,511(4.05)	7,418(5.45)	23,834(17.51)	136,099
XIX	56,051(61.70)	14,459(15.91)	2,184(2.40)	4,991(5.49)	13,169(14.49)	90,854
XX	64,538(70.91)	14,128(15.52)	1,157(1.27)	4,270(4.69)	6,923(7.61)	91,016
TOTAL	816,040(45.44)	402,232(22.40)	84,691(4.72)	232,679(12.96)	260,410(14.49)	1,796,052

SOURCE: Loua, *Atlas statistique*, p. 59. Loua's calculations are based on the 1872 census, with an important modification. He has included in his professional categories not only persons who earn their living directly by commerce, industry, etc., but also all dependents, family members and domestics alike. This involves some misrepresentation, especially as family size will vary from category to category, not to mention size of domestic staff.

leather factories on the south side of the Montagne Sainte-Geneviève, housed substantial industrial populations. Of the city's commercial arrondissements, then, the Ist, IInd, VIth and IXth were the most markedly bourgeois in character while the IIIrd, Vth and Xth tended to be, if not more working-class, at least more socially heterogeneous. The functional commercialization of Paris' core arrondissements was accompanied by a definite embourgeoisement of the resident population, a phenomenon most pronounced in the city center's western districts.

It was the needs of commerce that increasingly set the tone of public life in central Paris. Storeowners large and small, wholesalers and middlemen of all varieties claimed the heart of the capital for themselves, as a place of residence no less than as a place of work. The twin processes of commercialization and embourgeoisement created a distinctive social climate in the city's central arrondissements, a "world of intermediaries."[48] The cohesion of this emergent commercial "world" was reinforced by shared political convictions.

Ironically, central Paris, so much the product of Haussmann's handiwork, was emphatically republican in its sympathies. The republican antecedents of the *Syndicat général* and *Ligue syndicale* have already been discussed. Employees, according to one of Zola's informants, were reputedly hostile to the Empire.[49] But what of the chief beneficiaries of Haussmannization, the wealthiest strata of the parvenu bourgeoisie? According to one urban historian: "The new class of daring financiers, large-scale building contractors, big department store owners, hotel operators and the rest of the *nouveau riche* commercial breed had every reason to support and promote all aspects of the Second Empire program."[50] And yet, Boucicaut in 1859 put his name to a petition supporting Manin, the Venetian republican, and later, during the Commune, gave aid to the *Ligue d'union républicaine des droits de Paris*.[51] In 1872, a *Société des écoles laïques* was formed in Paris' Ist arrondisement. Three Masonic lodges were among its first subscribers, as were Chauchard and Hériot of the Louvre, Cognacq of La Samaritaine, and Rochard, the director of La Belle Jardinière.

[48] Gaillard, p. 556.
[49] BN NAF 10278, Zola, p. 216.
[50] Saalman, p. 113.
[51] Gaillard, p. 548.

Could such men, who publicly associated with Freemasons and ran the risks of reprisals from the government of Moral Order, have formerly been convinced Bonapartists? In 1881, thanks to the efforts of Méline, Tirard and Floquet, a familiar trio of republican politicians, the *Société* was officially declared "of public utility."[52] Zola in *Pot-Bouille* clearly situates Mouret, employee and future department-store owner, in the opposition to Napoleon III's regime. In a political debate over upcoming elections, the fictional Mouret is made to pronounce against the official candidate, M. Dewinck, a real personage who owned a prosperous chocolate business in the rue Saint-Honoré and who did in fact run for office on the Bonapartist ticket in 1852.[53] Whether fictional or real, department-store owners manifested a distinct coolness to Bonapartism, if not a genuine warmth for republican values. Napoleon III's investment in economic expansion, urban renewal and the creation of new wealth won the Imperial regime few friends in central Paris, even among those who profited most.

The transformation of Paris' urban core, then, engendered a coherent center-city milieu: commercial, middle class and republican. Haussmannization made it possible for intermediaries to conceive of themselves as a separate group with distinct economic and political interests. It prepared the ground for the massive commercial mobilization that was to find expression in the *chambre syndicale* movement. But the unity of this movement, as we have seen, was fragile, destined to dissolve in the 1880s as the center-city commercial community became polarized between the radical activism of the *Ligue syndicale* and the moderate conservatism of the city's commercial establishment. Even this division, however, had its roots in the urban transformations of mid-century. Haussmanniza-

---

[52] On the *Société des écoles laïques*, see Delcourt, "Les associations parisiennes de propagande," pp. 14, 20.

[53] Zola, *Pot-Bouille*, p. 248.

tion not only created the "world of intermediaries" that provided the critical mass behind commercial syndicalism, but at the same time, as we shall see, fixed the fault lines along which the syndical movement would eventually fracture.

NEW AND OLD DOWNTOWNS

The commercial milieu created by Haussmannization was by no means monolithic. *Grands magasins* took precautionary, paternalist measures to forestall employee unrest but did not always succeed. Paris' major department stores were struck in 1869. The strike ended in defeat; failure set back employee unionism for over fifteen years, but the event bore witness to the social tensions that threatened the republican unity of central Paris.[54] The harmony of the commercial world was undermined by a second and no less critical set of tensions. Haussmannization endowed Paris with a magnificent new retail area that stretched along the boulevards and avenues of the renovated city. The emergence of this new retail center, however, caused problems for older commercial streets. *Vieux Paris* had boasted one of Europe's most spectacular shopping districts, but this old district was overshadowed in the 1860s and 1870s as the city's new downtown siphoned off trade. Haussmannization then equipped Paris with two downtowns that coexisted uneasily in the marketplace, competing for trade.

The exact location of the city's old shopping district is not without significance. It was concentrated in three wards—the Faubourg Montmartre, Vivienne, and Palais-Royal—precisely the neighborhoods where the *Ligue syndicale* recruited with greatest success. This coincidence of geography points to a connection between the declining fortunes of Paris' old shopping district and the retailer mobilization of the eighties.

[54] On the strike, see Gaillard, pp. 550–553.

What inspired the *Ligue*'s formation, looked at from this angle, would seem to have been a desperate if not always clearly articulated commitment to preserve a decaying downtown area against the encroachments of a new one born of urban change.

The Palais-Royal, under the Restoration, had uncontestably been *the* gathering place for Parisians in search of amusement. Its cafés and restaurants, gambling dens and low dives drew fabulous crowds. Hawkers and street vendors of all kinds jammed the galeries, competing for space with the armies of prostitutes who came in the evening to "do the Palais." Entertainments to suit all tastes were available, from high-brow theater (the Comédie Française, the Théâtre du Palais-Royal and, until 1820 when it was moved to the rue Le Peletier, the Opéra) to cosmoramas, waxworks and magic shows.[55] And never far from entertainment, intellect, finance and commerce plied their respective trades. Balzac describes the famous Wooden Galleries of the Palace in their heyday (they were leveled in 1828):

> In this shameless, unblushing haunt, amid a babel of talk and the screams of wild mirth, an immense amount of business was transacted in the years between the revolutions of 1789 and 1830. For twenty years the Bourse was just opposite, on the ground-floor of the Palais, and public opinions and reputations as well as political and financial transactions, were made and unmade there. People used to meet in the Galleries after the Bourse. . . . Booksellers dealing in poetry, politics and prose, and the clothing trade, enjoyed a monopoly of the place, except for the prostitutes. . . .[56]

Louis-Philippe, who had lived in the Palace from 1815 to 1830 before moving over to the Tuileries, acted on accession

---

[55] Champier and Sandoz, *La Palais-Royal*, vol. II, pp. 147ff.
[56] Balzac, *Lost Illusions*, p. 274.

to power to clean up on his one-time residence. The police imposed dress regulations on the prostitutes; gambling was banned in 1837; and gay life began to emigrate toward the boulevards.[57] The opening of the rue Vivienne and recent construction of the Vivienne and Colbert arcades facilitated the movement northward.[58] The boulevards themselves, in the era of the July Monarchy, retained an aspect "half Parisian and half rural." They resembled more the "mall in front of a prefecture" than a major urban thoroughfare.[59] There were no sidewalks, only tree-lined pathways; gas lighting was not installed until 1857. Boulevardiers feared "and with reason, its effect on the time-honored shadows that constituted the charm of their favorite promenade."[60] The elegant restaurants and cafés that took up residence along the boulevards eschewed the gas lamp. In the evenings, one dined by candlelight and picked one's way home along avenues illumined by flickering street lamps. The boulevards were, in those days, an aristocratic preserve. It was here, before the Bois de Boulogne came into vogue, that gentlemen and ladies paraded their equipages. The dandies and literary men (often one and the same), who promenaded up and back along the shaded *allées* to the delight of café-goers, more often than not sported a title or at least a *particule*: Alfred de Musset, Roger de Beauvoir, Lord Seymour, the comte d'Orsay, Honoré de Balzac. This was a small world and an elegant one.[61]

For the noise of crowds, bright lights and the intoxication of commercial activity, the stroller was obliged to turn into the arcades that opened out onto the boulevards. The passage Jouffroy and the twin galleries of the passage de l'Opéra fed

[57] Augé de Lassus, *La Vie au Palais-Royal*, pp. 135–136.
[58] Reboux, *Histoire et les dessous de Paris*, p. 28; Claudin, *Mes Souvenirs*, p. 16; Gaillard, p. 526.
[59] Laut, "Le boulevard d'aujourd'hui," p. 15.
[60] *Ibid.*, p. 22.
[61] Claudin, *Paris*, pp. 119–120.

into the boulevards from the north. The Opéra galleries, much frequented by dancers and singers, were famed for their pastry and flower shops, but toiletries and fashionable clothing (perfume, dresses, boots, hats) could be had there as well.[62] The passage des Panoramas bisected the boulevards from the south at the Théâtre des Variétés. The arcade took its name from an ingenious exhibit opened in 1825 by one M. Boulogne. Two rotundas stood on either side of the *passage*. From a platform located in the middle of each rotunda, spectators gazed out on a set—an artful combination of *trompe l'oeil* mural and three-dimensional modeling—which suggested a panoramic view of a battlefield, a European capital or whatever. In the 1830s the Panoramas used sets modeled after designs by Robert Fulton, attracting enormous crowds and establishing the arcade's reputation. Modish boutiques flocked to the *passage*, as did the buying public. One went to Duvelleroy's for fans, to A la Duchesse de Courlandes' for bonbons, to Mme. Lapostole's for straw hats. Refreshments for the weary shopper were to be had at the Café Véron or Café des Variétés.[63] In tandem with the rue Vivienne which, subsequent to its opening in the thirties rapidly became a center for the wholesale trade of luxury goods, the Panoramas became "the heart of Paris, the *quartier* par excellence of fashion, *toilette* and feminine elegance.[64]

The rue de Richelieu, running exactly parallel to the rue Vivienne and the passage des Panoramas, was a major shopping thoroughfare in its own right, lined with "very elegant boutiques" that "bore witness to the growing importance of the luxury trade" under Louis-Philippe.[65] One historian of the

---

[62] Reboux, *Histoire et les dessous de Paris*, p. 27; Claudin, *Mes Souvenirs*, p. 19. The galleries linked the Opéra, recently moved from the Palais-Royal, to the boulevards.

[63] Bertaut, *Le Boulevard*, pp. 108–112.

[64] Malet, *Le Baron Haussmann*, p. 129.

[65] *Le Parisien chez lui*, p. 44.

boulevards has suggested a list of nineteen shops especially favored by the fashion-conscious ladies and gentlemen of the July Monarchy.[66] Six were located on the rue de Richelieu. Here is how the street appeared in 1852, slightly worn but still grand:

> And so it was with the rue de Richelieu. Many artisans . . . some employing workers of their own occupied the upper stories, but on the ground floor, the boutiques were more luxurious and bourgeois apartments more numerous. The Palais-Royal had suffered a loss of popularity, increasingly eclipsed by the boulevards from around 1830, but the street still remained busy, although perhaps without the luster of former days.[67]

Commercial activity, of course, was not confined to the *quartiers* Vivienne, Palais-Royal and Faubourg Montmartre. It spilled over into the Gaillon and Place Vendôme wards, especially in the passage Choiseul and along the north-south axis formed by the rue Castiglione, the Place Vendôme and the rue de la Paix. In the VIIth arrondissement, the clothing trade was especially brisk along the rue du Bac, the principal artery of communication linking the Left to the Right Bank. These additions, however, only reinforce the central point being made, namely that the city's old downtown area and the centers of *Ligue* recruitment coincide almost exactly. Roughly one in eight of the 256 shopkeeper militants inscribed on the *Le Commerçant* list of 1882 and the *Ligue* list of 1888 operated enterprises in the various *passages*, the Palais-Royal or on the rues du Bac, du faubourg Montmartre, de Richelieu and Vivienne.

Haussmannization utterly transformed the commercial geography of Paris. The spacious, new avenues that criss-crossed

---

[66] D'Ariste, *La Vie et le monde du boulevard*, pp. 228–243.
[67] Daumard, *Maisons de Paris*, p. 108.

the new city had been designed to handle the enormous volume of traffic, concentrated in the center, that was generated by urban expansion. By the end of the century, the avenue de l'Opéra handled per diem 36,185 horses drawing 29,460 conveyances of all kinds.[68] Traffic was so dense that pedestrians crossed at a risk the intersection of the rue and boulevard Montmartre, nick-named the *carrefour des écrasés* by Emile de Girardin.[69] From the planner's perspective, the crowds in the street, the pedestrians and passengers, were so many travelers whose movement had to be accommodated by a rational street plan. From the retailer's perspective, they were so many potential shoppers, a vast clientele in motion. In the new world of commerce, the smart shopkeeper did not wait for customers but went to them. He moved to the new streets in hot pursuit of his market. Ample provision had been made for his arrival. Haussmannic buildings, especially those located on major thoroughfares, came equipped with ground-floor premises specifically and admirably designed for commercial use. Ernest Levallois describes the couturiere shops that proliferated along the rue du Quatre-Septembre: "Luxurious stores, large offices well lit and airy, workshops and fitting rooms for our finest clothing designers, we had only to sit back and labor in peace, opulently, gloriously."[70] For spaciousness and design, for convenient access to the marketplace, premises along the newly opened boulevards offered distinct advantages. Urban renewal fostered a new network of downtown shopping streets—the *grands boulevards*, the boulevard Sébastopol, the avenue de l'Opéra, the rues de la Paix and de Rivoli—a network that has survived to this day with relatively few casualties (e.g. the rue du Quatre-Septembre) albeit a considerable loss of splendor. It was here that the new

[68] Boucard, *La Vie de Paris*, p. 344.
[69] Castelnau, *En remontant les grands boulevards*, p. 163.
[70] Levallois, *Paris propre*, p. 10.

world of commerce was born, with its brilliant lights, gold lettering and gaudy display.

Older, established streets suffered eclipse. The opening of the avenue de l'Opéra brought an end to decades of steeply climbing property values in neighboring commercial streets: the rue de Richelieu, passage Choiseul, rue des Petits-Champs, rue St.-Augustin.[71] Anthony Sutcliffe has estimated that, as a general rule, "land prices in old streets in any area were about half those current in new streets nearby."[72] Shopkeepers as well as property owners saw the bloom taken off their investments by the rise of the Haussmannic boulevard. The completion of the macadamized rue de Rivoli drew business away from the rue Saint-Honoré. The *percée* of the boulevard Sébastopol accelerated the decline of the rue Saint-Denis, already hurt by loss of trade to the rue du Sentier. Construction of the new Opera House bought ruin to the passage de l'Opéra.[73] And the Place de la République built its fortunes on the ruins of more than one old Paris street: "Here are everywhere to be found descendants of the unfortunate Palais-Royal; here also are to be found hatters in exile from the passage du Saumon and refugees from the rue du Caire where flowers and feathers were once sold but now only manufactured."[74]

The rue de Richelieu and, of course, the Palais-Royal were two of the principal victims of Haussmannization. Trade in women's clothing on the "unfortunate" rue de Richelieu was devastated by competition from the rue du Quatre-Septembre.[75] In 1851, of Paris' 59 *magasins de nouveautés*, 18 were situated on the rues de Richelieu, Montmartre and du Temple. Only four remained in 1869.[76] The spoils of the Palais-

[71] Daumard, *Maisons de Paris*, p. 154.
[72] Sutcliffe, p. 159.
[73] *Ibid.*, p. 155; Daumard, *Maisons de Paris*, p. 141.
[74] Montorgueil, *La Vie des boulevards*, p. 19.
[75] *Les Boulevards de Paris*, p. 106.
[76] Gaillard, p. 624n.

Royal were disputed by a host of contending successors. The Place de la République has already been mentioned. The rue de la Paix inherited "the luxury commerce that once lingered in the Palais-Royal," emerging under the Empire as one of Paris' most prestigious shopping streets.[77] But the chief beneficiary of the Palais-Royal's decline were the *grands boulevards*, "that great luxury thoroughfare which aspires to supplant the Palace, which has robbed it of its Morocco-leather shops and merchants of small bronzes."[78]

Haussmannization then would seem to offer a plausible explanation for the distinctive geographical pattern of *Ligue syndicale* recruitment. The *Ligue* mobilized small and medium businessmen, drawing support from areas of Paris that had once been centers of the luxury trade. These *quartiers* were in decline; Haussmannization had transferred the focus of commercial activity to other parts of the city. One of the virtues of the "Haussmannization thesis" is that it accounts not only for the *Ligue*'s highly localized appeal but also for its choice of the department store as a scapegoat. The *grand magasin* was in fact very much a by-product of Haussmannization. It was along the new streets of Haussmannized Paris that the department store set down its roots.[79] The big stores could not survive without a huge clientele; where else could customers be found in adequate concentrations but on the boulevards of new Paris. *Magasins de nouveautés* virtually monopolized the rue de Rivoli from end to end.[80] Jacques Ruel began his career in commerce as a cheapjack and then moved into wholesaling to street vendors. One vendor in particular, he observed, outsold the rest. Ruel leased a storefront on that very spot (rue des Archives and rue de Rivoli) in 1860 and went into retailing for himself as proprietor of the Bazar de l'Hôtel

[77] Reboux, *La Rue de la Paix*, pp. 57–58.
[78] Montorgueil, *op. cit.*, p. 19.
[79] Gaillard, p. 528; Sutcliffe, p. 154.
[80] Jarry, *Les Magasins de nouveautés*, pp. 69ff.

The Rue de Richelieu in the 1840s

2202. PARIS — Rue de Richelieu 1908

The Rue de Richelieu in 1908

de Ville.[81] The Grands Magasins du Louvre had opened up only five years earlier at the other end of the rue de Rivoli just across the street from the Louvre Palace. For years, the Place du Palais-Royal had been a muddy sink, virtually impassable to pedestrians. It was paved over in 1851; the rue de Rivoli was completed in 1854; and the Louvre department store opened the next year with the blessing and financial help of the Péreire brothers. A host of smaller stores, most now forgotten, lined the stretch of pavement between the Louvre and the Hôtel de Ville, from Au Nouveau Paris (!) at no. 72 to A la Tour St. Jacques and A Pygmalion at the boulevard Sébastopol, to Au Paradis des Dames at no. 10.

The rue Pont-Neuf, built in 1867, was intended to ease communications between les Halles and the Left Bank. The street attracted business as well as traffic. La Belle Jardinière opened a store here the very year the street was completed, occupying modest premises formerly the site of nine smallish houses with two- or three-windowed facades. La Samaritaine's beginnings were yet more humble. Ernest Cognacq, sometime employee and aspiring entrepreneur, had tried his luck and failed with a *magasin de nouveautés* on the rue Turbigo. In 1870, he sublet a storefront from a local café-owner on the rue Pont-Neuf at the rate of fifteen francs per day. The street treated the two newcomers well. La Samaritaine expanded to encompass virtually the entire west side of the rue Pont-Neuf, La Belle Jardinière virtually the entire east side.[82] Construction of the avenue de l'Opéra made the fortune of another big store, the Gagne-Petit. An old established business founded at the beginning of the century on the rue des Moineaux in the heart of the Palais-Royal ward, the Gagne-Petit fell on hard times in the 1860s and 1870s. But then the rue des

---

[81] For Ruel's story, see *ibid.*, pp. 69–70; Valmy-Baisse, *Les Grands Magasins*, p. 12; Coffignon, *Le Pavé parisien*, p. 64.

[82] On the origins of La Samaritaine and La Belle Jardinière, see Jarry, pp. 74, 83–84.

Moineaux was leveled to make way for the avenue de l'Opéra. The Gagne-Petit won an extremely favorable expropriation settlement, exchanging 2,500 m^2 of floor space for new premises, 3,700 m^2, with frontage on the new avenue. The business, in the words of one observer, was reborn "from its ashes, handsome and more resplendent than it had ever been. . . ."[83] Félix Potin began with a small grocery store on the rue du Rocher. In the 1850s, he moved the commercial part of his business to the brand new boulevard Malesherbes[84] and then in 1859 opened a second store on the boulevard Sébastopol virtually "in the middle of the demolitions."[85] And finally there is the case of Jules Jaluzot's Au Printemps, situated at the intersection of the rue du Havre and the boulevard Haussmann "in the very heart of *Paris nouveau.*"[86] The boulevard was completed in 1857; Au Printemps moved in eight years later. Proximity to the *grands boulevards,* however, does not fully account for the store's astonishing success. After all, the boulevard Haussmann until 1922 extended no further than the rue Taitbout, thus providing only indirect access to the city's busiest thoroughfare. It was rather the railroad that made the Printemps' fortunes. The Gare Saint-Lazare just a few short blocks away handled 62 percent of Paris' rail traffic in 1869, thirteen million passengers per year in all. Travelers poured in from the city's fanciest suburbs (Auteuil, Saint-Germain-en-Laye) and from well-to-do nearby towns (Versailles, Rouen), and more than one was on a shopping trip. The station acted as "a funnel sucking up travelers from France's entire Northwest and then discharging them into the Printemps department store."[87]

[83] Daumard, "L'avenue de l'Opéra," pp. 173–183.

[84] The rue du Rocher premises were used for packaging Potin products.

[85] For Potin's career, see du Maroussem, *Halles centrales de Paris,* pp. 161–166.

[86] Claudin, *Paris,* p. 252.

[87] *Printania,* p. 14.

The new streets of Haussmannic Paris were indeed mid-wives to the department store. Haussmann reequipped the city to handle a massive volume of new traffic and in the process fostered commerce on a new and grand scale. The kinship of *grand magasin* and new Paris, however, was perhaps most apparent in the realm of aesthetics. The department store, with its monumental and rectilineal façade, fit snugly into an urban landscape that stressed the identical architectural values. Elaborate and eclectic trimmings were added to appeal to a newly rich clientele with a taste for grand-opera magnificence. In donning baroque architectural clothing, the *grand magasin* laid claim to a place of honor in Paris' new "parvenu cityscape." Department store interiors, on the other hand, resembled more the daring bareness of les Halles or the Galérie des Machines than the high-flown pretentiousness of the Haussmannic apartment house. Bare metal staircases and vaulting glass skylights showed off the new materials of the industrial age to great effect, inevitably calling to mind parallel institutions of similar colossal structure: railroad stations, the Bourse du Commerce, etc. The *grand magasin* was but one of a host of new urban organisms designed to handle masses of people in a city built on a new scale.

Glass and iron, even though up-to-date and impressive, did not alone suffice to create a shopping environment. Fantasy and bright lights, color and display created the charged atmosphere that in turn generated high turnover. The department store transformed itself into a gigantic theater; the double, curving staircases in the main gallery of Au Bon Marché recalled the Grand Stairway at the new Opéra.[88] Customers who paraded up and down were at once actors and spectators in a fabulous drama. Commerce steeped in theater, of course, was not a recipe invented by the department store. The theater district of Imperial Paris, after all, was headquartered on the city's busiest commercial artery, the boulevards. A string

[88] Hautecoeur, "De l'échoppe aux grands magasins," p. 829.

of theaters extended from the Gymnase and Variétés in the east to the Nouveautés, Opéra Comique, Vaudeville and Grand Opera in the west. Stage and street alike trafficked in a commodity much coveted by a *nouveau-riche* clientele—spectacle, whether the visual delights of a well-dressed store window or the light-hearted pageantry of an Offenbach operetta. Commodity utopianism and *la gaieté parisienne* were two sides of the same coin. The mixture of business and theater concocted by the department store was then a second-hand edition of the genuine article to be found outside on the streets of new Paris. The boulevards of the *grand magasin* interior were so many extensions of the *grands boulevards* that stretched from the Madeleine to the Bastille. The department store, the city's new boulevards, the look and structure of *Paris nouveau* were interlocking phenomena, aspects of a single process.

Contemporaries recognized implicitly the interconnectedness of the changes wrought by Haussmannization. Haussmann's Paris, like the department store—the real city like the city in miniature—conjured up images of machines, tentacled creatures, phalansteries, barracks and agglomerations. City and store were bureaucratic, functionalized environments that slotted persons according to the jobs they performed, sundering bonds of social solidarity in the name of efficiency. Old Paris, by contrast, was seen as a congeries of narrow, winding streets, dirty perhaps, but also picturesque. People rarely strayed, it was believed, from their particular neighborhood. Residence and place of work were more often than not one and the same. Social hierarchy existed, to be sure, but people knew each other, and daily intercourse muted class tensions. In the words of Augustin Cochin: "Common place of birth, neighborliness, trade, daily encounters in the exercise of rights and discharge of obligations, little by little transformed each arrondissement into a small civil and industrial province."[89] Indeed, the city itself was conceived as a patchwork or fed-

[89] Cochin, pp. 83–84.

eration of such neighborhoods, each more or less self-suffi-cient and self-governing. The small shop had flourished in this environment, serving the needs of the local community, of-fering credit to customers short of cash and generally con-tributing to the neighborly mood that permeated *quartier* life. The storefront may not have sparkled like the fancy shops of the boulevard, but its quaint demeanor—handsomely com-plemented by a colorful, hanging-sign—blended in harmo-niously with local surroundings. As for the store owner, he was a man risen from the ranks, a worker still in many ways, who had an intuitive understanding of the wage earners in his employ. He was a family man, a model citizen and a good Frenchman. The values of the *quartier* were recapitulated in his person and in the way he conducted his business.

Contemporaries identified *petit commerce* with the old city, an identity expressed in the common descriptive language ap-plied to both. The department store and *Paris nouveau* were similarly linked. The two pairs constituted polar opposites, each the negative image of the other. The small-shop/old-city represented all that was small, local, familial, picturesque; the department-store/new-city all that was large, centralized, bu-reaucratic and rectilineal. Whatever the observer's sympa-thies, whether he decried the passing of the old as the death of community or welcomed the advent of the new as the triumph of modernity, commercial and urban change were woven together in the public imagination.

No contemporary was more acutely attuned to this inter-connectedness or exploited it to greater effect than Zola. Take the following passage from *La Curée* as an example. Renée and Maxime are riding in a carriage together:

> The lovers had a love for new Paris. They often ran about the city in a carriage, making a detour to travel along boulevards that they loved with a personal tenderness. They were enraptured by the tall buildings with sculpted

doorways, with balconies from which glistened in giant
letters of gold, names, signs, and company logos. The
unobstructed passage coursing toward the horizon . . .
that uninterrupted double file of *grands magasins* where
clerks cast smiles at lady shoppers, those humming and
shuffling crowds filled them little by little with an absolute satisfaction.[90]

Zola here conflates the department store, the boulevard and
new Paris. The artist's "description," of course, contains a
significant distortion. The boulevard is represented as an
"uninterrupted double file of *grands magasins*," whereas, in fact,
Paul Reboux's characterization—"an uninterrupted file of
boutiques"—is certainly more accurate.[91] Department stores
were liberally interspersed, but it was the boutique, the luxury shop that prevailed numerically along the city's new and
refurbished streets. And yet, to the observer, Zola, who sought
to decode Paris' new cityscape, the department store *appeared*
to predominate. *Grands magasins* set the tone of *Paris nouveau*;
they epitomized the profound transformations the city had
undergone and took on importance as symbols. Zola's vision
of the boulevards, while not a literal transcription of reality,
does capture a symbolic truth.

The department store as emblem of new Paris reappears in
Au Bonheur des Dames, not as a passing reference but as the
novel's central metaphor. The owner of Zola's fictional *grand
magasin*, Octave Mouret, is a mere twenty-six years old at the
outset of the story. He is a prophet of the new commerce who
dreams of constructing a magnificent facade on one of Paris'
spanking new thoroughfares:

As long as the grand entranceway faced onto the rue
Neuve Saint-Augustin, onto a darkened street of old Paris,

[90] Zola, *La Curée*, p. 276.
[91] Reboux, *Histoire et les dessous de Paris*, p. 62.

his work lacked consistency; he wanted to show it off to new Paris, on one of the brand new avenues where thronged in bright sunlight the fin-de-siècle crowd.[92]

Thanks to the timely assistance of Baron Hartmann, president of the Crédit Immobilier, Mouret finally obtains a site on the rue du Quatre-Septembre. The explosive expansion of the department store brings ruin to the small shops in the neighborhood: the lingerie store in the passage Choiseul, the milliner's on the rue Gaillon, the furrier's on the rue des Petits-Champs. The *quartier*'s misfortunes are recapitulated in microcosm in the lingering death suffered by Au Vieil Elbeuf. Zola describes the store as it appeared to the proprietor's niece on a rainy night:

> She took a step backward for a moment, taken with a chill, her heart constricted by the sight of the badly lit boutique, lugubrious at that hour. Humid exhalations, the breath of the old *quartier*, rose from the street: it seemed that the rain dripping from the umbrellas ran right up to the counters, that the street with its puddles and mud, entered into the shop, covering in mold the floor whitened with salt-peter. It was a vision of old Paris, soaked through and through. . . .[93]

Street, shop, *quartier*, the old city fuse in the girl's visionary experience. Au Vieil Elbeuf is drained of its particularity and achieves symbolic status, a countermetaphor to Au Bonheur des Dames, representing an antithetical complex of phenomena (*vieux Paris*, old streets, old commerce). Of course, the transformation of Au Vieil Elbeuf into an emblem of old Paris involves a distortion. Not all the shops of the old city, certainly not those of the *passages*, were ill lit and decrepit with

---

[92] Zola, *Au Bonheur des Dames*, p. 365.
[93] *Ibid.*, pp. 34–35.

age. Yet, to a stroller on the city's muddy, back streets, at a moment of heightened perception, how must the small shop have looked? Might not Au Vieil Elbeuf with its battered, discolored storefront have appeared the very embodiment of all that was old Paris? Zola's naturalism does not lie in the pursuit of literal truth, but in the creation of symbols that translate the literal into dramatic metaphor. Literal or historic processes can then be played out in symbolic drama. The transition from old Paris to new is staged in *Au Bonheur des Dames* as a contest between boutique and department store.

The *Ligue syndicale* viewed its own struggle in precisely these terms, but with this difference. It took its symbols—the small shop, the department store—seriously, as real historical actors, not for what they in fact were, fictional personae. In fiction, the metaphorical status of the drama is never in doubt. Ideological drama is no less metaphorical in character; it translates lived experience into symbolic conflict, but the act of symbol formation is completely denied in the process. Fictional truth is mistaken for the literal truth. *Ligue* ideology reproduced the symbolism of *Au Bonheur des Dames* but without consciousness of the historical process this symbolism dramatized.

The *Ligue*'s symbolic leap was understandable. Not just *ligueurs* but outside observers—apologists for Haussmannization and the department store, partisans of old Paris and *petit commerce*—made the same leap. The department store, given its location and appearance, could easily be taken as a symbol for the larger process of Haussmannization which was, in fact, the genuine source of the *ligueur*'s troubles.

The "Haussmannization thesis" then has several strengths. The reconstruction of central Paris gave birth to a new "world of intermediaries," to a coherent social and political milieu that was fertile ground for the formation of a distinctive retailer consciousness. The Haussmannization thesis, moreover, can account for the *Ligue syndicale*'s popularity in the *quartiers* that constituted Paris' old shopping district, and it provides an explanation for the shopkeeper movement's anti-department store animus. The thesis, however, does have weaknesses. There is firstly the question of timing. If Haussmannization is solely to blame, why did the *Ligue* form in 1888, eighteen years after the Second Empire's collapse and a full decade after completion of the last Haussmannic street. And then there is the more complicated issue of motive. Urban renewal did indeed transform central Paris, but it did not destroy at one stroke the city's old commercial geography.

The boulevard in the 1860s, despite commercialization, retained its appeal as a gathering place for bon vivants and litterateurs. The street was inundated with a flood of traffic, but the sidewalks remained the preserve of the leisurely stroller. On summer nights in the 1870s, crowds of idlers were to be found in front of the Gymnase, lounging on easy chairs rented for two sous an hour.[94] A well-bred exclusivity, moreover, still reigned at the cafés lining the route. "It was an audacious fellow or a boor," Georges Montorgueil wrote of the 1860s, "who dared set foot in the old Café de Paris without a sponsor. Tortoni's had its own set, and no one felt at home at the Grand Balcon until after the proper introductions had been made."[95] The after-theater crowd that assembled at the Café Anglais to celebrate into the wee hours was overwhelmingly aristocratic: the duc de Gramont-Caderousse, prince Galitzine, prince d'Orange, the marquis de Modène.[96] The literary men—Aubryet, Claudin, Charles Monselet, Aurélien Scholl—who gathered nightly for dinner and conversation at the Café Riche were not titled noblemen, but they made up in wit and style for what they lacked in pedigree (Scholl was famed for his perennial monocle).[97] And the boulevards still

[94] Ginisty, *Les Anciens Boulevards*, p. 39; Duvernois, *Le Boulevard*, pp. 8–9.

[95] Montorgueil, *op. cit.*, p. xi.

[96] Claudin, *Mes Souvenirs*, pp. 243–244; Bertaut, *op. cit.*, p. 7.

[97] Claudin, *op. cit.*, pp. 293–295.

boasted the headquarters of the city's most select dinner and gambling clubs: the Cercle agricole, the Cercle militaire, the Cercle de l'union and, of course, the Jockey.

The avenue was fast becoming a bourgeois playground, but the stamp of its aristocratic past was far from obliterated. What the boulevards had lost in refinement and *bon ton*, they regained in gaiety and excitement. Gentlemen, men of letters and wealthy parvenus merrily pursued their pleasures, as yet undisturbed by an excess of undesirables—tourists, foreigners, petits bourgeois and *faubouriens*. The transformation of the boulevard was only in its initial stages.[98] So, too, the decline of Paris' old downtown area.

Indeed, for the Palais-Royal, the Second Empire was, in the words of one observer, "one of the most brilliant phases of its history."[99] The business boom of the sixties brought an Indian summer of prosperity to the jewelry stores and luxury shops that lined the arcades of Louis-Philippe's one-time residence. While Parisians in increasing numbers sought their entertainment on the boulevards, the Palais-Royal got along handsomely on tourist revenues. "See the Palais-Royal and die," noted the *Paris-Guide* of 1867, "that's the fondest wish of every traveler in Europe."[100] The rue de Richelieu had indeed faded from its former elegance, but the neighboring rue Vivienne in 1877 still remained "one of the most animated streets in Paris." The arcades that abutted the Vivienne, the passage Colbert and Galérie Vivienne, were still "very busy, whatever the time of day."[101] Nor had fashion utterly deserted the city's other major *passages*. The passage Delorme, leveled in this century, formerly linked the rue de Rivoli and the rue Saint-Honoré in the vicinity of what is now the Place des Pyramides. In its heyday under the Empire, the *passage* had been ". . . one of the most brilliant in Paris, filled with modistes

[98] Bertaut, *op. cit.*, p. 7; Reboux, *Histoire et les dessous de Paris*, p. 35.
[99] Robert Hénard, *La Rue Saint-Honoré*, vol. II, p. 464.
[100] Cited in Champier and Sandoz, vol. II, p. 93.
[101] *Les Boulevards de Paris*, pp. 106–107.

The Théâtre du Gymnase in 1863

and toy stores and patronized by the wealthiest clientele."[102] Just to the north stretched the passage Choiseul, site of the Théatre des Bouffes where Offenbach got his start as theater director in the 1850s. Land values may have stagnated in this part of town under the Empire, but the arcade still retained its fairyland quality. Eduoard Fournier wrote in 1861: "Here, all is bustle, spectacle and pleasure. This is the passage Choiseul, with its boutiques so tightly squeezed together that the arcade appears a double row of shop windows stuffed with the most varied and enticing merchandise."[103] The Panoramas, too, retained their appeal and, indeed, still outshone the boulevards. In the *passage*, according to one historian, "the activity is more intense than on the boulevard, the elegance more breath-taking, the fashions more daring."[104]

The arcade then survived the Second Empire in grand style. Arcade building, in fact, did not come to a halt until 1860 with the completion of the passage Mirès, now passage des Princes. The staying power of Paris' arcades was manifest not just in the crowds they still drew but also in their continued grip on the Parisian imagination. In 1869, Tony Moulin published *Paris en l'an 2000*, a utopian vision of the socialist city of the future. Streets have been abolished save as traffic arteries for public transportation. Pedestrian traffic has been diverted to a network of marvelous glass-paneled *rues-galéries*, outfitted with a full panoply of shops. In twenty-first-century Paris, the happy *flâneur* never found himself obliged to quit the spectacular dreamworld of the *passages*. As a commodity utopia or a utopia *tout court*, the *passages* were by no means leveled by the initial thrusts of Haussmannization.[105]

Paris under the Empire was outfitted with two parallel

[102] R. Hénard, p. 475.

[103] Fournier, "Promenade dans Paris," p. 26.

[104] Bertaut, *op. cit.*, p. 108.

[105] Moulin, *Paris en l'an 2000*, pp. 9, 25–26, 42. See also Kahn, *L'Esthétique de la rue*, p. 193.

downtowns, one new, one old, one expanding rapidly, the other losing momentum. In the boom times of the 1860s, however, the emerging gap between the city's twin shopping districts was not as yet substantial. Was the old downtown's relative decline sufficient to mobilize a commercial protest movement of the *Ligue syndicale*'s dimensions? The impact of Haussmannization, I would argue, was not by itself brutal enough to generate such a massive outburst of retailer anger.

Urban transformation created a fissured commercial community riven with simmering social tensions between employees and department stores, between old and new downtowns. These conflicts were destined to explode, but it was not urban change that set off the explosion. To settle the unanswered questions of timing and motive, it is necessary to turn to a discussion of the economic slump of the 1880s and 1890s. At the end of the century the Parisian business world experienced a severe short-term crisis which brought its internal divisions to the surface, which splintered the commercial community into a variety of contesting factions, the *Syndicat général*, the *Ligue syndicale*, the *Chambre syndicale des employés*. It is against the immediate background of commercial crisis, indeed of economic depression, that the origins of the shopkeeper movement must be seen. Haussmannization was a necessary but not sufficient condition of retailer mobilization. It required the sting of hard times in the 1880s to motivate shopkeepers to take action.

4

. . .

The Economic Crisis
of the 1880s

THE FRENCH ECONOMY decelerated in the last quarter of the century. Throughout the decades of mid-century, a steady if unspectacular growth rate of 1.6 percent a year had been maintained, but in the 1880s, the rate tumbled to a dismal 0.6 percent.[1] There is no debate in France as there is in Britain about the "myth of the great depression." Why the French economy slowed down and the long-term structural consequences of the crisis, however, remain subjects of dispute, but two points seem clear. Firstly, on the question of the slump's origins, it is widely agreed that France's economic troubles were in large part attributable to the ravages of foreign competition. Relative newcomers like Germany and the United States produced with greater efficiency and at less expense, underselling French-made goods and driving them out of the market.[2] As for the long-term impact of the crisis, the comparative cheapness of foreign manufactures coupled with the defensive and often desperate efforts of French producers to cut costs depressed prices, resulting in a consumer revo-

[1] Lévy-Leboyer, "La décélération de l'économie française," p. 486.
[2] Caron, *An Economic History of Modern France*, pp. 105–112.

· 143 ·

lution or what Jacques Néré has called the *"révolution du bon marché."*[3]

How these processes unfolded needs to be spelled out in more detail before turning to a discussion of their impact on the Parisian economy and on its commercial sector in particular. The point has been made repeatedly in recent historiography that the French economy did not stagnate in the nineteenth century but that growth was concentrated in labor-intensive industries organized on a small-workshop basis and geared to the manufacture of high-quality goods. Two reasons are cited for the peculiar pattern of French industrialization.[4] England, as the first industrial nation, enjoyed a competitive edge in mining, metals and machine construction which dampened the expansion of France's infant heavy industrial sector. France was steered into a specialization in luxury manufactures such that the two economies, the French and the British, developed in complement rather than in opposition to one another. France, moreover, was endowed with a plentiful supply of highly skilled labor suited to luxury production. The very abundance of skilled manpower reduced incentives to mechanize and, as a consequence, France's specialty industries remained in the main labor intensive. Economic development in France then was by no means inimical to artisanal modes of production, and indeed, a numerous and prosperous artisanate specializing in the production of fine leather goods, handcrafted furniture, jewelry and *articles de Paris* survived into the third quarter of the century. Even in textiles, the most highly concentrated industry in France, labor-

[3] Néré, *La Crise industrielle de 1882 et le mouvement boulangiste*, vol. I, p. 133. On the end-of-century consumer revolution, see Williams, *Dream Worlds, Mass Consumption in Late Nineteenth Century France.*

[4] Lévy-Leboyer, "Les processus d'industrialisation," pp. 281–298; Lévy-Leboyer, "La croissance économique en France au XIXe siècle," pp. 788–807; Crouzet, "Encore la croissance économique française au XIXe siècle," p. 286.

intensive luxury production predominated.[5] France remained
a major exporter of heavy silk and fine linen, quality fabrics
prized for their durability and handsome finish. The materials
sold well but were costly in large part due to under-mecha-
nization. Spinning factories there were, but weaving remained for the most part the work of small-scale ateliers using hand-powered looms. In the silk industry, as late as 1875,
hand looms outnumbered power looms by a factor of 11.4 to
1 (80,000 to 7,000).[6]

France's high-quality manufactures enjoyed a position of
undisputed supremacy on luxury markets for most of the
nineteenth century. Foreign producers could not rival the exquisite and tasteful elegance of French handcrafted and hand-
woven goods. By replacing skilled labor with machinery and
substituting factory organization for the atelier, they could of
course produce the same items at less cost—a toy, a hat, a
bolt of silk cloth—but standards of quality were sacrificed in
the process. Luxury goods did not readily lend themselves to
machinofacture. Technical advances, however, undercut France's
position of dominance in the late nineteenth century, and it
was the Germans and the Americans who led the way.

Foreigners pioneered new processes and new machinery that
revolutionized labor-intensive artisanal industries from wall
paper to *articles de Paris*.[7] Goodyear perfected a machine to
sole footwear without damaging even the finest leather. The
Germans developed rubber toys. The *métier* Cotton, introduced in the eighties, could weave six to eighteen hats simultaneously at high speed.[8] Frenchmen, entrepreneurs and

[5] Caron, p. 155.

[6] *Ibid.*, p. 154.

[7] Chambre des Députés, Spuller Commission, testimony of the *Syndicat
des ouvriers de papiers peints*, p. 45, and of the *Chambre syndicale des industries
diverses*, p. 120.

[8] Du Maroussem, *Le Jouet parisien*, p. 69; Aftalion, *Le Développement de la
fabrique et le travail à domicile*, pp. 30, 53–54.

workers alike, acknowledged the superiority of foreigners at machinofacture.[9] The items produced were not up to the highest French standards; they lacked the detail and imagination of handcrafted work. More than one critic was prepared to dismiss the new goods as *la camelote*, as "shoddy," but machine-made hats and shoes were cheap and now, given technical progress, of reasonable quality.[10] And so in the eighties and nineties, a new generation of inexpensive foreign manufactures began to make inroads into the luxury market, once an exclusive French preserve.

The French textile industry, too, was losing its grip on the luxury market and for similar reasons. In the 1880s, lighter weight silks, cotton goods and blends deluged the market, underselling the high-quality fabrics in which French manufacturers had specialized. Foreigners, Germans in particular, outdistanced the French in the production of the new textiles. The formula of German success was straightforward. The fabrics produced were machine woven of cheaper materials. They cost less and, not least of all, gave the appearance of being well made. Light-weight Krefeld silk wore less well than Lyon heavy silk, but it was still silk after all and easier to tailor into the bargain.[11] Frenchmen of conservative temperament decried the "invasion" of the new goods, the "reign" of *la camelote*.[12] In previous times, it was lamented, "one [had] made children's breeches out of grandfather's overcoat; it was the age of silk dresses that 'stood up by themselves,' dresses

[9] Chambre des Députés, Spuller Commission, testimony of Senator Tolain, p. 127, and of the *Chambre syndicale des industries diverses*, p. 120; see also Worth, *La Couture et la confection des vêtements de femme*, pp. 95–96; Barberet, *Monographies professionnelles*, vol. III, p. 100.

[10] Chambre des Députés, Spuller Commission, testimony of A. Muzet, p. 60; Aftalion, pp. 105–108.

[11] Labrousse and Braudel, eds., *Histoire économique et sociale*, vol. IV, pt. 1, pp. 295–296.

[12] Domergue, *Comment et pourquoi les affaires vont mal en France*, p. 62; Garrigues, *Les Grands Magasins de nouveautés*, p. 132.

passed down from generation to generation."[13] However stiff or heavy the fabric, the clothing of yesteryear had lasted and was preserved as part of the family patrimony. Modern man, however, was losing his taste for solid and durable things; he coveted a "false luxury":[14] "once upon a time, our fathers cared about quality, but today people only want show."[15] From the point of view of many consumers, of course, cut-rate luxury was preferable to the genuine high-priced luxury of French-made *nouveautés*. "French industry," Jacques Néré has summed up, "founded on quality and high prices, adapted badly to a consumer demand that was democratizing."[16]

Foreign competition struck hard at France's specialty industries, luxury manufactures and high-quality textiles. France's response, however, was by no means passive. The textile industry undertook a rapid shift to mechanization in the late nineteenth century. In wool production, the artisan-weaver "virtually disappeared from the scene" in the 1880s.[17] The number of handlooms in the silk industry plummeted to 17,300 while the number of power looms shot up to 42,500. Between 1877 and the onset of World War I, the number of mechanized looms in the cotton industry more than doubled, rising from 60,000 to nearly 140,000.[18]

Foreign competition enforced basic changes in the structure and modus operandi of luxury industries as well. Pressures to reduce costs drove shoe manufacturers to abandon the labor-intensive small workshops of the Paris faubourgs. The center of the footwear industry shifted from the capital city

[13] Domergue, p. 11.

[14] Feyeux, "La question des grands et des petits magasins," p. 363; du Maroussem, *Ebénistes du faubourg Saint-Antoine*, p. 101.

[15] Duclos, *La Transformation du commerce de détail*, p. 138; Saint-Martin, *Les Grands Magasins*, pp. 116–118.

[16] Néré, vol. I, p. 193.

[17] Caron, p. 153.

[18] Labrousse and Braudel, eds., vol. IV, pt. 1, p. 296; Caron, p. 151.

to mechanized factories in the provinces.[19] Mechanization was not the only alternative available to cost-cutting entrepreneurs. Production by *fabrique collective* took on new importance at the end of the century. The garment industry was long familiar with this form of urban putting out. Low quality clothing—uniforms, work clothes, smocks, aprons—had been manufactured by *fabrique collective* since the 1830s. What was distinctive about the end of the century was the application of putting-out procedures to better quality clothing, menswear in particular, and a whole range of new trades: toys, *articles de Paris* and furniture.[20] For luxury manufacturers, the system had two advantages. The workshop craftsman earned the high wages of a skilled laborer. Converted into a home worker, he could be paid by the piece, and piece rates in the 1880s were unstable and declining.[21] The dissolution of the atelier in favor of the *fabrique collective*, moreover, shifted the burden of overhead costs to the employee. The worker, not the employer, was saddled with machinery maintenance and the payment of rent on business premises.

The foreign-led technical revolution, it should be added, created not only problems, but also fresh opportunities. Innovations in machine tools and metal-working, scientific advances in electricity and engine design, bred a whole range of new consumer durables: bicycles, electrical appliances and above all automobiles. In the eighties and nineties, these products were still luxury items, high-quality manufactures that required a skilled labor force to produce. France, with its pool of skilled labor and traditions of luxury production, was well placed to shift into these new industries, and shift it did, staking out a preeminent position that would

[19] Aftalion, p. 160.

[20] Du Maroussem, *Ebénistes du faubourg Saint-Antoine*, p. 209; *idem, Le Jouet parisien*, p. 119; Henri Bonnet, "La carte des pauvres à Paris," p. 415.

[21] Office du travail, *Le Vêtement à Paris*, p. 658.

pay off with the return of prosperity at the turn of the century.[22]

Machinofacture, sweating and innovation delimited the range of alternatives available to French luxury manufacturers under extreme external pressure. Opinions differ as to whether France adapted to the foreign challenge with sufficient vigor and foresight, but two points can be made with relative confidence. Domestic markets were flooded with relatively inexpensive consumer goods, a real gain for buyers whose livelihoods were not threatened by the crisis. For the numerous un- and underemployed, the eighties brought only misery, but for others who had full-time work and a modicum of good luck, life actually improved. Contemporaries spoke of a "democratization of luxury."[23] A ready-to-wear suit of clothes cost far less than tailor-made clothing. Ready-made shoes were cheaper than custom made. The introduction of low-cost quality goods brought articles "which formerly were purchased only by the privileged classes" (toys, toiletries, brush ware) within the price range of shoppers on fairly modest budgets.[24] The chief beneficiary of the shift to cheaper goods was the petite bourgeoisie. "The relative luxury" of the lower middle class, noted the vicomte d'Avenel in 1902, "dates only from yesterday."[25] But laboring men, too, profited from reduced consumer prices. Employers and public officials decried the habits of luxury to which working people were becoming addicted. Workers were now accustomed to taking coffee and smoking a cigar after dinner: ". . . some even manage to squeeze in

---

[22] Crouzet, "Encore la croissance," p. 288; Lévy-Leboyer, "La croissance économique en France," p. 799; and more generally, Landes, *The Unbound Prometheus*, p. 244.

[23] D'Avenel, *Le Mécanisme de la vie moderne*, vol. I, p. 66.

[24] See the deposition of M. Dupont, *fabricant de brosserie*, to the Mesureur Commission, AN C5498, 15 May 1891.

[25] D'Avenel, vol. IV, p. 5.

a so-called aperitif at bed-time."[26] Working man and petit bourgeois both, as we shall see, made their way as consumers onto the boulevards of Paris and into the city's department stores. The cafés-concerts that proliferated on the eastern fringe of the boulevard catered to a popular theater-going public, and yet never lacked for customers even in the worst years of the crisis.[27] The people, so long excluded, erupted into the closed world of commodity utopianism: "Once the boulevard was reserved for people of *bon ton;* then the bourgeois slipped in; and now it is the turn of the crowd."[28] Not everyone, of course, welcomed the arrival of a mass-buying public. The triumph of the factory (*fabrique collective* or *grande fabrique*) was interpreted by conservative critics as the triumph of junk over taste, of mediocrity over art. But whether the democratization of demand was to be praised or blamed, few doubted that France was in the throes of a consumer revolution.

As in every industrial crisis, there were winners and losers, and this is the second point that emerges from accounts of the slump's impact on French industry. In textiles, the impetus to mechanize spurred on industrial concentration. Cotton-spinning enterprises in the department of the Nord had averaged 13,300 spindles to the factory in 1865. By 1911, Lille boasted forty factories with an average of 51,500 spindles and eighteen with an average of 67,000.[29] The transition to mass production was by no means a smooth or painless process. Businesses plagued by labor problems or hamstrung by a shortage of capital were in no position to withstand the

---

[26] Chambre des Députés, Spuller Commission, testimony of Frédéric Bertrand, president of the *Syndicat des patrons charpentiers du département de la Seine,* p. 47, and of the *Chambre syndicale des entrepreneurs de démolitions,* p. 79; APP B/a 503, St.-Ambroise, 18 March 1886.

[27] Chambre des Députés, Spuller Commission, testimony of the prefect of police, pp. 329–330.

[28] Laut, "Le boulevard d'aujourd'hui," p. 2.

[29] Caron, p. 168.

competition of more efficient producers. François Caron has remarked of the textile industry in the last decades of the century: "there was a kind of vast redistribution of assets. The bankruptcies of some manufacturers enabled others to build rapid fortunes and concentrate the means of production."[30] What was true of individual entrepreneurs was no less true of entire towns, indeed entire regions. The woolens industry of Roubaix grew at the expense of the woolens industry of Fourmies. Alsace, with its large-scale and technically advanced spinning factories, "outclassed" Normandy which had once dominated the industry.

The drive to slash production costs divided the textile industry into survivors and victims, and the same process of polarization can be detected in the luxury goods sector. Businesses that made the change-over to mechanized mass production were able to weather the crisis, albeit not without difficulties. A clothier from Reims summed up the risks that mechanizing industries confronted:

> In our industry, for example, mechanical innovations have been so numerous and so rapid that only the largest firms have been able to keep their plant up-to-date. . . . The transformation has been exceedingly costly, and it was necessary to muster new capital investment to combat foreign industries, born for the most part after the 1870 war and whose brand-new machinery would have given them the edge had we hesitated to follow step by step the path of progress.
>
> We can produce cheaply only if we produce in quantity, and so it is imperative that we avoid work stoppages and temporary shut-downs.[31]

---

[30] *Ibid.*, p. 154 and pp. 148–155 for what follows.

[31] Testimony of A. Dauphinot, AN C5498, Mesureur Commission, 6 November 1891.

Mechanization, of course, was not the only route to survival. The putting-out sector knew a period of unparalleled expansion in the late nineteenth century. The ready-to-wear business in Paris may be cited as an example. It was a highly concentrated industry. The city's 120 largest ready-to-wear manufacturers (*maisons de confection*) in the mid-1890s subcontracted to 2,000–2,500 entrepreneurs who in turn employed upwards of 25,000 workers.[32] And for the sweaters, if not the sweated, the business of manufacturing ready-made clothing was highly profitable. The sales of ready-to-wear items in Paris more than doubled between 1871 and 1896.[33] Manufacturers of the new consumer durables fared even better. The first French automobile was assembled in 1884. Annual production rose to 1,850 in 1898 and then soared to 45,000 on the eve of the Great War.[34] Mechanized clothing factories, *maisons de confection* and automobile workshops survived the end-of-century slump. They manufactured new goods in new ways, cheap mass-produced items and finely engineered consumer durables; and they tapped new markets, an emergent mass-buying public and a fringe of luxury buyers avid for the most up-to-date products that modern industry could produce.

For manufacturers of old-fashioned luxury merchandise destined for established markets, however, the Great Depression proved a disaster. The artisanal sector which had grown steadily through the first three-quarters of the nineteenth century experienced a dramatic reversal of fortunes. German toys brought ruin to the French toy industry. High-quality French gloves, which had enjoyed a virtual corner on the U.S. market in the 1860s, lost out to foreign-made "factory-produced imitations." Luxury manufactures had accounted for 30 percent of the total value of French exports in the period 1867–

[32] De Seilhac, *L'Industrie de la couture et de la confection*, p. 223.

[33] Office du travail, *Le Vêtement à Paris*, p. 297.

[34] Fridenson, *Histoire des usines Renault*, vol. I, p. 26.

1871, but only 20 percent in 1909.[35] The sorry state of France's artisanal sector stirred lengthy and anxious public discussions about a *crise des métiers* and the decline of apprenticeship.[36]

The impact of the depression then was selective, sparing manufacturers who adapted to the foreign-led *révolution du bon marché*, hammering those who did not or could not. The slump's impact on the Parisian economy was no less selective. There were winners and losers, and it is worth sorting them out for two reasons. The losers, as I will show, were the very trades and neighborhoods that rallied to the *Ligue syndicale,* clearly establishing a link between shopkeeper mobilization and the crisis of the 1880s. As for the winners, their number included department stores, ready-to-wear manufacturers, and costume jewelers, all at one time or another objects of league resentment. To understand why the league felt the resentments that it did requires some awareness that the targets selected were the victors in a crisis from which shopkeeper militants had lost out.

THE CRISIS IN PARISIAN INDUSTRY

The Parisian industries that coped most effectively with the slump were precisely those which manufactured cheap consumer goods, goods designated as *la camelote*. The Spuller Commission of 1884 heard testimony of unremitting gloom from dozens of *chambres syndicales*, from both workers and employers, corroborating the depth and extent of the economic downturn. An exception, however, was the *Chambre syndicale de la bijouterie imitation* represented by, among others, Alfred Mascuraud. The deputy Langlois congratulated the *Chambre*

---

[35] For the preceding, see Caron, pp. 106–108.
[36] Labrousse and Braudel, eds., vol. IV, pt. 1, p. 476; du Maroussem, *Halles centrales de Paris* p. 221.

syndicale on its performance: "You represent a tendency toward the democratization of art. You are also one of the rare industries which has not complained."[37] Police sources in the Marais reported on the crisis in the local jewelry and woodworking trades, but noted that manufacturers of costume jewelry and simili-bronzes had somehow escaped serious difficulties.[38] So too with ready-to-wear items. Delegates from the *Chambre syndicale de la confection et de la couture* (M. Dreyfus and Gaston Worth) claimed in their deposition to the Spuller Commission that their industry, unlike others, showed no signs of crisis.[39] This optimism was not unwarranted. The value of women's ready-mades marketed abroad, for example, climbed sharply through the years of the slump from 10.4 million francs in 1878 to 74.5 million in 1893.[40]

The economic downturn of the 1880s did not affect all industries with equal severity. Employer organizations like the *Comité central des chambres syndicales de Paris* and the *Syndicat général* could deny the existence of a crisis altogether.[41] To the victims of a depressed economy, such complacent indifference was infuriating. Success, or so it seemed, was reserved for well-connected politicos (Mascuraud) and Jewish entrepreneurs who trafficked in junk goods (Dreyfus).[42] But to whom was success denied? If the winners were manufacturers of *la camelote*, who were the losers?

The slump was devastating to the labor-intensive luxury industries of central Paris, doubly hit by restricted domestic

[37] Chambre des Députés, Spuller Commission, p. 314.

[38] APP B/a 503, 15 April 1887; Folie-Méricourt, 11 March 1886.

[39] Chambre des Députés, Spuller Commission, p. 337.

[40] Office du travail, *Le Vêtement à Paris*, pp. 650–651.

[41] Chambre des Députés, Spuller Commission, testimony of Havard, president of the *Comité central*, p. 56, and of Muzet, president of the *Syndicat général*, p. 58.

[42] See Gaillard, *Paris, la ville 1852–1870*, p. 595n., for details of anti-Semitic attacks on Jewish clothing entrepreneurs.

demand and declining sales on foreign markets. Financial insecurity and investment losses in the wake of the Union Générale crash of 1882 obliged well-to-do consumers to reduce spending. Orders slumped, and luxury production went into a tailspin.[43] Output was reduced by as much as half in the hat and furniture industries.[44] Nearly thirty percent of the toy workshops in the Marais closed down altogether.[45] Police reports estimated that business fell off anywhere from fifteen to fifty percent in the jewelry trade.[46] Astronomical rates of unemployment were the inevitable consequence of workshop closings and production cutbacks. Employers laid off all but a core of loyal, long-time employees.[47] According to the president of the *Chambre syndicale patronale de l'ameublement*, a quarter of the industry's twenty to twenty-five thousand workers were jobless.[48] The jewelry trade reduced its labor force by as much as a third.[49] Four thousand hatters were out of work.[50]

Depressed domestic demand crippled luxury industries, but the most devastating losses were not incurred on the Parisian market. In the 1880s, luxury exports plummeted, a crushing blow to Parisian industry which lived above all by foreign sales.[51] In one year, from 1882 to 1883, the value of Parisian exports dropped over thirty percent, from 313 to 216 million

[43] Chambre des Députés, Spuller Commission, testimony of Senator Feray d'Essones and Dietz-Monin, president of the Paris Chamber of Commerce, pp. 113, 318.

[44] *Ibid.*, testimony of the *Chambre syndicale patronale de l'ameublement*, p. 99; Barberet, vol. III, p. 156.

[45] Du Maroussem, *Le Jouet parisien*, p. 46.

[46] APP B/a 503, Enfants-Rouges, 17 March 1886; Ste.-Avoie, 14 March 1886.

[47] *Ibid.*, Combat, 14 March 1886; 15 March 1887.

[48] Chambre des Députés, Spuller Commission, p. 99.

[49] *Ibid.*, testimony of the *Chambre syndicale de la bijouterie*, p. 310.

[50] Barberet, vol. III, p. 156.

[51] Chambre des Députés, Spuller Commission, testimony of Muzet, p. 58.

francs.[52] The furniture industry lost nearly sixty percent of foreign business over the course of the decade.[53] From 1876 to 1885 the per annum value of *articles de Paris* exports dropped seventy-four million francs, of leather goods exports twenty-four million francs.[54] In virtually every area—carpets, toys, artificial flowers—Parisian luxury manufacturers suffered severe setbacks abroad.[55] The loudest complaints were not directed at thrift-minded domestic buyers but at foreign competition. Parisian products, world-renowned for their fine craftsmanship, were undersold on foreign markets by cheaply made goods manufactured in Germany, Austria, Belgium, Japan and the United States.

The shrinkage of the domestic market and the loss of markets abroad stunned the Parisian economy. Local manufacturers scrambled feverishly to restore their competitive edge. To survive, firms could and did imitate their foreign competitors. Workshop expansion and mechanization raised overhead but also reduced dependence on skilled labor. Under the circumstances, a move out of the center city to the periphery or beyond made sound economic sense. Clothing workshops were transported to Belleville, Montmartre, Malakoff and Montrouge.[56] The toy industry left the Marais for the XXth arrondissement.[57] Shoe firms moved to Liancourt and Mouy in the Oise.[58] The chorus of complaints aroused by foreign com-

[52] *Ibid.*, testimony of Senator Feray d'Essones, p. 113.

[53] Du Maroussem, *Ebénistes du faubourg Saint-Antoine*, p. 167.

[54] Vachon, *La Crise industrielle et artistique*, p. 62.

[55] Drumont, *La France juive*, vol. II, p. 281; Chambre des Députés, Spuller Commision, testimony of the *Chambre syndicale des ouvriers tapissiers*, p. 262; *Union des fabricants des jouets*, p. 401; *Chambre syndicale des fleurs, feuillages, fruits et apprêts*, p. 158.

[56] D'Avenel, vol. IV, p. 94; Office du travail, *Le Vêtement à Paris*, pp. 24, 666.

[57] Du Maroussem, *Le Jouet parisien*, pp. 45–46; APP B/a 503, 15 March 1887.

[58] Aftalion, p. 58.

petition was soon swelled by attacks on suburban and provincial manufactures. Coach makers complained that chassis work had been exported to the Ardennes. Marble-cutting was now done in the Nord or Belgium.[59] Haussmannization had banished heavy industry from the city center. In the 1880s, labor-intensive industries in the throes of mechanization and under intense pressure to cut costs joined the exodus. Center-city trades threatened by foreign and provincial competition, of course, had other options besides a move to the periphery or beyond. A firm could slash production costs simply by intensifying exploitation. French workers might rebel at wage cuts, but foreigners could not afford to. "The Italian works at reduced prices," reported the police commissioner of the XIIIth. "The native worker would rather starve than abandon established wage rates."[60] And so Italians and Germans and Belgians were hired to replace Frenchmen, stirring deep, xenophobic resentments among Parisian workers who regarded the foreigners as little better than scabs.[61] For tasks requiring concentration or dexterity but not heavy work, a wage-cutting employer could also turn to female labor. A toy manufacturer in the XIth beat back his German competition by "feminizing" his work force. The local police commissioner wrote admiringly: "He has ingeniously replaced male labor with female labor. He pays the women less, and they are more industrious."[62] The thrift-minded entrepreneur's final coup was to transfer overhead costs to the laborer while still cutting his pay. The hallmark of this strategy, as we have seen, was production by *fabrique collective*. Gross exploitation of home workers, by no means a novelty in Paris, assumed such massive proportions in the eighties that a blinkered public

[59] APP B/a 503, Ternes, 27 March 1886; Chambre des Députés, Spuller Commission, testimony of the *Syndicat des ouvriers marbriers*, p. 40.
[60] APP B/a 503, Picpus and Bel-Air, 8 March 1886.
[61] Néré, vol. II, pp. 70ff.
[62] APP B/a 503, St.-Ambroise, 18 March 1886.

consciousness was obliged to take notice. A phrase was borrowed from the English to describe the phenomenon.[63] The "sweating system," by one estimate, employed upwards of a quarter million at the end of the century in the department of the Seine alone.[64]

The small center-city workshop then was squeezed between the large-scale factory and the sweatshop, and the squeeze was fatal. "In Paris," according to Lévy-Leboyer, "the years 1860–1880 marked a reprieve for many forms of [artisanal] activity (textiles, leather and wood) . . . but come the sharp business slump . . . of the 1880s, and the workshops of the city's faubourgs closed down. Their decline was irreversible."[65] Contemporaries bemoaned the passing of Paris' skilled artisanate. The social harmony of the workshop, it was claimed, was now forever lost, replaced by the "anonymity" of factories and garrets.[66] Du Maroussem wrote of "the end of an industrial era: the final decomposition of the independent atelier."[67]

Sweatshop entrepreneurs, manufacturers of ready-to-wear clothing and costume jewelers managed to scrape through the slump but not the *petit artisanat* of central Paris. Small workshops, wedded by tradition to a limited output of high-quality items, went under. Success or failure turned on a capacity to churn out mass quantities of inexpensive merchandise.

In Paris' commercial sector, success or failure similarly turned on a capacity to merchandise the new goods. Industrial transformation inundated the city's retail market with cheaply made consumables. Department stores and boulevard shops adapted

---

[63] See du Maroussem, *Ebénistes du faubourg Saint-Antoine*; and Mény, *Le Travail à domicile*, p. 7.

[64] Mény, p. 36.

[65] Lévy-Leboyer, "La décélération de l'économie française," p. 489.

[66] Mény, p. 41.

[67] Du Maroussem, *Le Jouet parisien*, p. 96; see also Brants, *La Petite Industrie contemporaine*, pp. 76–77.

accordingly. They undertook to create a new popular buying public, to find customers for ready-to-wear clothing, machine-made shoes and low-quality merchandise of all kinds. And the strategy paid handsome dividends. The commercial expansion of both boulevard and *grand magasin* at the end of the century was phenomenal. For luxury retailers, on the other hand, apart from a handful of top-flight stores, the slump was ruinous. Paris' old downtown area which had enjoyed a relative prosperity through the 1860s and 1870s entered a period of rapid and absolute decline.

Grands Magasins
AND BOULEVARD SHOPS

A visitor to the late nineteenth-century *grand magasin* would have been mystified by any talk of crisis. The major Parisian stores were doing more business than every before. In a scant eighteen years, 1877–1895, La Samaritaine's net receipts shot up from two to forty million francs.[68] Sales at Au Bon Marché rose from sixty-seven million in 1877 to 150 million in 1893.[69] Boucicaut had been reluctant to expand the number of Au Bon Marché's departments, but not so his successors.[70] The store branched out from *nouveautés* in the 1870s, adding a variety of new lines, toys, shoes, furniture, etc. The pace of diversification accelerated in the eighties. By the end of the century, Au Bon Marché boasted forty-seven distinct departments where there had been only four in 1852.[71] And diversification was not restricted to the Bon Marché. La Belle Jardinière, which had got its start selling work clothes, opened

[68] Laudet, *La Samaritaine*, p. 8.

[69] Martin Saint-Léon, *Le Petit Commerce français*, p. 15.

[70] D'Avenel, vol. I., p. 64.

[71] Miller, *The Bon Marché*, pp. 49–51; Cucheval-Clarigny and Flavien, *Etude sur le Bon Marché*, p. 30.

a sports clothes department and then a womenswear depart-ment.[72] Au Printemps advertised a menswear department for the first time in 1880, a home furnishings department in 1893, a children's clothing department in 1900.[73]

Department store expansion was most precipitous in the area of ready-to-wear items.[74] In the spring of 1875, in response to "interest expressed of late in *articles confectionnés*," the Bon Marché organized "a special exposition of ready-made dresses, gowns and apparel."[75] A store catalogue published the fol-lowing year referred to the ready-to-wear department as "the counter whose importance is growing day by day."[76] A Lou-vre publication dating from the late 1870s observed:

> Not so long ago, such clothes [womenswear], made haphazardly and without method, fit women badly. To-day, the Louvre department store has transformed this branch of industry. All sizes are prepared in advance so that women may find instantly the items that fit them to perfection.[77]

The growth of ready-to-wear departments did not mean that fabric sales were slackening; the silk counters at the Louvre still turned over eighteen million francs per year at the end of the century.[78] But the move to *articles confectionnés*, just getting underway in the late seventies and early eighties, was of enormous symbolic importance. An era, so it seemed, was passing. In the words of Urbain Guérin, a Catholic conserva-tive of the Le Playian school: "Today the reign of the shawl

---

[72] *La Vie d'une grande industrie moderne*, p. 23.

[73] *Printania*, p. 48.

[74] Pasdermadjian, *The Department Store*, p. 34.

[75] BHVP, Actualités, *Au Bon Marché*, "Exposition spéciale de robes toutes faites, costumes et confections," 1875.

[76] *Ibid.*, "Exposition spéciale de robes toutes faites, costumes et confec-tions pour dames et pour enfants," 1876.

[77] *Le Louvre. Grand hôtel et grands magasins*, p. 48.

[78] D'Avenel, vol. I, p. 66.

is finished; it has been dethroned by *la confection*."[79] The new goods, men like Guérin feared, were shoddily made and of low quality. Frenchmen, as we have seen, were deeply disturbed by what they called the "invasion of *la camelote*," an invasion that made a mockery of sound workmanship and threatened the corruption of public taste. But who was responsible for this state of affairs? Unscrupulous foreigners? Feckless consumers? More than one contemporary observer cited the department store as the principal agent of the nation's aesthetic and moral degeneration, as the chief architect of "the reign of the shoddy."[80]

The eighties witnessed changes not only in department-store merchandise but also in the character of the big stores' buying public. *Grands magasins* could sustain expansion only if they simultaneously expanded their clientele. Initially, stores like the Louvre, Bon Marché and Printemps cultivated a well-to-do clientele, newly rich, essentially Parisian and for the most part female. The end of century department store began to break out of this mold.

More foreigners and provincials than ever before were shopping at Paris's *grands magasins*. The stores earned a worldwide reputation which boosted mail-order sales phenomenally. Department stores also made concerted efforts to attract male shoppers.[81] All major establishments had, by the end of the century, opened counters for the sale of shirts, ties, haberdashery. Of far greater significance, however, were changes in the social composition of department store clienteles. The big stores, as one observer put it, were "democratizing." "The most leisured class," mainstay of the first *grands magasins*, had "given its maximum."[82] In an effort to widen their appeal,

[79] Urbain Guérin, *L'Evolution sociale*, p. 76.

[80] Duclos, p. 138; du Maroussem, *Ebénistes du faubourg Saint-Antoine*, p. 101; Garrigues, p. 132; Saint-Martin, p. 118.

[81] D'Avenel, vol. I, p. 67.

[82] Mény, p. 178.

The Coats and Ready-to-Wear Department of the Grands Magasins du Louvre in 1888

department stores turned "above all to the public-at-large, that is to the vulgar public."[83] The appearance of cheap consumer goods on department store shelves and the democratization of store clienteles were obviously related phenomena. But can the social profile of the big stores' new buying public be pinpointed with more precision? Zola provides a clue. He was told by one of his informants: "department stores are certainly responsible in large part for the modern-day extravagance, for the spending fever of the petite bourgeoisie."[84] Zola's own first-hand observations confirmed his informant's assessment. Describing the crowds at the Grands Magasins du Louvre, he wrote in 1881: "Moreover, the crowd is mixed. Little luxury on the whole, petit bourgeois and somewhat worn in appearance, not well fixed."[85] According to contemporary opinion, "the democratization of luxury which is the stock-in-trade of the department store"[86] profited most the lower middle class. Gambetta's new social strata, even as they claimed a share of political power, also claimed a place in the market as a consuming power. The department store and its ready-made goods assisted in their social ascension.

It was not only the petit bourgeois, however, who was newly initiated into the joys of consumerism. The lower middle-class market was cultivated by the city's most prestigious *grands magasins*, but other stores set their sights on a working-class clientele. Crespin-Dufayel's, located on the boulevard Barbès in the XVIIIth, a solidly working-class neighborhood, was known as "the poor man's department store."[87] The store had been founded in 1856 by a junk dealer, Crespin; Dufayel bought in later and quickly became the driving force behind

[83] Du Maroussem, *Ebénistes du faubourg Saint-Antoine*, p. 95.

[84] BN NAF 10278, Zola, p. 202.

[85] BN NAF 10278, Zola, p. 90.

[86] D'Avenel, vol. I, p. 66.

[87] Funck-Brentano, "Les causes et les conséquences de l'affaiblissement des classes moyennes en France," p. 552.

the store's expansion. By 1892, the enterprise was handling an estimated 700,000 customers per annum.[88]

At least for upper-crust visitors, the flood of new customers which poured into the fin-de-siècle department store poisoned the fairyland atmosphere. Denys Cochin, legitimist deputy from Paris and son of Augustin Cochin, complained of the "unhealthy air" in the Louvre department store. He cut short his visit, "worn out by the movement of the crowd."[89] And, indeed, the crowds were enormous, creating a din that "staggered" and "stunned" the hapless customer.[90] Persons of delicate constitution, it was feared, risked their mental equilibrium. Jostled by crowds and deafened by noise, lost in a "labyrinth of merchandise," they became unhinged. Women were particularly susceptible to emotional outbursts, seizures of uncontrolled weeping, wild shopping sprees and, of course, fits of kleptomania.[91] Gustave Macé, one-time *chef de service* at the *Sûreté*, estimated that Paris's thirty largest stores, taken together, were shoplifted six hundred times per day on the average.[92] Kleptomania, at the turn of the century, became an appropriate subject for scholarly and scientific study, and, of course, the department store was accorded special mention as principal breeding ground of the disease.[93] The *grand magasin* undermined normal restraints on human behavior. Some people became hysterical, others depraved. The promiscuity of the crowds led inevitably to sexual promiscuity. Illicit lovers could meet and lose themselves in the mass of shoppers without ever being noticed. Dubious characters of all sorts,

[88] Du Maroussem, *Ebénistes du faubourg Saint-Antoine*, p. 101; Saint-Martin, pp. 89ff.

[89] Cited in "Comptes-rendus," *La Revendication*, 10 January 1889.

[90] Giffard, *Paris sous la Troisième République*, p. 29.

[91] Coffignon, *Les Coulisses de la mode*, p. 197; Dubuisson, *Les Voleuses de grands magasins*; U. Guérin, p. 75.

[92] Macé, *Un Joli Monde*, p. 255.

[93] Miller, p. 200.

fetishists and mashers, could pursue their perverted interests without fear of discovery. Women who ventured into the department store did so at their peril. The *grand magasin* was an abyss, a Babel, a spider web: "With her little bird's head, the daughter of Eve enters into this inferno of coquetry like a mouse into a mousetrap."[94] Just as the development of new products generated a critique of the department store as an instrument of aesthetic corruption, so the democratization of the stores' buying public provoked accusations of moral turpitude. "The big bazaar," Macé concluded, "*c'est l'immoralité.*"[95]

The appearance of new classes of buyer in the halls of Paris' great commercial emporia was not of course a spontaneous occurrence. A diversified inventory retailed at bargain prices made possible an expansion of the big stores' clientele, but *grands magasins* had to campaign relentlessly to make sure that prospective customers came. Advertising was the department store's principal weapon in this campaign, and it set to the task with a remarkable and innovative zeal. The use of store dummies, indispensable for display of ready-to-wear items, became widespread in the 1880s.[96] While mannequins were fine for store windows, they were of no use when it came to advertising ready-made goods in the press. The invention of photoengraving in 1874 gave birth to a new medium, the illustrated magazine, which solved the problem. Images of flesh-and-blood mannequins could now be reproduced by the thousands and disseminated to a mass buying public via journals, newspapers or house publications.[97]

In adopting new forms of advertising, the *grand magasin* extended its reach. The mail-order catalogue introduced provincials and foreigners to big-store merchandise. The illus-

[94] Coffignon, *op. cit.*, p. 193; Giffard, pp. 6, 29.
[95] Macé, p. 254.
[96] *Printania*, p. 47.
[97] *Ibid.*, p. 36.

trated poster brought news of the commodity to the far corners of the city. Jules Chéret is credited with the development of mural chromolithography. He produced his first multicolored poster in 1858 at the age of 19—but the medium did not blossom into a major industry until the end of the century.[98] The first poster exhibition took place in 1884. In 1896, Maurice Talmeyr published in *La Revue des deux mondes* "L'âge de l'affiche," a hostile essay treating the poster as a sign of the degenerate times. The same year, Roger Marx, in collaboration with Chéret, began serial publication of *Les Maîtres de l'affiche*, a magnificent retrospective of poster art. The earliest poster in the series dates from 1875.[99] The department store exploited the new medium to full advantage. The city's largest stores—the Louvre, the Grande Maison de Blanc, A la Place Clichy—plastered posters all over the city advertising carpets, toys, *nouveautés*, giving notice of a white sale or simply announcing the arrival of the spring season. Eight of the two hundred odd posters in Marx's collection were executed for *grands magasins*.[100]

Product diversification, less expensive merchandise, adventurous advertising, *grands magasins* bent every effort to court a wider buying public. But the expense of expansion placed a heavy burden on department store budgets. *Grands magasins* went public in search of fresh capital. The Louvre had, from the beginning, operated as a *société anonyme*. Au Bon Marché, founded as a family enterprise, became a joint-stock company in 1880; Au Printemps incorporated in 1881.[101] By the midnineties, Au Gagne-Petit, A la Place Clichy, the Belle Jar-

[98] Baudin, *L'Enseigne et l'affiche*, p. 74.

[99] Marx's collection has been reprinted with an introduction and notes: *Masters of the Poster, 1896–1900*. See the introduction by Alain Weill, p. 3; the notes by Jack Rennert, p. 8; and pl. 81. For the Talmeyr article, see the reprint in Talmeyr, *La Cité du sang*.

[100] *Masters of the Poster*, plates 18, 141, 169, 185, 189, 191, 207, 211.

[101] Saint-Martin, p. 31; *Printania.*, p. 41.

dinière and A la Ville de Londres had all followed suit.[102]

The department store at the end of the century assumed a new form. Its juridical status changed; the variety and quality of its merchandise changed; the social complexion of the crowds changed. The crisis of the eighties motivated a radical transformation in the modus operandi of *grands magasins*. The big stores were "democratizing" to satisfy the urgent demands of industry for a mass market. Department stores accommodated industry, however, without becoming subservient to it. On the contrary, industries making the painful transition to mass production were heavily dependent on department-store custom and capital. M. Dupont, owner of a brush factory in the Oise, testified to a government commission investigating department stores: "The firm does 300,000 francs in business with department stores; it is a certainty it could not do 1,000 francs of business with 300 small shops." Edouard Laine and Co., a Beauvais carpet firm employing 1,800, claimed that department stores absorbed "more than half of our output." The Maison Tréfousse, based in Troyes, sold 40,000 pairs of gloves annually to the Bon Marché alone.[103]

Parisian putting-out industries were also beholden to department stores and for much the same reasons. Du Maroussem describes the relationship between department stores and clothing manufacturers:

These *"grands magasins"* . . . buy from the big ready-to-wear houses. But one can imagine on what terms. . . . A client whose 52 departments do more than one hundred million in business will take up a large place in a ready-to-wear manufacturer's annual sales, even in the sales of

[102] See the *Liste des membres adhérents de la Chambre syndicale du commerce de la nouveauté* (circa 1893), contained in AN C5607, Patentes.

[103] AN C5498, Mesureur Commission: Dupont, 15 May 1891; Laine, 26 June 1891; Maison Tréfousse, 3 July 1891.

a big firm—a place that would be hard to fill in case of a falling out. And so the manufacturers make concessions "to keep the business regular," which is one of the attractions and strengths of this terrible customer.[104]

Grands magasins used a strong bargaining position to push down wholesale prices. Manufacturers in turn depressed wages to preserve profit margins. Department-store orders sustained putting-out industries through the crisis but at the same time reinforced pressures on business to adopt sweating practices.

Department stores could also be sweaters in their own right. They operated as we have seen extensive *fabriques collectives* of their own, manufacturing a wide range of items, ready-to-wear clothing above all, but also to an increasing extent home furnishings and *articles de Paris*. In the eighties and nineties, independent craftsmen down on their luck, toymakers, cabinet-makers and the like, swelled the number of petty entrepreneurs who took in piece work from department stores.[105] Nominally self-employed, these entrepreneurs were in fact tributaries of the big stores, entirely dependent on them for work. To more than one observer, department store and sweating system were synonymous terms. Workers certainly blamed the big stores for the disintegration of the center-city artisan community. The *Chambre syndicale des ébénistes/meubles sculptés* could not contain its resentment: "We wish to reduce to ruin, if necessary, those scoundrels who force work at sixteen hours a day for onerous prices, disorganizing our faubourg in order to transfer it beyond Montreuil, Bagnolet, etc. . . ."[106]

The transformation of the department store provoked harsh, often bizarre criticism: the *grand magasin* traded in junk mer-

[104]Office du travail, *Le Vêtement à Paris*, p. 299.

[105]Du Maroussem, *Ebénistes du faubourg Saint-Antoine*, p. 99; Bernard, *Du Mouvement d'organisation et de défense du petit commerce français*, p. 44; APP B/a 503, Ste.-Marguerite, 17 March 1886.

[106]Cited in Miller, p. 206fn.

chandise, subverted social restraints, drove people to hysterical outbursts or to criminal behavior. The institution was corrupt and cosmopolitan. While only a handful of *grands magasins* were actually run by Jews—the Galéries Lafayette, Aux Classes Laborieuses, A la Ville de Strasbourg[107]—critics insisted on linking the department store with an insidious Jewish influence. Frantz Funck-Brentano alleged the chain store to be a Jewish invention.[108] "The Semitic question," du Maroussem claimed, "is very often mixed in with the department store question."[109]

Department-store growth paralleled and fed upon the radical commercialization of the boulevards. The city's new downtown area enjoyed a sudden surge of commercial activity in the fin-de-siècle era. New crowds appeared. New forms of entertainment emerged. Reaction to these changes echoed in tone and substance the accusations leveled at the *grand magasin*. Boulevard and department store were linked, as ever, in the public mind. And just as a visitor to the Bon Marché in the eighties or nineties would have been hard pressed to discover signs of commerical crisis, so with a visitor to the *grands boulevards*.

Business invaded the boulevards of fin-de-siècle Paris as surely as the Prussians had invaded France in 1870. Luxury shops, tailors, couturieres congregated to the west along the streets radiating from the Place de l'Opéra—rue de la Paix, avenue de l'Opéra, boulevard des Capucines.[110] Commission houses and export firms populated the eastern fringe of the boulevards from the rue Montmartre all the way to the Porte Saint-Martin, a stretch nicknamed *le boulevard des affaires*.[111] Boulevard businesses competed fiercely to maintain a fashionable,

[107] See the *Liste des membres adhérents de la Chambre syndicale du commerce de la nouveauté*, AN C5607, Patentes.

[108] Funck-Brentano, "Les causes et les conséquences," p. 553.

[109] Du Maroussem, *Ebénistes du faubourg Saint-Antoine*, p. 100.

[110] Montorgueil, *Le Vie des boulevards*, pp. 21–23.

[111] *Ibid.*, p. 182.

up-to-date appearance. English styles of shop design were popular, characterized by large plate-glass windows and slender, carved colonnades in precious woods.[112] Commerce was inescapable, a tinseled presence that offended *flâneurs* with memories of more elegant times. Perhaps what offended most deeply was the trumpery of the commercial show.[113] The gilding was "vulgar," the bronzes "imitation," the stones "fake."[114] "The pseudo-diamond gleams all along the route, too blinding, exaggerated and of a grossness that betrays its lying limpidity. It's a fevered frenzy and how symptomatic."[115] The fin de siècle was, indeed, the era of the costume jeweler.

The most visible symbols of a growing business presence on the boulevards, however, were not the lavishly decorated shops, the export houses or scurrying *gens d'affaires*, but rather the massive, new office buildings. The Crédit Lyonnais opened premises on the boulevard des Italiens in 1878 which, by the war, had been expanded to cover a full hectare of terrain.[116] The Comptoir d'Escompte, whose ornate and looming facade can be seen down the rue Rougement from the boulevard Poissonnière, was built around 1880.[117] Banks, insurance firms, maritime companies chose sites along the boulevards for their corporate headquarters. The boulevards, commented one observer, "industrialized."[118] The stroll from the Gymnase to the Madeleine, once the delight of the *flâneur*, was now punctuated by "zones of grey stone." "One has the sense of strolling among strong-boxes."[119]

[112] *Ibid.*, pp. vii–viii, 29–30.

[113] Claudin, *Paris*, p. 136.

[114] Bertaut, "Le boulevard d'autrefois," *L'Opinion*, 29 June 1912; Bernard, p. 37; Meyer, *Ce que mes yeux ont vu*, p. 181.

[115] Montorgueil, *op cit.*, p. 23.

[116] Sutcliffe, *The Autumn of Central Paris*, p. 162.

[117] Fournier, *Histoire des enseignes de Paris*, p. 440.

[118] Ginisty, *Les Anciens Boulevards*, p. 45.

[119] Reboux, *Histoire et les dessous de Paris*, p. 62.

The commercialization of the boulevards was not simply an affair of shops and office buildings. Trade spilled out into the street, covering the walls and kiosks with advertisements, littering the sidewalk with leaflets.[120] The illustrated poster was ubiquitous, a spectacle which disgusted Gustave Macé. "The filth is not only on the ground," he fumed, "it is spread around every kiosk, on every newsstand and is climbing up the walls."[121] Even the crowds in the street were liberally interspersed with representatives of the commodity—sandwichmen, distributors of handbills, newsboys—but it was the irregulars of commerce, prostitutes and peddlars (*camelots*), that chroniclers of the street scene returned to again and again.[122]

Maurice Barrès' description of the Left-Bank brasserie could apply just as well to a number of disreputable establishments, *embrasseries* as they were called, located on or just off the boulevards.[123] Claudin cites two or three such *maisons* on the boulevard des Italiens that remained open all evening, ablaze with light long after the rest of the boulevard had gone to sleep.[124] The rue du faubourg Montmartre, just north of the *carrefour des écrasés*, became notorious as a gathering place for pimps and their "girls."[125] To a moralist like Macé, the leap from pimping to peddling was small. The street peddlar would trade in flesh as willingly as in knick-knacks. But the *camelot* was no criminal. He was a young man, perhaps in his twenties and out of work, who tided himself over by selling odds and ends on the street: balloons, shoelaces, street maps, what have you. He plied his trade in the suburbs at Clichy or at a variety of locations in town: railroad stations, the Bourse, and,

[120] Montorgueil, *op. cit.*, p. 44; Kahn, *L'Esthétique de la rue*, pp. 240, 303.

[121] Macé, pp. 331–332.

[122] Coffignon, *Le Pavé parisien*, pp. 127–130.

[123] De Lannoy, *Les Plaisirs et la vie de Paris*, p. 35; Montorgueil, *op. cit.*, p. 204.

[124] Claudin, *op. cit.*, p. 212.

[125] Macé, pp. 300, 280.

The Boulevard des Italiens in the 1850s

The Crédit Lyonnais on the Boulevard des Italiens in 1906

of course, the boulevards.[126] Devotees of *la vie parisienne* romanticized the *camelot*. However miserable his condition, he was an independent spirit, a lover of the sidewalk, quick with his tongue and his wits. Like the ragpicker and the newsboy, to whom he bore a strong family resemblance—all three were in business for themselves—he was a fixture of the fin-de-siècle street scene, "a type quintessentially Parisian."[127]

To the resentful man of letters, it might well have appeared that the boulevards, his patrimony, had fallen prey to alien powers: to trade, to corporate enterprise—and to Jews. The financier was a favorite target of Aurélien Scholl's wit, and he laced his jibes with a sizeable dose of anti-Semitism.[128] Georges Montorgueil noted that the businesses at the Porte Saint-Martin were "almost all of Hebraic confession."[129] De Maupassant in *Bel-Ami*, published in 1885, embodied his vision of a money-grubbing age in the character of M. Walter, owner of *La Vie française*, a paper of the new boulevards that "steered its course through the waters of high finance and low politics." Walter himself is described as a "member of the Chamber of Deputies, a financier, a capitalist and businessman, a Jew from the Midi."[130]

What was no less disturbing, this ghastly invasion of commerce, business and "Jewish finance" had brought in its train hordes of disagreeable interlopers. Montorgueil, commenting on the proliferation of boulevard taverns in the eighties and nineties, remarked: "with the beer, democracy flows in full abundance."[131] Once a "salon," the boulevard had become a

---

[126] On *camelots*, see Bloch, *Types du boulevard*, p. 18; Castelnau, *En remontant les grands boulevards*, p. 273; Coffignon, *Le Pavé parisien*, pp. 47, 54; Macé, pp. 276, 283–286.

[127] Montorgueil, *op. cit.*, p. 49.

[128] Scholl, *L'Esprit du boulevard*, pp. 23–24, 73.

[129] Montorgueil, *op. cit.*, p. 184.

[130] De Maupassant, *Bel-Ami*, pp. 149, 47.

[131] Montorgueil, *op. cit.*, p. xi.

"fair"; once a "closed society," it had become a "mob."[132] The riding jacket and stovepipe hat made way for the evening jacket and the *blouse*, for the top hat and peaked cap.[133] Aging men of letters, "slow of step," found themselves in the company of harried businessmen, clerks on ninety francs a month and working men out for a good time.[134] And vulgar pleasure-seeking, not a cultured leisure, was the main pursuit of the new boulevard crowds, hence the flushed even wild look on their faces. People pushed and hurried. They gobbled sauerkraut and guzzled German beer. They wore cheap ready-made clothing that did not quite fit. They imitated English fashions and figures of speech.[135] The collapse of social barriers was a source of great satisfaction to an old revolutionary like Jules Vallès:

> The boulevard, that little old man determined to outlive himself, has yet one more weakness: as the rendezvous of journalists, artists and politicians, it thinks it represents the spirit and genius of France. It has forgotten that the crowd has erupted onto the scene, and that everyone has a place in public life. . . . Legitimists, bourgeois, aristocrats, merchants, workers, how many find themselves side by side on the sidewalk?[136]

But others deplored the egalitarianism of the sidewalks, none more than Xavier Aubryet. Montmartre, La Villette, and Belleville were only too well represented among the strollers.

[132] *Ibid.*, p. xi; Laut, "Le boulevard d'aujourd'hui," p. 22.

[133] *Les Boulevards de Paris*, p. x.

[134] Duvernois, *Le Boulevard*, pp. 8–9; Montorgueil, *op. cit.*, p. 26.

[135] Laut, "Le boulevard d'aujourd'hui," p. 4; Benjamin and Desachy, *Le Boulevard*, pp. 22–23; Claudin, *op. cit.*, pp. 55, 76; "C'était hier le boulevard," published in *Vrai* (December–January n.d.), p. 5. (A copy of this article can be found in the BHVP.)

[136] From *La Rue*, 7 December 1879. Cited in Vanier, *La Mode et ses métiers*, p. 251.

The boulevard, he complained, had become the "walk-way of the faubourgs."[137]

Xenophobia went hand in hand with snobbery. J. M. Laut performed a post-mortem on the boulevards published by *Le Figaro* in 1910: "And it's no longer as it was in Aubryet's day; the sensibility of Paris used to show itself there; now rather, it's sensuality which is offered up to the Metics come from every corner of the universe."[138] The expositions in particular, "that sinister trio of 1878, 1889, 1900," had attracted swarms of foreign visitors to the city.[139] Cosmopolitans, barbarians, half-breeds, invaded the bright world of the boulevards, importing foreign tastes and values into the sacred precincts of French culture. Nestor Roqueplan, dandy and *viveur*, had invented the word "Parisine" in 1847 to convey the limpidity and finesse of boulevard wit. Arthur Meyer pronounced the passing of Parisine in 1911.[140] "*L'esprit boulevardier*" perished with the fin de siècle, a casualty of "cultural democratization."[141]

As the boulevard became commercialized and as its public widened, an older form of boulevard life began to pass away. Wits and literary men had gathered in the days of the Empire at the Librairie Nouvelle, housed just beneath the Jockey Club on the boulevard des Italiens. "This refuge for boulevardiers," as Claudin called it, moved off the boulevards in 1897 to a new address on the rue Laffitte.[142] Tortoni's, also on the Italiens, went out of business in 1893. For over half a century, it had been the "most dandified café in Paris," the

---

[137] *Les Boulevards de Paris*, p. x.

[138] Laut, "Le boulevard d'aujourd'hui," p. 2.

[139] Bertaut, *Le Boulevard*, p. 8; Duvernois, *op. cit.*, pp. 8–9.

[140] Meyer, p. 174.

[141] Castelnau, *op. cit.*, p. 264.

[142] Claudin, *Mes Souvenirs*, pp. 165, 171; Billy, *L'Epoque 1900*, p. 383. The bookshop was purchased by Michel and Calmann Lévy in 1859.

"Temple of parisianism."[143] The Café de Paris, just across the rue Taitbout, shut its doors in 1896. In the sixties and early seventies, the Café de Madrid on the boulevard Montmartre had been a watering hole for opposition politicians. Here Jules Vallès, bohemian journalist and future Communard, had rubbed shoulders with Gambetta, commander-in-chief of the boulevard Radicals. The Café de Madrid closed in 1897. The Café de Suède, just across the street, closed in 1901.[144] Café society had begun to fade at the end of the century, but what was to take its place?

Old-timers were shocked and mystified by the pastimes and preferences of the new men of the boulevards. They did not take refreshment at the café but at brasseries and taverns.[145] They preferred a *bon bock* or aperitif to coffee or wine. Descriptions of the multicolored drinks—black bitters, red vermouth, green absinth—to which fin-de-siècle Parisians were addicted, sometimes literally, abound in the literature of the period.[146] Aubryet could barely contain his indignation at the changing mores of the boulevards: "By what right have they replaced the private houses and mansions with the grandiose pot-houses whose tables, piled with bocks and steins, are invading the asphalt. If the comte d'Orsay were still alive, how could he be expected to go for a stroll in this atmosphere of beer and absinth?"[147]

Dining, too, had lost the elegance and refinement of former times. Scholl, an habitué of Tortoni's and its last customer, remarked on the café's passing: "Everything's going. The great restaurants with exorbitant prices for a fastidious

---

[143] James, *The Princess Casamassima*, p. 335. The novel was first published in 1886. Reboux, *op. cit.*, p. 34.

[144] Bertaut, *Le Boulevard*, pp. 78–88; Billy, p. 382.

[145] Billy, p. 368; Bertaut, *Le Paris d'avant guerre*, pp. 143–144.

[146] Goudeau, *Paysages parisiens*, p. 115; de Maupassant, *Bel-Ami*, p. 27.

[147] *Les Boulevards de Paris*, p. xi.

bourgeoisie are disappearing one by one. *Bouillons* and brasseries are taking their place."[148] The Maison d'Or and the Café Anglais both closed their private dining rooms in the nineties.[149] The fin de siècle was, by contrast, a boom time for the *bouillons* Duval which opened a string of cut-rate eateries along the boulevards: 21 boulevard Montmartre, 11 boulevard Poissonnière, 27 boulevard Madeleine.[150]

Scholl, the disgruntled gourmet, was scarcely more sanguine about the future of entertainment on the boulevards. "In fifteen years," he prophesied in 1893, "all the theaters will be replaced by cafés-concerts."[151] Boulevard theater flourished at the end of the century, but Scholl was right enough in predicting the rise of more popular forms: the music hall, the follies, the café-concert. The Olympia Music Hall, one of the biggest in the city, opened for business on the boulevard des Capucines, not far from Garnier's opera house.[152] Even the most cursory examination of contemporary artwork suggests the profound impression these new forms made on the public imagination. Manet's "Bar at the Folies-Bergère" was first exhibited in 1882. De Maupassant's *Bel-Ami* contains a description of an evening at the follies as does Huysman's *Croquis parisiens,* published in 1886.[153] But of the new entertainments, the most pervasive in its impact was the café-concert. Degas painted the Café-concert des Ambassadeurs in

[148] Laut, "Le boulevard d'aujourd'hui," p. 12.

[149] The Maison d'Or closed definitively in 1908, the Café Anglais in 1913. Arbellot, *La Fin du boulevard*, pp. 20, 81; Benjamin and Desachy, p. 22; Laut, "Le boulevard d'aujourd'hui," p. 13.

[150] Baedeker, *Paris and Its Environs*, p. 16; also, Martin Saint-Léon, p. 56.

[151] Laut, "Le boulevard d'aujourd'hui," p. 12; see also Benjamin and Desachy, p. 23.

[152] Arbellot, p. 18. The Capucines were also the scene of the first cinema showing staged by the Lumière brothers at the Grand Café in 1895. Castelnau, *op. cit.*, p. 266.

[153] De Maupassant, pp. 36ff.; Huysmans, *Croquis parisiens*, pp. 3ff.

1877. In 1896, Paris boasted 274 such establishments. Maurice Talmeyr ruefully observed in 1902: "The café-concert, in a quarter of a century, has become the art form of the people."[154] And the most spectacular temples to this new art form congregated along the eastern end of the boulevards, the Alcazar at the rue du faubourg Poissonnière, the Eldorado at the boulevard de Strasbourg, etc. "The café-concert," remarked Montorgueil, "has its real headquarters on the boulevard. . . ."[155]

Afficionados of the old boulevard—and moralists—were scandalized by the café-concert. Gentlemen did not remove their hats; they smoked and drank in the presence of ladies. People of all classes mingled without regard for social distinctions. And the entertainment? The acrobatics and *tableaux vivants* were stupid, the songs and reviews depraved.[156] "The modern laugh!" protested Edmond Benjamin apropos of café-concert humor, "the kind of laugh we hear more and more of today, is no longer a frank, generous, healthy, gallic laugh; it's a snigger, ironic and sarcastic."[157] The new entertainments, it appears, were even a threat to the national character.

The boulevards in the closing decades of the century were transformed into a great, popular fairground, jammed with crowds, teeming with commercial enterprise. The *flâneur*'s familiar habitat had become inhospitable, but this did not mean his extinction. The man of leisure could retire to his club or seek his amusement elsewhere. He could move down the rue Royale or the rue de la Paix and head west toward the Champs-Elysées. The Ritz Hotel opened on the Place Vendôme in 1898,

[154] Talmeyr, "Cafés-concerts et music-halls," pp. 159, 161.

[155] Montorgueil, *op. cit.*, p. 164.

[156] See Alfred Fouillé, "Dégénérescence? Le passé et le présent de notre race," p. 22; and, of course, Talmeyr, "Cafés-concerts et music-halls," pp. 159–184.

[157] Benjamin and Desachy, p. 26.

Maxime's on the rue Royale in 1893. Diners who found the clientele at Maxime's too risqué—it was a favorite with *viveurs* and courtesans—could patronize soberer establishments just a short distance away: Durand's, Larue's, Weber's.[158] Those of more youthful, bohemian tastes took refuge in another part of town, the Butte Montmartre. The dance halls painted by the Impressionists closed down in the eighties, to be replaced by the cabarets and nightclubs preferred by an uppercrust or high-brow clientele.[159] The opening of the Moulin Rouge in 1889 was attended by Scholl, the prince de Sagan and the comte de La Rochefoucauld.[160] The fin de siècle was the heyday of the Butte. Montmartre, it was said, "has taken over from the Boulevard. It reigns over Paris, as over the entire world."[161]

The *flâneur* then survived, but not his favorite stamping ground, the boulevard. In its place emerged a new boulevard. A popular public asserted its presence in the precincts of commodity utopianism. The "uproar of pleasure and prosperity"[162] grew all the louder, the crowds all the denser. The *flâneur*'s cultural loss was the new consumer's material gain.

The emergence of the new boulevard invites comparisons with a parallel phenomenon, the transformation of the department store. Department store and boulevard alike experimented in new goods, cheaper merchandise that attracted a more popular, "democratic" clientele. The end-of-century department store assumed new juridical form, the *société anonyme;* it developed and expanded its marketing machinery. Along the boulevards, corporate headquarters and office buildings proliferated. Commerce made its presence felt as never before, on the walls, on the terraces, in the crowds, everywhere. To the observer's eye boulevard and *grand maga-*

[158] Arbellot, pp. 54–91; Meyer, p. 176; Sutcliffe, p. 171.

[159] *L'Esprit montmartrois*, p. 27; Roman, *Paris Fin de Siècle*, p. 58.

[160] Castelnau, *Belle Epoque*, p. 48.

[161] *L'Esprit montmartois*, p. 148.

[162] James, *Princess Casamassima*, p. 335.

sin evolved in tandem. The terms invoked to describe the one were equally applied to the other. Haussmannization established a symbiotic relationship between the two phenomena that was carried forward into the fin-de-siècle era. And however much *flâneurs* and moralists might grumble, the commercial nexus of department store and boulevard appeared to continue in strapping good health.

Both department store and boulevard owed their success to timely adaptation. Department-store proprietors and boulevard businessmen scrambled successfully to develop a mass buying public for the new goods. The "democratization" of Paris' new downtown area, however, was not achieved without jolts and setbacks. The Bon Marché in 1882 briefly suspended payment on all debts following the crash of the Union Générale bank.[163] La Belle Jardinière reduced its staff by fifty-five during the 1885–1886 season.[164] The winter months of 1889–1890 were an especially troubled period for all department stores. A flu epidemic raged at the Louvre.[165] A la Tour St. Jacques laid off personnel and closed down altogether in the spring. Aux Filles du Calvaire went under the following winter.[166] Even the shops on the boulevards, so prosperous in appearance, suffered from closings and layoffs. According to a police report of 1886, Barbédienne's on the boulevard Poissonnière, the city's largest dealer in bronze objects, "has done very little business in the last two years."[167] *La Crise commerciale,* a biased observer to be sure, wrote of "the numerous specialists who are going under each day from the rue Montmartre to the boulevard des Capucines."[168] But even the po-

[163] Gaillard, p. 540.

[164] APP B/a 503, St.-Germain l'Auxerrois, 12 March 1886.

[165] APP B/a 504, 15 December 1889.

[166] APP B/a 485, *rapports mensuels,* 1 March and 1 November 1890; B/a 504, 1 August 1889.

[167] APP B/a 503, Faubourg Montmartre, 15 March 1886.

[168] Louis Bréhant, "Commerce et beaux-arts," *Le Crise commerciale,* 15 January 1889.

lice acknowledge that profits on the boulevard were not what they once had been.[169]

The crisis then spurred commercial innovation, but innovation that was often costly. In the long run, the enormous financial rewards amply compensated for the pains of transformation and growth. Not all members of the commercial community, however, adapted with the department store's and the boulevard's success.

THE CRISIS IN COMMERCE

The commercial sector of the Parisian economy suffered a serious and prolonged recession in the 1880s and 1890s. *Patente* statistics at first glance do not seem to bear out this claim (see figure 5). The number of taxable enterprises in Paris multiplied rapidly from 1881 to 1884, leveled off and then in 1888 resumed its upward course. Stagnation there was in the mid-eighties, but it constituted little more than a brief interruption in a long-term trend towards growth—or so it seems. If the figures are broken down by arrondissement, a different picture emerges. In the VIIth-VIIIth and the XIth–XXth arrondissements, the number of taxable enterprises (*patentables*) climbed continuously over the period 1881–1895, but the city's core neighborhoods did not fare so well. They experienced not so much stagnation as actual decline. Over the five-year span 1884–1888, the total of taxable enterprises shrank absolutely in the VIth, IXth and Xth before returning to normal levels; and in the Ist–Vth, the number of *patentables* had still not recovered pre-depression levels as late as 1895. Central Paris had once accounted for the majority of taxable businesses in the city; this ceased to be the case after 1890. There was indeed a commercial depression, but its impact was largely confined to Paris' commercial core.

---

[169] APP B/a 503, Faubourg Montmartre, 15 March 1886.

Economic Crisis of the 1880s

FIGURE 5: *Patentables* in Paris, 1880-1895

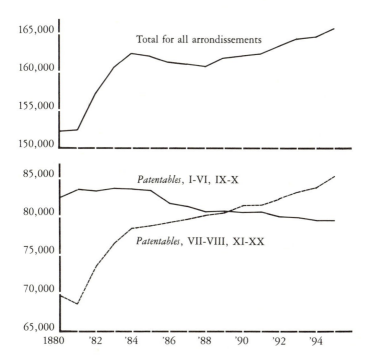

SOURCE: Annuaire statistique de la Ville de Paris (Paris, 1881-1897)

The center's difficulties are to be explained in the first instance by a contraction of demand and in particular of demand for the luxury goods and services in which the center
city specialized. A faltering stock market, bank closings and
an uncertain investment climate constricted luxury spending.[170] People entertained less. Wealthy tourists stayed away.

---

[170] APP B/a 503, Roule, 8 March 1886; Madeleine, 11 March 1886; Europe, 19 March 1886; Chambre des Députés, Spuller Commission, testimony of the prefect of police, p. 329.

The leisured classes wintered in the country instead of coming up to Paris for the season. Caterers and couturieres alike complained about the infrequency of balls and soirées.[171] In the worst moments of the crisis, occupancy at the grand hotels of the IXth sank to one third.[172] But the principal victims of the slump, according to police sources, were "those who deal in luxury items . . . jewelers, retailers of *objets d'art*."[173]

This is not to say that center-city luxury retailers suffered equally. A high-fashion tailor on the boulevard des Capucines, a first-rank jeweler on the rue de la Paix survived, even prospered through the slump. They owed their good fortune in part to superior location. In a period of restricted consumption, access to the market becomes a crucial advantage. Businesses situated on the splendid and spacious avenues of *Paris nouveau* attracted what customers there were. The losers in the crisis were rather second-rank luxury retailers who could not afford an advantageous location. And nowhere were *commerçants* of this description to be found in heavier concentrations than in the streets and arcades of Paris's old downtown area. The depression hit the center city with the greatest severity, and the shopping district of old Paris found itself in the very eye of the storm.

For the department store and the boulevard, the eighties were a period of troubled growth. For the city's old downtown, the end of the century brought commercial disaster. The Palais-Royal, which had preserved something of its former glory through the sixties and seventies, went into total eclipse. Edouard Drumont noted in the second edition of his elegiac *Vieux Paris*:

[171]Barberet, vol. V, p. 326; vol. VI, p. 66. See also Worth, pp. 23, 31.

[172]APP B/a 503, 1 January 1887; see also St.-Thomas d'Aquin, 12 March 1886.

[173]*Ibid.*, Madeleine, 11 March 1886.

1885 . . . The Palais-Royal is struggling: it says as the young woman captive, "I do not yet want to die, but I want to live in virtue," and we applaud such resolve with all our heart, without having any unnecessary illusions as to the final outcome.

1897 . . . The Palais-Royal no longer struggles. . . . All the great jewelers have moved out one after the other to the rue de la Paix and the rue Royale. . . . It's all over.[174]

The Palais-Royal, once the commmercial and cultural heart of Paris, had become a "necropolis," a "cadaver in stone."[175] Other commercial streets in the Palais-Royal ward—the avenue de l'Opéra excepted—fared little better. The passage Delorme, one of the liveliest corners of old Paris, was bought up by the Louvre department store and converted into a carpet workshop, "cold, sullen and deserted."[176] Monsieur Gohn, owner of a troubled shoe business on the rue Croix-des-Petits-Champs, sadly acknowledged that "trade ha[d] moved away." "[T]he rue Croix-des-Petits Champs," he lamented, "is no longer so central."[177]

The old commercial streets of the IInd arrondissement suffered no less severely from the displacement of trade. The hat trade, once so active on the rue du Caire, migrated elsewhere.[178] The rue de Richelieu, of course, had been ailing since the sixties, but the rue Vivienne's decline can be dated from the end of the century.[179] As for the passage Choiseul,

---

[174] Cited in Champier and Sandoz, *Le Palais-Royal*, vol. II, p. 207.

[175] Leroy-Beaulieu, *L'Art de placer et de gérer sa fortune*, p. 23; H. Deverin, *La Résurrection du Palais-Royal*, p. 7.

[176] Hénard, *La Rue Saint-Honoré*, vol. II, p. 475.

[177] AN C5498, Mesureur Commission, 20 March 1891.

[178] See remarks by Maury, municipal councillor, in "Séances des comités et groupes," *L'Union démocratique*, 27 October 1888.

[179] Champier and Sandoz, vol. II, p. 200.

Louis-Ferdinand Céline, who grew up in the arcade, described what life was like there around 1900:

> Horrible, horrible . . . I mean that we had hardly anything to eat, and we had to keep up appearances. For instance, in the passage Choiseul, we always had two showcases, but only one of them was lit up because there was nothing in the other.[180]

But the best known and most mourned of the IInd's casualties was the passage des Panoramas. The *passage* at the turn of the century exhaled "a smell of the provinces."[181] The arcade's most prestigious establishment, Duvelleroy's, had moved to the boulevard des Italiens. Vacant storefronts were not easily rented, and for the remaining tenants, trade was slack save on rainy days. Ill lit and, now, little frequented, the Panoramas became a haven for streetwalkers, a "covered market" for prostitution.[182] Visitors were astounded by the quiet and relative solitude, while the boulevards, just a few yards away, teemed with noisy crowds. "How many times," Ernest Levallois observed in 1910, "have you remarked to yourself on leaving the boulevards of an evening, those animated and lively boulevards, that the neighboring streets are hushed and almost mournful."[183]

This was true of the old shopping streets north, as well as south, of the boulevards. With the destruction of the old Opera House in 1873, the twin passages de l'Opéra ceased to attract crowds and stagnated.[184] The toy merchants of the passage

[180] See the interview with Céline in the introduction to Céline, *Castle to Castle*, p. x.

[181] A. V., "Les passages," *La République française*, 15 April 1900.

[182] Levallois, *Paris propre*, p. 91; Montorgueil, *op. cit.*, p. 125.

[183] Levallois, *op. cit.*, p. 95; see also A. V., "Les passages," *La République française*, 15 April 1900.

[184] "C'était hier le boulevard," *Vrai* (December–January n.d.), p. 21 (this clipping can be found in the BHVP).

The Galérie d'Orléans (Palais-Royal) in the 1840s

The Galérie Colbert at Mid-Century

The Passage Choiseul in 1908

Jouffroy complained bitterly of a business slowdown. The commissionnaires who populated the backstreets of the IXth enjoyed no better fortune.[185] Jules Vallès wrote in 1882 of the small shops in the Porte St.-Denis neighborhood: "Businesses which in twenty years had earned enough to pension off the owners at six thousand francs a year and allowed them to go plant cabbages out at St.-Mandé, these businesses are now starving to death."[186]

New and old downtowns had managed to coexist in the prosperous years of the Second Empire. In the eighties and nineties, the boulevards continued to grow, painfully to be sure, while the city's old shopping streets skidded into permanent and irreversible decline. The Palais-Royal was abandoned; the *passages* vegetated.[187] "Anemic," so Eugène Hénard, city-planner and son of the Palais-Royal himself, characterized the dismal state of commerce in the city's central *quartiers*.[188] Drumont mourned the passing of *vieux Paris;* others like Hénard and Levallois concocted schemes to revive commercial activity. No one, however, disputed that a problem existed, least of all the *Ligue syndicale.*

The *Ligue* contented itself for the most part with abstract denunciations of the department store, but from time to time intimations escaped of specific streets and *quartiers* where shopkeepers experienced hardship. Storefronts in the Palais-Royal remained vacant. The passages Delorme, Jouffroy, Verdeau were deserted. Entire buildings on the Sentier could not be rented. The faubourg Montmartre was "very hard hit" and so on.[189] To *ligueurs*, as to persons outside the commer-

---

[185] APP B/a 503, 1 April 1887; Faubourg Montmartre, 15 March 1886.

[186] Vallès, *Le Tableau de Paris*, pp. 39–40.

[187] Montorgueil, *op. cit.*, p. 23; Kahn, p. 194.

[188] Eugène Hénard, *Etudes sur les transformations de Paris*, vol. V, pp. 177–178.

[189] See testimony by A. Hamel, AN C5498, Mesureur Commission, 15 May 1891; and articles in *La Revendication*: R. Cadet, "Une plaie sociale,"

cial community, Paris' old downtown area was foundering in crisis. Shopkeepers watched once prosperous businesses wither as, not a hundred feet away, boulevard boutiques and department stores did a booming trade.

But the crisis was selective not only in its geographical impact. Certain trades were particularly hard hit as well: luxury goods, clothing, food, the commission business and bespoke trades. I have emphasized a softening of demand and the disadvantages of inferior location in my discussion of the demise of Paris' old downtown area. To account for the selective sectoral impact of the slump, I will stress rather the adverse consequences of the *révolution du bon marché*. The influx of cheap goods—ready-to-wear clothing, machine-made furniture, etc. —changed the structure of the market, inflicting permanent damage on a wide range of trades, the very trades in fact that were drawn to the *Ligue syndicale*.

For middlemen of all kinds—jobbers, commissionnaires, wholesalers—the crisis proved a disaster. The collapse of exports in the face of competition from abroad cut the bottom out of the commission business. M. Coutant, a commissionnaire headquartered on the rue de Réaumur, claimed that his trade had fallen off by two-thirds since the onset of the crisis, testimony confirmed by police reports from the IXth, the center of the city's export traffic.[190] Textile wholesalers on the rue du Sentier fared no better. The Sentier, as principal outlet for the textile industry, was crippled by the eclipse of high-quality French *nouveautés*.[191] Textile importers, in fact importers of all kinds, better absorbed the shock of the crisis, but as handlers of foreign goods, their success inspired distrust. They

---

15 December 1893; "Compte-rendu de la réception d'une délégation," 15 February 1896; "Comité de centralisation," 15–31 March 1894.

[190] Chambre des Députés, Spuller Commission, p. 277; APP B/a 503, Faubourg Montmartre, 15 March 1886; also 15 May 1887; and B/a 504, 15 February 1889.

[191] APP B/a 503, Mail, 9 March 1886.

were suspected as commercial spies and branded as cosmopolitans. It was taken as an affront that such men prospered while the old established commission houses of the Sentier and the IXth arrondissement foundered.[192]

Falling retail prices only exacerbated the difficulties of middlemen. To save money, manufacturers and retailers sought shortcuts to by-pass useless, cost-inflating intermediaries. A factory might open a depot in the city, as occurred in the ceramics industry,[193] or operate its own chain of stores, as did Les Incroyables shoe company. But to the outsider, it was the *grand magasin,* with its network of buyers, that caused greatest damage to the middleman. A Bordeaux wholesaler remarked: "All the commercial travelers and commission agents will be ruined or no longer exist because department stores—which handle their own purchasing and deal directly with the factory—have no use for them."[194] Less partial observers, du Maroussem and Zola, reached the identical conclusion: as the department store grew and developed, the commission business declined.[195] *Grands magasins* made no apologies, justifying the ruthless purge of middlemen in the name of economy. Plassard, an administrator at the Bon Marché, explained to the Mesureur Commission:

> Middlemen have suffered more than the retailer; for them the crisis is more acute because big and little commerce have abandoned them. They're the ones who have incited an unthinking fraction of *petit commerce* against the department store.
>
> Their disappearance will count as a step forward. Every

---

[192] Domergue, pp. 17, 38–39, 72.

[193] H. Cariot, "Encore les grands magasins," *La Crise commerciale,* 1 March 1888.

[194] Cited in Levallois, *Une France nouvelle,* p. 351.

[195] Du Maroussem, *Le Jouet parisien,* p. 62; BN NAF 10278, Zola, p. 224.

useless cog must be eliminated, especially in the machinery of society.[196]

The elimination of intermediaries, Plassard rightly points out, was not the special prerogative of *grands magasins*. Small shopkeepers as well as large and, as we have seen, manufacturers as well as retailers, shared an interest in reducing the costs of bringing goods to market. The commission business was a casualty not of the department store but of a shrinking export market and, on the domestic front, of rationalized marketing mechanisms. Plassard, however, was wrong on one point. He minimized shopkeeper ferment, attributing it to agitation by disgruntled middlemen, but merchants and tradesmen had ample reason to complain without encouragement from outside agitators.

The bourgeoning trade in ready-mades cut deeply into the market for custom-made goods. Shoemakers, cabinetmakers and tailors who dealt in what du Maroussem called "the solid and serious comfort of the middle class of old" lost business to department stores and other commercial outlets which sold low-priced, mass-produced merchandise.[197] Custom shoemakers, claimed *La Crise commerciale*, were losing clientele so rapidly that they would soon have only repair work to do. *Grands magasins* and shoe chains monopolized the market, but they sold only junk: "it's only ready-made goods (and often made abroad)," the paper pleaded, ". . . the shoemaker serves you better. He makes shoes to measure."[198] The situation in the furniture trade was no better. Artisan retailers, "veritable artists," could not compete with junk dealers trading in *la camelote*. Du Maroussem describes the case of a custom cabinetmaker, a one-time independent who had been reduced to the status of outworker in a department store *fabrique collec-*

[196] AN C5498, Mesureur Commission, 29 May 1891.
[197] Du Maroussem, *Ebénistes du faubourg Saint-Antoine*, p. 45.
[198] A. Marc, "Chaussures," *La Crise commerciale*, 15 July 1888.

tive. He had formerly operated a shop of his own, specializing in dining-room draw-tables, but the growing popularity of lightweight furniture, so-called *ballons* because "they are at once elegant in appearance and lacking in solidity," had robbed him of his bourgeois clientele.[199] As for tailors, a government report on the clothing industry described their circumstances in the following terms:

> . . . ready-made goods flowing into the domestic market are finishing off every day numbers of small, independent tailors. These tailors, working in their *arrière-boutiques*, are obliged to become, unbeknownst to the public, piece workers for ready-to-wear firms.[200]

Whether for trousers or for other articles of clothing—hats, shirts, bonnets—the custom-made shop could not match the prices offered at ready-to-wear stores.[201]

Grands magasins were not the only retailers of ready-made goods—Les Incroyables sold shoes, the *marchand d'habits neufs* sold ready-to-wear clothing—but they were the most conspicuous and as such focused on themselves the anger of victims of the new merchandise. M. Gohn, the store owner on the rue Croix-des-Petits-Champs, specialized in the sale of bespoke footwear. Despite his admission that the neighborhood was no longer as "central" as it had once been, he still wanted to lay principal blame for his misfortunes on the department store.[202] Business, he explained to the Mesureur Commission, had fallen off by half since the big stores opened shoe sections. The government's report on the clothing industry took note of the depth of antidepartment-store sentiment among tailors and, it is perhaps worth adding, du

[199] Du Maroussem, *Ebénistes du faubourg Saint-Antoine*, pp. 95, 99, 45–46.

[200] Office du travail, *Le Vêtement à Paris*, p. 208.

[201] Martin Saint-Léon, p. 63; Aftalion, pp. 295–297, 300.

[202] AN C5498, Mesureur Commission, 20 March 1891.

Maroussem's proletarianized cabinetmaker was also a member of the *Ligue syndicale*.[203]

The impact of the new merchandise did not, of course, bring ruin to all custom goods retailers. The jewelers and couturieres of the rue de la Paix, as we have seen, were not wanting for clients. Superior location accounts in part for their relative success, but the high quality of the merchandise they traded in must also be cited. The moneyed classes could still afford to pay custom prices, and their patronage sustained an aristocracy of first-class establishments. The competition of *articles confectionnés* or machine-made goods was stiffest for articles just below the highest quality. The new merchandise captured the lower reaches of the luxury market, stripping second-rank retailers who specialized not in haut luxe but in *le bon courant* (the everyday), of their clientele. This was true not only for the bespoke but for other luxury trades as well. The jewelry business is a good example.

M. Bloch, a jewelry exporter, observed to the Spuller Commission: "It's to be remarked that what we call *le bon courant*, that is, the jewel in between the expensive jewel and the cheap jewel, has completely disappeared. The public buys either expensive or bargain jewels; in fact, it's the bargain jewel that is preferred."[204] Cheap jewelry at the end of the century successfully penetrated French markets. Eighteen-carat was replaced by fourteen-carat gold, often refined outside Paris in the provinces or abroad.[205] But it was the so-called "invasion" of South African diamonds which affected the jewelry trade most profoundly. The stones were plentiful and cut cheaply in Amsterdam or London. The use of less expensive materials allowed substantial price reductions, making jew-

---

[203] Office du travail, *Le Vêtement à Paris*, p. 208; du Maroussem, *Ebénistes du faubourg Saint-Antoine*, p. 95.

[204] Chambre des Députés, Spuller Commission, p. 282.

[205] *Ibid.*, p. 281.

elry accessible for the first time to a new class of buyers.[206] The consequences were predictable. Alfred Hamel, a Palais-Royal jeweler and league member, summed up the change in the jewelry trade: "Once upon a time, the trade in jewelry and *objets de luxe* employed hundreds of merchants and man-ufacturers who strove to create unique objects of exquisite taste; today, they have been replaced by big factories which want to make cheap merchandise."[207] At the top of the market, the city's premier jewelers—Boucheron, Fontana, Mellerio—continued to manufacture artistic work, but for second-order businesses, for Palais-Royal jewelers, "one fell back on so-called *camelote*" or, worse, on costume jewelry which was not, prop-erly speaking, jewelry at all.[208]

The bottom of the market as well, although to a lesser ex-tent, was shaken by the influx of new merchandise. The used-clothing trade had centered on the Temple market since its opening in 1865. The ready-to-wear revolution brought new clothing within the price range of buyers who had previously had to settle for hand-me-downs. The Temple was by no means driven out of business, but trade fell off in the eighties.[209] In March of 1887, at the nadir of the depression, 618 of the Temple's 1,540 stalls were unoccupied.[210] Old, established merchants closed up shop and were replaced by new men who would accept, because they had no other choice, the marginal existence to which a second-hand dealer had been reduced. Martin Saint-Léon records this conversation with an Auverg-nat junk-man: "In ten years, we will be elbowed aside. We Auvergnats, thirty or forty years ago, we replaced the Nor-

---

[206] "Taille des diamants," *La Bijouterie*, 22 January 1888; Guerrand, *L'Art nouveau en Europe*, p. 164.

[207] AN C5498, Mesureur Commission, 15 May 1891.

[208] APP B/a 503, Palais-Royal, 8 March 1886.

[209] Coffignon, *Les Coulisses de la mode*, pp. 182–183; Sutcliffe, p. 162.

[210] APP B/a 503, 15 March 1887.

mans who had dominated the Temple; now it's the Jew-for-eigner's turn to take over."[211]

Another, yet humbler casualty of the new merchandise was the city's Christmas season street market. In the weeks before Christmas or on New Year's Day, Paris' main thoroughfares, the *grands boulevards* above all, were crowded with makeshift booths selling hand-made toys and knick-knacks. This venerable and "picturesque" custom, an opportunity for the poor to supplement family incomes during the holiday season, fell on hard times at the end of the century.[212] A police report of 1889 offered an explanation: "These small fry specialize in *articles de Paris* which can be found every day of the year at a department store counter for bargain prices, and so they have lost the vogue they once enjoyed."[213]

The new goods upset the commercial world of central Paris from luxury shops to street markets, from the Palais-Royal to the Temple. The *Ligue syndicale* rallied to itself the shopkeepers and middlemen who lost from commercial change. The *Crise commerciale* exhorted its readers: "*Négociants* under your arcades, merchants in your avenues, courage in the face of the enemy, and then for the Palais-Royal which is the rich man's Temple and for the Temple which is the poor man's Palais-Royal, there will be prosperity and good fortune."[214] The enemy, however, was not the department store but cheap goods, marketed by *grands magasins* to be sure, but by others as well.

The *révolution du bon marché*, on the other hand, does not fully explain the crisis in food retailing at the end of the century. Preserved, refrigerated and processed foods were only just

[211] Martin Saint-Léon, p. 71.

[212] Coffignon, *Le Pavé parisien*, pp. 15–16, 21–22; Montorgueil, *op. cit.*, pp. 46–47.

[213] APP B/a 504, 15 January 1889.

[214] Montaigu, "Le Temple et le Palais-Royal," *La Crise commerciale*, 1 November 1888.

beginning to undercut the fresh food market. Prices for necessities, moreover, for bread, wine and potatoes, dipped only modestly in the eighties.[215] Critics of the *Ligue syndicale* and even some friends blamed the commercial crisis of the 1880s on an overabundance of small, inefficient shopkeepers.[216] This assertion, without validity for luxury trades, does make sense when applied to the food industry.

Du Maroussem, in his monograph on les Halles, repeatedly makes the claim that the food trades were swamped by out-of-work craftsmen in search of an alternative livelihood. The *crise des métiers*, he observed, had turned the unemployed, especially women, toward that form of commerce accessible to all: the food-and-drink business.[217] Petty entrepreneurs who had failed in other lines of business could take refuge in food retailing, "that last cartridge of the *petit commerçant*" as *La Revendication* called it.[218] Drapers, mercers and hatters declined in numbers but not bakers and fruit-sellers.[219] The proliferation of wineshops was a source of particular consternation to moralists,[220] but even the wine merchants themselves conceded that their numbers had grown excessively. Paris' commercial directory, which listed fifteen pages of wineshop-keepers in 1878, listed fifty in 1884.[221] But shopkeeper concern focused above all on the swelling army of street vendors. According to a representative of the *Comité de l'alimentation*,

[215] Néré, vol. I, p. 259.

[216] Duclos, pp. 150–151; U. Guérin, pp. 84–85; Saint-Martin, p. 43; AN C5498, Mesureur Commission, testimony of Frédéric Honoré, 5 June 1891.

[217] Du Maroussem, *Halles centrales de Paris*, pp. 11, 93.

[218] Calixte Camelle, "Liquidation," *La Revendication*, 15 December 1894.

[219] Garrigues, p. 10.

[220] *Ibid.*, p. 10; Paul Leroy-Beaulieu, "La répartition de la population par professions en Allemagne et en France," *L'Economiste français*, 5 July 1884, p. 3.

[221] Chambre des Députés, Spuller Commission, testimony of the *Chambre syndicale des débitants de vins de la Seine*, p. 363.

the number of pushcarts swarming the streets of Paris sky-rocketed from 6,000 to 20,000 in the eighties.[222] And the hordes of street peddlars, it was claimed, were not even proper Frenchmen. "These itinerants," complained the butchers' weekly, "belong almost all of them to the tribe of Israel."[223] Foreigners, cosmopolitans and Jews were infiltrating the world of commerce from every side, or so it seemed. They took over the street as they had *grand commerce* and the commission house.

The rapid growth of the cooperative movement exacerbated the problems of overcrowding in the food business. Charles Gide, the nation's leading exponent of cooperation, identified 1885 as the moment of take-off for the movement. From 1867 to 1883, perhaps a hundred co-ops in all were formed nation-wide, Paris and Lyon accounting for the vast majority.[224] By 1900, the national Labor Office counted 1,463 consumers' cooperatives in operation.[225] In Paris, the organizations served an essentially working-class clientele resident in the outer ar-rondissements. Co-ops for civil servants and military officers did exist, but they paled beside institutions like La Moisson-euse, an enormous enterprise located in the XIIth with a membership in excess of fifteen thousand.[226]

Food retailers under pressure because of overcrowding shifted the blame onto the cooperative and the supermarket, massive institutions which, to all appearances, grew and prospered through the crisis. Displacement of affect was not, as we have seen, uncharacteristic of shopkeeper thinking at the end of the nineteenth century. Middlemen and luxury retailers as well as greengrocers and wine merchants used large-scale compet-

[222] "Comptes-rendus," *La Revendication*, 21 February 1889.

[223] "Les irréguliers du commerce," *Journal de la Chambre syndicale de la boucherie*, 9 July 1899.

[224] Charles Gide, *Les Sociétés coopératives de consommation*, pp. 28–30.

[225] Vouters, *Le Petit Commerce*, p. 182.

[226] D'Avenel, "Le mécanisme de la vie moderne. Les magasins de l'ali-mentation," p. 833.

itors as scapegoats for a commercial crisis brought on by economic depression. The problem was not the department store or the supermarket, but a shrinking export market, structural change in consumer goods production, an influx of new merchandise, overcrowding in the food trades, and all this compounded by a cyclical business contraction.

A select cluster of *commerces* then bore the brunt of the end-of-century crisis. This observation is borne out by bankruptcy statistics. In the food, clothing, luxury and commission trades, the number of business failures soared in the 1880s, peaking in 1886–1887 (see Figure 6). The rate of business closings slowed in the next two or three years returning to normal levels in 1889–1890, but then shot up again in the early nineties. The end of the century was certainly a rocky period for these trades, but was it any worse for them than for other sectors of Paris' commercial community? When totals for the food, clothing, luxury and commission trades are added together and compared to the composite bankruptcy rate for all other trades (banking, building, etc.), three points emerge with striking clarity (see Figure 7). The period 1882–1884 was difficult for all sectors. For building, banking and the like, however, the crisis subsided quickly; it had bottomed out by 1885 while in food, clothing, etc., pre-slump levels of business failure were not approximated until 1888–1889. Nor was the depression yet over. It was for builders and bankers, but not for luxury retailers and clothiers whose bankruptcy rates began to climb again in 1892. For the trades that rallied to the *Ligue syndicale*, the economic downturn of the eighties was real and more thoroughgoing than it was for other sectors of the business community.

The Great Depression shattered the dual structure of industrial and commercial life engendered by Haussmannization. Under pressure, *grands magasins* and boulevard businesses had developed new lines of merchandise and new merchandising techniques to attract and accommodate a wider buying public. For the enterprises involved, whether large or small, adaptation was not only a question of profit-mongering but of survival. The eighties were a difficult period even for the winners. The losers in this commercial drama were tailors, jewelers and shoestore owners hard hit by the *révolution du bon marché*. They ran poorly located second-rank businesses sited in the city's old downtown area. While the new shopping district born of Haussmannization survived the slump, the streets and arcades of *vieux Paris* suffered eclipse, strangled by a lack of trade.

The bitterness and frustration felt by the victims of the crisis spilled into the retailer mobilization of the 1880s. The anger of retailer militants was directed above all at the department store, and the choice of target is understandable. To *ligueurs* as to contemporaries, it appeared that the commanding heights of commerce had fallen into the hands of foreigners and cosmopolitans who built vast fortunes selling shoddy merchandise to an unwitting public—and at prices that brought ruin to old-line luxury retailers. If honest merchants had fallen on hard times, if public taste was corrupted and public morality menaced, was it not because of the disloyal business practices of commercial speculators and monopolists? But *ligueurs* and contemporaries alike erred on two counts in blaming the slump on the *grand magasin.* The big stores were not the only purveyors of the new merchandise. *Grands magasins* grew rich in the depression years, but so did costume jewelers and ready-to-wear manufacturers like Mascuraud and Dreyfus. In drawing a parallel between the *grand magasin* and boulevard, contemporaries implicitly recognized that what was at issue was not just department-store growth but a widespread commercial transformation, a consumer revolution of which department store growth was but one manifestation. This consumer revolution, moreover, had its roots not in the changing business practices of *grands magasins* or even of the department store/boulevard nexus but in changes in the structure of French

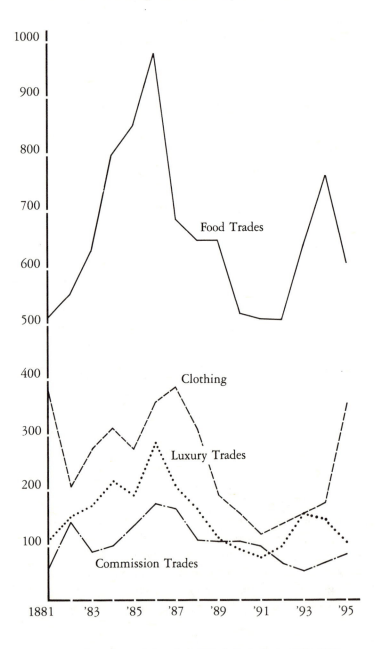

FIGURE 6: Bankruptcies in Paris by Trade, 1881-1895

Food Trades

Clothing

Luxury Trades

Commission Trades

1881   '83   '85   '87   '89   '91   '93   '95

SOURCE: Annuaire statistique de la Ville de Paris (Paris, 1881-1897)

FIGURE 7: Bankruptcies in Paris, 1881-1895

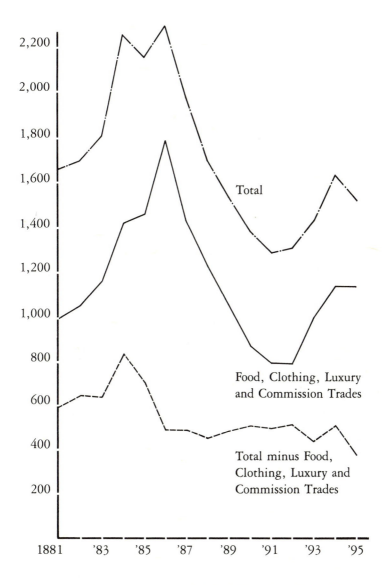

SOURCE: Annuaire statistique de la Ville de Paris (Paris, 1881-1897)

industry imposed by foreign competition and technical innovation. The transformation of commerce was a response to, and not the cause of, the economic downturn of the 1880s, and so it is to the slump that the ultimate origins of the *Ligue syndicale* must be traced.

Urban transformation provides the beginnings of an explanation for the *Ligue syndicale*'s peculiar geographical and professional profile. The divisions which culminated in the break-up of central Paris' commercial community at the end of the century were sown in part by Haussmannization. But this break-up was triggered by the economic crisis of the eighties. A full explanation of the sources of retailer discontent requires an understanding of the polarizing impact of the Great Depression which sundered Paris' business community, bringing good fortune to some and hardship to others. The losers, hard hit by urban transformation and economic change, made a final effort through the *Ligue syndicale* to stave off disaster.

5

. . .

The Crisis of
the Palais-Royal:
A Local Study

URBAN RENEWAL and economic crisis fragmented the commercial community of central Paris. The outlines of this process have already been sketched in using qualitative evidence, in particular the testimony of urbanists, literary men and social critics. A statistical description of the phenomenon requires exploitation of quantifiable sources detailing changes in commercial and residential life on a street-by-street basis. Sources of this nature—electoral lists and *patente* registers—do exist but, because of the staggering quantity of entries, are difficult to use save for the study of a single arrondissement or still better, of a single *quartier*. In the case of the shopkeeper movement, the choice for a local study would logically fall on one of the center-city wards in which the *Ligue syndicale* recruited with greatest success: the Palais-Royal, Vivienne or Faubourg Montmartre.

I have selected the Palais-Royal for several resaons. The *quartier* (see figures 8 and 9) housed two of Paris' largest department stores, the Louvre and the Gagne-Petit. It was also the site of the last great public-works project of the Haussmannic era, the construction of the avenue de l'Opéra. And finally, business activity in the ward was heavily weighted in favor of the luxury and clothing trades, the trades hardest hit by the Great Depression. The Palais-Royal ward then offers an excellent proving ground for the hypotheses advanced in the preceding chapters. A street-by-street breakdown of business and residence in the *quartier* will show: (1) whether department stores did, in fact, smother trade in their immediate vicinity; (2) whether Haussmannization promoted residential embourgeoisement and a shift in commercial activity away from closed spaces like the Palais-Royal in favor of the broad, new boulevards of renovated Paris; (3) whether the Great Depression attacked all streets and neighborhoods and all sectors of the commercial community with equal ferocity. Fortunately, the documentation necessary to such an investigation is available and adequate. The *patente* series of the Palais-Royal is complete and as for electoral lists, only the poll-book of 1894 is missing.

These sources, to be sure, have their limitations. *Patente* registers list the address, name and occupation of every person exercising a taxable trade or profession within a particular *quartier*. Tax assessments are also recorded. Assessments represent a percentage of the rentable value of business premises as determined by a complicated formula. In some instances, businesses were required to pay according to the number of personnel employed. Taxes on department stores and other large-scale operations were calculated in this way, but such cases were exceptions. If deciphered, the tax figures listed in the *patente* would at best yield a picture of business rents in a given locality. Overhead costs, however, are a poor indicator of the size or prosperity of an enterprise. A jeweler with a booming trade would probably pay less rent than a furniture dealer on the skids. In this respect, *patente* registers are not especially helpful. Nor do they present a complete description of the business life of a *quartier*. Certain kinds of industrial enterprise, home work in particular, were tax-exempt and so were not entered onto the tax rolls. No major exceptions were made, however, for commercial operations. Wholesalers as well as retailers, liberal professionals as well as stall-keepers (*étalagistes*) paid the *patente*. The entries, moreover, include a fairly precise characterization of the profession exercised. *Patente* registers, with all their limitations, can provide a reasonably accurate and detailed account of the structure of commerce in a given neighborhood. Unfortunately, no registers prior to 1885 exist, and after 1885, registers have only been preserved on a quinquennial basis: 1885, 1890, 1895, etc. Short-lived enterprises in operation for only a year or two may escape the researcher's detection. This is not a serious limitation where changing structures over time, not business turnover, is the major concern.

Electoral lists present far more serious problems. Poll-book entries include an interesting range of information: place of residence, date and place of birth, as well as a declaration of occupation made by the registrant. Electoral lists can be used to determine the social compostion of a resident population, but a few cautionary remarks are in order. Firstly, a citizen was entitled to register only after an extended period of settled residence. Transients do not appear in the poll books and, as a consequence, certain forms of employment, e.g. casual employment, are bound to be underrepresented. Women were also excluded from the franchise with similar consequences. Entries for modistes, seamstresses, and lingerie retailers are not likely to be numerous. Foreign residents, of course, do not appear on electoral lists, nor do citizens who for one reason or another neglected to register. Census manuscripts would not be marred by lacunae of this nature, but they are as yet closed to public consultation. Electoral lists can give only a rough and skewed indication of residence patterns, but they are the best available source.

Keeping the limitations of the sources in mind, then, what can be said about the changing structures of business and residence in the fin-de-siècle Palais-Royal?

TABLE 7. Distribution of *Patentables* in the Palais-Royal Ward,
1885–1900

BUSINESS AND LIBERAL PROFESSIONALS

	Liberal profs.	Stockbroker, discounter, money changer	Middle-man	Large-scale enterprises	SUB-TOTAL
1885	151	21	53	53	258
1890	148	23	54	29	254
1895	161	18	49	35	263
1900	139	16	53	27	235

LUXURY TRADES

	Jewelry	Watches	Gilding/ engraving	Articles de Paris	Leather goods	Flowers & feathers	SUB-TOTAL
1885	153	27	31	90	10	25	336
1890	152	26	24	87	13	25	327
1895	122	21	25	68	14	26	276
1900	113	13	30	74	11	25	266

CLOTHING TRADES

	Nouveautés, cloth & garment wholesaling	Shoes (manu.)	Shoes (sales)	Clothing (manu.)	Clothing (sales)
1885	50	33	22	7	26
1890	32	20	19	10	22
1895	31	15	14	11	20
1900	28	12	11	6	36

Crisis of the Palais-Royal

	Lingerie	Dress-making	Tailoring	Men's hats	Women's hats	SUB-TOTAL
1885	19	96	136	19	35	443
1890	16	82	122	15	37	375
1895	13	88	105	16	45	358
1900	11	87	92	12	48	343

OTHER TRADES

	Notions	Toilette	Household goods	Home furnishings	Printing	Books
1885	31	25	29	21	18	39
1890	36	19	30	27	17	34
1895	38	23	24	21	13	34
1900	41	31	23	20	14	31

	Cards/paints	Food	Services	Mil. equip./instruments	Packing	Building	Raw mats.	SUB-TOTAL
1885	15	363	70	28	13	38	15	705
1890	14	361	59	27	17	39	17	697
1895	15	361	62	26	10	33	13	673
1900	18	342	67	22	9	35	18	671

MISCELLANEOUS

	Stall keeper	Other	SUBTOTAL	TOTAL
1885	30	46	76	1,818
1890	25	59	84	1,737
1895	19	56	75	1,645
1900	20	68	88	1,603

SOURCE: AS D⁹P², *Palais-Royal, Patente* registers for 1885, 1890, 1895, 1900

Origins of Shopkeeper Protest

THE DEPARTMENT STORE THESIS

The commercial community of the Palais-Royal ward was shaken by a severe crisis in the concluding decades of the nineteenth century. While the number of taxable enterprises in Paris as a whole rose from 162,144 in 1885 to 171,287 in 1900, in the Palais-Royal ward, the total of *patentables* slipped from 1,818 to 1,603 (see Table 7). The *quartier's* loss of commercial vitality is in part attributable to demographic decline. Resident population fell from 14,316 to 13,199 in the 1885–1900 period. But the correlation between the ward's demographic and commercial difficulties is not a strong one. Firstly, how important is a sizeable resident population to the commercial well-being of a centrally located shopping district like the Palais-Royal ward that drew business from all over the city? Downtown areas do not depend on local customers for the bulk of their trade. And in any event, the rate of commercial decline in the ward outstripped the pace of population shrinkage such that in 1900, there was one *patentable* for every 8.23 inhabitants whereas fifteen years earlier the ratio had been 1/7.87.[1] Even granting the relevance of demographic factors, population loss cannot fully account for the dramatic fall-off in the *quartier's* stock of taxable enterprises. Nor does population loss answer the question of why the ward's commercial decline was so selective in its impact. The garment and the luxury trades were particularly hard hit. The number of clothing businesses of all sorts (shoes, hats, lingerie, etc.) collapsed from 443 in 1885 to 343 at the turn of the century. The fall-off in the luxury trades, from 336 to 266, was no less pronounced. The crisis was selective not only with respect to profession but also to geographic location. The arcades of the Palais-Royal were devastated. For decades the

[1] *Annuaire statistique de la Ville de Paris*, 1885 and 1900 (Paris, 1887 and 1902).

center of the Parisian jewelry trade, the Palace suffered a precipitate and irreversible decline at the end of the century. In
1890, its galleries housed 200 businesses, of which 81 specialized in the sale or manufacture of jewelry and watches. By
1900, these figures had been reduced to 146 and 48 respectively.[2] If demography does not offer a satisfactory explanation of the ward's commercial crisis, what alternatives remain?

It would be easy to attribute—as did the *Ligue syndicale*—
the ward's commercial problems to the rise of the department
store.[3] After all, two of the city's largest retail establishments, the Grands Magasins du Louvre and the Gagne-Petit,
were located in the *quartier*. The big stores were major retailers of clothing and luxury goods. Surely they drained trade
from neighboring streets. Haberdashers, shoe stores and curiosity shops simply could not withstand the competition. And
indeed, the number of hatters in the *quartier* dwindled from
19 to 12. Retailers of *articles de Paris* declined from 90 to 74,
and so forth. In the last fifteen years of the century, trade
slowed appreciably in the immediate vicinity of the Louvre.
The number of *patentables* on the rue de Rivoli dropped from
100 to 70, on the rue Saint-Honoré from 129 to 112. The
Palais-Royal, situated just across the street from the Louvre,
naturally suffered the heaviest casualties. How could small and
medium-sized merchants carry on business in the shadow of

[2] All *patente* figures have been culled from: Archives de la Seine D⁹P², *Palais-Royal, registres de patente*, 1885, 1890, 1895, 1900. A word needs to be said also about the boundaries of the Palais-Royal ward. The rue Saint-Roch separates the ward from the quartier de la Place Vendôme to the west. The rue des Petits-Champs marked the ward's northern border, the rue Croix-des-Petits-Champs its eastern border. Even-numbered addresses on the rue Saint-Roch are not part of the Palais-Royal ward, and so are not counted in the table above. Similarly with the odd-numbered addresses on the rues des Petits-Champs and Croix-des-Petits-Champs.

[3] A. Trépreau, "En Arrière! En Avant!!," reprinted from *La Revendication* in *Affiches tourangelles*, 13 December 1900.

838. – PARIS – Les Grands Magasins du Louvre et la Rue de Rivoli   C. M.

The Grands Magasins du Louvre in 1906

giants like the Louvre which in 1910 was grossing nearly 150 million francs per annum?[4] This interpretation of events, however, is unsatisfactory for three reasons.

Firstly, a number of trades in direct competition with department stores held their own or actually increased in numbers in the 1885–1900 period. Dressmaking experienced only a modest contraction from 96 to 87 enterprises, while the number of milliners rose from 35 to 48. Furriers increased from 5 to 8, wig-dealers from 8 to 10 and retailers of corsets and support undergarments from 8 to 18. These gains to be sure were not adequate to offset the massive losses in wholesaling (50 to 28), shoes (55 to 23), lingerie (19 to 11) and tailoring (136 to 92). But if the department store was to blame for the collapse of the clothing business in the *quartier,* it played the villain's part with a curious inconsistency.

The department store thesis, moreover, cannot satisfactorily explain the peculiar rhythm with which the crisis unfolded. The decline in luxury goods, for example, was neither steady nor unbroken but occurred in one major spasm between 1890 and 1895. From 1885 to 1890, the number of enterprises in this sector declined only imperceptibly from 336 to 327. The collapse, precipitate and devastating, came in the ensuing half decade. The luxury sector shrank by 51 businesses, but then stabilized. The decline continued after 1895 but at a much reduced rate. In the ward as a whole, luxury goods registered a loss of only 10 enterprises from 1895 to 1900. The Louvre department store dated back to 1855; the Gagne-Petit was still older. If these stores did in fact exert a malignant influence on the luxury-goods sector, why did this sector collapse in 1890 and not at some earlier date? And why, for that matter, did the sector stabilize after 1895?

Finally, while commercial activity may have slackened in the vicinity of the Louvre, it flourished or at least stayed its

[4]Martin Saint-Léon, *Le Petit Commerce français*, p. 15.

ground in the vicinity of the Gagne-Petit. The number of taxable enterprises on the avenue de l'Opéra, site of the Gagne-Petit, jumped from 120 in 1885 to 135 in 1900.[5] The increase was heavily concentrated in the clothing trade—in wholesaling and *nouveautés*, shoes and women's hats. Where there had been 21 clothing businesses in 1885, there were 38 a decade and a half later. The Opéra, it is true, was relatively new (the avenue was completed only in 1877) and just beginning to develop its commercial potential. But other streets in the area were not; how can one explain their relatively solid performance? The number of enterprises on the rue Sainte-Anne rose from 56 to 62, on the rue des Pyramides from 81 to 83. The increases were small, but compared to the eastern end of the *quartier* and to the totals for the ward as a whole, business fared well in the Gagne-Petit area. Proximity to a department store was by no means a sentence of death for the luckless retailer.

A commercial crisis battered the Palais-Royal ward in the closing years of the century. But the department store thesis cannot account for the timing of the crisis, which reached its peak of intensity in 1890, nor for its conspicuous selectivity. The eastern end of the ward was affected more profoundly than the western, jewelers and haberdashers more than retailers of ladies' apparel and accessories. Haussmannization and the Great Depression, far more than *grands magasins*, shaped the *quartier*'s peculiar evolution in the fin de siècle.

HAUSSMANNIZATION

The completion of the avenue de l'Opéra transformed the face of the Palais-Royal ward (see figures 8 and 9). The impact of Haussmannization on residential life was immediate and ap-

[5]These figures refer only to that portion of the avenue de l'Opéra contained in the Palais-Royal ward.

parent. The *quartier*, once an agglomeration of socially diverse neighborhoods became increasingly the preserve of the middle class, of doctors and businessmen, wholesalers and employees. How urban change affected the commercial life of the ward is harder to characterize in the absence of *patente* records antedating construction of the Opéra. The new avenue and neighboring thoroughfares generated a surge of business activity. Established shopping streets in the *quartier* were shaken by competition from the Opéra but managed, for the moment, to stave off commercial collapse. Haussmannization generated tensions in the ward's business community, but local life was, as yet, not sharply polarized.

The Palais-Royal ward at mid-century was a labyrinth of densely populated narrow streets. According to the Chamber of Commerce survey of 1872, the *quartier* housed over 18,000 residents, squeezed into a mere 28.45 hectares.[6] Business and commerce, moreover, competed fiercely with population for space; in 1865, roughly one dwelling in nine was "used exclusively for commercial or industrial purposes."[7] In the western end of the ward, it was residence, not trade, which predominated, and for good reason. No major thoroughfare crisscrossed the block of cramped, winding streets bordered west and east by the rues Saint-Roch and de Richelieu. *Flâneurs* who strayed into this isolated enclave, the Butte des Moulins as the neighborhood was known, entered another world, "a city apart."[8]

[6]Chambre de Commerce de Paris, *Enquête sur les conditions du travail en France pendant l'année 1872*, p. 315.

[7]Sutcliffe, *The Autumn of Central Paris*, p. 156. The ⅑ ratio cited by Sutcliffe in fact applies to the Ist arrondissement as a whole. It may fairly be assumed, however, that the situation in the Palais-Royal ward roughly approximated the situation prevailing across the arrondissement in its entirety.

[8]Daumard, "L'avenue de l'Opéra," p. 167; Lottin, *Conséquences du percement de l'avenue de l'Opéra*, pp. 10–11.

FIGURE 8: Map of the Palais-Royal Ward in 1868

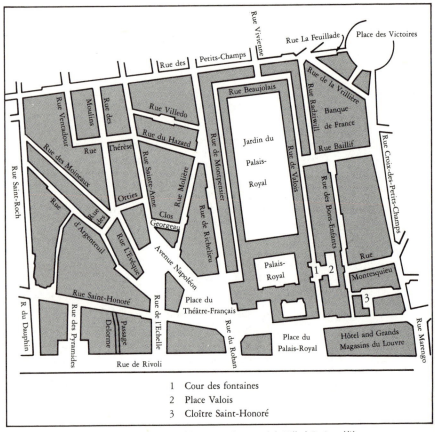

1   Cour des fontaines
2   Place Valois
3   Cloître Saint-Honoré

SOURCE: *Atlas administratif des 20 arrondissements de la Ville de Paris, publié d'après les ordres de M. le baron G.E. Haussman, Sénateur, Préfet de la Seine* (Paris, 1868).

Luxury shops lined the streets on the periphery of the Butte, along the rue de Richelieu and the rue Saint-Honoré. The rue des Petit-Champs, "multiple bazaar," was jammed with boutiques "so diverse and so animated."[9] Commercial activity *on* the Butte, however, was of another variety. The street scene

[9]Fournier, "Promenade dans Paris," p. 26.

FIGURE 9: Map of the Palais-Royal Ward in 1895

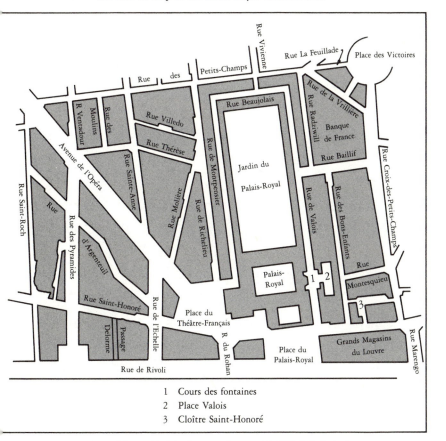

1   Cours des fontaines
2   Place Valois
3   Cloître Saint-Honoré

SOURCE: *Atlas municipal des vingt arrondissements de la Ville de Paris dressé sous l'administration de M. E. Poubelle, Préfet, sous la direction de M. Alphand, Inspecteur Général* (Paris, 1895). The Palais-Royal ward has remained virtually unchanged since the turn of the century. The Cloître Saint-Honoré no longer exists, nor does the passage Delorme. The rue Montesquieu has been extended into the place Valois; and finally, the name of the rue Baillif has been changed to the more patriotic, rue du Colonel-Driant.

did not lack in variety or color, but the goods retailed were staple items strictly for local consumption. The terrain rose gently as one moved eastward off the rue Saint-Roch, reaching a height of six meters at the crossroads where the rues

Moineaux, Moulins, Orties and l'Evêque intersected. Here street vendors and secondhand dealers noisily plied their trades blocking traffic and attracting crowds. Grocery stores, coal dealers and wineshops abounded, drawing their clientele from the substantial working-class population in the vicinity. The Butte des Moulins was, indeed, a proletarian stronghold in the very heart of the Imperial capital. With its ramshackle buildings and crooked streets, it had become in the 1870s a neighborhood of last resort for center-city working people displaced by Haussmannization.[10]

The picturesque bustle which animated the top of the Butte dissipated as one descended eastward toward the rue de Richelieu. The streets adjoining the rue de Richelieu—the rues Thérèse, Villedo and Molière—were deserted, their somber silence undisturbed by commercial or pedestrian traffic. The neighborhood was "stiff," respectable, and drab.[11] The streets smelled of petty officialdom, of clerks and bureaucrats in starched clothing. Edouard Fournier remarked of the *quartier*: "It has an odor of the courthouse about it which makes you think you are in some provincial town not far from the Palace of Justice."[12] What a contrast with the elegant shops and flats of the rue Saint-Honoré. What a contrast with the rues de Richelieu and des Petits-Champs, busy commercial streets, housing a heterogeneous population of artisans and bourgeois, of tailors and liberal professionals.[13] The commercial surge which swept over the Palais-Royal ward under the Empire by-passed the Butte des Moulins. Working-class and petit-bourgeois neighborhoods survived, vestiges of *vieux Paris* isolated amidst the rush and roar of downtown Paris.

East of the rue de Richelieu, however, the progress of commercialization went unchecked. The Palais-Royal, of

[10] See Lottin, p. 11, for a description of the Butte.
[11] Fournier, *op. cit.*, p. 26; Daudet, *Paris vécu*, p. 80.
[12] Fournier, *op. cit.*, p. 26.
[13] Daumard, *Maisons de Paris*, p. 108.

course, was already well established as a center of shopping and exchange, long before Haussmannization. For night life and entertainment, "the palace of jewels and diamonds," had no equal. Nowhere in the world, claimed one booster, could be found "side by side such an accumulation of riches."[14]

The pace of commercial life, however, was far more feverish in neighboring streets. Commercial traffic clogged the rue des Petits-Champs, causing a perpetual jam exasperating to pedestrians as much as to coachmen and carters.[15] Textile firms which had migrated from the rue Saint-Denis, as we have seen, colonized the rue Croix-des-Petits-Champs and the Place des Victoires. As for the rue Saint-Honoré, it was no less active at this end of the *quartier* than in the west. But here, there were no elegant shops catering to the *bon ton*. Rows of wooden booths selling knick-knacks and bric-à-brac thronged the sidewalks. The buildings housed, not bourgeois, but a teeming population of artisans—shoemakers, framers, tailors—piled into "unspeakable lodgings where the sun rarely shines, save for a shaft of light that creeps into some courtyard, itself little better than a foul well into which kitchen waters have been discharged."[16] In the east end of the Palais-Royal ward, all was commerce and industry, and not just on the main thoroughfares.

The spacious and handsome mansions in the vicinity of the Palais-Royal, relics of the *quartier*'s aristocratic past, were converted for business use under the Empire. The venerable rue Montesquieu, the rue des Bons-Enfants and the Cour des Fontaines were buried under a mudslide of vulgar commerce. So it appeared to Fournier who lamented the passing of the area's great *hôtels*: "All, in effect, have been destroyed or metamorphosed; they have suffered the same fate as the *quartier*,

[14] A. du Perron, "Le Palais-Royal," *Le Premier Arrondissement*, 27 October 1889.

[15] Lazare, *Les Quartiers pauvres de Paris*, p. 21.

[16] R. Hénard, *La Rue Saint-Honoré*, vol. II, p. 379.

which, once aristocratic, is now industrial and mercantile; they have been replaced by some tall building penetrated by *l'esprit de boutique* from the sidewalk to the eaves; or else, what is no less a profanation, they have surrendered the remainder of their vast galleries to counting-houses and stores."[17]

The Palais-Royal ward, with its odd assortment of neighborhoods and trades appealed to a *flâneur* like Fournier who unashamedly preferred *"le pittoresque au confortable."*[18] To the planner's eye, however, the *quartier* was overcrowded and congested. The Butte des Moulins was a slum without light or air whose "filthy alleys dishonor the center of Paris."[19] The ward's narrow streets, moreover, were inadequate to cope with the mounting volume of traffic. Completion of the rue de Rivoli relieved some of the pressure on the major transverse arteries, the rue Saint-Honoré and the rue des Petit-Champs,[20] but traffic moving north-south was virtually confined to a single street, the rue de Richelieu. To improve circulation and at the same time eliminate an unsightly slum, the baron Haussmann planned construction of a major new thoroughfare, to cut right through the Butte des Moulins, linking the boulevard des Capucines to the Place du Théâtre Français. The new street was to bear the Emperor's name, the avenue Napoléon.

Work on the project, begun in 1866, moved slowly. At the outbreak of the war with Prussia, only seven buildings in all had been erected. For five years, construction was suspended, until the republican government threw its full weight behind Haussmann's scheme. In under two years, 37,000 square meters of terrain were expropriated, sixty-eight buildings demolished, and a spanking new avenue laid out, at an

[17] Fournier, *op. cit.*, pp. 28, 35–36.

[18] *Ibid.*, p. 54.

[19] Cited from an 1870 petition voted by the *Corps législatif*, urging completion of the avenue de l'Opéra. See Daumard, "L'avenue de l'Opéra," p. 161.

[20] Fournier, *op. cit.*, p. 56.

expense to the taxpayer of thirty million francs. The street, rechristened the avenue de l'Opéra, was inaugurated in September of 1877.

Critics and boosters alike predicted a brilliant commercial future for the Opéra, and their expectations were not disappointed.[21] Luxury retailers snapped up the roomy and well-fitted storefronts that lined the new avenue. Clothing boutiques, delicacy shops and art galleries proliferated. Opéra shops catered to persons of refined and expensive tastes, to a moneyed clientele who fancied antiques and Gallé lamps, fine art and *chinoiserie*. Commercial activity, of course, was not confined to the ground floor. Tailors and couturieres rented out showrooms upstairs. Commissionnaires and wholesale agents, doctors and lawyers maintained offices. As for corporate enterprise, it was an ever-expanding presence as apartment houses along the avenue were increasingly claimed for office space. From 1885 to 1914, the number of financial institutions on the street edged up from seven to ten; the number of insurance companies more than doubled, from five to eleven.[22] To be sure, business did not monopolize the Opéra, but its predominance was incontestable, manifest even in the complexion of the new avenue's relatively small residential population. The luxury flats of the Opéra housed neither aristocrats nor functionaries. Rentiers there were, but it was the successful businessman, the textile magnate and the grain merchant who enjoyed pride of place.[23]

As a commercial thoroughfare and traffic artery, the Opéra

[21] Doctor Moura, *La Butte des Moulins*, p. 24; *L'Estaffette*, 16 October 1876, cited in Daumard, "L'avenue de l'Opéra," p. 167.

[22] Daumard, "L'avenue de l'Opéra," p. 175. Daumard's figures refer to the number of *patentables* along the entire length of the avenue de l'Opéra and not just on that portion contained in the Palais-Royal ward.

[23] The story of the avenue de l'Opéra's construction and subsequent evolution is admirably recounted in Daumard, "L'avenue de l'Opéra," pp. 172–181.

The Rue des Moulins around 1866

The Avenue de l'Opéra in 1908

equaled, even surpassed the *grands boulevards*. It was lacking in cultural amenities, in cafés and theaters, but for window-shoppers and businessmen the new avenue was scarcely distinguishable from its more time-honored rivals. An illustrated guidebook to the splendors of downtown Paris, published in the 1880s, naturally featured drawings of the boulevards but included as well fold-outs of the rue de la Paix and the avenue de l'Opéra.[24] The Opéra was constructed as an extension to the Haussmannic boulevard system; it quickly established its reputation as a brilliant addition to the city's refurbished downtown area. And the Opéra looked its part.

With its "generous and uniform proportions," its rectilineal construction, its monumental vista terminating in Garnier's neobaroque Opera House, the new avenue was the very embodiment of Haussmannic aesthetic values, the "ultimate and supreme expression of progress."[25] The contrast with the old Butte des Moulins, razed to make way for the Opéra, could not have been more brutal. New Paris steam-rollered over the remains of the old city, tearing open the Palais-Royal ward and utterly transforming the life of the *quartier* in the process.

Urban renewal destroyed the working-class character of the ward's west end. The streets of the Butte des Moulins, if not leveled as the rues Moineaux, Orties and l'Evêque, were drastically amputated. The thrust of the Opéra through the Butte lopped off stretches of the rues des Moulins, Ventadour and Thérèse. The rue Argenteuil survived intact; it was even upgraded by widening, but the improvements pushed up rents to the prejudice of low-income tenants.[26] The new housing in the neighborhood, luxury flats on the rue des Pyramides and the avenue de l'Opéra, was simply beyond the means of

[24] *Les Boulevards. L'avenue de l'Opéra et la rue de la Paix.* A copy of this illustrated guidebook can be found in the BHVP.

[25] R. Hénard, vol. II, p. 541.

[26] Daumard, *Maisons de Paris*, p. 154.

displaced Butte residents. A shoemaker or piece-rate tailor could handle rents in the 400–600 franc range, but he could not afford, even remotely, the prices charged for Opéra flats which let for 3,500 francs on the average.[27] For the poor and working class, Haussmannization meant demolished and truncated streets, scarce and expensive housing. It meant homelessness and ultimately emigration in search of a more hospitable neighborhood.

The construction of the Opéra drained the Palais-Royal ward of population. In 1875, 4,490 residents were registered to vote, only 3,086 ten years later.[28] The Butte des Moulins neighborhood sustained the heaviest losses. The Palais-Royal ward can be divided into three sets of streets: (1) streets west of the rue de Richelieu (essentially the Butte des Moulins); (2) streets east of the rue de Richelieu (the Palais-Royal area); (3) major transverse and lateral arteries (the rues des Petits-Champs, de Rivoli, Saint-Honoré, and de Richelieu). In 1875, west-end streets housed a preponderance of the *quartier*'s population; 47.11 percent of registered voters lived on or near the Butte des Moulins as against 27.08 percent living east of the rue de Richelieu and 25.81 percent along the ward's major traffic arteries. Ten years later, a new residential topography had emerged. The Palais-Royal area and major through streets had lost approximately 100 voters each; the Butte des Moulins' total had tumbled by nearly 1,200 from 2,115 to 929 (see Table 8).

The evisceration of the Butte des Moulins radically altered the social balance of the Palais-Royal ward. A *quartier* once heavily dominated by the trades, in particular the clothing trades, became increasingly bourgeois. Developing evidence to substantiate this generalization poses problems. Electoral

[27] Daumard, "L'avenue de l'Opéra," p. 178.

[28] All statistics on the voting population of the Palais-Royal ward have been drawn from: AS D₁M², *Premier Arrondissement, Listes électorales*, 1875, 1885, 1895.

TABLE 8. Distribution of Registered Voters in
the Palais-Royal Ward, 1875–1895

Year	East-end streets	(% of Total)	West-end streets	(% of Total)	Transverse and lateral arteries	(% of Total)	TOTAL
1875	1,216	27.08	2,115	47.11	1,159	25.81	4,490
1885	1,118	36.23	929	30.10	1,039	33.67	3,086
1895	1,062	34.60	968	31.54	1,039	33.86	3,069

SOURCE: AS D_1M^2, *Premier Arrondissement, Listes électorales* for 1875, 1885, 1895

lists do not permit a complete breakdown of population along class lines. Liberal professionals, rentiers and middlemen can safely be categorized as bourgeois; employees, white-collar workers and civil servants as lower middle class. At the other end of the scale, it is certainly fair to characterize boy labor, day labor and skilled labor (blacksmiths, tinsmiths, turners and the like) as working class. In between, however, in the murky social region I have labeled the trades, distinctions are harder to make. *Patrons* and *ouvriers* are not clearly distinguished in all instances. Is a "jeweler" bourgeois or proletarian? It cannot be known whether he owns a jewelry store, runs a workshop or earns his living as a simple craftsman. But the trades can at least be broken down by sector: luxury goods, clothing, food, furniture and construction to name the most important. If the voting population is classified along these lines, the professions and strata hardest hit by urban renewal can be pinpointed with some precision.

There can be no mistaking that the trades were the principal victims of Haussmannization. (For the social composition of the voting population in the Palais-Royal ward, see Table 9). The number of voters employed in all trades plunged

TABLE 9. Social Composition of the Voting Population
in the Palais-Royal Ward, 1875–1895

	Liberal profs.	Rentier/ proprietor	BOURGEOISIE Entre- preneur	Middleman	Wholesaler	SUBTOTAL
1875	254	129	12	87	60	542
1885	240	71	37	49	88	485
1895	243	65	24	60	117	509

	Employee	LOWER MIDDLE CLASS Other white- collar	Civil servant	Policeman	Concierge	SUBTOTAL
1875	664	91	132	16	155	1,058
1885	580	46	49	42	99	1,301
1895	518	51	65	50	94	1,287

	Jewelry	Watches	LUXURY TRADES Gilding/ engraving	Articles de Paris	Leather goods	Flowers & feathers	SUB- TOTAL
1875	178	51	50	44	8	15	346
1885	171	38	44	21	5	8	287
1895	140	34	40	21	8	11	254

TABLE 9. Social Composition of the Voting Population
in the Palais-Royal Ward, 1875–1895 (*Continued*)

| | | CLOTHING TRADES | | | | | |
	Drapery	Shoes	Hats	Ready-to-wear goods	Tailoring	Other	SUBTOTAL
1875	35	140	30	16	467	57	745
1885	10	61	21	10	230	37	369
1895	6	50	13	5	214	29	317

| | | OTHER TRADES | | | | |
	Notions	Toilette	Household goods	Home furnishings	Printing	Books
1875	46	13	83	29	50	48
1885	34	6	30	11	36	37
1895	30	8	23	13	25	30

	Food	Services	Mil. equip./ instruments	Building	Raw mats.	SUBTOTAL
1875	384	67	18	164	26	928
1885	230	44	14	75	9	526
1895	243	42	10	77	9	510

| | | WORKING CLASS | | | |
	Boy labor	Day labor	Skilled labor	Domestic service	SUBTOTAL
1875	277	27	137	45	486
1885	183	16	67	33	299
1895	193	14	61	39	307

	Soldier	Student	Artist	No prof.	Retired
		MARGINALS			
1875	128	32	38	16	27
1885	88	51	15	8	24
1895	183	43	13	32	22

	Cleric	Misc.	SUBTOTAL	TOTAL
1875	28	116	385	4,490
1885	19	99	304	3,086
1895	10	91	394	3,069

SOURCE: AS D_1M^2, *Premier Arrondissement, Listes électorales* for 1875, 1885, 1895

dramatically in the brief span of ten years, falling from 2,019 in 1875 to 1,081 in 1885. Luxury goods, with the exception of *articles de Paris*, withstood the impact of urban change with a minimum of damage, but no other sector fared as well. For food-and-drink men, shrinking population meant a tighter market and an inevitable contraction in employment. Completion of the Opéra cut the bottom out of the construction business. The fall-off in home furnishings and furniture was equally drastic, but the clothing trades, given their weight and importance in the local economy, sustained by far the heaviest losses. The number of voters employed in this sector tumbled in a decade from 745 to 369. The drop was most precipitate among tailors (467 to 230), shoemakers (140 to 61) and drapers (35 to 10). The ward as a whole was of course losing population, but the rate of decline in the trades far exceeded that of the *quartier*. In 1875, nearly 45 percent of registered voters had earned their living in the trades; in 1885, only 38.32 percent. Construction of the Opéra was a disaster for cabinetmakers and cobblers, for tailors and stonecutters. Bourgeois, however, weathered the storms of Haussmannization in fine shape. The number of liberal professionals in the *quartier* shrank imperceptibly. Rentiers and middlemen dwindled in numbers, but these losses were compensated by the growing importance of entrepreneurial types, managers and wholesale merchants. Indeed, bourgeois life in the *quartier* was undergoing a subtle, internal transformation. The business-man, representative of a more energetic, muscular capitalism, replaced coupon-clippers and commissionnaires as the ward's typical middle-class resident. While the trades declined as a percentage of the total resident population, the bourgeoisie increased its representation form 12.07 to 15.72 percent.

Lower middle-class occupations registered a similar rise from 23.56 to 26.44 percent. In absolute numbers, to be sure, the ward's white-collar population declined. Civil servants, in particular, were affected. But in spite of losses, the *quartier*'s lower middle-class contingent improved its relative position. It shrank much less rapidly than other categories of resident, owing in large part to the staying power of the employee class and to a significant expansion of the resident police force. The embourgeoisement of the *quartier* can even be detected in the changing composition of the working-class population. All working-class categories registered a drop in numbers from 1875 to 1885, but the decline was most marked among day and skilled laborers. Domestics, errand boys, *garçons de café* and the like held their own. In a *quartier* increasingly domi-nated by bourgeois, work in an office, restaurant or house-hold was relatively plentiful. In the old ward, it was the *pro-priétaire* or commissionnaire who had topped the social hierarchy, with tradesmen a rung below and skilled laborers at the bottom. The social structure of the new quartier du Palais-Royal accorded pride of place to the businessman, the employee next and the office boy last of all.

Haussmannization was the catalyst for these transforma-tions. Residential life in the ward's east end, undisturbed by demolitions, remained numerically and socially stable. It was in the west end, site of the new avenue de l'Opéra, that the most marked changes occurred. The percentage of bourgeois among the local population nearly doubled. The numbers of voters who earned a living in the trades was slashed from 975 to 284 (see Table 10). Haussmannization delivered a crushing blow to the old Butte des Moulins. Just how devastating the blow was can be seen in a comparison of the Opéra's residential population (Table 11) with that of the three streets—the rues Moineaux, Orties and l'Evêque—utterly razed to make way for the new avenue (Table 12). The poll-book of 1875 indicates that one resident in four on the old Butte des Moulins had been a tailor or shoemaker. The trades and working-class population combined had accounted for 60 percent of all registered voters. What became of these people? They certainly did not move to the Opéra. In 1885, this "masterwork in town-planning" housed 177 voters, less than half as many as the former streets of the Butte. And these 177 were overwhelmingly middle class. Twenty-nine percent can be classified as bourgeois, twenty-five percent as petit bourgeois. Haussmannization altered the internal balance of the ward. The east remained what it had been since mid-century, a busy center of commercial activity. The west, however, underwent a shattering metamorphosis. Once a labyrinth of heavily populated, residential streets, it became a comfortable haven for wealthy bourgeois. Population was considerably thinned out in the process. The Opéra neighborhood lost much of its residential flavor as local life increasingly assumed a business orientation.

The imprint left by Haussmannization was as indelible as it was profound. The social structure of residence in the *quartier* did not change significantly in the ensuing decade from 1885 to 1895. Indeed, the Palais-Royal in the late nineteenth century probably bears a stronger resemblance to the ward of today than to the old *quartier* of the 1870s, as yet untouched by Haussmannization.

The Opéra's impact on local commercial life is much more

TABLE 10. Geographic Distribution of the Voting Population in the Palais-Royal Ward, 1875–1885

	Bourgeoisie (%)	Lower middle class (%)	Luxury trades (%)	Clothing trades (%)	Other trades (%)	Working class (%)	Other (%)	TOTAL
EAST END								
1875	127(10.45)	303(24.92)	139(11.43)	156(12.83)	224(18.42)	172(14.15)	103(8.47)	1,216
1885	134(11.99)	315(28.18)	146(13.06)	108(9.66)	188(16.82)	126(11.27)	101(9.03)	1,118
WEST END								
1875	237(11.21)	485(22.93)	131(6.19)	385(18.20)	459(21.70)	220(10.40)	190(8.98)	2,115
1885	195(20.99)	245(26.37)	65(7.00)	84(9.04)	135(14.53)	99(10.66)	109(11.73)	929
TRANSVERSE AND LATERAL ARTERIES								
1875	178(15.36)	270(23.30)	76(6.56)	204(17.60)	245(21.14)	94(8.11)	92(7.94)	1,159
1885	156(15.02)	256(24.64)	76(7.34)	177(17.04)	203(19.54)	74(7.12)	97(9.34)	1,039

Crisis of the Palais-Royal

TABLE 11. Social Composition of the Voting Population on
the Avenue de l'Opéra, 1875–1895

	Liberal profs.	Rentier/ proprietor	Entre- preneur	Middleman	Wholesaler	SUBTOTAL
			BOURGEOISIE			
1875	2	1	0	0	0	3
1885	24	15	3	3	8	53
1895	26	11	4	1	16	58

	Employee	Other white- collar	Civil servant	Policeman	Concierge	SUBTOTAL
			LOWER MIDDLE CLASS			
1875	1	0	0	0	2	3
1885	21	5	1	0	18	45
1895	20	5	3	0	11	39

	Jewelry	Watches	Gilding/ engraving	Articles de Paris	Leather goods	Flowers & feathers	SUB- TOTAL
				LUXURY TRADES			
1875	0	0	0	0	0	0	0
1885	6	2	0	3	0	1	12
1895	4	0	0	1	0	0	5

TABLE 11. Social Composition of the Voting Population on
the Avenue de l'Opéra, 1875–1895 (*Continued*)

CLOTHING TRADES

	Drapery	Shoes	Hats	Ready-to-wear goods	Tailoring	Other	SUBTOTAL
1875	0	0	0	2	0	0	2
1885	0	0	1	1	7	3	12
1895	1	0	0	0	7	0	8

OTHER TRADES

	Notions	Toilette	Household goods	Home furnishings	Printing	Books
1875	0	0	0	0	0	1
1885	0	1	0	0	0	1
1895	0	5	0	0	0	0

	Food	Services	Mil. equip./ instruments	Building	Raw mats.	SUBTOTAL
1875	0	0	0	0	0	0
1885	5	0	2	0	0	9
1895	2	2	4	0	0	18

WORKING CLASS

	Boy labor	Day labor	Skilled labor	Domestic service	SUBTOTAL
1875	0	0	2	3	5
1885	14	0	4	6	24
1895	14	0	3	5	22

| | MARGINALS | | | |
	Soldier	Student	Artist	No prof.	Retired
1875	0	0	1	0	1
1885	4	10	0	1	4
1895	18	6	1	6	3

	Cleric	Misc.	SUBTOTAL	TOTAL
1875	0	0	2	16
1885	0	3	22	177
1895	0	1	35	185

SOURCE: AS D_1M^2, *Premier Arrondissement, Listes électorales* for 1875, 1885, 1895

TABLE 12. Social Composition of the Voting Population on the Rues Moineaux, Orties and l'Evêque, 1875

| | BOURGEOISIE | | | | | |
	Liberal profs.	Rentier/ proprietor	Entre- preneur	Middleman	Wholesaler	SUBTOTAL
1875	10	2	0	4	2	18

| | LOWER MIDDLE CLASS | | | | | |
	Employee	Other white- collar	Civil servant	Policeman	Concierge	SUBTOTAL
1875	94	6	12	5	8	125

TABLE 12. Social Composition of the Voting Population on the Rues Moineaux, Orties and l'Evêque, 1875 (*Continued*)

LUXURY TRADES

	Jewelry	Watches	Gilding/ engraving	Articles *de Paris*	Leather goods	Flowers & feathers	SUB-TOTAL
1875	1	9	4	0	4	0	18

CLOTHING TRADES

	Drapery	Shoes	Hats	Ready-to-wear goods	Tailoring	Other	SUBTOTAL
1875	0	27	2	1	76	3	109

OTHER TRADES

	Notions	Toilette	Household goods	Home furnishings	Printing	Books
1875	6	0	11	1	1	1

	Food	Services	Mil. equip./ instruments	Building	Raw mats.	SUBTOTAL
1875	39	5	0	24	3	91

WORKING CLASS

	Boy labor	Day labor	Skilled labor	Domestic service	SUBTOTAL
1875	24	2	24	1	51

	MARGINALS			
Soldier	Student	Artist	No prof.	Retired
1875				
14	0	1	1	2

	Cleric	Misc.	SUBTOTAL	TOTAL
1875	0	5	23	435

SOURCE: AS D_1M^2, *Premier Arrondissement, Liste électorale* for 1875

difficult to gauge for want of *patente* information prior to 1885. This much is certain: the new avenue quickly established its position as the principal business artery of the ward. In 1885, the Opéra and rue des Pyramides together accounted for more than half of the ward's large-scale enterprises, nearly one-quarter of its liberal professionals and over a fifth of its *articles de Paris* retailers.[29] A shopper in search of curios or fine jade might still try the rue de Rivoli first, but if one had business with the notary, financial problems or just bad teeth, the Opéra and environs were the place to go. What a change from the wineshops and pushcarts of the old Butte des Moulins. To know the meaning of Haussmannization, of the transition from *vieux Paris* to *Paris nouveau*, Palais-Royal residents did not have to look far. Urban renewal flattened the mom-and-pop stores of the *quartier*'s old west end. A new commercial world was built on the rubble, a world dominated by big business, big banks and insurance companies. But there was more to the commercial life of the old ward than the local trade which had once flourished on the Butte. The *quartier* boasted, after all, several of Paris' smartest shopping streets and, of course, the still magnificent Palais-Royal. Haussmannization brought

---

[29] Sixteen of 33 large-scale enterprises, 37 of 151 liberal professionals, and 20 of 90 dealers in *articles de Paris*.

ruin to the humble boutiques of the Butte; how did it affect the ward's long-established luxury trade?

The new Opéra, outfitted with a splendid array of shop-fronts and bustling with pedestrians, inevitably drew trade away from the *quartier*'s older commercial areas. The nearby rue Saint-Honoré, it is true, benefitted from the overflow of activity generated by the Opéra, but other streets were hard pressed.[30] Business slackened noticeably on the rue de Rivoli.[31] The loudest complaints, however, originated from disgruntled Palais-Royal residents. "Construction of the avenue de l'Opéra," one wrote, "has struck the Palais-Royal a definite blow."[32] Outsiders as well—Eugène Hénard and Ernest Levallois—remarked on the connection between the fading fortunes of the Palace and completion of the Opéra.[33] In 1879, on the initiative of Gustave Sandoz, a one-time student of Breguet and a jeweler of world-wide reputation, local merchants formed the *Syndicat du Palais-Royal* in the interests of "restoring the Palace to its former vogue."[34] The *Syndicat* organized evening and afternoon concerts to attract visitors. Night-time security was tightened and lighting facilities improved with installation of electric in place of gas lamps. But the crowds never materialized, and businesses began to move elsewhere. The Café de la Rotonde, the Palace's best known coffeehouse, closed down in 1884. The tailoring firm, A la Ville d'Amiens, vacated to new premises on the avenue de l'Opéra. The Librairie Dentu moved out en route to the bou-

[30] R. Hénard, vol. II, p. 542.

[31] Evenson, *Paris: A Century of Change*, p. 10.

[32] Un Vieux Locataire du Palais-Royal, "Le Palais-Royal," *Le Premier Arrondissement*, 24 December 1893.

[33] Hénard, *Etudes sur les transformations de Paris*, vol. V, p. 150; Levallois, *Paris propre*, p. 112.

[34] "Le dégagement du Palais-Royal, rapport de M. Gaston Hénard (architecte)," *Bulletin du Palais-Royal*, October 1882.

levard Saint-Michel.[35] As early as 1883, the baron Despatys, municipal councillor of the neighboring Place Vendôme ward, remarked on the commercial exodus from the palace:

> The opening of the avenue de l'Opéra has attracted a part of the luxury trade, principally the jewelry business which used to be the glory of the Palais-Royal. Tourists no longer go there, and business has fallen off to a considerable degree.[36]

The Palais-Royal, however, should not be written off prematurely. In 1883, local merchants still grossed a hefty twenty-five million francs per annum, an enormous sum and proof of the Palace's continuing vitality.[37] Shopfronts in 1880 commanded rents in the five to seven thousand franc range, and there were as yet no vacancies.[38] Businesses left, but replacements could still be found. From 1885 to 1890, the number of taxable enterprises in the Palais-Royal did not shrink. Several restaurants did indeed close their doors, but the jewelry business held firm, the baron Despaty's claim notwithstanding. As for the claim that the Opéra inherited business from a hemorrhaging Palais-Royal, there is no evidence of this, at least not in the first quinquennium for which *patente* registers exist. The Opéra in 1885 boasted a mere seven jewelry stores to the Palais-Royal's sixty-seven. Five years later, the proportion had altered but in the Palace's favor, six to seventy-three. There is no doubt that construction of the Opéra created serious and disturbing problems for the Palace, as evidenced by

[35] Champier and Sandoz, *Le Palais-Royal*, vol. II, p. 188; Jarry, *Les Magasins de nouveautés*, p. 92.

[36] Cited in "Conseil Municpal, séance du 25 juin 1883," *Bulletin du Palais-Royal*, December 1883.

[37] "Assemblée générale du 7 décembre 1883, allocution de M. Gustave Sandoz," *Bulletin du Palais-Royal*, December 1883.

[38] Champier and Sandoz, vol. II, p. 192; Levallois, *op. cit.*, p. 122.

the fevered efforts of the *Syndicat du Palais-Royal* to drum up business. But the Palais-Royal did not collapse.

Haussmannization created a new shopping street, the avenue de l'Opéra, which overshadowed but did not obliterate its rivals. Two shopping districts confronted one another in open and as yet unresolved competition. This was Haussmann's legacy to the Palais-Royal ward as it was to the entire commercial community of central Paris. It was the Great Depression which finally brought the conflict to a head, reducing the city's old shopping district—and the Palais-Royal—to a semideserted backwater.

THE GREAT DEPRESSION

The department store thesis and Haussmannization cannot account for the peculiar rhythm of commercial change in the Palais-Royal ward. The *quartier* and above all the luxury trades were seized by a sudden and precipitous contraction of business in the years 1890–1895. If construction of the Opéra and department store expansion were responsible, surely the breakdown would have occurred at an earlier date, in the late seventies or early eighties. The timing of the crisis is better explained by the Great Depression. The Parisian business community, as we have seen, suffered in the grips of a profound and enduring economic slowdown which persisted into the late 1880s and well beyond in the city's central wards. The commercial disaster which befell the Palais-Royal ward in the early 1890s was a local manifestation of this larger crisis.

Commercial life in the quartier du Palais-Royal revolved around the clothing and luxury trades which together accounted for 779 or 42.85 percent of the ward's taxable enterprises in 1885. These were also the business sectors hardest hit by the end-of-century crisis. One might well expect the depression years to have been particularly painful for the Palais-Royal ward, and indeed they were.

The jewelry stores and workshops of the *quartier* were world renowned. Boucheron, Fontana, Sandoz, Lalique, all maintained businesses locally. Mme. Loisel, in de Maupassant's short story "The Necklace" (1880), turns to a Palais-Royal jeweler in search of a diamond necklace to substitute for the borrowed one she has lost. The item sets her back a staggering thirty-six thousand francs. For elegant and expensive jewelry, the Palais-Royal was still the place to go. In 1885, the manufacture and sale of gems and jewelry occupied over one *patentable* in twelve throughout the ward, 153 in all. By the turn of the century, only 113 firms remained. Lalique had not abandoned the ward, evidently satisfied with his location on the corner of the rue Thérèse and the avenue de l'Opéra. But Boucheron and Fontana had relocated to the rue de la Paix and Place Vendôme. Gustave Sandoz died in 1891. His son and heir, Gustave-Roger, moved the family business to new premises on the rue Royale.[39]

The number of jewelry businesses in the *quartier* declined by 25 percent, but this percentage does not fully convey the disaster which struck the industry. The *patente* registers list jewelry firms under a variety of classifications, from manufacturers to piece workers, from retailers of fine stones to costume jewelers. The structure of the jewelry trade in the Palais-Royal ward can be broken down as shown in Table 13. Clearly, the depression did not affect all levels of the trade with the same intensity. Indeed, for costume jewelers whose numbers nearly doubled, the depression years were a boom time. Major retailers who designed and manufactured their own merchandise (merchant-manufacturers) managed to hold their own, as did stonesetters and cutters at the bottom end of the trade. It was the men in between—piece workers,

---

[39] Champier and Sandoz, vol. II, pp. 193–194.

The Palais-Royal in 1850

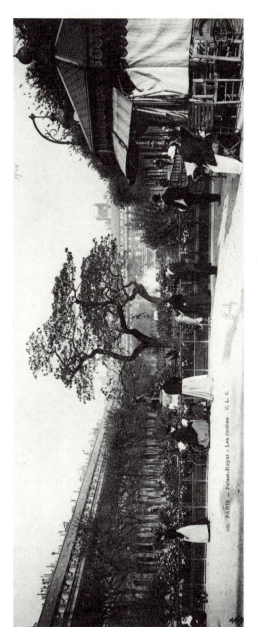

50. PARIS — Palais-Royal — Les Jardins C. L. C.

The Palais-Royal in 1904

TABLE 13. Structure of the Jewelry Trade in
the Palais-Royal Ward, 1885–1900

	1885	1890	1895	1900
Merchant-manufacturer	4	6	7	5
Merchant	58	58	46	35
Manufacturer	38	30	26	25
Piece worker	25	23	18	13
Stone-setter	10	14	6	8
Costume jeweler	14	19	18	26
Other	4	2	1	1
TOTAL	153	152	122	113

SOURCE: AS D^9P^2, *Palais-Royal, Patente* registers for 1885, 1890, 1895, 1900

manufacturers and merchants—who bore the brunt of the crisis. The number of enterprises in these categories was reduced by nearly 40 percent in just fifteen years.

A similar selectivity operated in the clothing trades (Table 14). The custom-goods sector sustained the heaviest casualties. The number of tailors plummeted in fifteen years (1885–1900) from 136 to 92, a drop of nearly one-third. The losses, moreover, were not spread evenly throughout the trade. *Tailleurs à façon* who mended garments or fitted ready-made clothes did not diminish in number. It was the custom-tailor who encountered the greatest difficulties. A *tailleur sur étoffes* sold cloth by the bolt on the premises: a customer made his selection from the tailor's merchandise and was then outfitted with a suit of clothes made to order. A *tailleur sur échantillon*, by contrast, did not stock cloth. He, too, made clothes to order but out of material chosen by the customer from a sample-book and then ordered from a wholesaler. Both categories of

TABLE 14. Structure of the Tailoring Trade in
the Palais-Royal Ward, 1885–1900

	1885	1890	1895	1900
Tailleur à façon	27	26	24	27
Tailleur sur échantillon	53	47	37	35
Tailleur sur étoffes	56	49	44	30
TOTAL	136	122	105	92

SOURCE: AS D^{9}P^2, *Palais-Royal, Patente* registers for 1885, 1890, 1895, 1900

custom-tailor declined in the fin-de-siècle era, from 53 to 35 for *tailleurs sur échantillon*, from 56 to 30 for *tailleurs sur étoffes*.

Custom-made shoes fared no better. The shoe trade was virtually wiped out by the depression (Table 15). At almost every level, numbers fell off sharply. The simple cobbler was eliminated; the number of piece-work shoemakers dropped from 11 to 0. Bespoke shoemakers suffered 65 percent casualties. It did not pay to run a shoe store, but shoe merchants, of all major categories in the trade, experienced the least hardship.

The crisis in custom goods had serious implications for other sectors of the clothing trade (Table 16). In former times, a man in the market for a new suit of clothes went to a tailor who in turn bought from a draper or cloth wholesaler. The tailor's decline meant serious difficulties for the wholesaler of *nouveautés*. In 1885, the *quartier* boasted seven wholesale drapers, twenty-five cloth wholesalers and five cloth retailers. Only sixteen businesses can be counted in 1900. Wholesale firms registered the greatest losses, of 70 percent and 60 percent respectively. In the fin-de-siècle era, the tailor/wholesaler nexus was clearly in crisis.

Not all sectors of the clothing trade, of course, registered

TABLE 15. Structure of the Shoe Trade in
the Palais-Royal Ward, 1885–1900

	1885	1890	1895	1900
Merchant shoemaker	18	15	11	9
Other sales	4	4	3	2
Bespoke shoemaker	20	14	11	7
Piece-work shoemaker	11	2	0	0
Other manufacturer	2	4	4	5
TOTAL	55	39	29	23

SOURCE: AS D⁹P², *Palais-Royal, Patente* registers for 1885, 1890, 1895,
1900

TABLE 16. Structure of the Cloth and Garment Trade in
the Palais-Royal Ward, 1885–1900

	1885	1890	1895	1900
Wholesale draper	7	1	1	2
Cloth wholesaler	25	19	12	10
Cloth retailer	5	1	7	4
Ready-to-wear wholesaler	12	10	10	9
Ready-to-wear retailer	0	0	1	1
Warehouser	1	1	0	2
TOTAL	50	32	31	28

SOURCE: AS D⁹P², *Palais-Royal, Patente* registers for 1885, 1890, 1895,
1900

decline. The overall figures for the hat trade show a slight increase from fifty-four to sixty enterprises. If the trade is subdivided into hatters and milliners, a more nuanced picture emerges. Menswear stands out as a declining sector in contrast to the buoyant growth in ladies' hats. Similarly in the needle trades, tailoring fared worse, far worse, than dressmaking. The number of couturieres remained fairly steady, hovering in the vicinity of ninety while the number of tailors, as we have seen, took a dramatic plunge.

One is inclined to attribute this selectivity to the growing importance of ready-to-wear items in the clothing business. Custom-goods dealers of all kinds were confronted with new difficulties but more so in men's than in women's apparel. The influx of ready-made merchandise did not strip the custom sector in womenswear of its market because of the overwhelming importance of fashion. The market for custom-made menswear, however, was not protected in this way and consequently was vulnerable to the depredations of the *révolution du bon marché*.

The crisis of the 1880s operated selectively. The depression ravaged menswear, jewelry and *articles de Paris* while sparing costume jewelry and women's clothing. The depression's impact on the ward's commercial geography was no less selective. The avenue de l'Opéra and its tributaries, the rue des Pyramides and rue Sainte-Anne, were apparently unaffected. The number of businesses sited on these streets grew from a total of 257 in 1885 to 280 in 1900. The increase in commercial activity was most pronounced along the Opéra. For doctors, dentists and other liberal professionals, the new avenue was a choice location, and their numbers multiplied by half in a brief fifteen years (see Table 17). The clothing business, so sickly in other parts of the *quartier*, flourished. The number of shoe stores and *marchands de nouveautés* increased, and even tailors held their own. It is true that the luxury sector registered a decline from 25 to 19 enterprises, but the

TABLE 17. Distribution of *Patentables* on the Avenue de
l'Opéra, 1885–1900

| | BUSINESS AND LIBERAL PROFESSIONALS | | | | |
	Liberal profs.	Stockbroker, discounter, money changer	Middleman	Large-scale enterprises	SUBTOTAL
1885	20	3	4	11	38
1890	22	4	5	8	39
1895	32	4	2	10	48
1900	30	3	4	6	43

| | LUXURY TRADES | | | | | |
	Jewelry	Watches	Gilding/ engraving	*Articles de Paris*	Leather goods	Flowers & feathers	SUB-TOTAL
1885	7	0	0	14	3	1	25
1890	6	0	0	7	3	2	18
1895	4	0	0	7	3	0	14
1900	7	1	1	7	3	0	19

| | CLOTHING TRADES | | | | |
	Nouveautés, cloth & garment wholesaling	Shoes (manu.)	Shoes (sales)	Clothing (manu.)	Clothing (sales)
1885	0	0	0	0	1
1890	1	0	1	0	3
1895	3	0	1	0	0
1900	3	1	3	0	4

	Lingerie	Dressmaking	Tailoring	Men's hats	Women's hats	SUBTOTAL
1885	1	8	9	0	2	21
1890	1	7	7	0	5	25
1895	1	6	10	0	11	32
1900	0	8	9	0	10	38

OTHER TRADES

	Notions	Toilette	Household goods	Home furnishings	Printing	Books
1885	0	6	3	3	0	3
1890	1	4	6	3	0	3
1895	0	6	5	4	0	2
1900	0	4	2	3	1	4

	Cards/ paints	Food	Ser- vices	Mil. equip./ instruments	Packing	Building	Raw mats.	SUB- TOTAL
1885	0	13	2	2	0	1	1	34
1890	0	9	2	3	0	4	1	36
1895	0	11	1	3	0	2	2	36
1900	1	11	1	3	0	1	1	32

MISCELLANEOUS

	Stall keeper	Other	SUBTOTAL	TOTAL
1885	0	2	2	120
1890	0	1	1	119
1895	0	3	3	133
1900	0	3	3	135

SOURCE: AS D^9P^2, *Palais-Royal, Patente* registers for 1885, 1890, 1895, 1900

slump was confined to *articles de Paris*. The jewelry trade escaped without casualty although in the ward as a whole, the jewelry business was in serious trouble. The crisis seemed to pass over the Opéra and neighboring streets.

Elsewhere in the ward, however, the impact of the depression was crushing. In 1888, a shopkeeper newspaper, the *Crise commerciale*, reported on a rash of vacancies along the rue Croix-des-Petits-Champs; 17 boutiques closed, 52 industrial rentals vacant, "that's what I've seen in a street that counts 55 house numbers . . . one of the most commercial in Paris."[40] In 1885, 4 businesses on the Place des Victoires had specialized in *nouveautés* and garment wholesaling, 5 on the rue Baillif and 8 on the rue des Bons-Enfants. In 1890, the figures were 1, 1 and 4 respectively. But the collapse of the clothing business in the ward took its heaviest toll on the streets in the vicinity of the Palais-Royal: the rue and Place Valois, the rue des Petits-Champs and the rue de Richelieu. In 1885, this area accounted for just under half of the shoes businesses in the *quartier*, 26 out of 55. Only 12 firms remained in business fifteen years later. The crisis in the tailoring trade was particularly telling on the rue des Petits-Champs and the rue de Richelieu. The number of tailors on the Petits-Champs dropped from 21 to 12. The situation on the rue de Richelieu was slightly more complicated.

The needle trades represented a substantial percentage of taxable enterprises on the street, nearly one in four. This proportion remained constant through the turn of the century, but one should not be misled by an appearance of stability. If the category of needlework is broken down into dressmaking and tailoring, it becomes apparent that tailors at the end of the century fared much worse than couturieres. In 1885, three-fourths of all *patentables* in the needle trades worked in men's clothing. The proportion had slid to two-thirds in 1900.

---

[40] E. Berry, "Aux propriétaires," *La Crise commerciale*, 15 March 1888.

TABLE 18. Structure of the Needle Trades on
the Rue de Richelieu, 1885–1900

	1885	1890	1895	1900
Tailleur à façon	2	4	5	8
Tailleur sur échantillon	18	17	16	14
Tailleur sur étoffes	25	27	20	13
Subtotal	45	48	41	35
Dressmaker	17	17	17	19
TOTAL	62	65	58	54

SOURCE: AS D^9P^2, *Palais-Royal, Patente* registers for 1885, 1890, 1895, 1900

The actual number of tailors dropped from 45 to 35, perhaps not a cataclysmic fall-off, but the blow to the trade was heavier than these figures reveal (see Table 18). *Tailleurs sur étoffes* who occupied the highest and most prestigious position on the professional hierarchy suffered a disastrous decline. Their numbers were nearly halved, dropping from twenty-five to thirteen. The middle ranks of the trade, *tailleurs sur échantillon*, took fewer losses, and the men at the bottom, *tailleurs à façon*, actually quadrupled in numbers from two to eight. The tailoring trade on the rue de Richelieu was shrinking and of equal importance, it was increasingly dominated by piece workers working out of fourth- and fifth-floor apartments, men whose wealth and status scarcely exceeded those of the proletarian.

The commercial decay which set in in the vicinity of the Palais-Royal was as nothing compared to the problems of the Palace itself. The restaurants were the first to leave. From 1885 to 1900, the number of dining establishments in the Palace declined from 15 to 8. The jewelry stores which had sus-

TABLE 19. Distribution of *Patentables* in the Palais-Royal, 1885–1900

	BUSINESS AND LIBERAL PROFESSIONALS				
	Liberal profs.	Stockbroker, discounter, money-changer	Middleman	Large-scale enterprises	SUBTOTAL
1885	4	5	2	0	11
1890	6	5	2	0	13
1895	4	3	4	0	11
1900	4	2	2	1	9

	LUXURY TRADES						
	Jewelry	Watches	Gilding/ engraving	Articles de *Paris*	Leather goods	Flowers & feathers	SUB-TOTAL
1885	67	6	4	23	0	0	100
1890	73	8	2	25	0	0	108
1895	56	7	2	15	0	0	80
1900	46	2	3	23	0	0	74

	CLOTHING TRADES				
	Nouveautés, cloth & garment wholesaling	Shoes (manu.)	Shoes (sales)	Clothing (manu.)	Clothing (sales)
1885	0	1	1	0	2
1890	0	1	1	0	1
1895	0	1	0	0	1
1900	0	0	0	0	2

Crisis of the Palais-Royal

	Lingerie	Dressmaking	Tailoring	Men's hats	Women's hats	SUBTOTAL
1885	1	0	3	1	1	10
1890	1	1	2	1	0	8
1895	0	1	1	0	1	5
1900	0	1	1	0	1	5

OTHER TRADES

	Notions	Toilette	Household goods	Home furnishings	Printing	Books
1885	0	4	1	0	1	6
1890	0	3	1	0	0	4
1895	0	3	1	0	0	3
1900	1	3	2	0	1	3

	Cards/ paints	Food	Services	Mil. equip./ instruments	Packing	Building	Raw mats.	SUB-TOTAL
1885	2	31	1	7	0	0	0	53
1890	2	28	1	6	0	1	0	46
1895	3	22	2	5	0	0	0	39
1900	2	16	2	5	0	0	0	35

MISCELLANEOUS

	Stall keeper	Other	SUBTOTAL	TOTAL
1885	19	5	24	198
1890	20	5	25	200
1895	17	4	21	156
1900	16	7	23	146

SOURCE: AS D^{9}P^2, *Palais-Royal*, *Patente* registers for 1885, 1890, 1895, 1900

tained the Palace's reputation for over forty years moved out en masse in the early nineties (see Table 19). In 1890, the Palace housed 81 establishments which specialized in the sale of watches and jewelry. This figure had fallen to 48 in 1900. The crowds had just stopped coming; even the tourist trade had been reduced to a trickle. But not all businesses in the Palace suffered. Costume jewelers nearly doubled their numbers, increasing from 10 to 19. Retailers of *la camelote* supplanted the splendid shops of a former epoch, and with the new commerce came a new clientele. Bon vivants, men of letters and wealthy tourists were displaced by stamp collectors and "the newly decorated" come to purchase a medal or "button-hole ribbon."[41] The prostitutes and bankers who had populated the arcades in Balzac's day were long gone. The Palais-Royal in the nineties belonged to lovers of military music drawn by the afternoon concerts, but, above all, to children and their nursemaids who appreciated the relative calm which prevailed throughout most of the day.[42] Turn-of-the-century observers who could still remember something of the Palais-Royal's former glory bemoaned the loss of a familiar stamping ground. The Palace, once the focal point of Parisian life, had become another Place des Vosges, a desert, a necropolis.[43]

The depression of the eighties shattered the commercial community of the Palais-Royal ward. Along the Opéra business continued unabated by crisis, but to the east, in and around the Palais-Royal, trade stagnated and showed no signs of imminent recovery. The polarization of local life generated powerful feelings of resentment. The Louvre and Gagne-Petit, expansive and successful in the midst of depression, were natural targets for such feelings. If the Palais-Royal was going

[41] De Lannoy, *Les Plaisirs et la vie de Paris*, p. 15.

[42] Champier and Sandoz, vol. II, p. 114.

[43] *Le Petit Journal* cited in *La Revendication*, 25 October 1888; de Lannoy, p. 15; Deverin, *La Résurrection du Palais-Royal*, p. 7; Levallois, *op. cit.*, p. 122.

under, residents complained, it was because of "the clamor-
ous competition of those out-sized department stores."[44] "These
tentacled monsters" were sucking "the wealth, the glory, the
very life" out of the Palace.[45] Perhaps, it was suggested, the
crowds would return if the Palais-Royal lifted its prohibition
on gambling and prostitution.[46] But most residents rejected
a compromise with vulgarity:

> The kind of crowds who frequent the rue de Rivoli, that's
> what suits the Palais-Royal best and not the swarm of
> cosmopolitan night owls who "enliven" the boulevard
> Montmartre from sundown.[47]

The Palace was different from the grandiose streets of Haussmannic Paris. Its flowers, plants and dignified galleries were
"a jarring contrast to the banality of rectilinear streets, without freshness and all in stone."[48] Why should the Palais-Royal
destroy its charm and distinctive character by imitating the
coarse practices of the competition? No, what the Palace needed
was a tourist attraction, a spectacle that would attract curi-
osity-seekers and potential customers. Perhaps a sports palace, a zoo or a crystal tower would be just the thing.[49] Perhaps the entire structure could be glassed over and converted
into a greenhouse.[50]

   Urbanists like Henri Deverin and Eugène Hénard advo-

[44]"La destruction du Palais-Royal," *Le Premier Arrondissement*, 5 January
1890.

[45]"Le futur conseil," *Le Premier Arrondissement*, 30 March 1890.

[46]"Discours de M. Wilfrid de Fonvielle," *Bulletin du Palais-Royal*, December 1883.

[47]"Palais-Royal. 'Paris' contre 'Paris,' " *Le Premier Arrondissement*, 26
January 1890.

[48]"Palais-Royal. 'Paris' contre 'Paris,' " *Le Premier Arrondissement*, 26
January 1890.

[49]BHVP CP 3430, *Palais-Royal, Pièces diverses*, 1896, *Mémoire de F. J.
Pillet, ingénieur*; "La Tour de Crystal," *Le Premier Arrondissement*, 27 April
1890.

[50]Lazare, p. 22.

cated more drastic changes. The Palace had faltered because it was out of the way; it was lacking in easy access routes and could not accommodate a large volume of traffic. These problems could be resolved, Deverin believed, if the rue Vivienne were extended through the Palace, intersecting with the rue de Rivoli just in front of the Conseil d'Etat.[51] Hénard favored a yet more ambitious scheme. Central Paris, he argued, was suffocating because of poor circulation. Construction of an "aortic artery right in the heart of the city" would infuse much needed "new blood." This artery was planned to run from east to west along an expanded rue Rambuteau, straight through the Palais-Royal and then smack into the avenue de l'Opéra. Hénard appropriately named his projected avenue, the avenue du Palais-Royal.[52]

In the final decade of the nineteenth century, saving the Palais-Royal had become something of a *cause célèbre*, occupying the minds and imaginations of residents, sympathetic *vieux parisiens* and visionary urbanists. The issue naturally injected itself into local politics. The local municipal councillor was inevitably obliged to promise his full support for any and all projects "tending to facilitate access to the Palais-Royal and to restore to it the public and commercial activity that ought to reign there."[53] In the 1890 municipal elections, a Palace jeweler was moved to enter the race and challenge an incumbent deemed unresponsive to local needs. The contest pitted Alfred Hamel a "radical" against Alexis Muzet "of moderate persuasion."[54] Hamel was also a shopkeeper militant and founding member of the *Ligue syndicale* while Muzet

[51] Deverin, *op. cit.*, pp. 2–7. See also Guy Tomel, "Le Palais-Royal," p. 170. This article is a clipping from the *Monde moderne* (1899), and can be found in the BHVP.

[52] E. Hénard, vol. V, pp. 156–178.

[53] From the electoral platform of M. Levée, municipal councillor of the Palais-Royal ward, cited in Ernest Gay, *Nos Ediles, 1904–1908*, p. 42.

[54] "Aux électeurs," *Le Premier Arrondissement*, 27 April 1890.

headed the city's most influential businessmen's association, the *Syndicat général*. Hamel, the challenger, lost, but his candidature was indicative of an emergent split in the local commercial community.[55] Businessmen like Hamel, angered over the declining fortunes of the Palais-Royal and its environs, were increasingly ready to mobilize in opposition to commercial notables and their Opportunist allies, often, as in the case of Muzet, one and the same man.

CONCLUSION

The *Ligue syndicale* scored its greatest successes in neighborhoods like the Palais-Royal ward, polarized by urban and economic transformation. It was not the rise of the department store which fragmented the local commercial community but Haussmannization and the Great Depression. The shopkeeper movement's most fervent recruits were businessmen like Alfred Hamel who had lost from change, men whose present well-being and future prospects had been undermined by changes in commercial geography and the *révolution du bon marché*.

How must the world have appeared to such men? One can imagine how the Palais-Royal jeweler and rue de Richelieu tailor, threatened with bankruptcy, must have interpreted their experience. They knew, or thought they knew, the real meaning of Haussmannization. It meant the triumph of *sociétés anonymes* and art nouveau boutiques with exotic, un-French names like Au Mikado or Bernheim's. It meant the triumph of big business over the old-fashioned tradesman, of the mon-

[55] Hamel managed a fourth-place finish on the first *tour de scrutin* with just under 20 percent of the vote. Muzet finished at the top of the list with 31.5 percent, followed by the Boulangist candidate, Cère, who garnered 24.9 percent. See, E. Gay, p. 43.

umental over the picturesque, of the straight over the crooked. The depression only brought the message home with greater clarity. It was the monopolist, the tentacled bloodsucker retailing bargain-basement merchandise, who profited from hard times. Speculators without taste, purveyors of costume jewelry and *la camelote*, these were the scoundrels who made scandalous fortunes while decent and loyal citizens were unable to make ends meet. And if one had to pick a symbol to represent the vile injustice wrought by urban and economic change, what better symbol than the department store?

This interpretation of events is full of distortions, but it does translate, and with some truth, the lived experience of the Palais-Royal jeweler and the rue de Richelieu tailor. But there is no need to speculate as to the content of shopkeeper consciousness. The *Ligue syndicale* was prodigal in its ideological outpourings. An analysis of its doctrine will help to clarify the peculiar relationship between shopkeeper experience and shopkeeper consciousness. And it will help to clarify a second issue as well.

What, after all, was the precise political orientation of the retailer mobilization of the 1880s? If the *Ligue* was formed in revulsion against urban and economic change, if retailer thinking was riddled with nostalgic yearnings and xenophobic resentments, it would seem reasonable to situate the nascent shopkeeper movement on the reactionary right. Yet how does such a conclusion square with the radicalism of an Alfred Hamel or indeed with the Radical antecedents of the *Ligue syndicale* itself? The retailer movement appears torn between reactionary impulses and Radical commitments. Where then is the *Ligue*'s political center of gravity to be located, on the right or on the left? One avenue of approach to this question lies through an analysis of retailer ideology.

II

...

THE POLITICS
OF SHOPKEEPER
PROTEST

6

. . .

Shopkeeper Republicanism: The Ideology of The *Ligue Syndicale*

SHOPKEEPERS, artisans, disaffected petits bourgeois of every description have been accused of antimodernism, of a dogged and regressive hostility to the values and institutions inevitable in an urban, industrialized world.[1] The origins of antimodernism are most often traced to the end of the century. Western Europe and North America in the 1880s and 1890s did indeed witness a powerful, sometimes spectacular outburst of small-owner protest. Farmers, craftsmen and, of course, shopkeepers (*commerçants*) mobilized en masse against the depredations of an emergent corporate capitalism. But was this movement irredeemably reactionary? Does small-owner discontent translate directly into a politics of reaction as the antimodernist thesis suggests? Or is it possible to imagine a small-owner politics in reaction against urban and economic change, yet at the same time left-wing in its commitment to democratic and social reform? The *Ligue syndicale* presents a handy and challenging opportunity to put such competing claims to the test.

[1] See, for example, Volkov, *The Rise of Popular Anti-Modernism in Germany*, pp. 15ff., and pp. 343–353.

SHOPKEEPER REPUBLICANISM

The *Ligue syndicale*, it must be said straightaway, was emphatically republican, devoted to the principles of '89 and ever ready to invoke the nation's revolutionary heritage. Shopkeepers, of course, interpreted republican values from a self-centered, self-serving perspective. The Le Chapelier law of 1791 had abolished the guilds and corporations of the ancien régime, inaugurating a new era of commercial liberty. Freedom afforded all decent, hard-working patriots the opportunity to make something of themselves, above all to win respectability and earn their independence through accession to the ranks of the propertied.

The forces of privilege, scattered by the Revolution, had begun to regroup in the late nineteenth century. A new feudality, based this time on capital not land, asserted its arrogant power. Modern-day monopolies, "capitalist bastilles" were grim reminders of the military prisons of the ancien régime.[2] A new class of seigneurs was emerging, who, like their forebears, treated the people with high-handed contempt, *"comme espèces taillables et corvéables à merci."*[3] To preserve the Republic, the progress of monopoly had to be arrested, and with what better weapon than specialization? "Everyone," declared Léopold Christophe, "ha[s] the right to practice the métier of his choice and to change jobs if he so pleases . . . but no one has the right to practice MORE THAN ONE MÉTIER."[4] The Revolution had advanced the cause of *morcellement*. This had been its principal objective and achievement.

[2] E. Girard, "14 Juillet," *L'Union démocratique*, 14 July 1888.

[3] Destréguil, *La Crise commerciale et industrielle*, p. 62; E. G., "L'irresponsabilité regrettable," *Journal de la Chambre syndicale de la boucherie*, 14 May 1899.

[4] L. Christophe, "A Monsieur le vte. d'Avenel," *La Revendication*, 15 December 1894.

In demanding specialization, shopkeepers simply demanded that the nation remain true to its revolutionary past.[5]

The notion of *morcellement* was shot through with powerful moral overtones. The Revolution, *ligueurs* firmly believed, had involved not just a redistribution of property but the construction of a new form of community. *Ligue* vice-president Louis Gazon sketched in the outlines of the new society:

> . . . if the hatter does business with her neighbor the shoe merchant, and the shoe merchant reciprocates, then both will make money and be all the more willing to do business with the neighborhood butcher, *charcutier* and wine-seller.
>
> In helping your neighbors to earn a living, you are making customers for yourself and creating an environment of mutual respect.[6]

The local community was conceived as a virtual autarky, self-enclosed and self-sustaining. Money spent at the corner store did not leave the neighborhood but inevitably found its way back into local circulation. A portion of the retailer's gross was reserved to pay overhead costs. The *commerçant* purchased his inventory from an artisan or manufacturer, a businessman much like himself. Both merchant and producer were independents, and relations between the two evolved on a strictly "equal to equal" basis.[7] Overhead expenses paid, the retailer

[5] For the *Ligue*'s version of the French Revolution, see *La Revendication*: La Rédaction, "Programme de *La Revendication*," 5 July 1888; M. L. Christophe, "Quelques lignes historiques," 9 February 1890; G. Fabius, "Les libertés commerciales au XIXe siècle," 24 August 1890. See also E. Girard, "14 Juillet," *L'Union démocratique*, 14 July 1888.

[6] Louis Gazon, "A votre tour, mesdames," *La Revendication*, 31 October 1896; see also "Aux dames de la province," *La Crise commerciale*, 1 November 1889.

[7] F. Pontonnier, "Rapport lu à la Chambre syndicale de la ganterie," *La Revendication*, 28 March 1889; A. T. "Questions économiques," *La Revendication*, 15 August 1893.

pocketed the remainder of his income and entered the marketplace as a customer. He did not reinvest his profits in the interests of expansion but consumed them, and, as consumer, assured the well-being of other local merchants. The innumerable face-to-face transactions which constituted the local economy nurtured powerful feelings of mutual solidarity. Shopkeepers congratulated themselves that the great revolutionary values of liberty, equality, and fraternity were fully realized in their neighborhood life. The *quartier* was autonomous; its leading citizens were independent businessmen, men of roughly equal stature whose unceasing industry generated a climate of mutual esteem and general good will.

The *quartier*, however, was more than an agglomeration of autonomous individuals cemented by exchange and lacquered over with a veneer of fellow-feeling. With his peers, the shopkeeper insisted on perfect reciprocity, according no more respect than he demanded, but not all persons in the local community were peers. The *petit commerçant* was an employer and paterfamilias. He exercised supreme authority over two overlapping and, to his mind, scarcely distinguishable institutions, the workshop and the family. If the shopkeeper was an understanding, even affectionate employer, it was in part because he had once been a wage earner himself. *Ligueurs* never missed an opportunity to invoke their working-class origins.[8] They had come up the hard way and knew what it meant to labor in another man's service. But as their own achievement showed, the status of wage earner was by no means permanent. An employee with patience and a taste for work could hope to get on in the world; every worker was a potential *patron*.[9] The worker's expectations and the shopkeeper's past,

---

[8] *La Revendication*: "Voleurs!," 29 November 1888; "Réunion extraordinaire de la Ligue," 15 December 1893; "2e Réunion extraordinaire de la Ligue," 15–31 March 1894.

[9] *La Revendication*: "Statuts de la Ligue," 23 February 1890; "Elections municipales," 15 April 1893.

ligueurs believed, reduced the social gap which existed between them. An overlay of family feeling defused whatever residual tensions remained. The shopkeeper addressed his employees as "my boys"; he shared his table with them and was even prepared to welcome the ablest into his family as a son-in-law. To the paternal bonhomie of the *patron*, employees were expected to respond with deferential appreciation and filial respect. [10]

If the workshop was a happy family, the family was a supremely efficient production unit. Everyone made a contribution. Sons and sons-in-law were set to learning the trade in preparation for the day they would succeed "papa" or strike out on their own. Wives and daughters were pressed into service, working the cash register, doing accounts or selling merchandise. All performed their allotted tasks under the watchful eye of the *patron*. The superimposition of work relations on family relations did not threaten intimacy. On the contrary, the familiarity and coziness of the hearth spilled over into the shop. An ordered household in the classic, paternalist mold buttressed the structure of authority in the workplace. [11]

The shopkeeper occupied a strategic position in the moral life of the community. His enterprise and authority assured the continued existence of *quartier*, workshop and family. Without him neighborhood life would disintegrate, the Republic crumble, and society sink into anarchy and sexual disorder. Shopkeepers warned that this grim perspective was no distant possibility. Department stores threatened *petits com-*

---

[10] F. Limoge, "Un homme de bien," *Le Commerçant*, 18 March 1882; "Compte-rendu de la séance du 15 nov. 1891," *La Revendication*, 22 November 1891.

[11] In the estimation of one *ligueur*, the family was no less than "the veritable pivot of all organized society." Henri de Vouvray, "Immoralité," *La Revendication*, 18 April 1889.

merçants with extinction. The time had come once again to sound the revolutionary alarm: *La Patrie est en danger.*[12]

DEPARTMENT STORES

The *Ligue syndicale*'s critique of the department store has a familiar ring. *Ligueurs* liberally employed the language of *Gemeinschaft/Gesellschaft* to describe the shopkeeper's struggle against the *grand magasin*. The *quartier*, workshop and family were enlisted on the side of *petit commerce*. The department store was associated with a complex of opposing forces: *sociétés anonymes*, large-scale industry and bureaucracy. But shopkeeper militants were also republicans and interpreted the conflict between community and organization in frankly political terms. The *grand magasin* was an aristocratic device designed to rob the people of their democratic birthright. Organization was the driving wedge of a new feudalism that endangered the communitarian basis of the Republic.

The rise of the *grand magasin*, *ligueurs* protested, sapped the vitality of local life. The big stores were vampires, octopi, manchineels, tentacled monsters ruthlessly draining the life blood from neighborhood markets: "Behind a facade of anonymity they cynically monopolize everything for themselves . . . already they have overrun their neighbors, indeed entire streets; it's a veritable invasion."[13] Shopfronts were vacant, street life withered: "Certain *quartiers* were like a desert; the city is in decay."[14] And the rot, "like an inkspot," was

---

[12] Louis Bréhant, "Pas de politique," *La Crise commerciale*, 15 February 1889.

[13] "La maison des nouveautés," *La Crise commerciale*, 1 October 1887. *La Revendication*: J. Hucbourg, "Un peu de lumière," 6 September 1888; L. Christophe, "A nos amis et à nos ennemis," 26 June 1892. Léon Chartier, "Féodalité moderne," *La Crise commerciale*, 15 July 1888.

[14] The author of this remark, Eugène Delattre, was a deputy and reliable *Ligue* ally. "Un document législatif," *La Revendication*, 25 October 1888.

spreading.[15] Department stores ran full-page ads in the press; kiosks were plastered with their brightly colored posters. *La Revendication* sneered at department stores as "permanent expositions."[16] Who could escape or resist the pervasive and enticing promises of commercial paradise? The *Ligue* hated the puffery of public relations. *La Revendication* accepted advertising only with the greatest reluctance, even from fully paid subscribers.[17] The *Crise commerciale* scorned the kiosk as "the idiot's mirror" and demanded legal action against the poster. The day the public authorities seriously enforced the warning "Post No Bills," "That day . . . we will see no longer those advertisements that steal into our homes, robbing us of our livelihood and taking the bread from our children's mouths."[18] But if, as seemed likely, no steps were taken to brake department store expansion, neighborhood shops were doomed: "Where there had been life, only a necropolis would remain."[19]

The dissolution of the *quartier* condemned the workshop to extinction. In former times, the manufacturer had sold to a myriad of *petits commerçants*, small-scale entrepreneurs much like himself. But now, with the precipitate collapse of petty retailing, department stores were coming to monopolize the market, and they used their power to dictate prices. The *fabricant* had little choice but to submit, and in so doing lost his status as an independent. He became little better than a foreman, his employees little better than serfs.[20] Manufactur-

[15] Bréhant, "Dépopulation," *La Crise commerciale*, 15 April 1889.

[16] "Le droit des pauvres et les expositions du Louvre, Bon Marché, Printemps, etc., etc.," *La Revendication*, 31 July 1893.

[17] "Comptes-rendus," *La Revendication*, 6 September 1888.

[18] Bréhant, "Une idée," *La Crise commerciale*, 1 December 1888.

[19] Rabasse, "La question de l'intermédiaire, *La Revendication*, 12 January 1890.

[20] See the anonymous pamphlet reprinted by Rabasse in *La Revendication*, 26 January 1890.

ers who resisted department store domination were ruthlessly
undercut. Undeterred by patriotic scruples, *grands magasins*
turned to foreign suppliers. As *Ligue* president Léopold
Christophe explained: ". . . in the event a producer refuses
to submit to the conditions set by a department store buyer,
the store will not hesitate to have an imitation of the French
article, so fine, so coquette, made abroad in Belgium, in
Germany."[21] The big stores were downright anti-French,
"antipatriotic," "the Germany of commerce."[22] "These feudalities," concluded the *Union démocratique*, "are in effect cosmopolitan."[23] And what foreigners could not supply, *grands
magasins* were prepared to manufacture for themselves. Their
"industrial pretensions" enraged shopkeepers who accused the
big stores of every conceivable labor abuse.[24] Mendicity and
prostitution awaited the unfortunates who sweated out their
lives in department store workshops. But the *grand magasin*'s
final coup was to eliminate the independent master, the "spe-
cialist worker," entirely. He could be replaced by a machine,
his workshop by a factory. "Capital," shopkeepers argued, "in
its drive for exclusive control, has eliminated the tool-owning
worker who labors at home, transplanting him—and his wife
and children—to gigantic factories and immense stores."[25]

[21] AN C5498, Mesureur Commission, 24 (29?) February 1891.
[22] "Comité de centralisation," *La Revendication*, 24 August 1890; Bréhant, "Quand même," *La Crise commerciale*, 15 January 1888.
[23] A. Girard, "Démocratie et féodalité," *L'Union démocratique*, 11 February 1888.
[24] A. Girard, "Ligue syndicale contre les grands magasins," *L'Union démocratique*, 10 March 1888. On the fate of department store employees,
according to the *Ligue*, see: AN C5498, Mesureur Commission, 6 November 1891; "Réunion extraordinaire de la Ligue," *La Revendication*, 31 March
1895; Léon Chartier, "Différence des temps," *La Crise commerciale*, 15 April
1888.
[25] AN C5498, Mesureur Commission, testimony of the *Chambre syndicale
du commerce de détail et des spécialistes des industries diverses*, 5 June 1891. See
also "Comptes-rendus," *La Revendication*, 20 September 1888; A. T.,
"Questions économiques," *La Revendication*, 15 August 1893.

To the shopkeeper, big commerce and big industry were indivisible. The department store was an agent of machinism; indeed, it was itself constructed in the very image of an immense machine. Employees were numbers or cogs whose movements were regulated "in advance like those of a clock."[26] The proprietor was unknown to his workers; he lived off the premises and was perhaps ignorant of the day-to-day operations of his enterprise. Regimentation and anonymity, these were the dominant features of Paris' great commercial factories. And what kind of future could wage earners look forward to in a world dominated by machines and absentee millionaires? The elimination of the *petit patronat* swelled the ranks of the working class and condemned the growing mass of proletarians to a lifetime of unremitting servitude. The workshop cultivated camaraderie, ambition and initiative. The crushing weight of factory life bred only despair, bitterness and class hatred.

The *grand magasin* poisoned social relations, destroying all bonds of commonality. Even the family, last refuge of moral value, was threatened. The shopkeeper's litany of accusations on this score does not deviate from the commonplaces of the day save in shrillness of tone. The death of family enterprise upset the harmony and hierarchy of domestic life. Imagine father in the factory, mother in the department store, and the children left to fend for themselves. The family gathered together only in the evening and then in a state of exhaustion and general irritability. The consequences were as harsh as they were inevitable: drunkenness, vice, delinquency. It was, of course, working conditions in the department store which most exercised the shopkeeper's lurid imagination. Sales personnel were not allowed to sit; the noise was deafening and the air fetid; and worst of all, men and women in the full vigor of life worked in intimate proximity. The female constitution

---

[26] *La Revendication*: de Vouvray, "Immoralité," 18 April 1889; "Compte-rendu de la séance du 15 nov. 1891," 22 November 1891.

was delicate and inevitably cracked under the strain of department store work. Hysteria and neurosis attacked the mind. Reproductive organs atrophied, and the blood thinned out. The unfortunate shopgirl, too weak-willed to save herself, slid into promiscuity, morphinomania and, eventually, prostitution.[27] The fate of the female customer was no less grim. These poor "daughters of Eve," "hypnotized" by "all the apples of coquetry" so artfully displayed, yielded themselves up to temptation.[28] They developed a wasteful taste for luxury; they bought wildly; they stole. The family budget was ruined, the family honor compromised. What husband would expose his beloved wife, what father his adored daughter, to the moral corruption of the *grand magasin?* The big stores were "ghouls and satyrs which lived on and off of women."[29] They threatened French womanhood with madness and sterility. They threatened the nation with depopulation and decadence.[30] To the *petit commerçant*, bound up in his tightly knit world of work and family, the *grand magasin* symbolized all the perils of emotional release: impotence, disease and insanity.

France's future was gloomy indeed. Factories, warehouses, department stores, barracks, in a word, organization was

[27] De Vouvray, "Insalubrité et danger public," *La Revendication*, 11 April 1889. See also *La Revendication*: de Vouvray, "Charlatanisme," 16 May 1889; Fabius, "Les libertés commerciales au XIXe siècle," 4 May 1890; L. Marot, "Servages de femme," 23 April 1887; V. Bazin, "Employés et employées," *L'Union démocratique*, 18 August 1888.

[28] Anonymous pamphlet reprinted by Rabasse in *La Revendication*, 26 January 1890.

[29] Bréhant, "Aux femmes de France," *La Crise commerciale*, 1 September 1888; Chartier, "Les grands bazars et leur moralité," *La Crise commerciale*, 1 November 1888; de Vouvray, "Contagion," *La Revendication*, 25 April 1889.

[30] De Vouvray, *op. cit.*; "Assemblée générale annuelle et extraordinaire," *La Revendication*, 7 February 1892. The *Ligue*, in a fit of indignation, was moved to pledge its support to Jacques Bertillon's *Alliance nationale pour le relèvement de la population française par l'égalité des familles devant l'impôt. La Revendication*, 31 May 1896.

coming to dominate the national landscape.[31] Every sphere of human activity had been staked out by engulfing institutions, and woe to the unfortunates, the marginals and pariahs who lived beyond the pale of corporate life. Liberal economists like Paul Leroy-Beaulieu and Ernest Brelay might applaud the triumph of *Gesellschaft*. They defended the new "corporate regime"[32] in the name of science and progress, but shopkeepers rejected such arguments.[33] Big business, they feared, was bound to abuse its massive power and conspire to impose monopoly prices. Consumers, dispersed and disorganized, would never be able to protect themselves from the most ruthless exploitation. Worse still, the encroachments of organization meant the growth of bureaucracy. To secure a better future for their offspring, careworn shopkeepers pushed their children into the liberal professions but above all into government service. Bureaucracy mushroomed. The functionary, in shopkeeper mythology, was a grotesque creature, an indolent parasite without enterprise or virility.[34] Desk work softened the brain and sapped a person's energies. This was not progress but atrophy, degeneration and decay.[35]

[31] For the use of the word "barracks" (*caserne* in French), see de Vouvray, "La gare Saint-Lazare," *La Revendication*, 15 November 1888.

[32] Rabasse, "La question de l'intermédiaire," *La Revendication*, 12 January 1890.

[33] This line of argument particularly infuriated shopkeepers. Fayet attacked Leroy-Beaulieu (editor of *L'Economiste français*), Ernest Brelay (also of *L'Economiste français*) and Edmond Demolins in a series of articles in *La Revendication*: "La science sociale et la question des grands magasins," 15 June 1890; "Chiffres et documents," 23 March 1890. Christophe took on the vicomte d'Avenel: "A Monsieur le vte. d'Avenel," *La Revendication*, 15–31 August and 15 September 1894. Gazon took on Yves Guyot: "Aux défenseurs du petit commerce," *La Revendication*, 15–30 September, 15 October 1896.

[34] Rabasse, "Choses et autres," *La Revendication*, 24 August 1890.

[35] *La Revendication*: Rabasse, "18 novembre," 22 November 1888; Martin, "Lettres d'un ligueur," 13 July 1890; Rabasse, "Fonctionnarisme," 13 December 1891.

From the *Ligue syndicale*'s perspective, philanthropists and drawing-room socialists represented an improvement on the liberal economists. They, at least, had the perspicacity and courage to repudiate the evils of laissez-faire, to recognize the existence of a "social question." But their cure for the disease was wrong-headed. Charitable spirits like the comte d'Haussonville and the comte Albert de Mun, were right to attribute pauperism and class hatred to the brutal Social Darwinism of the marketplace.[36] But the solution was not, as they advocated, to fortify the "unfit" through organization; "association, cooperation, participation, the phalanstery, the familistery, etc., etc." only exacerbated the root problem: overinstitutionalization.[37] In large-scale operations of any kind, whether commercial, charitable or cooperative, there was no accountability. Who was in charge? A labyrinthine bureaucracy? An anonymous board of directors? Shopkeepers held in deepest suspicion corporate enterprise, *sociétés anonymes*, "joint-stock companies where it's impossible to find out who has the final word."[38] Institutions destroyed any sense of personal responsibility without which a genuine individuality was impossible. France had been a nation of citizens, independent and self-governing; it was fast becoming an undifferentiated mass of sheep, brutes and serfs, shepherded and fleeced by a handful of monopolists and financiers.[39]

Capitalist concentration was progressively grinding down the independent petite bourgeoisie, a class which in happier

[36] "La vérité vraie," *La Revendication*, 20 December 1888; Fayet, "Les élections municipales," *La Revendication*, 20 April 1890; Rabasse, "Choses et autres," *La Revendication*, 10 August 1890. See also AN C5498, testimony of the *Ligue syndicale*, 24 (29?) February 1891.

[37] A. Prével, "Question sociale," *L'Union démocratique*, 9 April 1887.

[38] Chartier, "Les grands bazars et leur moralité," *La Crise commerciale*, 1 November 1888.

[39] Un groupe d'économistes rémois, "La plaie sociale," *La Crise commerciale*, 1 October 1889; M. Anquetin, "L'art, la bienfacture et la pacotille," *La Revendication*, 11 October 1888.

times had acted as a "link," as a "buffer" muffling the shock of class conflict.[40] In due time, the complex and variegated hierarchy of national life would resolve itself into two bitterly hostile, mutually uncomprehending classes, on the one hand "a few capitalist caesars," on the other "a flock of proletarians who will be fed and clothed like sheep."[41] Originality and character could not long survive in a polarized environment. Nor could the Republic.

Shopkeepers closely identified themselves with the stalwart citizens of republican Rome. Militants entitled articles "Vae Victis" and "Vae Soli," cited Cicero and signed their names Mucius Scaevola and Fabius.[42] The mother of Republics taught a lesson as terrible as it was apposite. Concentrated wealth had destroyed Roman virtue, dissolving the bonds of civic life in a riot of luxury and vice. The rich wallowed in corruption, while the plebs, ever more numerous, seethed with bitter resentment. Decadent and devoured by social hatred, the Roman Republic had collapsed in a paroxysm of prolonged and bloody civil war. Only a tyrant, only Caesar had been able to restore order. A similar fate awaited republican France unless drastic measures were taken.

Liberal economists might chatter on about consumers and producers, "elevated souls" about philanthropy and pauperism, but the real issue turned on the survival of community and independence in a world administered by anonymous bureaucracies and "commercial agglomerations."[43] "The strug-

[40] *La Revendication*: Rabasse, "Responsabilités," 25 January 1889; "Quatrième réunion générale," 1 June 1890.

[41] Rabasse, *La Revendication*, 6 September 1888; "Quatrième réunion générale," *La Revendication*, 1 June 1890.

[42] A. Blondel, "Sainte Annonce," *Le Commerçant*, 25 March 1882; Mucius Scaevola, "Les employés de commerce," *Le Commerçant*, 25 February 1882; Fabius, "Les libertés commerciales au XIXe siècle," *La Revendication*, 24 August 1890; L. N. "Vae Soli," *La Crise commerciale*, 1 February 1889.

[43] The phrase "commercial agglomerations" was used by the *Ligue* in its deposition to the Mesureur Commission, AN C5498, 6 November 1891.

gle," declared a shopkeeper militant, "has always pitted monopoly against small ownership; it's no surprise today that the fight is between capitalism and *la démocratie morcellaire*."[44] At the center of this struggle stood the shopkeeper, the neglected and victimized guardian of republican virtue. The modern aristocracy, "the bourgeois aristocracy," was plotting a new "famine pact," but "the humble," the "little folk" would block their path.[45] In the name of republican justice, the people would rise up as "one *fascis* to strike down their new oppressors, the seigneurs of commerce."[46] The "producing third estate" would prove to itself and to the world that "thanks to its unity, energy, and virility," it had the strength to defend its historical heritage.[47] The time for "a (commercial) '89" had come. It was a republican duty to close down the department store.[48]

The shopkeeper/department store struggle was easily transposed into the language of *Gemeinschaft* vs. *Gesellschaft*. Both sets of oppositions were in turn filtered through the vocabulary of an inherited political discourse: republicanism. On this

[44] A. Girard, "Elections municipales et revendications commerciales," *Les Droits du peuple*, 7 April 1890.

[45] E. G., "Les affaires et la politique," *L'Union démocratique*, 18 August 1888; letter to the editor of *La Lanterne, La Crise commerciale*, 1 January 1888. *La Revendication*: Un groupe d'économistes rémois, "La vie à bon marché," 21 February 1889; Fayet, "M. Anatole de la Forge," 18 May 1890.

[46] For the use of the word *"faisceau,"* see "Compte-rendu de la séance du 15 nov. 1891," *La Revendication*, 22 November 1891.

[47] Cited from a *Ligue* flier, n.d., BHVP Actualités, série 119, Commerce et Industrie. *"Tiers Etat producteur"* (Girard, "Le droit au commerce," *L'Union démocratique*, 26 March 1887) was only one among numerous similar self-referents employed by shopkeepers. Other favorites included: "The Great Party of National Labor," "The Producing Democracy," and more ambitiously, "The Entire People." A. Bodinier, "Aux ligueurs," *La Revendication*, 5 July 1888; E. G., "Les affaires et la politique," *L'Union démocratique*, 18 August 1888; Bodinier, *La Revendication*, 13 September 1888.

[48] Paul Pilon, "Un 89!" *La Revendication*, 2 August 1888.

scheme, the small shop, local community and *"la démocratie productrice"* were lined up against an imposing array of enemies: department stores, bureaucracy, and "the new feudality." Urban and economic transformation, I have argued, utterly reshaped the shopkeeper's field of experience in the late nineteenth century. Contemporaries interpreted these twin phenomena as a sequence of transitions, from old to new Paris in the case of Haussmannization, from solid quality to shoddy quantity in the case of the *révolution du bon marché*. The shopkeeper movement incorporated these formulations with predictable results. Old Paris and artistic production took their place alongside boutique and *quartier* as embodiments of republican virtue.

Vieux Paris v s. *Paris nouveau*

Louis Boeuf ran for municipal office in the local elections of 1890. A campaign poster underscored his Parisian origins, obviously a point of some pride: "Son of Paris, having always lived in this great city, my speech bears no trace of an exotic origin. Raised in the class of the people, of the laboring people, I know and share the aspirations of the Parisian democracy."[49] A true *ligueur* was Paris-born; he spoke the idiom of the people. He savored the public balls on Bastille Day, the picturesque scenes of faubourg life at holiday time.[50]

A jealous protectionism characterized *Ligue* attitudes toward the capital city. Shopkeepers took a lively interest in Paris' archaeological heritage. The *Union démocratique* reported faithfully on the meetings of the *Vieux Montmartre* society, one of the city's first preservationist associations.[51] But shopkeeper

---

[49] APP B/a 963, poster.

[50] Georges Mity, "14 juillet. Scène parisienne," *La Revendication*, 12 July 1888; "Le 14 juillet à Paris," *L'Union démocratique*, 21 July 1888.

[51] *L'Union démocratique*: "Séances des comités et groupes," 31 January 1887; "Une promenade archéologique à Montmartre," 1 October 1887.

concern for old Paris was inspired by more than antiquarianism. Paris was the moral and spiritual capital of the nation. *Ligueurs* were repulsed by the base ugliness of Zola's portrait of urban life; nor could they understand his unrepentant optimism in the face of such ugliness.[52] Shopkeepers turned instead to the moral grandeur and sentimentality of Victor Hugo's vision. Hugo had admirably summed up the place of the capital city in national life: "Paris," he wrote, "is a sower."[53] Political ideas, artistic and intellectual movements fermented and took form in the heady and spiritual atmosphere of the capital city, then radiated outwards to the provinces, nourishing and inspiring the nation as a whole. All that was gross and profane was alien to Paris, the "City of Light." And yet, of late, an earth-bound and vulgar Mammonism had muddied the ethereal genius of Parisian life. Political and economic concentration was upsetting the fine balance between capital and country.[54]

Paris' fabulous wealth, *ligueurs* complained, had lured millions from the countryside. Fields lay fallow for want of laborers to work them. The peaceful malls of the nation's small towns, it was feared, would soon be restored "to the state of virgin forest."[55] People abandoned the soil, and for what, for the superficial glamour of urban life? Paris was fast becoming a city of power and luxury, swarming with parasites, money-

[52] *La Revendication*: Mipza, "Franc parler. L'art," 18 July 1888; Fayet, "L'esprit du temps," 20 December 1888.

[53] Cited in Léon Marot, "Le parti de la guerre et la Ligue des patriotes," *L'Union démocratique*, 5 November 1887. For shopkeeper appreciations of Hugo, see also: F. Limoge, "L'alliance des couturières de Paris," *Le Commerçant*, 18 February 1882; de Vouvray, "Les drames de la misère," *La Revendication*, 22 August 1889.

[54] Bréhant, "Aux femmes de France," *La Crise commerciale*, 1 September 1888. See also Bréhant, "Ça me vient de Paris," *La Crise commerciale*, 15 December 1888.

[55] Rabasse, "Beautés de la centralisation," *La Revendication*, 21 January 1892.

grubbers and a mass of unemployed. Vital energies were wasted in getting and spending. Rousseau had warned that urban life undermined the health and reproductive powers of the race, and so it would be with Paris. "Paris," observed the *Crise commerciale*, "is the brain of France, . . . but when all the blood rushes to the head, there is a danger of brain-stroke and death."[56]

France would be better served if Paris contented itself with moral leadership and refrained from monopolizing the political and economic life of the nation. As Gustave Mesureur explained to an audience of *ligueurs:*

> To everything in France, its place. We want only that the capital remain the seat of government, the city of generous ideas, the most beautiful and marvelous city in the world, and that it leave to us the little *patrie* where we were born and where we want to remain something, so that we may count for a little in the great *Patrie française.*[57]

Shopkeepers envisioned a Paris of autonomous neighborhoods set in a nation of autonomous regions, the whole bound by a common Frenchness and a profound republican patriotism.[58]

It was this obstinate localism that informed shopkeeper attacks on the Universal Exposition of 1889. The "real" city, *La Revendication* claimed, was disgusted by the phony spectacle and cardboard fantasy of the Champ de Mars. "I almost like better," one *ligueur* wrote, "the stalls at the hog and ham fair. It smells bad, that's true; it's not genteel, that's

[56] E. Ramel, "Lettre de Tours," *La Crise commerciale*, 1 October 1888. See also Rabasse, "Beautés de la centralisation," *La Revendication*, 21 January 1892.

[57] "Assemblée générale annuelle et extraordinaire," *La Revendication*, 7 February 1892.

[58] Bréhant, "Décentralisation," *La Crise commerciale*, 1 September 1888; Brodel, *La Revendication*, 17 January 1889.

also true; but at least there's the surprise of the unexpected."[59] The world's fair was just a razzle-dazzle show, a dreadful exercise in bad taste staged by *accapareurs* to boost their profits. Only well-connected merchants were awarded concessions; only the big shots won prizes in the gold medal competitions. Provincials and foreigners flocked to the Champ de Mars while the city's merchant community went begging for business. *La Revendication* addressed an urgent appeal to the fair-going public: "You'll find nothing in the arcades of the Exposition as charming and tasteful as you'll see in the arcades of the Palais-Royal."[60] But could one really expect foreigners, crude Chicagoans who spent their lives gutting pigs, to distinguish between "the vulgar cosmopolitan products" peddled at the fair and "works of pure Parisian taste."[61]

Of all the "marvels of the Champ de Mars," it was the Eiffel Tower which incited the bitterest recriminations. This "pasteboard bastille," this "metal asparagus" was the harbinger of a new iron age.[62] "That rude metal," wrote *La Revendication*, "has given its name to an age in which the strong physically crush the weak. It's only natural that iron has reached its apotheosis in a century and in a country . . . where the wealthy have all the advantages and the little people all the sufferings."[63] Eiffel, it was said, had built his tower with Italian labor. During construction he had opened a canteen for the workmen, robbing neighborhood merchants of business. And the final outrage, he had sold the reproduction rights for the

[59] Mousseline, "Mondanités," *La Revendication*, 25 April 1889.

[60] Mousseline, "Mondanités," *La Revendication*, 25 April 1889. See also L. Massart, "89!", *La Revendication*, 10 January 1889; Bréhant, "Misère," *La Crise commerciale*, 1 April 1889; Montaigu, "Les étrangleurs du commerce," *La Crise commerciale*, 30 June 1889.

[61] E. R., "L'exposition de 1889," *La Revendication*, 7 February 1889.

[62] "Encore une gaffe," *La Crise commerciale*, 1 March 1889; Mousseline, "Mondanités," *La Revendication*, 25 April 1889.

[63] E. R., "L'exposition de 1889," *La Revendication*, 7 February 1889.

tower to that vampire Jules Jaluzot. Department stores, machine architecture, foreign influences and vulgar cosmopolitanism—the Eiffel Tower represented a host of interlocking evils.[64] It symbolized as no other monument the conquest of old Paris by concentrated and centralized economic power.

Construction of the Métropolitain, no less than the exposition of '89 and its hated Eiffel Tower, mobilized shopkeepers in the name of *quartier* life to resist the centralizing schemes of monopolists and bureaucrats. A variety of métro schemes were mooted in the 1880s, generating heated and time-consuming debates which delayed realization of the project until 1900. Should the municipality or state government undertake the project? Should a subway or elevated system be constructed? But above all, should the new métro be designed principally to serve the local transportation needs of Parisian residents or to facilitate the penetration of suburban and provincial rail traffic into the city's downtown area?[65] The national government favored the latter, more ambitious scheme but was opposed by the Parisian municipal council, which wanted a strictly local system, a system, as the prefect of the Seine observed, which "Parisians can call by its first name."[66] Retailer militants sided with their municipal representatives, fearing that an overly centralized transportation system would ruin "neighborhood merchants."[67] The specter of a Paris-necropolis was once again raised by the cassandras of the shopkeeper movement. And who would profit from a public works project of such gargantuan proportions: "cosmopolitan fi-

[64] *La Crise commerciale*: L. B., "La grève de la Tour Eiffel," 1 October 1888; Louis Philippe, "Aux syndicats commerciaux et industriels de France," 15 December 1888; "Encore une gaffe," 1 March 1889.

[65] See Alain Cottereau, "Le métro et les mouvements municipaux," pp. 776–786.

[66] *Ibid.*, p. 778 fn.

[67] *La Revendication*: "Une liberté," 11 October 1888; "Comité de centralisation," 15 December 1895.

nance," the railway companies, and, of course, the most powerful financier and railroad magnate of them all, Alphonse de Rothschild.[68] Louis Pagèze, businessman and *ligueur*, railed against the government's project as a vast Jewish conspiracy:

—Who owns the banks?
The Jew.
Who owns the transport system?
The Jew.
Who owns the mines?
The Jew.
Who owns the advertising business?
The Jew. . . .
While waiting for the entire country to fall into the Jew's hands, isn't it only fitting that he also have a monopoly on the Paris Métropolitain?[69]

The surest defense against centralization, monopoly, and cosmopolitanism was a restoration of local liberties. Thiers' government, in reaction against the Commune, had taken steps to rein in the nation's fractious capital. Paris was to have no mayor, and administration of certain municipal functions, the police in particular, was vested in the prefect of the Seine, a government appointee responsible to the Ministry of the Interior. Shopkeepers were outraged and insisted on Paris' right to "communal autonomy": "Faithful to the principles of the Revolution, we favor decentralization; we want to revive local liberties."[70] The tutelage of the central government violated municipal autonomy as vouchsafed by the Revolution; it was an act of despotism, and the *Union démocratique* cited approv-

---

[68] Rothschild was chairman of the board of the Chemin de fer de la Grand Ceinture.

[69] Louis Pagèze, *La Ruine de Paris par le métropolitain*, pp. 13–14; see also pp. 8, 23.

[70] *L'Union démocratique*: A. Girard, "L'autonomie communale," 7 May 1887; J. Ulrich, "Banquet de l'autonomie communale," 11 June 1887.

ingly Jules Ferry's attack on prefectoral authority "as an institution that traced its descent in direct line to the Caesars of the [Roman] decadence."[71]

With autonomy, the Parisian municipal council would come into possession of the necessary powers to rescue the city's economy from plundering interlopers. The *octroi*, which *ligueurs* felt discouraged industrial activity within city limits, ought to be abolished straightaway. An extensive municipal works program would absorb the bulk of Paris' unemployed on terms favorable to the workers. Gazon insisted that contractors who did business with the city fix wages and hours at rates determined by the municipal government. From the shopkeeper's point of view, local autonomy promised tax relief and aggressive public action to control monopolies. A city council, genuinely concerned to defend the commonweal, would cut back on public expenditures and cut down on borrowing. As for monopolies, some *ligueurs* supported outright municipalization. A city-owned gasworks, it was expected, would provide services at much reduced rates. And lest the city council betray the public trust, shopkeeper militants, the *Union démocratique* group in particular, advocated the municipal referendum as a necessary instrument to enforce the genuine will of the people.[72]

[71] "Séances des comités et groupes," *L'Union démocratique*, 14 February 1887.

[72] For the various municipal reforms advanced by shopkeeper militants, see: APP B/a 1092, *Programme municipal*, formulated by Gazon during his '93 election campaign to win a seat on the municipal council for the Ternes ward in the XVIIth arrondissement; APP B/a 1092, 23 April 1896, electoral meeting; "Mouvement socialiste," *Les Droits du peuple*, 24 March 1890; Un Ligueur, "L'abaissement possible du prix de gaz," *La Revendication*, 28 February 1894. *L'Union démocratique*: Ulrich, "Les travaux de Paris," 19 March 1887; A. Prével, "A propos des travaux de Paris," 19 March 1887; A. Girard, "La production parisienne au Conseil Municipal," 14 May 1887; "Programme de *L'Union démocratique*," 23 June 1888; Girard, "La fédération," 17 November 1888.

Ligueurs resisted the triumph of *Paris nouveau* in the name of community values, but their resistance ought not to be dismissed as pure reaction. Shopkeeper hostility to the new city was clothed in the language of republicanism; the program of local reforms advanced by militants, moreover, smacked peculiarly of municipal socialism. A similar ambiguity, a similar melange of reaction, republicanism and social reformism, characterized shopkeeper reaction to the end-of-century depression.

THE GREAT DEPRESSION

To shopkeepers, no less than to more highbrow contemporaries, the department store appeared as a corrupter of public taste. Twenty years ago, *Le Commerçant* observed in 1882, shoppers still cared about "a well-made product . . . good quality, and it must also be added, business morality," but no more.[73] *Grands magasins*, in the interests of high turnover, catered shamelessly to the cosmopolitanism of contemporary taste, to the public's regrettable weakness for "the hollow and the false."[74] "These establishments," claimed *La Revendication,* "far from favoring the article of taste, denature it and destroy it. It's not the beautiful they want but the apparently beautiful; they are not interested in elegance but in effect."[75] Shopkeeper militants vainly insisted that "a woman's hat [was] not the same things as a soldier's kepi," but the regimentation, the degradation of public taste progressed unabated.[76] Expositions, advertising, but above all department stores

[73] Senente, "Les grandes entreprises commerciales," *Le Commerçant*, 25 February 1882.

[74] A. Girard, "Vrai et faux socialisme," *Les Droits du peuple*, 2 June 1890.

[75] Anonymous pamphlet reprinted by Rabasse in *La Revendication*, 26 January 1890.

[76] A. de Briori, "5, 25–15, 75," *La Revendication*, 12 July 1888.

conspired to foist shoddy merchandise on an undiscriminating public unappreciative of the value of quality and solidity.[77]

Ligueurs suspected the most sinister influences behind the department-store-led *révolution du bon marché.* In more lucid moments, they attributed the decline in public taste to the mechanization of consumer industries,[78] but explanations usually took a more xenophobic turn. Money-hungry *grands magasins*, it was claimed, had prostituted themselves to foreign manufacturers. The big stores shamelessly replaced "high quality French merchandise with goods manufactured abroad, with German-made junk (*camelote*) in particular."[79] Belgium and the U.S. were also implicated in the scheme, but the principal malefactor was Germany. The Germans were brutal barbarians who raged at the beauty and delicacy of French civilization. Having defeated France militarily in 1870, they were plotting a "commercial Sedan," a commercial masterstroke that would ruin the French economy. German-inspired speculation had finished off the Union Générale. The Comptoir d'Escompte nearly closed its doors in March 1889 after a rash and costly attempt to corner the world copper market. The Cail metal works at Grenelle were shut down in the middle of the same year. Was it not Bismarck who had engineered these disasters or near disasters in order to undermine France's financial and industrial power?[80]

[77] See the series of articles written by Anquetin under the title, "L'art, la bienfacture et la pacotille," *La Revendication*, 6 September, 20 September, 11 October 1888.

[78] Anquetin, "L'art, la bienfacture et la pacotille," *La Revendication*, 6 September 1888.

[79] Letter from Léopold Christophe, printed in the *Journal de la Chambre syndicale de la boucherie*, 12 January 1896.

[80] De Vouvray, "Révélations et enseignement," *La Revendication*, 14 March 1889; Pierre le Chercheur, "Ça et là," *La Revendication*, 11 July 1889; Barberon, "Revue économique," *La Crise commerciale*, 1 August 1889.

In all their machinations, the Germans were seconded by Jewish bankers from Berlin and Frankfurt. Indeed, German and Jew easily traded places in the *Ligue*'s cast of villains. Perhaps it was not Bismarck after all who manipulated the Jews, but quite the contrary: "Now then; isn't it true that the Jews with a twitch of the eyebrows can ruin institutions like the Union Générale and a host of others as in the Panama Affair? And isn't it so that they have bent the government to the service of their resentments and insatiable avarice?"[81] The Jews controlled the street trade as well as the Bourse. From top to bottom, "the Jewish International" had fixed its blood-sucking grasp, its "greedy fingers," on the commercial body of France.[82] *Ligueurs* insisted repeatedly that their attacks on "the Jewish Feudality" ("*la juiverie*" for short) were not directed at practitioners of any particular religion, but at persons of any persuasion—Catholic, Protestant or Israelite—who worshiped the golden calf at the expense of the fatherland.[83] Such disingenuous disclaimers only underline the economic, rather than biological or religious, inspiration of shopkeeper anti-Semitism.

A vast foreign-sponsored conspiracy then had been mounted against the French economy, and shopkeepers claimed the plot was working only too well. In a former epoch, the artisan had doubled as an artist. The product of an extended apprenticeship, he had been a man of refined taste and aesthetic judg-

---

[81] L. N., "Vae Soli," *La Crise commerciale*, 1 February 1889.

[82] "L'Internationale juive et l'accaparement des blés de France," *La Revendication*, 6 September 1891; Christophe, "Aux adversaires de la Ligue," *La Revendication*, 21 February 1889. See also Cassandre, "Où allons-nous?" *La Revendication*, 9 February 1890; "Aux dames de la province," *La Crise commerciale*, 1 November 1889.

[83] "La réunion au Cirque d'Hiver," *Journal de la Chambre syndicale de la boucherie*, 25 February 1894; Christophe, "La maison dite de nouveautés," *La Revendication*, 26 July 1888; Anquetin, "L'art, la bienfacture et la pacotille," *La Revendication*, 26 July 1888.

ment, a guardian of the nation's artistic patrimony, but this era was passing. Department stores selling cheaply made foreign merchandise ruthlessly undersold the craftsman, driving him to bankruptcy. The artisan/producer was now little better than a sweated laborer. "And the worker," asked *La Crise commerciale*, "what's become of him? He's lost his shop. It's at the back of some dark and obscure courtyard that he's taken refuge. He no longer sells but works by the piece or by the day."[84] Implicated in the artisan's demise, compromised by his ruin, were the wholesalers and retailers who had once brought his goods to market. The department store, with its low standards of craftsmanship, threatened the "inventive genius" and originality of the race, but more, it worked the ruin of an entire structure of production.[85] And it was not only the small owner—the artisan, the shopkeeper—who had suffered from the invasion of *la camelote*.

Foreign competition exerted a terrible downward pressure on wages in Paris. Desperate workers defended their position through union and strike activity.[86] Employers, however, responded with massive lay-offs, replacing the native born with foreign riff-raff, with Germans and Italians for whom paltry wages in Paris represented an improvement over what they were paid at home. *La Revendication* spoke unsympathetically of last century's "guest-workers": "No doubt they bring with them, packed away in their trunks, their Uhlan's or Bersag-

<hr>

[84] Joannes, "Le commerce et l'exposition," *La Crise commerciale*, 15 June 1889.

[85] For the *Ligue*'s version of the changing structure of artisanal production, see H. Bonnel, "Guerre aux bazars," *La Revendication*, 26 July 1888; *La Crise commerciale*: Chartier, "Différence des temps," 15 April 1888; A. Marc, "Tapisserie et ameublements," 15 June 1888; "Tué par ses obligés," 1 January 1890. See also Girard, "La décadence de l'apprentissage," *L'Union démocratique*, 9 July 1887; AN C5498, testimony of M. Blasset, delegate of the *Chambre syndicale des patrons tapissiers*, 19 June 1891.

[86] A. Girard, "Les grèves," *L'Union démocratique*, 11 August 1888.

liere's uniform, so that when the signal's given, they'll have only to change clothes to be on the spot to shoot their employers the inevitable day that the Germans and Italians declare war on us."[87]

The native worker, in the meantime, robbed of employment by cheap, foreign labor, was thrown back on his own resources. He might emigrate or, as a stopgap, try his hand at trade. Just a few francs would suffice to set up a makeshift odds-and-ends shop or to purchase the contents of a pushcart. The *Ligue syndicale* complained of outsiders, uncertain characters without business experience or regard for standards, who flocked to the commercial sector in hard times, stiffening competition for established merchants and giving trade a bad name.[88] It was with a bad conscience that the *Ligue*, self-styled champion of *petit commerce*, attacked pushcart vendors. But the street trade—shifting, irregular and unsupervised—roused shopkeeper suspicions. "Street vending," one *ligueur* wrote, "is so badly regulated that it has become the conduit of a cosmopolitan infiltration into France. . . . The trade hides many adventurers who are rightly suspected *of performing discreet and secret missions!*"[89]

On the *Ligue*'s understanding of the crisis, it was no one class in particular that suffered but the "people" as a whole: independents and workers alike. Shopkeepers and artisans were undersold and proletarianized. Wage earners confronted unemployment, competition from foreign labor and demotion to the dubious ranks of an ever more numerous lumpen-proletariat. *Grands magasins* certainly bore a heavy responsibility

[87] Pierre le Chercheur, "Ça et là," *La Revendication*, 8 August 1889.

[88] E. C., "Attentat contre les commerçants sédentaires, de détail des villes," *La Crise commerciale*, 30 June 1889; Ernie, "Réponse aux critiques contre l'alimentation," *La Revendication*, 30 June 1893; "Les sociétés coopératives," *Journal de la Chambre syndicale de la boucherie*, 16 February 1896.

[89] A. T., "Questions économiques," *La Revendication*, 15 September 1893.

for this dismal state of affairs, but behind the department store lay a wider, foreign-led conspiracy which worked its will through importation of cheap, machine-made merchandise and through the awesome power of monopoly. Shopkeeper militants concentrated their anger on the *grand magasin* above all, but at moments they dimly perceived that the department store menace was but one feature of a more generalized threat arising from foreign competition and large-scale enterprise. If this were so, however, would simple destruction of the big stores suffice to bring the retail crisis to resolution? To the extent that *ligueurs* felt their way beyond a narrow and exclusive focus on the department store, they recognized that broader and more thoroughgoing measures were required. But what kind of measures were envisioned?

First and foremost, the invasion of foreign goods had to be halted. All merchandise from abroad—wheat from America and Russia, wine from Italy, industrial products from Germany—was to be slapped with crippling import duties. *Ligueurs* demanded abrogation of all existing trade treaties, above all the infamous Treaty of Frankfurt which a triumphant Germany had imposed on France in the aftermath of 1871.[90] All imports, of course, could not be proscribed, but those products allowed to enter France would have to bear a country-of-origin stamp.[91] As for foreign workers, shopkeepers

[90] For examples of shopkeeper protectionism, see Berry, "Aux propriétaires," *La Crise commerciale*, 15 March 1888. *La Revendication*: P. L. C., "Les vins d'Italie," 20 June 1889; Pierre le Chercheur, "Ça et là," 25 July 1889; de Vouvray, "Des gens embarrassés," 15 August 1889; Meilhac, "Commerçants et fabricants," 15 August 1889; "Comptes-rendus," 12 September 1889. See also A. Girard, "Le comité autonomiste, radical, socialiste et commercial du quartier Bonne-Nouvelle," *L'Union démocratique*, 16 July 1887.

[91] Chambre des Députés, Spuller Commission, testimony of A. Girard, p. 123.

advocated a discriminatory "alien residence tax." Foreigners were to be barred altogether from state and municipal employment.[92] The most extreme and menacing measures, however, were reserved for Jews:

> Since 1790 and certainly since 1871, *la JUIVERIE*, like a plague of locusts, has descended on us from the four corners of the earth and eaten away at our guts. Democratic and Social France one day will find it necessary to take self-protective, delousing measures against the descendants of Abraham, an alien *financial* caste.[93]

The chilling racism of this remark was extreme for the shopkeeper movement, but it suggests the radical xenophobia, the deep hatred of anything or anyone deemed "alien," which resonated through shopkeeper thinking in the 1880s.

It was not enough, of course, to lash out at foreigners. What of their agents and imitators of native descent, sons of France who had sold out their fatherland for hard cash? The nation, under external influences to be sure, had bred its own class of fat cats and bloodsuckers. These men would be made to pay for their greed through tax reform. An upward revision of the *patente* was only one dimension of the fiscal package shopkeepers had put together. A turnover tax, a tax on profits or, best of all, a progressive and steeply proportional income tax would, it was hoped, savage monopolists while sparing decent Frenchmen who earned only a modest living.[94] Indeed,

---

[92] Pierre le Chercheur, "Ça et là," *La Revendication*, 6 October 1889; APP B/a 1092, Louis Gazon, *Programme municipal*, 1893 local elections, Ternes ward.

[93] E. T., "L'équilibre du budget," *L'Union démocratique*, 11 June 1887.

[94] Chambre des Députés, Spuller Commission, testimony of A. Prével, p. 121; Girard, "Le comité autonomiste . . . du quartier Bonne-Nouvelle," *L'Union démocratique*, 16 July 1887; A. Girard, "A la Salle de Rivoli," *L'Union démocratique*, 24 January 1888; APP B/a 1092, Gazon file, 16 and 22 April 1896.

a soak-the-rich policy coupled with high tariffs would probably make possible a real tax cut for the average Frenchman. In some instances, shopkeepers conceded, monopoly was unavoidable or useful. In such circumstances the state was within its rights to nationalize and administer the monopoly in the interest of the people. The postal service and tobacco industry were already in the hands of the state, and rightly so.[95] Nor did shopkeeper militants scruple to call for a "democratic reorganization of the Bank of France."[96] The national railway system as well was slated for public ownership. Louis Gazon, in the name of democracy, was prepared to go yet further, to nationalize mines, in fact, "anything that is of public interest or service."[97] Middle-of-the-roaders, like Christophe, recoiled at such extremism, but there should be no mistaking shopkeeper determination to demolish private monopoly, even at the expense of property rights.

This attitude accounts in no small degree for the *Ligue*'s outspoken support of the labor movement in the eighties and early nineties. The *Crise commerciale* spoke up on behalf of the London matchgirls strike in 1889.[98] *La Revendication* backed a walkout of Paris omnibus workers in '91.[99] When miners struck at Carmaux in 1892–1893, Gazon assured the Carmausins of shopkeeper solidarity and even suggested that the miners take over the baron Reille's enterprise and run it for themselves.[100] And it was not only on the issue of strikes that shopkeeper militants lent their support to working-class de-

[95] Christophe, "A propos de la question du gaz à Paris," *La Revendication*, 4 September 1892.

[96] Girard, "Le comité autonomiste . . . du quartier Bonne-Nouvelle," *L'Union démocratique*, 16 July 1887.

[97] Gazon, "Aux ligueurs," *La Revendication*, 15–30 November 1891.

[98] Marc, "Les grèves de Londres," *La Crise commerciale*, 15 September 1889.

[99] Rabasse, "Un drôle de résultat des coopératives," *La Revendication*, 31 May 1891.

[100] Gazon, *La Revendication*, 15 February 1893.

mands. The exploitative practices of private placement bureaux were roundly condemned in *La Revendication*.[101] The *Union démocratique* urged establishment of departmental Chambers of Labor to fix minimum wages; and Gazon, the most fervent partisan of an artisan/shopkeeper entente, spoke up repeatedly for worker-run pension funds.[102] Working people and shopkeepers, it was argued, were natural allies in the struggle against monopoly. "If among us—the humble, the little folk of the commercial world—," wrote Gazon in *La Revendication* in 1893, "there are people too stuck up, too inflated with pride to make alliance with the workers, . . .they are false friends. We must let them smother themselves in the flab of the overstuffed bourgeoisie."

Working-class alliance, punitive legislation—these were the preferred lines of attack against monopoly. Shopkeepers, by contrast, expressed only a lukewarm interest in measures to revitalize the small business sector. There was talk of public action to ease the perennial credit squeeze. Apprenticeship programs and professional schools, it was hoped, might sharpen the competitive edge of French small industry. And the state could help out by sponsoring research and encouraging inventions "that would promote worker ownership of tools and machinery that can be used at home."[103] But extensive government intervention in the affairs of small enterprise unnerved shopkeepers who dreaded the emergence of an omnipresent and omnicompetent "providential state."[104] The

---

[101] Hugonet, "Les bureaux de placement," *La Revendication*, 12 July 1891.

[102] "Programme de *L'Union démocratique*," *L'Union démocratique*, 28 July 1888; APP B/a 1092, Gazon, *Programme municipal*, 1893 local elections, Tenes ward and electoral meeting, 22 April 1896; Gazon, "Aux ligueurs," *La Revendication*, 15–30 November 1893.

[103] A. Girard, "Paris industriel," *Les Droits du peuple*, 28 April 1890; Girard, "Le comité autonomiste . . . du quartier Bonne-Nouvelle," *L'Union démocratique*, 16 July 1887.

[104] Fayet, "La Ligue et les futures élections," *La Revendication*, 21 August 1892.

machinery of power could be wielded to strike down monopoly and extirpate foreign influences, but that was the limit of its usefulness.

In its early years, the *Ligue syndicale* did not recoil at the epithet "socialist."[105] *Ligueurs* accepted welfare and labor reform, the necessity of nationalization, an expanded state role in the big business sector, but their socialism was of a peculiar variety. They repudiated collectivism with its *ouvriériste* and internationalist overtones as a false doctrine concocted by politicians and ideologues. A true or pragmatic socialism would defend not just a class, but the nation as a whole, the "productive democracy" of shopkeepers and laborers. But the ultimate perversity of collectivism lay in its indifference, if not hostility, to private property. "They have no idea of possession," one *ligueur* lamented. Collectivism aimed to improve, "the lot of workers as workers, but not to help them acquire possession of economic property."[106] To *ligueurs*, on the contrary, the ultimate goal of social reform had to be increased mobility not improved welfare. An increase in public power was justified to overthrow monopoly which blocked the movement of workers into the *petit patronat*, but not to destroy the promise of private property for all.

POPULAR DEMOCRACY

Ligueurs, to be sure, focused their frustrations on the department store, but the wide range of reforms advanced by militants suggests that far more was at stake for shopkeepers than the obliteration of unwelcome competitors. The *Ligue*'s municipal program was designed to rescue old Paris from the sinister agents of centralization: high finance, big business and

[105] *La Revendication*: "Comptes-rendus," 13 September 1888; "Comité de centralisation," 24 August 1890.

[106] A. Girard, "Vrai et faux socialisme," *Les Droits du peuple*, 2 June 1890.

the state. On the national level, shopkeeper militants aimed to revive a sagging economy through protectionism, a legislated xenophobia and destruction of private monopolies. These changes were, of course, proposed in the interest of *petits commerçants*, but they had a broader intent as well. The shopkeeper's gain translated into a victory for *quartier* life and aesthetic standards; but more importantly, the preservation of *vieux Paris* and the restoration of national prosperity offered the surest guarantees against a monarchical restoration. A. Girard insisted on the urgency of reform in these terms:

> We believe that these few reforms will help relaunch the economy and that as a consequence they will immunize the middle class, the worker against the monarchical parties which will be forced to abandon their ambitions.[107]

But how was the *Ligue*'s program to be put into effect?

The question of implementation posed a particularly difficult problem, for the rot that poisoned urban life and sapped the nation's productive energies had infected France's political institutions as well. The Republic itself had fallen victim to the scheming of monopolists, monarchists and Jews. Shopkeeper newspapers were sprinkled with derogatory references to the "capitalist republic," to "our bourgeois republic."[108] The nation's representatives were held in the deepest suspicion; they had sold out to capital, if they were not themselves "millionaire capitalists."[109] Indeed, *Ligue* militants showered a steady stream of abuse on the loudmouths, spendthrifts and poseurs of the Chamber of Deputies.[110] The problem with

[107] Chambre des Députés, Spuller Commission, testimony of A. Girard, p. 123.

[108] A. B., "Le commerce et les grands magasins," *L'Union démocratique*, 26 May 1888; Rabasse, "M. Drumont," *La Revendication*, 26 June 1892.

[109] Girard, "Situation nouvelle," *L'Union démocratique*, 25 August 1888.

[110] *La Revendication*: Rabasse, "Causerie hebdomadaire," 6 October 1889; Fayet, "Nos élus. Trop de non-valeurs," 15 May 1892. See also Verdier,

parliament was that it recruited among lawyers, doctors, and teachers, liberal professionals who knew nothing of commerce and industry. They frittered their time away in petty political maneuverings, while the nation's economy ground to a standstill.[111] And what hope was there of awakening the Chamber of Deputies from its careless slumber? Jewish millions subverted the electoral process. The parties—the Opportunists of course, but even to some extent the Radicals—were dominated by coteries and sects, by oligarchs and demagogues more concerned with their personal power than with the public welfare.[112] Nor could the press, so-called tribune of the people, be counted on in the struggle against corruption. Journalists, unhappily, were no less venal than politicians. The newspapers said nothing against department stores, creeping cosmopolitanism and the decay of public taste because Jews and monopolists had bought their silence.[113] All the paraphernalia of representative democracy—elections, parties and the press—had not saved the Republic from the domination of monopoly. "From parliamentarism," one militant remonstrated, "no remedy is to be expected."[114]

Municipal and economic reform, then, appeared highly improbable as long as the political power of monopoly remained unchallenged. The Constitution of '75 choked expression of the popular will and lent itself to the manipu-

---

"Quartier de La Chapelle," *Les Droits du peuple*, 24 March 1890; "Civilisation-progrès," *La Crise commerciale*, 1 May 1890.

[111]"Chambre syndicale de la boucherie de Paris," *Journal de la Chambre syndicale de la boucherie*, 9 April 1899. *La Revendication*: "Incompétence," 16 August 1888; Ratel, "Le virus," 25 January 1889; Christophe, "Autre temps, mêmes moeurs," 31 July 1894.

[112]*L'Union démocratique*: "Démocratie," 3 January 1887; Girard, "La situation politique," 21 July 1888; Girard, "Notre politique," 4 August 1888.

[113]Arces, "Comment on écrit l'histoire," *L'Union démocratique*, 7 October 1887. *La Revendication*: Anquetin, "L'art, la bienfacture et la pacotille," 6 September 1888; Christophe, "Les nouveaux collaborateurs de la Ligue," 3 April 1892.

[114]E. T., "L'équilibre du budget," *L'Union démocratique*, 11 June 1887.

lations of capitalists and oligarchs. It needed to be rewritten. Léopold Christophe ran for the Senate in 1894; he listed at the top of his political program: "Revision of the Constitution in a republican sense by a constituent assembly."[115] Republican revision meant in practice the elimination of appointive offices or offices filled by indirect elections. The Senate had to go, and A. Girard advocated abolition of the presidency as well. Legal proceedings, it was felt, ought to be directed by elected judges and verdicts rendered by juries of the people. Direct elections and active citizen participation assured a maximum of popular control. In a genuine democracy, of course, citizens exercised vigilance year-round and not just at election time. Shopkeeper militants advocated recall of officials who exceeded their mandate. "A deputy unrestrained by popular veto," Girard argued, "is to be feared as much as a monarch."[116] Issues of public import, perhaps all legislation, were to be submitted to popular referendum. Shopkeepers were particularly anxious to "establish the pecuniary and penal responsiblity of functionaries," though there was little agreement as to how to proceed on this question.[117] But no one doubted that government was developing a corporate interest of its own which did not coincide with the general will, and that something urgently had to be done. Democratic reform represented the essential first step toward economic and municipal reform and toward an eventual restoration of popular sovereignty. Every phase of the operation, it was hoped, would revive and strengthen the nation, securing the foundations of republican France for generations to come.[118]

[115] "La candidature du président de la Ligue au Sénat," *La Revendication*, 31 December 1893.

[116] Girard, "Notre politique," *L'Union démocratique*, 4 August 1888.

[117] E. G., "L'irresponsabilité regrettable," *Journal de la Chambre syndicale de la boucherie*, 14 May 1899.

[118] For details of shopkeeper plans to overhaul the machinery of government, see *L'Union démocratique*: A. P. "Sus au Sénat," 10 January 1887;

CONCLUSION

At first glance, the accusations of reactionary antimodernism leveled against petit-bourgeois protest movements would appear to be justified in the case of the *Ligue syndicale*. Urban transformation and the Great Depression spurred the growth of large-scale organization—heavy industry, joint-stock enterprise, high finance. The *Ligue* flew in the face of inevitable change and rejected the world of organized capitalism, and it did so in a spirit of backward-looking nostalgia for a happy and fictionalized past.

Quartier life was never as *ligueurs* described it: autonomous and autarkic. What a bizarre notion for a movement of middlemen and downtown merchants who operated in the city's principal shopping district. The *Ligue*'s vision of the happy workshop, functioning harmoniously in the midst of Europe's most revolutionary city, must also have required a strenuous effort of imagination. As for the petit-bourgeois family, the *Ligue*'s heart-felt rhapsodizing ought not obscure the repressed conflicts and simmering resentments which have earned this institution such an unfortunate reputation. What could be more reactionary than the wish to preserve a past that was vanishing if indeed it had ever existed?

The *Ligue*'s rejection of organized capitalism, moreover, took the form of an all-out and irrational campaign against department stores. Implicit in the *Ligue*'s attack on *grands magasins* was a hide-bound resistance to mass consumerism and the dynamism of the modern metropolis. Expressions of resistance were highly charged wtih xenophobic and anti-Se-

---

Girard, "Le comité autonomiste . . . du quartier Bonne-Nouvelle," 16 July 1887; L. Guillemin, "Plus de députés," 24 March 1888; Girard, "Notre politique," 4 August 1888; "La Ligue syndicale, section du 6e arrondissement," 16 February 1889. See also "Revue de presse," *La Crise commerciale,* 1 February 1889; Fayet, "L'obstacle," *La Revendication,* 21 January 1892.

mitic sentiments; Jews, foreigners and *grands magasins* made convenient scapegoats for larger and more diffuse social phenomena, difficult to grasp let alone master. It is possible, of course, to understand why the *Ligue* chose the targets it did.

Hostility to outsiders is not uncommon in closely drawn communities, whether city-states, small towns or neighborhoods. Imagine such communities in dissolution, genuinely endangered by powerful economic forces that escaped local control. *Ligueurs* experienced firsthand the consequences of Haussmannization. They witnessed the depression's pervasive impact on commercial and industrial life. It was only too easy for them to blame it all on the competition, on department stores. But were they wildly off the mark? The big stores owed their success to Haussmannization; they were, moreover principal merchandisers of the new goods in the late nineteenth century.

The *Ligue*'s animosity toward Germans and Jews can be made sense of in a similar manner. It was German manufacturers who spearheaded the *révolution du bon marché*. As for Jews, what of Dreyfus' confection house, the Galéries Lafayette and, of course, Rothschild's financial empire? Need it be said that not all Jewish businesses prospered in the latter part of the century, that Germans did not hold an exclusive patent on the manufacture of cheap goods, that department stores did not monopolize the retail of *la camelote*? But there was just a glimmer of truth in each proposition. What did the Palais-Royal merchant who stepped out onto the avenue de l'Opéra see: the Gagne-Petit selling German clocks, Bernheim's selling japonaiserie? *Ligueurs*, of course, were not unique in their anti-Semitic and anti-German biases. A distrust of Jews had deep roots in segments of French public opinion. Animosity toward Germany was a given of French public life since the humiliating defeat of 1870–1871. The economic crisis of the end of the century brought to the surface or exacerbated such resentments. The shopkeeper's animus against Jews and Germans, while rooted in his particular experience, fed upon and drew added strength from a climate of opinion conducive to prejudice.

Shopkeepers recognized the signs of a massive social transformation, but they mistook symptoms for causes, the parts for the whole. Department stores, foreigners and Jews operated as "collective images," as stand-ins for urban and economic transformation. The condensation of experience into collective imagery vastly simplified the task of understanding and promised intellectual and emotional relief to men under intense pressure. The end-of-century crisis could, of course, be reduced to yet more manageable proportions. The department store was melted down and recast in the figure of Jaluzot. Krupp stood in for the Germans, Rothschild for the Jews. In the persons of Jaluzot, Krupp and Rothschild, corporate capital—big commerce, heavy industry, high finance—took on human proportions, assumed a flesh-and-blood existence which could be isolated and focused upon.[119] It is possible, knowing the particulars of shopkeeper experience, to comprehend why certain institutions and persons were singled out for abuse. The selection of scapegoats is not arbitrary, but the fundamental irrationality of scapegoating must not be underestimated. Condensation and personalization, the mechanisms through which the selection of victims is made, are distorting processes. And for the antimodernist argument, this is precisely the point. Shopkeeper ideology is not only reactionary in its idealization of the past and rejection of the present, but hopelessly irrational in its mode of argument.

This view, while not wrong, is one-sided. Firstly, the *Ligue*

[119] Schneider, of course, could personify heavy industry as well as Krupp; and Boucicaut could substitute for Jaluzot. See Marot, "Le parti de la guerre et la Ligue des patriotes," *L'Union démocratique*, 5 November 1887; Bréhant, "En grève!" *La Crise commerciale*, 15 August 1888; Bréhant, "Vous avez la parole," *La Crise commerciale*, 15 March 1889.

remained firm in its commitment to republicanism, however reactionary its opposition to new Paris and mass consumerism. The Revolution surely cannot be taken as a symbol of tradition. Nor can one dismiss shopkeeper demands for direct democracy, municipal socialism, welfare and tax reform as simple manifestations of antimodernist reaction. Referendum and recall, local autonomy, the income tax, minimum wage legislation, nationalization of natural monopolies—these items have been and still are standard features of social democratic and progressive platforms. As this range of reforms suggests, shopkeepers implicitly recognized that revision of the *patente* did not offer a sufficient solution to their present difficulties. More had to be done because the problem went deeper than the *grand magasin*. Shopkeepers groped toward a fuller comprehension of their situation and came close in their critique of *Paris nouveau*, of cheap consumer goods and of the growing power of large-scale organization. They did not pin down Haussmannization's impact on commercial geography or the origins of the Great Depression, but some understood that urban and economic transformation were at the root of the current crisis. And they were right. Shopkeepers succumbed only too often to the temptations of scapegoating, but an untempered verdict of irrationality is excessive.

The *Ligue syndicale* and parallel movements were not liberal in their thinking and attitudes, and it is perhaps this fact which has inspired liberal-minded observers to raise the specter of antimodernist reaction. If the antimodernist label, however, seems inappropriate, what term is preferable? The *Ligue*'s passion for direct democracy, its commitment to *morcellisme* and its fierce patriotism place it squarely, I think, in France's radical republican tradition. Liberals see an irreconcilable conflict between state and individual, but the radical republican is ever determined to merge personality and community. Freedom is guaranteed and practiced for the republican through active and unmediated participation in public affairs, not through preservation of a private space exempt from government intervention. It is the general will of all right-thinking citizens which rules a properly constituted popular democracy. The wider the range of private rights, the narrower the sphere in which the people may exercise their sovereignty. For this reason, radical republicans view with suspicion the passion for rights, for dissenting minorities which liberals exhibit from time to time. But does this suspicion betoken a total lack of regard for individuality? Is it a sign of incipient totalitarianism? The *Ligue syndicale* incessantly harped on the theme of personal independence. Real individuality, real citizenship, meant property ownership. If a man owed his livelihood to another, his liberty was compromised. To the radical republican, the polarization of society into bourgeoisie and proletariat represented a far graver threat to public freedom than the suppression of dissent or the punishment of undesired minorities. Liberty in a democratic community depended more on rough equality of ownership than on a bill of rights. On this scheme, the citizen derived his freedom, indeed his very individuality, from the small-owning community. Preserving its tightly knit, egalitarian constitution was a question of self-preservation. Hence the unswerving and, to liberals, unsettling patriotism of radical republicans, a patriotism rooted in local life and distrustful of laissez-faire attitudes and cosmopolitan influences alike. In their more exuberant moments, shopkeepers liked to imagine a patriotic democracy of petty proprietors, a commercial version of Rousseau's contractarian utopia.[120]

As a radical republican movement, it is appropriate to classify the *Ligue syndicale*, at least at its outset, as a movement of the left. But it is critical to recognize at the same time that the radical republican tradition in which the *Ligue* was steeped

[120] Shopkeepers were very much aware of the Rousseauan model. Paulin Sarrut, "Le droit de vivre," *La Crise commerciale*, 15 November 1889.

had entered a period of flux and uncertainty in the 1880s and 1890s. At mid-century, the dream of small ownership for all might well have appeared within the grasp of an increasingly prosperous and propertied nation. But toward the end of the century, the emergence of an organized, industrial capitalism apparently banished this vision of republican life from the realm of possibility. *Ligueurs* wanted to arrest the progress of events, but it was not a stubborn traditionalism which inspired their actions. Rather, they struggled to defend a conception of property relations appropriate to one epoch in the development of capitalism against new forms of social and economic organization inimical to small-owner utopianism. They defended expectations, reasonable perhaps at mid-century, but which were losing their validity in an increasingly corporate world.

The uncertain status of the radical republican vision is reflected in the divided character of shopkeeper thinking. In conformity with radical republican tradition, *Ligue* militants demonstrated a willingness to endorse working-class demands and an attachment to direct democracy. This tradition, however, was now on the defensive, a loss of self-confidence evident in the *Ligue*'s extreme xenophobia. A patriotic parochialism, I have argued, is a common feature of radical republican movements. But in the case of the *Ligue syndicale*, patriotic sentiment had begun to harden under the pressure of urban and economic dislocation into a shrill and inward-turning chauvinism. *Ligue* ideology sanctioned democratic, even socialist reform, but it also bore the marks of an incipient radical nationalism alien in its resentful extremism to the radical left tradition. The *Ligue syndicale* was radical republican, but the contradictory impulses at work in its thinking signaled a crisis in the radical republican heritage.

A similar melange of democratic, socialist and chauvinist tendencies is to be found among militants and publicists on the radical fringe of French politics. In the late eighties, it was a rare socialist who balked at playing up to popular anti-Semitism. Demagogic journalists like Henri Rochefort and ultra-patriots like Paul Déroulède inveighed against the parliamentary Republic for its indifference to genuine democracy and to the social welfare of the people. Nowhere was the ambiguity of radical politics in the waning decades of the century more perfectly expressed than in Boulangism. And no movement in the 1880s came closer to sundering shopkeeper ties to Radical-Socialism than the Boulangist movement.

7

. . .

The Boulangist Interlude

GENERAL BOULANGER has been dismissed as a comic-opera Bonaparte, as a "Saint-Arnaud of the café-concert" in Jules Ferry's apt and cutting phrase.[1] As Minister of War in the Freycinet cabinet (January–December 1886), Boulanger revived the republican practice of reviewing the troops on Bastille Day. A great military parade filed from Longchamp down the Champs-Elysées, July 14, 1886, an event commemorated in a wildly popular song, "En r'venant de la r'vue," first performed by Paulus at the Alcazar. The General's enormous popularity and obvious political ambition inspired the jealousy and suspicion of Opportunist politicians who moved to block his career. Boulanger resisted, launching a nation-wide campaign to revise the constitution and topple the Opportunist establishment from power. He won a decisive victory in the January 1889 by-elections in Paris, defeating the official candidate Edouard Jacques by over 80,000 votes. On the night of January 27, the Boulangist party gathered in celebration at Durand's. While outside an enthusiastic crowd of 30,000 chanted "Vive Boulanger!" the General's lieutenants encouraged him to attempt a coup.[2] Instead, he retired

[1] Cited in Beau de Loménie, *Les Responsabilités des dynasties bourgeoises*, vol. II, p. 162.

[2] Dansette, *Le Boulangisme,* p. 248. According to Seager, on the other hand (*The Boulanger Affair*, p. 207), no evidence exists to substantiate the claim that a coup was discussed on the evening of January 27.

to an upstairs salon with his mistress Marguerite de Bonne-mains.

In a little over two months, a skillfully orchestrated campaign of official repression had frightened the General into mortifying exile. Leaderless and under police pressure, the Boulangist movement did not perform well in the legislative elections of September–October 1889 and subsequently collapsed amidst mutual recriminations. The General himself never returned to France. His beloved Marguerite, who had followed him into exile, died of tuberculosis in July 1891. Grief-stricken, Boulanger killed himself at her graveside three months later. The Boulanger Affair began with a parade and hit tune and ended, ignominiously, in humiliation and suicide.

Boulangism is hard to take seriously if one focuses on the person of General Boulanger. From this angle, the affair adds up to disappointing tragicomedy: an ultrapatriotic citizenry nearly catapults into power a dashing but foolish General who in the end prefers romance to politics. Boulangism on this account appears an amusing but trivial episode, a fitting prelude to the frivolous nineties.

Recent historical research has substantially revised this assessment. The affair, it turns out, was of the utmost political and social significance, although there is considerable disagreement as to wherein that significance lies. On one interpretation Boulangism was a movement of the far right that ominously prefigured the fascist movements of the twentieth century. Boulanger's January '89 campaign was masterfully conducted by the Bonapartist Georges Thiébaud who employed all the techniques of modern mass politics—advertising, sloganeering, spectacle—to fasten the public's attention on the General's personality. While Boulanger presented himself to the public as a loyal republican, he at the same time conspired with and accepted the covert financial support of royalist and Bonapartist backers.[3] The General owed his

---

[3] Levillain, *Boulanger*.

landslide victory of January '89 in large part to voters in Paris' VIIth and VIIIth arrondissements, the wealthiest and most conservative neighborhoods in the city. To be sure, he also received a substantial vote from working-class constituencies on the city's periphery, but here his support came not from factory proletarians but from *gens de métier* employed in small-scale handicrafts and from poorly paid casual laborers (dockers, ditch diggers and the like).[4] Those sectors of the Parisian working class hard hit by unemployment and foreign competition proved most responsive to the revisionist appeal. An unsteady coalition that brought together old elites and a panic-stricken, volatile populace, this was the hallmark of Boulangism as it would be of far right movements between the two world wars in the twentieth century. And finally, it is pointed out, Boulanger's best known supporters—Henri Rochefort, Maurice Barrès, Paul Déroulède—all turn up once again at the end of the century as anti-Dreyfusard Nationalists. Zeev Sternhell's recent study of the "revolutionary right" has elaborated at length the case for approaching Boulangism as a political and ideological overture to the Dreyfus Affair and the emergence of a new Nationalist and protofascist right.[5]

A case can also be made, however, for seeing Boulangism as a movement of the left, not as the forerunner of an ominous fascist future, but as a watershed in the evolution of Parisian popular politics from republicanism to socialism. If the revisionist campaign made use of the most up-to-date electioneering techniques, it lacked utterly the centralized and hierarchical organization of a modern mass party. In Paris, the revisionist cause inspired a wild outburst of committee activity. *Comités boulangistes, comités révisionnistes, comités répub-*

[4] Englund, *The Origins of Oppositional Nationalism*, pp. 477–478; Perrot, *Les Ouvriers en grève*, vol. I, pp. 94, 179, 384, 393; vol. II, pp. 437–438.

[5] Sternhell, *La Droite révolutionnaire.* See also Sternhell's *Maurice Barrès et le nationalisme français*; and Thomson, *Democracy in France Since 1870*, p. 157.

licains nationaux proliferated, sometimes two or three to the *quartier*. The Boulangist leadership, organized in the *Comité républicain national* (CRN), struggled to impose structure on the anarchy of local activity but to no avail. Local committees suspected the intentions of the General's entourage and blocked leadership efforts to centralize control.[6] But rank-and-file Boulangists were prepared to establish ties with revisionist associations that operated independently of the CRN.

It was independent associations like Déroulède's *Ligue des patriotes*, the *Fédération des groupes républicains socialistes de la Seine*, and the Rochefortists that assured the triumph of Boulangism in Paris. All three organizations antedated the revisionist campaign of 1888–1889 by several years. The *Ligue des patriotes* had been founded in 1882. The Rochefortist group was an offshoot of the Blanquist *Comité central révolutionnaire* which dated back to 1881. The *Fédération* represented the revisionist rump of a Radical organization constituted in 1884. Their conversion to the General's cause assured the Boulangist campaign an essential minimum of organizational coherence. The *Fédération*, the *Ligue*, the Rochefortists operated as intermediaries in a ramshackle, three-tiered structure, linking the national leadership to a protean mass of local committees. Indeed, the patchwork organization of Boulangism calls to mind less the bureaucratic innovations of twentieth-century mass politics than the federalist and decentralized club movements of 1848 and 1871.

There should be no mistaking, moreover, the left republican character of much of Boulangism's electoral clientele, at least in Paris. The working-class voters who constituted the bulk of the General's constituency in the capital city had in previous elections cast their ballots for Radicals. The revi-

[6] APP B/a 1466, "Comité révisionniste du IXe," 10 October 1888; see also "Comité républicain national révisionniste du VIIe," 13 December 1888; and APP B/a 1519, "Comité révisionniste républicain socialiste du XVIIIe," 14 December 1888.

sionist movement, which inspired such popular enthusiasm but which Radicals for the most part refused to endorse, detached the Parisian working class from its radical republican moorings. And it should be emphasized that working-class electors who voted for Boulanger were in no way making a conscious choice for the right. The ambivalence of the conservative press toward the General obscured the revisionist movement's right-wing connections. Rank-and-file Boulangists, moreover, knew nothing concrete of the General's financial dependence on royalist backers, learning of it only in 1890 on publication of Gabriel Terrail's exposé *Les Coulisses du boulangisme*. Finally, in the wake of the movement's collapse in 1889–1890, working-class revisionists veered sharply to the left, hardly the appropriate path had they in fact been protofascist in their sympathies. Paris' outer arrondissements, from which Gambetta and Clemenceau had launched their political careers, henceforth gave their votes to socialist candidates from the moderate Millerand to the Blanquist revolutionary Edouard Vaillant.[7]

A parallel course was pursued by many of the politicians and publicists in the General's personal entourage. Boulanger's lieutenants were all, with the exceptions of Thiébaud and the comte de Dillon, men of impeccable republican credentials, veterans of radical politics and the social struggles of the 1880s.[8] They sat in parliament with the *extrême gauche* as did Alfred Naquet and Charles Laisant or with the *groupe socialiste* as did Planteau, Georges Laguerre, and Alfred de Susini. Francis Laur and the Blanquist E. Roche, both Boulangist notables, had played conspicuous roles in the agitation on behalf of striking Decazeville miners in 1886. CRN members

[7] Mayeur, *Les Débuts de la IIIe République*, pp. 179–180.

[8] On the radical background of Boulanger's entourage, see Néré, *La Crise industrielle de 1882*, vol. II, pp. 121–161, 194–195, 365–384; and Néré, *Le Boulangisme et la presse*, pp. 229–232; Jacques Kayser, *Les Grandes Batailles du Radicalisme*, p. 164.

Henri Michelin and Maurice Vergoin had taken active part in the often violent antiplacement bureaux campaigns of 1886 and 1888. Roche and de Susini, it is right to point out, re- surfaced at the end of the century as anti-Dreyfusard National- ists, but most Boulangist deputies who survived the elec- toral debacle of 1889 drifted leftward into the socialist fold.[9] From this perspective, Boulangism appears as the last hurrah of the Parisian radical republican tradition and as a forerunner not so much of the radical right as of a nascent socialist movement.[10]

Did Boulangism then mark the debut of a new form of right- wing politics or the expiration of a radical tradition dominant in Parisian politics for almost a century? Did revisionism pre- pare the way for anti-Dreyfusard Nationalism or was social- ism its principal heir and beneficiary? The history of shop- keeper relations with the Boulangist movement suggests an interesting combination of answers. Yes, Boulangism was rooted in the tradition of radical republicanism, but it is also true that the break-up of this tradition set the stage for the emergence not only of a new socialist left but also, and per- haps more significantly, of a new radical right.

SHOPKEEPERS AND BOULANGISM

The *Ligue syndicale* was all but swept away in the revisionist campaign. Certainly shopkeepers were viewed by contempor- aries as Boulangist sympathizers. Three days before the Jan- uary '89 by-election, Boulanger received a delegation of *petits commerçants* who pleaded the shopkeeper's case against the de-

[9] Doty, "Parliamentary Boulangism after 1889," pp. 265–268.
[10] Dansette, *op. cit.*, p. 376; Hutton, "Popular Boulangism," p. 97; Hutton, *The Cult of the Revolutionary Tradition*, pp. 143–161; Nicolet, *Le Radicalisme*, pp. 27–28.

partment store.[11] *La République illustrée* published a full-page graphic of the encounter to the delight of the shopkeeper press.[12] The meeting moved Etienne Basly in *La Nation* to denounce retailer collusion with Boulangism.[13] In February, the Possibilist *Parti ouvrier* warned its readers to shun association with the *Ligue syndicale*: "This *Ligue* just like Déroulède's has been infiltrated by *la Boulange*."[14] Christophe, in an interview with *La Plaine Monceau* denied charges that "the *Ligue* is Boulangist," but did not succeed in laying the rumor to rest.[15] A fictionalized account of the Boulanger Affair can be found in Book v of Anatole France's *Penguin Island*. France tells the story of an Emiral Châtillon, a thinly disguised Boulanger, who conspires to overthrow the Penguin Republic. The account begins with an observation:

> Every regime creates malcontents. The republic, or commonwealth, produced them first among the nobles.
> . . . It created malcontents also among the small merchants who no longer earned a living because of deeply underlying economic causes, but who blamed the republic, which at first they had worshipped and from which they grew more disaffected each day.[16]

Much like the historical Boulanger, Châtillon was the syndic of Penguin Island's "malcontents." In fiction as in the press,

[11] A. Prével, "Les commerçants chez le général Boulanger," *L'Union démocratique*, 26 January 1889.

[12] *La République illustrée*, 24 January 1889. *La Crise commerciale*: Montaigu, "Le commerce chez le général Boulanger," 1 February 1889; "On n'a pas répondu," 1 March 1889.

[13] Basly, "Boulanger et les petits commerçants," *La Nation*, 26 January 1889.

[14] F. Privé, "Les ligueurs du petit commerce," *Le Parti ouvrier*, 17 February 1889.

[15] B. de L., "Les revendications du petit commerce parisien," *La Plaine Monceau*, 29 March 1890.

[16] France, *Penguin Island*, p. 119. For the expression *"syndic des mécontents,"* see Dansette, *op. cit.*, p. 368.

shopkeepers could not escape accusations of Boulangism, and the accusations were not far off the mark.

Militants connected with the *Crise commerciale* and the *Union démocratique* were indeed fervent revisionists. Louis Bréhant was the General's principal advocate on the staff of the *Crise commerciale*. Bréhant made no secret of his Déroulèdist sympathies. He sang the praises of Déroulède's volume of patriotic poetry *Les Chants du soldat* and entitled articles with *Ligue des patriotes* slogans: "En Avant" and "Quand Même."[17] Voters had turned to Boulanger in the January by-election, Bréhant claimed, to punish the free-traders and liberal economists who had brought France to the brink of economic ruin. The people looked to the General, as did *La Crise commerciale,* for relief: "He will know how to pull us out of the terrible crisis we are in, to usher in a new era of labor and business activity. He will bring an end to political wrangling and institute the reforms we need so urgently."[18]

Such sentiments were forcefully seconded in the pages of *L'Union démocratique.* Boulangism, the paper firmly believed, was a genuine people's movement that drew its strength from the outrage and desperation of honest citizens hard hit by the economic slump.[19] The regime, corrupt and caught up in sterile political debates, had failed to respond to the crisis, and so the people had had no choice but to turn to the General. Girard, the *Union démocratique*'s editor-in-chief, excoriated "our rulers who think more of their own pockets than of the nation's business."[20] On election day in January 1889, the paper printed an appeal to voters:

[17]*La Crise commerciale*: Louis Bréhant, "Difficile!" 15 June 1888; "En Avant," 1 February 1888; "Quand Même," 15 January 1888.

[18]Bréhant, "L'élection du 27 janvier," *La Crise commerciale*, 1 February 1889.

[19]"Une faute," *L'Union démocratique*, 17 March 1888.

[20]A. Girard, "La nation et le parlementarisme," *L'Union démocratique*, 19 May 1888.

The parliamentarians, the promoters of Jacques' candidacy, have concluded tariff treaties without reciprocity that are ruinous to national labor.

They have depressed the wages of working men by a total of forty billion francs annually, which amounts to so many transactions the less for domestic commerce.

They have voted the *patente* law of 15 July 1880, regressive in its impact on tax-payers; they have condoned monopolistic practices advantageous to department stores and disastrous for retailers.

Their misguided economic policies have allowed Bismarck to plot once again the ruin of France, this time by an *Industrial Sedan.*[21]

Boulanger had not thwarted income-tax legislation. It was not he who had imposed the oppressive *patente* of 1880 or rejected the *Ligue syndicale*'s petition for redress. There was no doubt, the *Union démocratique* concluded, that shopkeepers, manufacturers and workers would vote "en masse" for the General, and the by-election returns of '89 did not disappoint the paper's hopes.[22] It did not hesitate to ascribe the General's success to "the retail sector," which had "suffered so much in recent years."[23] The hardships brought on by the economic slowdown and the infuriating incompetence of parliament in the face of the crisis, these were the motives that had turned shopkeepers, indeed all the productive classes, to Boulanger.

La Revendication's position vis-à-vis Boulangism was more circumspect. As the official organ of the *Ligue syndicale,* the paper was forbidden by statute to indulge in partisan polem-

---

[21] "Commerçants et industriels," *L'Union démocratique*, 27 January 1889.

[22] A. Girard, "Le commerce et l'élection de la Seine," *L'Union démocratique*, 22 January 1889.

[23] A. Girard, "Le commerce et les élections du 27 janvier," *L'Union démocratique*, 31 January 1889. See also E.Girard, "Commerce et politique," *L'Union démocratique*, 5 February 1889.

ics. And yet, in October 1888, one of the paper's regular contributors ventured a partial, if oblique, endorsement of the General: "It is perhaps regrettable that people who have complaints to make have turned to a single individual rather than undertake the task themselves. But is there any alternative? Do the voters know of one?"[24] As the election of January '89 approached, moreover, *La Revendication* increasingly allowed its reserve to drop. Boulangism was known as the "party of malcontents," and the *Ligue syndicale* no longer scrupled to make known its solidarity with that party. "The *Ligue*," declared a *La Revendication* editorial, "is one great faction of malcontents, determined and convinced."[25] An article of 10 January 1889 enumerated the weaknesses and deficiencies of the "parliamentary republic": unfair taxes, economic oppression, government corruption. Boulanger was a doubtful character, an unknown quantity with peculiar political connections, but "frankly, what have we to lose, is it so precious that we must fear so much the unknown? . . . The moment has come to move out of the incubation period and into the period of action."[26] 1889, shopkeeper militants warned, might prove a repetition of 1789, and the politicians—"as uncaring as they are careless"—had better take heed.[27]

It is not just in the press that evidence of the *Ligue syndicale*'s prorevisionist sentiments can be detected. A number of prominent *ligueurs* took out membership in Boulangist organizations or stood as Boulangist candidates in the 1890 city council elections. Boeuf and Pagèze belonged to the *Fédération des groupes républicains socialistes,* as did A. Girard, who for

[24] A. Fayet, "Pas de mécontents!" *La Revendication*, 4 October 1888.
[25] Le Comité de Rédaction, *La Revendication*, 17 January 1889.
[26] E. Rabasse, "N'est-ce pas le moment?" *La Revendication*, 10 January 1889.
[27] A. Girard, "La crise économique," *L'Union démocratique*, 20 February 1889; Fayet, "La journée de dimanche et la Ligue," *La Revendication*, 31 January 1889.

a brief period served as the organization's treasurer.[28] In 1890, Boeuf and Pagèze ran for municipal office in the IVth on the revisionist ticket.[29] Digard, president of the *Ligue*'s XVth arrondissement section, campaigned as a revisionist in the quartier Necker.[30] Louis Gazon, president of the XVIIth arrondissement section, was slated to run in the Ternes ward, but the local Boulangist committee selected a replacement at the last minute, Henri Galli of the *Ligue des patriotes*.[31]

The *Ligue syndicale,* moreover, was not the only retailer organization implicated in the revisionist campaign. *L'Auvergnat de Paris,* mouthpiece of the powerful and commercially oriented *Ligue auvergnate,* lent unstinting support to the Boulangist cause. Louis Bonnet, the paper's editor-in-chief, set the example. He organized a revisionist committee in Paris' Ist arrondissement, led a delegation of wineshopkeepers to pay respects to the General in March 1889, and in 1890 made an unsuccessful bid for municipal office as a Boulangist candidate in the quartier des Halles.[32] Boulanger was unquestionably popular among the metals traders, junk dealers and *marchands de vins* so numerous in the auvergnat community of Paris. Indeed, wine retailers as a group, whether of auvergnat descent or not, proved one of the General's most fertile—and most useful—constituencies.

Marchands de vins occupied a strategic position in end-of-century ward politics. Wine merchant support assured a candidate premises on which to hold political meetings as well as liquor to soften up prospective voters. In the absence of

---

[28] APP B/a 963, 3 December 1889 and 16 January 1890; B/a 1092, 31 May 1892 and 13 June 1893; B/a 1517, 5 October 1892.

[29] APP B/a 1465, CRN slate for 1890 municipal elections.

[30] APP B/a 1467, XVth arrondissement, 12 February 1890; "Comité de centralisation," *La Revendication,* 2 August 1888.

[31] APP B/a 1092, 13 December 1889; B/a 1468, "Comité républicain national révisionniste des Ternes et de la Plaine Monceau," 15 March 1890.

[32] Raison-Jourde, *La Colonie auvergnate de Paris,* pp. 268–270.

party organization, a politician could not dispense with the services furnished by the local *marchand de vins,* accordingly nicknamed "the Great Elector."[33] In the early eighties, the great beneficiary of wineshopkeeper patronage had been, predictably, Gambetta. No republican politician knew better how to woo the votes of *commerçants,* and he was a favorite of the leading wineshopkeeper association, the *Chambre syndicale des débitants de vins.* In the wake of Gambetta's death, the *Chambre syndicale* veered to the left, passing first into the Radical camp. It mounted a vigorous campaign against legislation mandating prison terms for *marchands de vins* convicted of selling adulterated wine, and it took its campaign into the streets. A march on parliament was staged in 1887 which nearly ended in a riot. The president of the *Chambre syndicale,* a M. Taillard, subsequently steered the organization into the Boulangist camp.[34] The government fought back and, with a promise of amnesty for wineshopkeepers charged under the adulteration law, dissuaded wine merchants from formally endorsing Boulanger in the January '89 election.[35] But sympathy for the General remained strong in the ranks of the *Chambre syndicale.* Eugène de Ménorval, a revisionist militant and resident of the IVth, boasted that thirty four of thirty-six local members of the organization supported the revisionist cause.[36] And Boulangists capitalized on this support to reassert their influence in the *Chambre syndicale.* A police informer reported in May 1889: "In a few days, the National Committee will at-

[33] On the place of the *marchand de vins* in local politics in the late nineteenth century, see: Macé, *Un Joli Monde,* p. 115; Talmeyr, "Le marchand de vins," in *La Cité du sang,* pp. 152–154; Benoist, *Souvenirs,* vol. III, p. 11.

[34] For the evolution of wineshopkeeper organization in the eighties, see Barberet, *Monographies professionnelles,* vol. VII, pp. 282ff.

[35] APP B/a 1466, "Comité républicain national du 7e arrondissement," 26 January 1889.

[36] APP B/a 1137, Eugène de Ménorval, 19 October 1890.

tempt to seize control of the union of wineshopkeepers. A good number of wineshopkeepers are most certainly Boulangists."[37] Taillard himself, in 1890, ran as a Boulangist candidate for municipal councillor in the Ist arrondissement.

The sympathy of shopkeepers and shopkeeper organizations provided Boulangism a core of militants to relay the revisionist message to the level of ward politics. The composition of local committees reflected the involvement of *petits commerçants* in the General's cause. The revisionist committee of the XVth was organized by a baker and three *marchands de vins*. In October '88, the police noted that committee membership had expanded to twenty-two, "all local merchants, retailers or butchers."[38] The attendance at a Boulangist gathering in the Ist was composed "for the most part of *commerçants* from the les Halles vicinity."[39] Petits bourgeois and domestics predominated at meetings in the XVIth, butchers from La Villette at meetings in the quartier du Pont de Flandre (XIXth).[40] According to police records, seventy-eight persons belonged to the *Comité républicain national du XVIIe.*[41] Professions were listed for sixty:

Rentier/*Propriétaire*	4
Liberal Professions	5
Manager/Wholesaler	5
Merchant/*Commerçant*	5
Food	7
Coiffeur	3

[37] APP B/a 1465, 23 May 1889.
[38] APP B/a 1467, XVth arrondissement, 9 November and 7 October 1888.
[39] APP B/a 1465, Ist arrondissement, 3 April and 5 December 1890.
[40] APP B/a 1467, "Comité national du XVIe," 24 February 1889; B/a 1468, "Comité républicain révisionniste du quartier du Pont de Flandre," 7 February 1889.
[41] APP B/a 1467, "Liste des membres du Comité républicain national du XVIIe."

Accountant	2
Housing	6
Metals	2
Coachman	15
Other Transportation	4
Other	2
TOTAL	60

Coachmen represented twenty-five percent of the membership, a fact accounted for in part by the presence of a major omnibus depot in the arrondissement. Small business (*commerçants,* food retailers and coiffeurs) made up another twenty-five percent. Even in the city's outer arrondissements, the XVth, XVIIth and XIXth, the commercial sector made a substantial contribution to the body of Boulangist militants. The upper echelons of Boulangism were staffed with deputies and journalists, but the movement's rank-and-file activists were heavily recruited among shopkeepers, accountants, *marchands de vins* and the like.

MOTIVES

The retailer press, shopkeeper organizations, individual militants and local merchants acting on their own account lent critical if not always unreserved support to the General's cause. But how is shopkeeper support for revisionism to be accounted for?

The explanation lies in part in a lack of attractive alternatives. Opportunism was clearly an unsatisfactory option. Moderate republicans like Eugène Spuller refused even to acknowledge the existence of a commercial crisis. *Petits commerçants* were dismissed by Opportunist politicians as "incompetents" and the shopkeeper's struggle as hopeless and

undeserving of sympathy.[42] And the final insult, Opportunism's candidate in the quartier Notre-Dame at the time of the 1890 municipal elections was none other than Jacques Ruel, the hated proprietor of the Bazar de l'Hôtel de Ville.

More discouraging to *ligueurs* than Opportunist contempt, however, was the apparent indifference of many Radicals to the shopkeeper cause. Henri Brisson shrugged off the *Ligue*'s antidepartment store campaign as unworthy of consideration because it was "not a political question."[43] Brialou, a Radical municipal councillor, told an amazed and furious retailer audience that he "put little stock in the *Ligue*'s success."[44] But perhaps most disillusioning of all was Radicalism's decision to renege on its long-standing commitment to constitutional reform. In early 1888, leading Parisian Radicals joined forces with the reviled Opportunists to defend the existing constitution, an unholy alliance in shopkeeper eyes that signaled a Radical betrayal of democracy and a triumph for oligarchy. *Ligue* militant E. Girard reacted with an outburst of anger: "They have sacrificed national labor to the foreigner; they have fovored time and again the machinations of the feudalities. . . . The democracy has been plied with pretty speeches and false promises, but all the while it has been subjected to the unrestrained exploitation of capital, of a money power aided and abetted now by the radicals no less than the opportunists."[45]

The shopkeeper movement, disgusted with Opportunism and its faith in Radicalism shaken, felt itself abandoned by the republican mainstream. Boulangist organizations acted

[42] A. Girard, "Le commerce et l'élection de la Seine," *L'Union démocratique*, 22 January 1889; "Comptes-rendus," *La Revendication*, 11 October 1888.

[43] Boeuf, "Le congrès du commerce français contre les grands magasins," *L'Union démocratique*, 4 February 1888.

[44] "Comptes-rendus," *La Revendication*, 11 April 1889.

[45] E. Girard, "Une conspiration," *L'Union démocratique*, 24 March 1888.

swiftly to exploit retailer dissatisfaction, and none with greater zeal than the *Fédération des groupes républicains socialistes.*

The *Fédération,* a loose association of Radical committees dating back to 1884, was converted to the revisionist cause in the fall of 1888.[46] The decision prompted the resignation of the organization's best-known Radical office holders (including Mesureur) as well as the secession of sixteen of its twenty-seven member committees.[47] But the *Fédération*'s fortunes had revived by year's end. Jacques Néré has observed that formation of local revisionist committees in Paris occurred in two waves, the first in the spring, the second in the winter of 1888. The second-wave committees, he notes, were drawn principally to the *Fédération des groupes républicains socialistes.*[48] Indeed, the organization had sufficiently recovered from the October schism to play a critical role in the Boulangist victory of January 1889. "[T]he forces of the *Fédération.* . . ," remarked one police report, "exercised a preponderant influence on the outcome of the January 27 elections."[49]

The organization was particularly well placed to understand the shopkeeper's problems. Its ranks were populated by retailer activists like Boeuf and Pagèze. In the municipal elections of 1890, the *Fédération* fielded fourteen candidates. Five advertised themselves as merchants and three as accountants. The center city, moreover, was well represented on the *Fédération* slate. Emile Cère, an editor of the prorevisionist *La France,* ran in the Palais-Royal. L.-H. Petit ran in the IInd, Boeuf and Pagèze in the IVth, Larcher in the Vth, Teyssèdre in the IXth and Dagonet in the Xth.[50] The commercial com-

---

[46] Néré, *La Crise industrielle,* vol. II, pp. 427–428; "Séances des comités et groupes," *L'Union démocratique,* 20 October 1888.

[47] On the split, see APP B/a 497, *rapport,* n.d.

[48] Néré, *La Crise industrielle,* vol. II, pp. 453–454.

[49] APP B/a 1465, 27 April 1889.

[50] On the *Fédération*'s slate of municipal candidates, see Boeuf, "Pas de division," *Les Droits du peuple,* 21 April 1890; APP B/a 1465, CRN slate

munity of central Paris constituted the *Fédération*'s principal base of operations. Little wonder then that the organization evinced a peculiar sensitivity to the concerns of militant retailers.

In the municipal campaign of 1890, for example, *Fédération* militants reverted time and again to the question of commercial defense. Larcher, *Fédération* candidate in the quartier de la Sorbonne (Vth), outlined his biography to a meeting of revisionist constituents. He had worked since thirteen he said, either "in the government, in banking, or as a meterman. In due time. . . , I had a little capital at my disposal, and here I am—today a small shopkeeper struggling against misery and department stores like M. Ruel's Bazar and the Louvre and the Bon Marché (applause)."[51] Louis Boeuf ran in the quartier Saint-Merri. A Boeuf poster, *"Aux Commerçants, Aux Industriels,"* dismissed "purely political questions" as passé. Economic issues were the order of the day, and Boeuf, as a founding member of the *Ligue syndicale* and secretary of the *Fédération,* was the man for the job: "merchants and manufacturers, a vote for Louis Boeuf is a protest against the monstrous and monopolistic practices of the big bazaars and centralizing *grands magasins.*"[52] Pagèze adopted a similar tone. A candidate in the quartier Saint-Gervais, he pledged to constituents his support for *patente* reform, touting himself as the "adversary of privilege, monopoly and government borrowing."[53]

The battle lines were drawn. On the one side, the *Fédération* argued, stood "the worker, the *commerçant,* the manufacturer, the employee, in a word, the entire working people;

for 1890 municipal elections; "Fédération des groupes républicains de la Seine," *L'Union démocratique,* 15 September 1888; B/a 497, *rapport,* n.d.

[51] APP B/a 1518, "Comité republicain révisionniste de quartier de la Sorbonne," 24 April 1890.

[52] Reproduced in *Les Droits du peuple,* 5 May 1890.

[53] "Mouvement socialiste," *Les Droits du peuple,* 24 March 1890.

on the other, a new race of idle kings," coupon clippers and speculators with no experience of productive labor: "Rothschilds, Lebaudys, Ephrussis, Says, Grévys, Wilsons, Louvres, Bon Marchés."[54] A *Fédération* militant, Henri Gâté, envisaged two possible resolutions to the confrontation of capital and the people: the destruction of small commerce and small industry or "that liberating cataclysm we call the social revolution."[55]

Echoes of the *Fédération*'s antidepartment store campaign reached local revisionist committees throughout the city. Candidates without affiliation to the *Fédération* declared themselves shopkeeper partisans.[56] Blanquists and Déroulèdists joined in. *Fédération* agitation elevated *patente* revision and commercial defense to principal themes of the 1890 campaign.

It was not only in 1890 that *Fédération* militants busied themselves recruiting shopkeeper support. In July 1889, Vth arrondissement revisionists, led by Georges Girou and Larcher, engineered a take-over of the local section of the *Ligue syndicale.* On July 25 at a meeting of the *Comités révisionnistes du Ve,* militants resolved to attend a *Ligue* reunion scheduled later in the day. Political issues were not be be discussed. "There are many undecided retailers in the *quartier,"* it was explained. "They must be shown that we understand their needs, their demands, and that we will join in their campaign. This is the way to lead them imperceptibly into the national party."[57]

[54] APP B/a 963, Boeuf poster for 1890 municipal elections; Gâté, "Socialisme et révolution," *Les Droits du peuple,* 10 March 1890; A. P., "La Question sociale," *Les Droits du peuple,* 3 March 1890.

[55] Gâté, "Socialisme et révolution," *Les Droits du peuple,* 10 March 1890.

[56] Coulon in les Halles, APP B/a 1465, 5 February 1890; Caussade in the Faubourg Montmartre, B/a 1466, 18 April 1890; Digard in the quartier Necker, B/a 1467, 12 February 1890.

[57] APP B/a 1517, "Réunion des comités révisionnistes du Ve arrondissement," 25 July 1889.

Fédération members duly appeared in force at the Salle de l'Ermitage where *ligueurs* were assembling to hear a speech by President Christophe. Larcher found occasion to inform the meeting of "the general's solicitude for all the oppressed in the social struggle."[58] The maneuver was a success; the Boulangist press in August announced with satisfaction that a revisionist had been elected vice-president of the *Ligue* local in the Vth and that three Boulangists, including Larcher, sat on the section's propaganda committee.[59]

The *Fédération*'s campaign to mobilize shopkeepers was enthusiastically supported by CRN treasurer Maurice Vergoin. Vergoin was Republican Socialist in his sympathies and briefly served as an officer in the *Fédération*. It was he who arranged for the General to meet with a delegation of shopkeepers on the eve of the January '89 by-election. And in the aftermath of Boulanger's victory, Vergoin had every reason to gloat: "unions, trade associations and labor groups managed this time to vote according to their economic interests . . . Boulanger's election has become . . . an election of working-class, commercial and industrial protest."[60] In February, a follow-up meeting brought the General together with fifty shopkeepers from the IIIrd.[61]

Vergoin had taken it upon himself from the very beginning to improve Boulangist ties to the shopkeeper movement. The CRN was formed in April 1888. The following month, Vergoin, in conjuction with A. Cinqualbre, a former official of the *Ligue des patriotes,* organized the *Fédération républicaine révisionniste.* The new grouping was designed to at-

[58] APP B/a 1517, Vth arrondissement, 25 July 1889.

[59] APP B/a 1517, clipping from *Le Ve*: Larcher, "Le petit commerce dans le Ve," 17–23 August 1889; see also police report of 28 March 1889.

[60] M(aurice) V(ergoin), "Souveraineté reconquise," *L'Union démocratique*, 28 January 1889; A. Prével, "Les commerçants chez le général Boulanger," *L'Union démocratique*, 26 January 1889.

[61] "S'unir et non se liguer," *La Crise commerciale*, 15 March 1889.

tract small businessmen. "I was trying above all," Vergoin explained, "to recruit small shopkeepers and employees on a citywide basis regardless of *quartier* or arrondissement."[62] The *Fédération révisionniste* had collapsed by mid-1889, the victim of factionalism and CRN interference. Vergoin next turned his attention to the organization of traveling salesmen.[63] Since May 1887, he had served as general counsel to the *Syndicat des voyageurs de commerce.* The CRN encouraged Vergoin to use his influence to convert the *syndicat* to Boulangism. Salesmen were invaluable propagandists. They had in the past ably served Gambetta in this capacity. Why not Boulanger? Vergoin undertook the assignment and succeeded. With the approval of the *syndicat* and funding from the General, he launched a newspaper in August 1889, *Le Syndicat des voyageurs,* which doubled as a corporative journal and revisionist organ. Between Vergoin and the *Fédération des groupes républicains socialistes* few opportunities were missed to bring men of commerce into the revisionist fold.

Boulangist attentions flattered and tempted the shopkeeper, and the revisionist appeal was all the more powerful for the language in which it was couched. The themes and preoccupations of much of Boulangist rhetoric, particularly in Paris, bore an unmistakeable likeness to shopkeeper ideology.

Boulangists insisted time and again on the genuinely republican character of the revisionist movement. They did not hanker for a military dictatorship whatever their opponents might say. De Ménorval, a one-time Radical and veteran of the Barodet campaign of 1873, defended Boulanger against

[62] On Vergoin's *Fédération révisionniste*, see APP B/a 1292, Vergoin, "Notes sur mon rôle dans le mouvement boulangiste," Bruxelles, 10 December 1890, pp. 49–51.

[63] On this episode, see *ibid.*, pp. 100–101. Odile Rudelle, too, has argued that the Boulangist movement operated strictly "within the framework of republican legitimacy." Rudelle, *La République absolue*, pp. 217, 222, 232.

accusations of Bonapartism: ". . . in the old days, people conjured up the bogeys of anarchy and the red Republic . . . the same thing is being done today when fears of Caesarism are stirred up to avoid the consequences of Republican government and an immediate revision of the Constitution."[64] If revisionists rejected the regime *en place,* it was not because of an ill-concealed craving for authority but because "the monarchical constitution of 1875" in Naquet's words bore no resemblance to genuine "legislative government as understood by the French revolution or by any existing republic save our own."[65] The institutions of the Third Republic, Boulangists claimed, short-circuited the expression of the popular will and made it easy for special interests to exploit the political process for private gain. A degenerate "industrial feudality"— "*nouveaux riches* Jews, corrupt financiers"—manipulated public power to serve their selfish ends.[66] They kept the Chamber of Deputies, "parliamentary bastille," well stocked with toadying politicians, "doctors without patients, lawyers without cases."[67] An unguarded public treasury was pillaged with impunity by place-seekers and do-nothing bureaucrats. Radical politicians and the "independent" press, so-called friends of the people, raised no cry of protest.[68] The parliamentary regime was rotten with corruption and parasitism. The entire operation had to be scrapped so that France might begin anew.

[64] "Réponse catégorique," *L'Union démocratique,* 23 June 1888. For details of de Ménorval's political past, see APP B/a 1137.

[65] Cited in Néré, *Le Boulangisme et la presse,* p. 95.

[66] Georges Laporte, a member of the CRN, published a book entitled *La Féodalité industrielle* in 1886: Néré, *Le Boulangisme et la presse,* p. 230. Maurice Vergoin, "Le serment de 20 juin," *L'Union démocratique,* 23 June 1889.

[67] Néré, *Le Boulangisme et la presse,* p. 210; Maurice Vergoin, "La fin d'un rêve," *L'Union démocratique,* 23 January 1889.

[68] Vergoin, "L'influence de la presse," *L'Union démocratique,* 9 June 1888; Louis Andrieux, former chief of the Paris police and Boulangist militant, spoke of "*une presse vendue*": "Comité de centralisation," *La Revendication,* 13 July 1890.

Boulangists campaigned under the slogan "Dissolution, Constituent Assembly, Revision." A constitutional convention, with a clear-cut mandate and plenary powers, would not fail in its appointed task—the restoration of popular sovereignty.

The institutional framework of the new regime, in particular the form and duties of the executive, were a matter of some debate, but most Boulangists favored a directly elected unicameral legislature, a *"régime d'assemblée."*[69] The most democratic proposals for constitutional reform came from the *Fédération des groupes républicains socialistes*. A *Fédération* poster explained to voters on the eve of the January '89 election: "Two political courses are available, the one, parliamentarism with its impotence and deceptions, the other genuine democracy, restoring to the people through the 'referendum' control over its own interests."[70] Institutions that thwarted expression of the popular will, the Senate, the presidency, were slated for abolition. An *"assemblée unique,"* elected directly and bound to submit controversial legislation to a plebiscitary vote, that was the essence of republican democracy.[71] It is perhaps odd, but Blanquists, too, expressed a commitment to democratic reform. In the September '89 elections, the ex-Communard Elie May ran as a revisionist candidate in the XIIth arrondissement. May's program included a plea for direct democracy. A whole battery of political reforms was proposed: suppression of the Senate, of course, but also an extension of the jury system, direct election of judges, referendum and recall. Déroulède, to be sure, did not sympathize with such radical democratic aspirations.[72] He favored a centralized regime with a powerful executive, but even Déroulède, the most

[69] Néré, *La Crise industrielle*, vol. II, p. 299.

[70] "L'élection de la Seine," *L'Union démocratique*, 22 January 1889.

[71] Louis Andrieux, "Ce que nous sommes," *Les Droits du peuple*, 3 February 1890; "Comité républicain radical socialiste du Xe arrondissement," *L'Union démocratique*, 16 June 1888.

[72] APP B/a 1466, XIIth arrondissement, Elie May poster.

authoritarian of the revisionists, framed his demand for strong government in the language of republicanism. He had worshiped Gambetta and saw in Boulanger a reincarnation of "that great advocate [*avocat*] of *la patrie*."[73] The General was looked to as a symbol of republican authority. "I welcome you," Déroulède apostrophized Boulanger, "as Cromwell. I will not tolerate you as Monck."[74]

It was, of course, France's own revolutionary republican traditions, more than England's, from which the revisionists drew greatest inspiration. In June 1889, the *Fédération* staged a rally to commemorate the centenary of the Tennis Court Oath. The revisionist committees which took part were encouraged to draw up *cahiers des doléances*.[75] Boulangist militants consistently modeled themselves on their Jacobin forebears, not the desperate and besieged men of the Terror, but the revolutionaries of 1792 who had swept aside the vestiges of monarchical government and framed the most democratic constitution the world had ever known. Vergoin warned the Radicals and Opportunists who opposed revision: "understand us well, sons of revolutionaries, revolutionaries ourselves, it's by 1792 that we swear."[76] And not only by 1792. In December 1888, an anniversary procession organized by the *Fédération* marched to the site of the barricade where Louis Baudin had died in 1851 resisting Louis-Napoléon's coup d'état.[77] Republican Socialist militants revered the memory of the Second Republic and acknowledged their debt to the

---

[73] Sternhell, *Maurice Barrès*, p. 67.

[74] Cited in Ducray, *Paul Déroulède*, p. 174.

[75] "Les cahiers de la démocratie française en 1889," *Les Droits du peuple*, 3 February 1890; Néré, *La Crise industrielle*, vol. II, p. 464; APP B/a 963, pamphlet, June 1889.

[76] Vergoin, "Le serment de 20 juin," *L'Union démocratique*, 23 June 1889.

[77] Louis Boeuf, "Manifestation en honneur de M.Baudin," *L'Union démocratique* 8 December 1888.

past in raising the old *quarante-huitard* battle cry: "Long live the Democratic and Social Republic."[78]

A plea for constitutional revision, legitimated by invocations of the First and Second Republics, was the cornerstone of Boulangism's political platform. A movement born in the midst of depression, of course, could ill afford to ignore the social question, and Boulangists were firmly persuaded that they had an answer to France's festering economic problems. Two themes recur persistently in the revisionist economic program: small-owner utopianism and a powerful xenophobia. The nation's economic ills, it was explained, were the work of foreigners and speculators. Vergoin denounced *grands magasins* as agents of internationalism.[79] German Jews, at Krupp's behest, had forced the closing of the Cail works.[80] Unemployment and low wages were blamed on immigrant Italian labor.[81] Barrès railed against "the financial feudality," and Laur pledged a "war without pity on the big banks and high finance."[82] National salvation necessitated the elimination of foreign influences—"France for the French!"[83]—and the destruction of monopoly. The measures proposed were predictable. Barrès pushed tariff reform and a tax on foreign workers.[84] Laisant and Naquet talked of profit-sharing and cooperation, of schemes to promote "the democratization of

[78] "L'élection de la Seine," *L'Union démocratique*, 22 January 1889.

[79] Vergoin, "Les grands magasins," *La République*, 2 October 1889.

[80] Clipping from *La Presse*, 27 June 1889, in APP B/a 1518, XIVth arrondissement.

[81] Néré, *La Crise industrielle*, vol. II, pp. 82–91; Sternhell, *Maurice Barrès*, p. 159.

[82] Barrès, *Scènes et doctrines du nationalisme*, vol. II, pp. 180–182; Laur's remark was made to a Boulangist audience in the XIXth, APP B/a 1468, 11 July 1889.

[83] Vergoin, "Le commencement de la fin," *L'Union démocratique*, 28 January 1889.

[84] Barrès, vol. II, pp. 165–166.

mechanical power" and worker ownership of light machinery.[85] In some instances—mines, railways, the Bank of
France—nationalization was contemplated, but Boulangists
in general favored measures to deconcentrate industrial property and disperse great fortunes.[86] It was in this spirit that
Barrès advocated *patente* revision, and Michelin a progressive
income tax.[87] The revisionist movement envisaged a France
purged of foreigners and speculators. Boulangism promised,
in the words of one militant, "the reconciliation of all good
patriots, of all honest folk, against the enemy: the Prussians
abroad and shady speculators at home." But who were the
"honest folk," the "good patriots?"[88]

Boulangists claimed to speak in the name of the people,
and they had a rough-and-ready notion of what the term meant.
When revisionists demanded the eight-hour day or six-day
week, when they supported the right to strike or an extension
of trade-union rights, they made plain their commitment to
the welfare of the honest working man.[89] Boulanger knew well
how to play on the economic discontents of his working-class
following. He expressed heartfelt support for striking ditch-
diggers and for the food-workers' campaign against placement bureaux. On the eve of the January '89 by-election, he
welcomed a delegation of sixty workers representing fourteen
chambres syndicales and, to cries of "Vive la République! Vive
Boulanger!" demanded amnesty for the myriad victims of
parliamentarism: striking miners at Denain, striking textile
workers at Amiens, and political prisoners of all varieties.[90]

[85] Sternhell, *Maurice Barrès*, pp. 89–90.
[86] *Ibid.*, pp. 89–90.
[87] *Ibid.*, pp. 158–160; Seager, p. 137.
[88] A. Taillard, "Aux commerçants," *L'Union démocratique*, 27 January 1889.
[89] See, for example, the program of the Rochefortist A. Crié, APP B/a
1468, "Comité républicain révisionniste du XVIIIe," n.d.; and Louis Boeuf's
comments in APP B/a 963, 21 August 1890.
[90] "Chez le général Boulanger," *L'Union démocratique*, 27 January 1889;
Néré, *La Crise industrielle*, vol. II, pp. 397ff.

The working class, however, was not the only target of Boulangist blandishments. A meeting of the *Ligue des patriotes* in the IXth shortly before the '90 municipal elections decided "that the principal theme of the election struggle will be an attack on *grands magasins* in the interest of small shopkeepers."[91] The *Ligue's* candidate in the quartier Petit Montrouge of the XIVth opened the *partie économique* of his program with three demands:

> Severe repression of *engrossers* and *speculators* to protect public and private finances against cosmopolitan Jew-dealing. Reform of the *patente* law to the advantage of small shopkeepers. Progressive suppression of monopolies.[92]

A. Crié, an editor at Henri Rochefort's *L'Intransigeant,* ran in 1890 as a Boulangist in the Grandes Carrières ward of the XVIIIth. In addition to standard demands for the "suppression of all monopolies," he recommended: "Revision of the *patente* to tax department stores progressively on the basis of the number of different articles sold. Reduction of the *patente* on small shopkeepers."[93] The *petit commerçant,* no less than the hard-pressed proletarian merited the solicitude of Boulangist candidates, and revisionists saw no contradiction in defending the interests of both wage earners and shopkeepers. Archain, a typographer and Blanquist hopeful in the quartier Saint-Fargeau (XXth), spoke of his profound attachment "to the cause of labor and of *petit commerce,* whose needs are identical, and whose interests are intimately linked and indistinguishable."[94]

---

[91] APP B/a 1466, IXth arrondissement, 13 March 1890.
[92] APP B/a 1518, poster for Janin, Déroulèdist candidate in the XIVth.
[93] APP B/a 1468, "Comité républicain révisionniste du XVIIIe," n.d.
[94] APP B/a 1469, "Comité socialiste constituant de quartier de Charonne et Saint-Fargeau," n.d.

A rhetoric of popular solidarity, not the language of class struggle, prevailed in revisionist discourse. "The aim of the *Ligue des patriotes*," a Déroulèdist explained to a meeting of wood sculptors, "is to establish concord between employers and employees such that the workshop door will be closed to German workers. If we achieve this goal, . . . there will be no more unemployment."[95] The depression had ravaged the proletariat, but workshop owners and shopkeepers, too, had suffered. All were victims of the capitalist bourgeoisie, of foreigners and high finance, of Jews and department stores. A caste of aliens and do-nothing monopolists had, like a colony of parasites, infested the productive body of the nation. The salvation of France required the abolition of large-scale organizations like the department store and the eradication of foreign influences through various forms of protectionism. The principles underlying the revisionist economic program constituted a coherent and readily recognizable social vision. It was the small-owner vision of a nation of independent workshops and boutiques bound in equal citizenship by a common patriotic fervor.

Boulangist thinking was a synthesis of nationalist, small-owner and democractic republican commitments, and as such, was tailor-made to a retailer audience that shared the identical values and concerns. But a shared republican heritage and small-owner vision were not all that the revisionist and shopkeeper movements held in common. The *Ligue syndicale* detested *Paris nouveau* and the new world of mass consumerism born of the end-of-century slump. These were themes no less congenial to Boulangists. Revisionism, in Paris at least, was as much a movement of cultural reaction as of republican protest. This dimension of Boulangism has not been fully explored by historians, and it is worth looking into in some detail for the light it sheds both on the revisionist movement itself and on the movement's appeal to shopkeepers.

[95] APP B/a 1337, 13 September 1883.

BOULANGISM AND CULTURAL REACTION

Sentiments of cultural reaction ran strongest in the boulevard milieu, from the boulevard proper to its outposts on the rue Royale and Butte Montmartre. The revisionist movement flourished in this environment, set down firm roots and swept all opposition before it. The origins of boulevard Boulangism are to be found in a profound revulsion against the commercializing impact on boulevard life of Haussmannization and the *révolution du bon marché.*

The boulevard press in the 1880s boiled with resentment against the vulgarity of *Paris nouveau* and low-brow materialism of public taste. In 1887, *Le Figaro,* located at the corner of the rue Drouot and boulevard Montmartre, printed a broadside "Le Manifeste des cinq" protesting the gross sensualism of Zola's *La Terre,* recently serialized in *Gil Blas.*[96] The attack on naturalism was followed in 1889 with publication of the infamous "artists' petition." A score of France's best-known writers, architects and painters—de Maupassant, Dumas fils, Garnier, Gounod, the Parnassian poets Leconte de Lisle and Sully-Prudhomme—signed their names to an hysterical denunciation of "the useless and monstrous Eiffel Tower": "The city of Paris, how long will it associate itself with the baroque and mercantile fantasies of a machine builder, only to dishonor and disfigure itself irreparably." The petitioners compared the tower to a "column of bolted sheet-iron," "a black and gigantic factory chimney." A monument to industry, brutal and barbarous, had no place amidst the historic splendors of old Paris.[97]

The Café Anglais occupied the corner just opposite *Le Figaro;* the offices of Arthur Meyer's royalist *Le Gaulois* were housed upstairs. Meyer was an afficionado of the old boulevards, a bon vivant and friend of the titled nobility. No less

---

[96] Billy, *L'Epoque 1900,* pp. 39–40.
[97] For the artists' petition, see Braibant, *Histoire de la Tour Eiffel,* p. 84.

than the signatories of the artists' petition, he decried the passing of "our dear old Paris." On Sundays, *faubouriens* swamped the boulevards. A *flâneur* had no room to stroll. "My poor boulevard," he lamented, "I look at you from my office window; you too, you are a king in exile."[98] Even *Gil Blas*, "the journal par excellence of the demimonde," made a modest contribution to the wave of cultural reaction. Headquartered on the boulevard des Capucines, the newspaper specialized in *"le genre galant,"* salacious stories, double-entendres and backroom gossip.[99] It was here that Maurice Talmeyr, the critic of poster art and cafés-concerts, got his start. De Maupassant—signatory of the artists' petition and author of *Bel-Ami* which unsparingly exposed the corruption of the new boulevards—published regularly in the *Gil Blas*. The paper's staff included a long list of cultural malcontents from the satirist Etienne Grosclaude who, in *L'Exposition comique*, heaped ridicule on the exposition, the Galérie des Machines and, of course, the Eiffel Tower,[100] to the caricaturist Forain, described by his biographer in these terms: "It seemed that he spoke over the heads of the parliamentarians and the men of position directly to the people—not to the body of politically conscious citizens, but to the simple folk, respectful, submissive, full of good sense and natural delicacy."[101]

Aurélien Scholl, a master of boulevard journalism, lent his talents and reputation to the chorus of antibourgeois complaint. Scholl was the perfect boulevardier, a combination of aristocratic affectation and fractious wit. He was a gourmet who dined only in the most select company. He had also been an opponent of the Empire in the 1860s; and, indeed, it was

---

[98] Meyer, *Ce que mes yeux ont vu*, pp. 173, 181.

[99] On the *Gil Blas*, see Billy, p. 47; Talmeyr, *Souvenirs de la comédie humaine*, pp. 2–8.

[100] Grosclaude, *Exposition comique*, pp. 7, 9, 26; see also Capus, *Boulevard et coulisses*, pp. 29, 31; and Talmeyr, *Souvenirs d'avant le déluge*, p. 127.

[101] Vaillat, *En écoutant Forain*, pp. 14, 114–115.

thanks in part to Scholl's financial generosity that Jules Vallès managed to scrape through a decade of London exile in the aftermath of the Commune.[102] Speculation and high finance were Scholl's particular bêtes noires. In the sixties, *La Presse* began regular publication of a stock-market page. This was the paper founded by Emile de Girardin, the paper that had launched Alexandre Dumas and Joseph Méry: "All right then, let's admit that the Bourse has become the great obsession of the French nation, but is it really necessary to show off the wound and in some sense to take pride in it?"[103] Scholl's contempt for vulgar money-making was tainted with an anti-Semitism of the most primitive variety. He liked to tell the story of an alleged encounter with one Moïse Burgos, a Jewish shipbuilder from the provinces. There were five hundred Jews in his home town, recounted Burgos, but no synagogue: " 'we meet at the 100,000 Overcoats [a reference to a Jewish-owned store in Paris, the 100,000 Chemises].' " "Doesn't the temple chosen," commented Scholl, "perfectly capture the spirit of the Jew? The good Lord and confection, the psalms and commerce!"[104]

A cultural malaise then settled over the boulevards at the end of the century. Scholl and his colleagues intoned against the commercialization of boulevard life. They expressed an uncompromising disdain for naturalism, high finance, ready-to-wear goods and all the symbols of so-called modernity from the Eiffel Tower to the Jew. But the pressrooms of boulevard newspapers were not the only place where the apostles of cultural reaction congregated. The new mood was no less pervasive on the boulevard fringe, on the Butte Montmartre above all, but here it was through the cabaret, not the press, that the voice of cultural discontent made itself heard.

---

[102] On Scholl, see Bertaut, *Le Boulevard*, p. 268; Billy, p.22.

[103] Scholl, *L'Esprit du boulevard*, p. 24.

[104] Scholl, p. 73.

The nightclubs that made Montmartre famous got their start in the 1880s. The prototype of the cabaret montmartrois was established by Le Chat Noir, founded in 1881 by a band of Latin Quarter refugees, by Left Bank artists and poets dedicated to the bohemian life. They reveled in their independence and high spirits: not for them the prosaic and mercantile concerns, the high-minded seriousness of their fathers' generation.

The Chat Noir's decor reflected the self-conscious irreverence of its founders. The interior was divided into two rooms, in front the Salle Henri IV, in back the Institut. The staff who waited on tables predictably wore the green palms of Academicians.[105] The cabaret's pseudo-Renaissance accoutrements—colored windows, tin and copper place settings, heavy wooden furniture—were calculated to evoke "an old Paris atmosphere."[106] A mural entitled "Parce Domine," painted by the graphic artist Willette, covered one entire wall and showed a band of revelers, in various poses of abandon, led by a reluctant Pierrot. Willette, *artiste révolté* and son of an infantry colonel, adopted the Chat Noir as the last refuge of youth and innocence in a city corrupted by foreigners and stockjobbers. "[W]hat the Chat Noir really was," he explained, was "a last-ditch resistance against the invasion of foreign influences."[107] Naturalism, Ibsen, the art of social realism, all offended Willette's dreamy sensibilities. He preferred to sketch the idyll of adolescent tenderness, the romances of Pierrot and Pierrette. Pierrette was conceived in the image of "a daughter of Paris, the sister of Gavroche, her heart on her sleeve, a smile on her lips." Pierrot, of course, was a poet, "facetious and sensitive," out of his element in the modern metropolis.[108]

[105] On the cabaret's interior, see Montorgueil, *Le Vieux Montmartre*, pp. 142–150.

[106] Donnay, *Autour du Chat Noir*, p. 13.

[107] Willette, *Feu Pierrot 1857–19.?*, p. 122; see also pp. 115, 129.

[108] Warnod, *Ceux de la Butte*. pp. 85–86.

The entertainment, no less than the decor, conveyed the Chat Noir's dedication to fantasy and iconoclasm.[109] An evening's program included patter, songs and in later years a shadow play. The master of ceremonies, Rodolphe Salis, provided the patter. Salis was, by all recollection, a fabulous *bonimenteur,* insolent and droll with a flair for neologism and slang. The songs, by turns sentimental and *frondeur,* told of the faubourgs and corruption in high places. They romanticized the picturesque and melancholy details of popular life. As the scene shifted from the quays and *les fortifs* to the splendors of the Elysée Palace, the sentimentality turned to ridicule. The people, "the humble folk," so the message went, were the unfortunate dupes of politicians and robber barons. It was in 1885 that the Chat Noir first introduced the Theater of Chinese Shadows. Silhouettes, made of cardboard and later zinc, were projected onto a screen to the accompaniment of music or a read script. The first production in zinc (1887) was entitled "Epopée," a celebration of Napoleon's greatest military victories written and designed by the graphic artist Caran d'Ache. The audience responded enthusiastically. The *"je m'en fichisme"* which characterized the Chat Noir style did not preclude expressions of patriotic emotion.[110] Indeed, for Willette, the cabarets of Montmartre represented a last bastion of patriotism: "It was here that the young, not the old, kept alight the sacred flame of the fatherland, as had the Vestal Virgins of Rome!"[111] Love of country all too easily shaded into xenophobia and anti-Semitism. In 1891, Maurice Donnay, later to become a successful boulevard playwright, presented a revue at the Shadow Theater entitled "Ailleurs," a résumé of mankind's evolution in twenty tableaux. Tableau 17 showed a silhouette of the Paris Bourse. The narrator's voice explains

[109] On the program of entertainment offered at the Chat Noir, see *L'Esprit montmartrois*, p. 33; Montorgueil, *op. cit.*, p. 171.
[110] *Guide de l'étranger à Montmartre*, pp. 69–71.
[111] Willette, pp. 115–116.

that the stock market has collapsed and a song is sung to the tune of "L'Amant de la Tour Eiffel":

> But the golden calf only sleeps
> It is not dead,
> It can be awakened again:
> For it's here, in this establishment
> That is earned one's daily matzah![112]

The Chat Noir inspired a dozen imitators: the Divan Japonais (where Yvette Guilbert's career was launched), the Cabaret de l'Enfer, and of course Aristide Bruant's Mirliton. The cultural politics of the imitators, if the Mirliton may be taken as an example, were identical to those of the Chat Noir. Bruant—*bonimenteur,* song writer and one-man show—posed as the essential bohemian, booted, with red scarf, black velvet costume and broad-brimmed hat. His act was an astounding combination of insult and song. He stood on a table abusing in the lowest slang the high-life audience which had come for a an evening in the mud. The most brutal assaults were reserved for "the snobs and nabobs" and above all the politicians. His music was equally brutal. He sang the "heroes of low life and prostitution," of dopers, pimps and toughs. Not for Bruant the charm and light fantasy of the Chat Noir *chanson.* His singular brutality, his *nostalgie de la boue* did not, however, set him apart in essentials from other artists on the Butte. He shared with the likes of Willette and Caran d'Ache a "fanatical and jingoist" patriotism.[113] His vision of popular life lacked the melancholy of the Chat Noir school, but in its way was no less romantic and picturesque.

The lore of popular life, a sentimental patriotism tinged with xenophobia and anti-Semitism, a profound contempt for

---

[112] The text of the shadow play is to be found in Donnay; for this quotation, see *op. cit.*, p. 183.

[113] *L'Esprit montmartrois*, p. 107.

avant-garde art, politicians and high finance, these were the common themes of the Montmartre cabaret. The mood on the Butte, with adjustments made for the energy and violent temper of youth, was little different from the mood on the boulevards. The high spirits of the cabaret milieu concealed a pervasive hostility to *Paris nouveau* and the vulgarization of cultural life.

The transformation of the boulevards under the impact of urban and economic change generated a powerful backlash of cultural resentment. Boulangism fed on this backlash. It absorbed the malcontents of the boulevard milieu into the revisionist campaign, making the cause of cultural protest its own and incorporating the themes of cultural protest into its appeal.

Certainly, Boulangism exercised a singular attraction on the journalists, men of letters, and cabaretiers who made the boulevards and its Montmartre branch office their home. Take Henri Rochefort as an example. He is today remembered as a seedy and vicious anti-Dreyfusard, as a "prince of the gutter press."[114] But Rochefort's descent into the gutter was a consequence of declining years and declining popularity. In his youth, it was otherwise. In the 1860s and 1870s, Rochefort enjoyed a reputation as France's most sparkling, most radical journalist, a writer and wit whose cultural tastes and fractious politics identified him unmistakably as a man of the boulevards.

Rochefort, the son of a marquis, was a true Parisian, raised in the bustling and popular quartier Saint-Denis (Xth). His father wrote vaudevilles, and young Rochefort grew up in the theater, "initiated from childhood in the secrets of the backstage."[115] The theater was for Rochefort an enduring passion.

[114] The following biographical sketch is based, unless otherwise noted, on material from Roger L. Williams, *Henri Rochefort*, and A. Daudet, *Trente ans de Paris*.

[115] A. Daudet, p. 198.

He produced eighteen light comedies, collaborated at one time with Offenbach and Halévy and landed his first job in journalism as theater critic for the *Charivari*. "It's easy to imagine," recollected Maurice Talmeyr, "a Rochefort taken up and obsessed with politics, but in reality he was much more so by the turf, the theater, and all that was antique furniture and old paintings."[116]

Nevertheless, it was as a political journalist that Rochefort made his name. From the *Charivari*, he transferred to Scholl's *Nain jaune* and in 1864 to de Villemessant's *Le Figaro*. He worked on and off at the paper for four years, graduating a *chroniqueur* of formidable talents. He churned out a torrent of acerbic and informed articles that mercilessly lampooned the Imperial government and ultimately got him fired. In 1868, Rochefort struck out on an independent course. As editor first of *La Lanterne* (described as "the rage of the boulevards")[117] and then of the provocatively titled *La Marseillaise*, he established a reputation for himself as an unswerving apostle of the republican cause—a reputation that did not tarnish in the 1870s. He was deported to New Caledonia in 1873 for pro-Communard activities but engineered a heroic escape commemorated in painting by Manet. With the amnesty of 1880, Rochefort resettled in Paris and immediately launched *L'Intransigeant*, serving notice that he remained unflinching in his radicalism. He resumed his former life not only as a journalist but also as a man about town. Afternoons were spent at Auteuil, evenings at the theater or Café Napolitain and the wee hours in the pressroom composing satirical attacks on the bourgeois Republic.[118]

The young Rochefort was not a gutter journalist but a

---

[116]Talmeyr, *Souvenirs d'avant de déluge*, p. 142.

[117]R. L. Williams, p. ix.

[118]Talmeyr, *Souvenirs d'avant le déluge*, pp. 141–142; Arbellot, *La Fin du boulevard*, pp. 26–27.

boulevardier, very much in the manner of Aurélien Scholl. He combined a caustic and polemical contempt for authority with a taste for the stage, gossip, and café life. Nor was Rochefort the only prominent Boulangist to emerge from the boulevard milieu. When Paul Déroulède entered politics in the 1880s, he was already a famous man, a playwright and poet feted by café society and welcome in Paris's literary salons.

Déroulède was born into a well-to-do bourgeois family, resident in the quartier Saint-Germain l'Auxerrois of Paris's Ist arrondissement.[119] His father, a prominent attorney, intended the boy for a career at the bar, but young Déroulède fancied himself a man of letters. He published his first verse in 1867; he debuted as a dramatist at the Comédie Française in 1869. Déroulède was well connected in the theatrical world through his uncle, Emile Augier, an enormously successful comic playwright. He whiled away his afternoons on the boulevards, at the Librairie Nouvelle in the company of Dumas fils, Meilhac and Halévy.[120] The outbreak of war in 1870 did not interrupt Déroulède's literary career so much as alter its direction. Déroulède served in the army from 1870 to 1874, first as an enlisted man, then as an officer. In 1872, while still in uniform, he published a book of poems celebrating the soldier's life, *Les Chants du soldat*. The volume made his reputation. It was crowned by the Académie française. Gounod judged the young poet's work worthy to be set to music.[121] Déroulède even merited an honorable, if oblique mention in *Les Contemporains*, a collection of portrait essays on contemporary artists, published in the eighties by Jules Lemaître principal critic at the prestigious *Journal des débats*.[122] Dér-

[119] For details of Déroulède's early career, see the relevant pages of Ducray; and Jean and Jérôme Tharaud, *La Vie et la mort de Déroulède*.

[120] Claudin, *Mes Souvenirs*, p. 171.

[121] Roman, *Paris Fin de Siècle*, p. 55.

[122] Lemâitre, *Les Contemporains*, p. 59.

oulède, like Rochefort, straddled two worlds, the world of radical politics and the world of theater, literature and journalism centered on the boulevards.

A focus on individuals, however, even on outstanding figures like Rochefort and Déroulède, does not fully convey the extent of the Boulangist presence in the boulevard milieu. Here were located the principal Boulangist newspapers: Meyer's *Le Gaulois, La Presse* on the boulevard des Capucines (not to be confused with de Girardin's paper), *La Cocarde* just off the boulevards on the rue Montmartre, and virtually next door, Rochefort's *L'Intransigeant.* Boulanger first announced his conversion to the cause of constitutional revision in April 1888 in the wake of a by-election victory in the Nord. The declaration banquet was held on the premises of the Café Riche, boulevard des Italiens. The elite of Boulangism was in attendance, Michelin, Laguerre, Rochefort—and Aurélien Scholl.[123]

Boulangism closed, as it opened, on the boulevards. In August of 1890, *Le Figaro* began publication of an embarrassing and anonymous exposé of the revisionist movement, in fact written by one of the General's closest associates, Gabriel Terrail (Mermeix). The series of articles under the title *Les Coulisses du boulangisme* revealed that the Boulangist campaign had been generously and secretly financed by royalists. The boulevard, of course, specialized in "behind the scenes" gossip. It was the seat of Paris' theater district and not far from the Bourse where, it was said, *coulissiers* (backstairs operators) manipulated stock prices from the wings. What more appropriate title then than *Les Coulisses du boulangisme* for a political exposé published in one of the leading boulevard newspapers? An emergency session of the Boulangist general staff was convoked to denounce Mermeix's accusations. The session met, of course, on the first floor of the Café Riche.

---

[123] APP B/a 1465, clipping from *Le Figaro*, "Au Café Riche," 5 September 1890.

Scholl and Laur remained downstairs, seated together on the terrace.[124] From beginning to end, the boulevard and its inhabitants occupied center-stage of the revisionist movement.

Boulangist activity was no less intense at the outposts of boulevard life, on the rue Royale and Butte Montmartre. The rue Royale, of course, was the site of Durand's, the restaurant at which the Boulangist general staff awaited election returns on the night of January 27, 1889. Enthusiastic crowds thronged the streets, up and down the boulevards from the rue du faubourg Montmartre to the Place de la Concorde. Adrien Dansette recounts an incident, indicative of the evening's high spirits. In front of Barbédienne's, on the boulevard Poissonnière, Dansette writes, "a stage-door Johnny [*un gommeux*] cried: 'Vive Boulanger!; a ragamuffin [*un loqueteux*] did the same; they fell into one another's arms . . . a pair symbolic of the union of classes under the aegis of Boulangism."[125] The choice of characters—a man about town and a ragamuffin—is apt. They were stock figures of the boulevard scene and well suited for the part of Boulangist walk-ons.

The smart set of the boulevards paraded *en équipage* on the boulevard Madeleine, dined at Larue's or Maxim's on the rue Royale, and if sufficiently wellborn and well connected, hobnobbed at the Jockey Club, rue Scribe. The young bucks of the Jockey had booed the opening of Wagner's *Tannhäuser* in 1861. *Lohengrin,* which opened at the Eden-Théâtre in '87, was greeted with a protest demonstration at the Place de l'Opéra. Larue's was owned by the duc d'Uzès whose wife poured millions into the revisionist campaign. As for the carriage parade, the most spectacular demi-daumont of the lot belonged to comte Boni de Castellane—dandy, Boulangist and future Maecenas of the anti-Dreyfusard movement. Revision-

[124] APP B/a 1465, clipping from *Le Figaro*, "Au Cafe Riché," 5 September 1890; also two police reports dated 5 September 1890.

[125] Dansette, *op. cit.*, pp. 242–243.

ism could indeed count on the support of Paris' aristocratic and irresponsible men about town.[126]

The lower depths of the boulevard no less than the high life fed recruits to the revisionist campaign. The *camelots,* who hawked newspapers and knick-knacks to boulevard strollers, flocked to the General's banner. Bohemians, *frondeurs,* irregulars, they took delight in Boulanger's attack on established authority. They sported the pink carnation, symbol of the revisionist campaign. In the words of Montorgueil, "they set aside their professional skepticism," to form the "avant-garde of the General's army, the escort of honor for the man on horseback."[127] The comte de Dillon, one of Boulanger's campaign managers, was no stranger to the techniques of popular electoral politics. He arranged distribution of millions of pins, pipes and photos bearing the General's name or likeness. *Camelots* "by the batch" were enlisted to accomplish the task.[128] The *camelots du roi* of the *Action française* were a weak imitation of the genuine article, the boulevard *camelot* who made his political debut in the service of General Boulanger.

The crowd that gathered in front of Durand's on the evening of January 27 was well sprinkled with boulevard types, an odd assortment of aristocrats and bohemians. The embrace of *gommeux* and *loqueteux* symbolized not so much the "union of classes under the aegis of Boulangism" as the solidarity of the boulevards in confrontation with the bourgeois Republic, overfed and pot-bellied. It has been said that Boulangism missed an opportunity to seize power that night. Others have argued that the possibility of a coup was never even remotely

---

[126] Arbellot, pp. 17, 55–56, 86, 95; Castelnau, *En remontant les grands boulevards,* p. 253. On Boni's connection to the Boulangist movement, see Sternhell, *La Droite révolutionnaire,* p. 114.

[127] Montorgueil, *La Vie des boulevards,* p. 40; see also *idem, Paris au hasard,* pp. 116–117.

[128] Bertaut, *Les Dessous de la "Troisième,"* p. 94; J.–M. Mayeur, *op. cit.,* p. 175.

considered by the General, his lieutenants or the celebrating crowds outside.[129] The possibility of a coup, however, was very much on the minds of Boulangists on the eve of the September 1889 legislative elections. The CRN was scheduled to await returns, once again, at Durand's. A police informant reported the balance of the plan:

> The *Ligue des patriotes* in its entirety will be massed on the boulevard, with *camelots* and hired riff-raff scattered along the route.
>
> If the news is good for the Boulangists, at midnight, a rising will be attempted the full length of the boulevards.[130]

If Boulangism was launched and dissolved at the Café Riche, its battle headquarters were located on the rue Royale at Durand's. For amusement, *la Boulange* marched to the other end of the boulevards and up the Butte Montmartre.

Jehan Sarrazin, director of the Divan Japonais, described audience conduct in the heat of the revisionist campaign of 1888–1889: "Every time an artist was about to begin his act, the entire audience on cue began to sing: 'En r'venant de la r'vue,' punctuating each couplet with shouts of: Vive Boulanger."[131] The majority of spectators wore the Boulangist pink carnation. Boulanger himself preferred the show at the Chat Noir. The General, in civilian dress, took his amusement on the Butte at Salis' establishment. And he was an honored guest. Salis addressed him as "Sire," to the amusement of the future Edward VII, another habitué of the Chat Noir.[132] In the general elections of '89, Willette ran in the IXth as an anti-Semite. He felt little enthusiasm for Boulanger but was an admirer of

---

[129] See note 2.
[130] APP B/a 1465, 20 September 1889.
[131] Sarrazin, *Souvenirs de Montmartre*, p. 112.
[132] Dansette, *op. cit.*, pp. 298–299.

Déroulède.[133] Indeed, the *Ligue des patriotes* was extremely popular on the Butte. André Warnod who spent a turn-of-the-century boyhood in Montmartre, remembered how he and his friends carried on at Déroulèdist meetings and disported themselves as patriotic toughs, complete with the mandatory leaded canes.[134] It is not known whether Willette's colleagues, Caran d'Ache and Maurice Donnay, opted for Boulangism.[135] At the turn of the century, of course, they sided with the anti-Dreyfusard cause, as did Bruant. Zola, after publication of *J'accuse,* was savaged by contemporary songwriters, with Bruant in the forefront.[136] What is certain, however, is that Boulangism prospered electorally in the XVIIIth.

In January 1889, the quartier Clignancourt, bordered on the south by the boulevard Rochechouart, gave 4,841 votes to Boulanger as against 3,374 to Jacques. In September, an exiled Boulanger was obliged to conduct an absentee campaign. Of all possible electoral districts in France, he chose to run in the quartier Clignancourt, site of the Mirliton, seat of Sacré Coeur. The General's opponent was a well-known antrevisionist, the Possibilist Charles Joffrin. Clignancourt voted for Boulanger, 8,000 to 5,500. The Boulangist campaign in the XVIIIth was conducted by the *Fédération des comités révisionnistes du XVIIIe.* A strategy meeting held by the *Fédération* at the Moulin de la Galette inspired a malicious *chansonnier* to write:

> It used to be to conquer Paris
> It was necessary to take Belleville;

---

[133] Seager, p. 179; Willette, pp. 115–116.

[134] Warnod, *Fils de Montmartre*, pp. 19ff.

[135] Caran d'Ache collaborated with Forain on the viciously anti-Semitic *P'stt!*, at the time of the Dreyfus Affair. Donnay, in 1903, produced an anti-Semitic play, *Retour de Jérusalem*, which played at the Gymnase.

[136] Barbier and Vernillot, *Histoire de France par les chansons*, vol. VIII, p. 131.

The Boulangists have understood
That it's not an easy trick.
At Montmartre, they moon about
Dreaming up plans of conquest,
And whiling away the hours . .
At the Moulin de la Galette.[137]

Whatever Boulanger's popularity in Belleville, he succeeded in winning the votes of Montmartre. The General's popularity on the boulevard and the boulevard fringe imparted gaiety and wit to a movement that drew its support from strata hard hit by depression. Boulangism, however, assimilated not only the high spirits of the boulevard but its cultural discontents as well.

Boulangists styled themselves defenders of Paris' revolutionary traditions, of the city's political autonomy and aesthetic heritage. De Susini, a member of the CRN, claimed for the movement the patronage of "Blanqui, Ledru-Rollin, Victor Hugo."[138] Revisionists deplored Paris' subjection to prefectoral authority as an affront to a freedom-loving city. A police informant jotted down details of Vergoin's political program—the urgency of constitutional revision, the necessity of a limited executive—and concluded his report with the remark: "the remainder of the program is absolutely decentralist: communal liberty, cantonal liberty, etc., etc."[139] In the local elections of 1890, revisionist candidates of every persuasion, from Blanquists to Republican Socialists, mounted a vigorous campaign for a restoration of municipal autonomy.[140]

[137] Millot, *La Comédie boulangiste*, p. 237.
[138] Paul de Susini, "Les droits du peuple," *Les Droits du peuple*, 3 March 1890.
[139] APP B/a 1292, 23 July 1889; see also Vergoin, "Election de la Seine," *L'Union démocratique*, 24 January 1889.
[140] Seager, p. 244; see also A. Crié's campaign material, APP B/a 1468, Comité républicain révisionniste du XVIIIe," n.d.; Georges Girou, "Les droits de Paris," *Les Droits du peuple*, 17 March 1890.

Boulangists to be sure never avowed themselves *vieux par-isiens,* but they bristled at the encroachments of *Paris nouveau* and scorned the symbols of its triumph. The Eiffel Tower was, of course, a prime object of their ridicule. Gyp, a woman of letters and ardent Boulangist, invented the character Bob, a sharp-tongued youth in the image of Hugo's Gavroche, full of gallic verve and plebeian witticism. He poked fun at flabby politicians, sang the praises of *le brav'général,* and puzzled over the grotesque stupidity of the Eiffel Tower: "Darn it all! . . . a train, maybe it's ugly as sin, but it's useful . . . a thresher, a hay-maker, any old machine . . . they're always ugly 'cause they're machines, but anyways, they do something . . . but an Eiffel Tower, now I ask you, what does it do, an Eiffel Tower?"[141] As for the exposition itself, the revisionist press agitated vigorously to rouse popular sentiment against the fair.[142] Paul de Cassagnac, editor of the Bonapartist and pro-Boulangist *L'Autorité,* blasted the "new city on the Champ de Mars" in the name of "true Paris."[143] In the spring of 1889, Cassagnac's paper, in conjunction with *Le Gaulois* and *La Presse,* collected five thousand signatures on a petition to close down the exposition during evening hours.[144] The *Ligue syndicale* was delighted with the effort. *La Revendication* expressed approval, and the *Crise commerciale* was outright enthusiastic.[145] Indeed, revisionists found themselves under some pressure from militant shopkeepers to push the anti-exposition campaign one step further and demand a complete shutdown of the fair three days a week.

[141] Gyp (comtesse Martel de Janville), *Bob à l'exposition,* p. 46; see also pp. 24, 57.

[142] Néré, *La Crise industrielle,* vol. II, p. 450.

[143] APP B/a 119, clipping from *L'Autorité,* 21 May 1889.

[144] APP B/a 119, clipping from *L'Autorité,* 21 May 1889, and *Le Gaulois,* 25 May 1889.

[145] Shopkeepers had been debating such a proposal for several years prior to the Exposition. See "Communications," *L'Union démocratique,* 13 March 1887; "Lettre à Cassagnac," *La Crise commerciale,* 15 May 1889.

Boulangists were no less hostile to plans for métro construction. In every phase of the métro debate, revisionists figured prominently in the opposition. In the early eighties, argument centered on a proposal to erect an elevated system. Old Paris loyalists feared the scheme would disfigure the beauties of the Parisian cityscape and formed a committee to block the project, the *Société des amis des monuments parisiens*. Victor Hugo served as honorary president. The society's efforts were seconded in the municipal council by the Blanquist Alphonse Humbert, Georges Berry (a Parnassian poet and future Boulangist), and Eugène de Ménorval.[146] De Ménorval's energy and dedication won him the abiding gratitude of preservationists. His love for the old city was compared to Hugo's, and in 1892 on his death, the *Socété des amis* dutifully sent a representative to attend his funeral.[147] Announcement in 1886 of the national government's métro plans fired a second round of protest. Blanquists denounced the proposal.[148] The *Fédération des groupes républicains socialistes* branded the *"métro d'intérêt general"* a capitalist device to enrich speculators and financiers.[149] The state's proposal was combatted in the city council by Georges Berry, once again, and Armand Grébeauval, a Boulangist from the XIXth. "I declare," argued Berry, "that the métro will create a void in the center of Paris."[150]

Why shopkeepers were attracted to the revisionist cause, then, has a variety of explanations. In the late eighties, retailer militants had few political alternatives to Boulangism.

[146] Lavedan, *Histoire de l'urbanisme à Paris*, p. 508.

[147] APP B/a 1137, Eugène de Ménorval, clippings from *L'Eclair*, 21 and 30 October 1897.

[148] See remarks by Paulin-Méry attacking the métro "Guyot-Eiffel-Rothschild," APP B/a 1467, "Comité républicain socialiste révisionniste du XIIIe," 15 August 1890.

[149] APP B/a 1468, remarks by Larcher, XIXth arrondissement, 7 December 1889; B/a 1518, "Comité des travailleurs républicains socialistes du VIIe," 25 October 1889.

[150] Cited in Lavedan, p. 512.

Only the General, it appeared to many, was prepared to take up seriously the question of commercial defense. His supporters, moreover, presented themselves as ardent small-owner republicans, heirs to a tradition in which the *Ligue syndicale* shared. And not least of all, the revisionists proferred a cultural program—defense of the old city against urban change and the encroachments of mass consumerism—with a powerful appeal to center-city retailers suffering the consequences of Haussmannization and the Great Depression.

CONCLUSION

For a brief moment, in 1888–1889, it appeared the two movements, revisionist and shopkeeper, had merged. The deputies most sympathetic to the shopkeeper cause, Vergoin, Planteau, Michelin, were all leading Boulangists (Mesureur was an exception). Boulangist candidates advertised themselves as shopkeepers and shopkeepers as Boulangists. One of the principal retailer newspapers, *L'Union démocratique,* had placed itself almost entirely at the disposal of the revisionist campaign. Both movements, moreover, recruited cadres from a common pool of militants. A number of *ligueurs* held concurrent membership in the *Fédération des groupes républicains socialistes:* Boeuf, Pagèze and Girard. Wineshopkeepers, traveling salesmen, local tradesmen of all varieties gave their support to Boulanger as organizers and propagandists. This is not to say, however, that retailer support for the General's cause was unanimous or durable.

A fraction of the shopkeeper movement remained indifferent to the revisionist appeal. The pro-Boulangist declaration published January 10, 1889 in *La Revendication* drew an angry response from a *Ligue* vice president. He denounced the futility of politics, "an ugly and scarred old-maid."[151] A *Ligue*

---

[151] A. Hugonet, "Faisons nos affaires nous-mêmes," *La Revendication*, 25 January 1889.

meeting in the XIIth silenced a Boulangist candidate who preached the revisionist gospel with what was judged excessive zeal.[152] In April, *La Revendication* printed an article written by Rabasse, author of the January 10 statement. The upcoming legislative elections were discussed, and this time, Rabasse advised *ligueurs* to put aside the issue of constitutional revision: "We must be content with existing institutions." A discussion of political reform, he wrote, "would unleash the whirlwind."[153]

Boulangism had attracted the support of *ligueurs,* but not engulfed the entire movement. The fraction of shopkeeper independents, moreover, expanded rapidly after the January 1889 by-election. A renewal of Radical commitment to promotion of *patente* reform was instrumental in bringing an end to the shopkeeper movement's flirtation with revisionism. The events of 1888–1889 had alerted Radicals that retailer support could not be taken for granted and stirred the republican left to adopt a more forthcoming stance on the shopkeeper question. Accordingly, on 24 February 1890, Gustave Mesureur submitted a *patente* reform proposal to the Chamber of Deputies. The project was signed by anti-Boulangist republicans of every stripe with Radicals in the majority: from Opportunists like Emile Ferry, through Radicals like Lockroy, Brisson and Clemenceau, to socialists like Millerand. An attached *exposé des motifs* acknowledged the urgency of commercial defense. Department stores, it was conceded, did indeed pose a threat to the small shopkeeper. If *petit commerce* was denied relief, a new round of political disorders was certain to follow. The conclusion was obvious, though unstated: to forestall a repetition of Boulangism, it was necessary to placate shopkeeper discontent with *patente* revision.[154] The project infuriated Boulangists, who

---

[152] "Comptes-rendus," *La Revendication*, 28 February 1889.

[153] E. Rabasse, "Tactique électorale," *La Revendication*, 4 April 1889.

[154] AN C5498, "Exposé des motifs (déposé par M. E. Lockroy et plusieurs de ses collègues. Proposition d'un projet de loi sur la modification de la loi sur les patentes)," 24 February 1890.

maneuvered to recapture the initiative. In December, the revisionist Georges Leveillé submitted to the Chamber a Boulangist scheme for a revision of the business tax complete with insulting asides aimed at free-traders, speculators and Jews.[155] Revisionists like Naquet and Louis Andrieux put in appearances alongside Barodet and Mesureur at *patente* reform rallies and competed with the likes of former Minister of Commerce Edouard Lockroy in expressions of support for the shopkeeper cause.[156] But efforts to arrest the erosion of retailer Boulangism met with little success. The *Ligue syndicale* maintained a scrupulous neutrality between Radicals and revisionists in the 1890 municipal elections, and as the Mesureur bill began to make progress in the Chamber, the *Ligue* abandoned the cause of constitutional revision altogether to concentrate its energies on passage of tax-reform legislation.[157] There were limits to revisionism's claims on the shopkeeper. Not every *ligueur* was a Boulangist. Radical discovery of the tax-reform issue, moreover, persuaded shopkeeper militants to back away from radical protest in favor of a parliamentary and reformist approach. The upsurge of revisionist sentiment in 1888–1889 had all but transformed the *Ligue syndicale* into a Boulangist front. By the early 1890s, however, the shopkeeper movement had shifted back once again in the direction of Radicalism and regained its independence of action.

The extent and limits of shopkeeper revisionism cast an interesting light on the problem of Boulangism's political significance. Viewed from below, from the perspective of the Parisian shopkeeper militant, revisionism appeared a movement of the left committed to social and democratic reform, a

[155] AN C5498, George Leveillé, *projet de loi,* 20 December 1890.
[156] *La Revendication*: E. R., "Causerie parisienne," 20 October 1889; "Comité de centralisation," 17 November 1889; Un ligueur et la rédaction, "Un double lâchage," 15 December 1889.
[157] "Avis important," *La Revendication*, 20 April 1890.

movement that drew its strength from a popular coalition of discontented workers and *commerçants*. The revival of shop-keeper Radicalism in the wake of the Affair underscores the "progressive" character of the revisionist campaign. Boulang-ism did not signal an abrupt shopkeeper shift to the right but constituted a brief interlude in the history of retailer Radi-calism. The popular constituencies mobilized by the Gener-al's campaign—*commerçant* and working class alike—were not transformed by the experience into fodder for movements of the right. The social, republican and genuinely popular char-acter of Boulangism places it in a long tradition of radical re-publicanism stretching backward in time through Gambetta and the Mountain of 1849 to the republican revolutionaries of 1792. But at the same time, there should be no mistaking the reactionary potential of the revisionist movement. Xeno-phobia, small-owner utopianism and cultural reaction figured prominently in the rhetorical arsenal of Boulangism, and these were themes pregnant with right-wing possiblities. Imagine Boulangism stripped of working-class support and confronted with powerful working-class organizations committed to col-lectivist principles. Imagine Boulangist rhetoric with the stress not on republican regeneration but on cultural reaction, fear of foreigners and defense of the *petit patronat* against collectiv-ism. What would remain of revisionism in the wake of these alterations: a coalition of shopkeepers and cultural malcon-tents, united by patriotic sentiment and a common rejection of avant-garde art, working-class collectivism and corporate capitalism—in short, Nationalism. From one angle, Bou-langsm appears the culmination of a time-honored tradition of republican dissent, from another the breeding ground of a Nationalist politics destined to come to fruition with the outburst of the Dreyfus Affair.

The double-edged character of revisionism points up the political ambiguities not just of Boulangism but of the shop-keeper movement itself. The *Ligue syndicale,* democratic and republican in its heritage, was at the same time riddled with resentments: against foreigners and big business, against parliamentary governement and cultural change. It is easy to conceive how these fears and anxieties might be mobilized in the service of far right causes, but the realization of the shopkeeper movement's right-wing potential was not the work of Boulangism. It was rather the 1890s that witnessed the movement's gradual drift to the right. In 1890, shopkeeper militants still stood on the left. By the turn of the century, however, they found themselves squarely planted on the right, allied with cultural conservatism and the forces of order. This rightward evolution is the theme and focus of the next two chapters.

8

• • •

The Shopkeeper Movement
Adrift

THE SHOPKEEPER MOVEMENT drifted out of the radical republican orbit in the 1890s and passed into the camp of the far right. Two lines of argument will be explored to account for this shift of political allegiances. The Third Republic is often thought of as the little man's Republic, as a regime peculiarly sensitive to the needs and interests of the small owner. The treatment meted out to the shopkeeper movement in the late nineteenth century, however, does not fully bear out this assessment. An emasculated version of the Mesureur bill was indeed enacted into law in 1893, but it proved a bitter disappointment to retailer militants. The *Ligue syndicale* had lobbied strenuously to secure passage of a much tougher measure and continued after 1893 to press for additional and more satisfactory legislation, but to no avail. Worse still from the shopkeeper's point of view, public attention which had once been riveted on the question of commercial defense was increasingly turning to new and alien concerns. The meteoric rise of socialism in the nineties polarized the parliamentary community along class lines. The left no longer focused on the perennial republican conflict of people vs. aristocracy, but on the working-class struggle for economic liberation. The *nouvelles couches sociales*, which had so worried the partisans of order in the early days of the Republic, now seemed far less threatening than the militant proletariat. For conservatives, the task at hand at the end of the century seemed to be two-fold: to finesse the "working-class question" and to combat socialism. As the structure of political alternatives evolved in the 1890s, the shopkeeper issue was pushed to the margins. The unhappy fate of *patente* reform and more generally of the question of commercial defense explains in part the shopkeeper movement's *virage à droite.*

The other part of the explanation lies in the efforts of men of the far right to woo retailer support. Marginal politics in the nineties were the affair of anarchists, royalists, anti-Semites and Christian Democrats. Shopkeepers abhorred the anarchist outrages of 1893–1894 and found royalism no less repellent. Anti-Semitism and Christian Democracy, however, made serious overtures to the shopkeeper movement. The *Ligue syndicale* became the focus of the far right's solicitations, and shopkeepers welcomed the attention, reciprocating with a show of gratitude and friendship. If the *Ligue* made a shift to the far right, it was not only because retailer militants felt betrayed by the republican mainstream but also because they found on the right a sympathetic haven in an increasingly hostile world.

Patente REFORM IN THE 1890S

In 1890, the *Ligue* had had good cause to be optimistic about the prospects of *patente* reform. The shopkeeper movement emerged from the Boulanger Affair in a position of great strength. The *Ligue*'s membership was expanding rapidly and would shortly exceed a hundred thousand. The issue of *patente* reform had been placed on the Chamber of Deputies' agenda. The department store question, du Maroussem wrote in 1892, was "the dominant economic question" of the day.[1] Radicals

---

[1] Du Maroussem, *Ebénistes du faubourg Saint-Antoine*, p. 100.

and revisionists competed in expressions of support for the shopkeeper cause. The Boulanger crisis had awakened the parliamentary left to the urgency and political appeal of *patente* revision, and the *Ligue syndicale* acted decisively to exploit its advantage.

The *Ligue* in the early nineties mounted an impressive offensive against the department store. In the '93 elections, it campaigned vigorously on behalf of candidates—Radicals and ex-Boulangists for the most part—pledged in support of *patente* reform. A broad-based pressure-group coalition was organized by the *Ligue* to back up its parliamentary allies. The *Comité de l'alimentation* and the *Chambre syndicale des employés* were enlisted in the antidepartment store campaign. Medium-sized *marchands de nouveautés,* worried about the potential ill effects of *patente* revision, were reassured that the *Ligue*'s principal targets were not stores of secondary importance but commercial giants like the Bon Marché and the Louvre.[2] In the event that political and interest-group pressure failed to produce the desired results, *ligueurs* were even prepared to threaten a tax strike or street demonstrations.[3]

The initial results of the antidepartment store campaign were encouraging. The Chamber, in June 1890, appointed a commission of twenty-two members to study *patente* reform. Mesureur was selected chairman and the Radical Emile Jamais *rapporteur.* Jamais left the commission in 1892 to join the Loubet government as Under-Secretary of Colonies but was replaced by another Radical, Louis Terrier.[4] The Mesureur Commission, controlled by Radical deputies, accorded the *Ligue* ample opportunity to present its case. The *Ligue syndicale* was

---

[2] "Comité de centralisation," *La Revendication*, 10 August 1890.

[3] *La Revendication*: "Comité de centralisation," 20 September 1891; "Causerie syndicale," 20 March 1892.

[4] On the make-up of the Mesureur Commission, see Daugan, *Histoire et législation des patentes*, pp. 113ff.; Chambre des Députés, *Terrier Report*, p.3; AN C5498, 14 March 1892.

called in to testify on more than one occasion. Individual *lig-ueurs*—two jewelers and one shoestore owner—who preferred to speak on their own behalf were granted separate hearings. A host of *Ligue* affiliates—the *Chambre syndicale des patrons tapissiers,* the *Chambre syndicale des magasins de bijouterie,* the *Chambre syndicale du commerce de détail*—submitted evidence to the Commission, as did independent bodies sympathetic to *patente* reform such as the *Chambre syndicale des employés* and medium-sized *marchands de nouveautés.* The range of witnesses mobilized by the *Ligue* represented a fair cross-section of shopkeeper movement militants: small and middle-sized center-city retailers, specializing in the sale of luxury goods, home furnishings, clothing and accessories.[5] The shopkeeper movement, however, was unable to monopolize the proceedings of the Mesureur Commission.

Jules Jaluzot, deputy of the Nièvre and owner of Au Printemps, sat on the Commission and saw to it that department store and allied interests were not neglected. A parade of department store owners and managers—M. Honoré of the Louvre, M. Plassard of the Bon Marché, M. Bessaud of the Belle Jardinière—was marched before the committee to argue the case against *petit commerce.* They were seconded by the *Chambre syndicale de la nouveauté* and a dozen provincial factory owners who sold in quantity to Paris *grands magasins;* businessmen from Grenoble, Beauvais and Reims, manufacturers of gloves, brushes and *tissus* assured the Mesureur Commission of the department store's indispensability as a commercial outlet.[6] Not surprisingly, Paris' commercial establishment weighed in on the side of *grand commerce.* The *Comité*

[5] For the testimony of witnesses in favor of *patente* reform, see AN C5498, letter of 19 March 1891, and verbal communications of 20 October 1890, 20 March 1891, 15 May 1891, 5 and 19 June 1891, 21 October 1891, 6 November 1891.

[6] For testimony in opposition to *patente* to reform, see *ibid.,* 20 February 1891; 15 and 29 May 1891; 5 and 26 June 1891; 6 November 1891.

central des chambres syndicales opposed any major change in *patente* legislation. The *Ligue*'s demands were dismissed in the business press as "utopian dreams."[7] A percentage of commercial notables hoped to sidestep the question of business-tax revision altogether by demanding outright abolition of the *patente*. Jaluzot advanced this position and was supported by Alexis Muzet of the *Syndicat général*. The Mesureur Commission dismissed the proposal out of hand. Yet, in one way or another, whether through foot-dragging or outspoken opposition, Paris' most influential business associations made known their antagonism to business-tax reform.[8]

Provincial Chambers of Commerce delivered a final blow to the *Ligue*'s hopes for tax relief. The Mesureur Commission, in addition to taking testimony, circulated questionnaires to business organizations throughout the country. *Chambres syndicales* expressed a modest interest in *patente* revision, but Chambers of Commerce were almost unanimous in expressions of satisfaction with the current legislation.[9] A powerful array of interests then lined up in opposition to the *Ligue syndicale:* department stores and their dependents, the Parisian commercial establishment, and provincial Chambers of Commerce.

The Mesureur Commission did not doubt that the current *patente* law was manifestly unfair. The Bon Marché, Jamais concluded, paid .37 percent of turnover in taxes while stores that grossed in the vicinity of 100,000F paid as much as 2 or 2.5 percent. The balance of pressure-group forces, how-

---

[7] "Ligue syndicale pour la défense du travail, de l'industrie et du commerce," *L'Union nationale*, 11 October 1890.

[8] For business establishment opposition to *patente* reform, see AN C5498, 20 November 1891; letter from the *Comité central des chambres syndicales*, 2 March 1891. See also AN C5498, letter from the *Union nationale*, dated 31 December 1890; "Syndicat général, 14 décembre 1892," *L'Union nationale*, 7 January 1893.

[9] AN C5498, questionnaires.

ever, clearly opposed a radical overhaul of the tax system. Jamais was forced to conclude: "There does not appear to be a majority among the interested parties, save for a limited reform."[10] And it was precisely a limited reform that the Mesureur Commission proposed in mid-1892.

The Mesureur bill broke new ground in that it adopted the principle of specialization so strenuously argued for by the *Ligue syndicale*.[11] The proposal outlined sixteen specialties ranging from food to military equipment. A store was required to pay a tax for every specialty it retailed. The bill, moreover, included a provision to tax all businesses on the basis of number of sales personnel employed. But otherwise, the proposal left the legislation of 1880 intact. The Mesureur bill, as *rapporteur* Terrier explained, was not designed to punish department stores.[12] It made a modest step in the direction of specialization and, more importantly, attempted to redistribute the burden of *patente* assessment to the advantage of stores with a small sales staff. Terrier feared that even such a moderate reform would encounter obstacles in parliament. The *Ligue syndicale* was irritated by Terrier's hesitations and accused him of lukewarm commitment to the shopkeeper cause. Nor was the *Ligue* happy with the Mesureur proposal and arranged an appearance before the Commission to express its disappointment.[13]

Terrier's doubts about the project's fate in parliament were not ill founded. The first hurdle was the Chamber of Deputies. The Mesureur proposal was reported out of commission

[10] Chambre des Députés, *Terrier Report*, pp. 4, 38; AN C5498, E. Jamais, "Résumé des réponses."

[11] On the terms of the Mesureur bill as reported out of committee, see Daugan, pp. 116–120.

[12] AN C5498, 7 February 1893.

[13] On the *Ligue*'s reaction to the Mesureur bill, see AN C5498, 21 November 1892; and A. Fayet, "La Ligue et ses alliés," *La Revendication*, 26 June 1892.

in February 1893, in spite of last-minute efforts by the Tirard government to impose a substitute bill without a specialization clause.[14] Once in the Chamber, the Mesureur project was challenged on the left by Boulangist deputies Naquet and Leveillé. Naquet called on his colleagues to multiply the number of taxable specialties from 16 to 70, Leveillé from 16 to 102.[15] Naquet and Leveillé's zealotry were mightily appreciated in the shopkeeper press and embarrassed the Radicals.[16] Yet more embarrassing to pro-shopkeeper Radicals was Yves Guyot's opposition to *patente* reform. Guyot was Radical deputy of Paris' commercial Ist arrondissement. He attacked the Mesureur bill in debate in the name of free trade and consumer welfare. *Ligueurs,* who had considered him a friend, were outraged.[17] Terrier, assisted by Mesureur, parried Guyot's challenge. The *patente* bill was finally brought to a vote, February 22, 1893, and passed by a large majority, 370 to 52.[18] But Radical credibility in the retail community was beginning to show signs of strain.

Matters were made worse by the Senate's resistance to *patente* reform.[19] The Senate wanted to restrict application of the specialization clause to stores employing over 200 sales personnel and insisted in addition that the steepness of the employee tax be reduced. The Chamber caved in to the Senate's demands and a modified version of the Mesureur bill was enacted into law on 28 April 1893.

[14] For the government's last-minute attempt to sabotage the Mesureur bill, see AN C5498, 16 February 1893.

[15] *JOC*, 17 February 1893, pp. 601ff, and 20 February 1893, pp. 639–644.

[16] *La Revendication*: "Comité de centralisation," 13 December 1892; "Compte-rendu," 1 January 1893.

[17] A. Fayet, "Actualité," *La Revendication*, 6 March 1892.

[18] For the debate in the Chamber of Deputies, see *JOC*, 17 February 1893, pp. 603–607, and 18 February 1893, pp. 620ff.

[19] On the Senate's treatment of the Mesureur bill, see AN C5498, 29 March 1893; and Daugan, pp. 132–139.

The Senate's emasculation of *patente* reform angered the *Ligue syndicale*.[20] It judged the law of April 28 with equal severity: "For most department stores, the law of April 28, 1893 has been . . . a tax-relief law."[21] The *Ligue*'s assessment was in fact perfectly correct. In the provinces, 231 stores employed a sales staff in excess of ten. The cumulative tax burden of these stores was reduced by the Mesureur bill from 432,279F in 1890 to 271,261F in 1893. The situation in Paris was more nuanced. The assessment on stores employing more than 200 sales personnel (seven stores altogether) increased from 673,833F to 1,818,282F. On the other hand, firms which maintained a sales staff of between 11 and 200 enjoyed a sizeable tax reduction. Sixty-five businesses fell into this category, and their total assessment in the 1890–1893 period dropped from 441,990F to 298,286F. From the *Ligue*'s point of view, the experience of *patente* revision had been a disappointment.[22] *Ligueurs* felt they had been treated with "humiliating disdain," "like an under-age child," and all they had to show for the ordeal was a so-called reform which in reality lightened department stores' tax burden in all but a handful of cases.[23]

Ligueurs, for want of an alternative, pressed for a further revision of business-tax legislation. In 1890, Radicals had seized the initiative on the question of *patente* reform. This time ex-Boulangists took the lead. In June 1895, Georges Berry, elected deputy of the IXth in 1893, submitted a bill to parliament to increase the number of taxable specialties from 16 to 67. The measure was applicable to stores employing 50 or more in Paris, 25 or more in cities with a population of 100,000

[20] "2e Réunion extraordinaire de la Ligue," *La Revendication* 15–31 March 1894.
[21] "Modifications diverses d'impôts," *La Revendication*, 30 November 1894.
[22] Sénat, *Gauthier report*, p. 98.
[23] "Conséquences de la loi du 28 avril 1893 sur les patentes," *La Revendication*, 15 August 1893.

plus and 15 or more elsewhere.[24] Berry's bill met stiff opposition in the Chamber and was unceremoniously voted down. Despite the setback, shopkeepers were delighted with Berry's performance. *La Revendication* applauded Berry as "our valiant friend and defender."[25] The shopkeeper movement had discovered a new champion, an ex-royalist, ex-Boulangist and, as of 1893, professed *rallié*.

Radicals, however, were not prepared to concede the shopkeeper movement to men of Berry's persuasion. The formation in November 1895 of the all-Radical Léon Bourgeois ministry resurrected the issue of *patente* reform. Mesureur was appointed to the cabinet as Minister of Commerce. The *Ligue*'s attitude toward the Bourgeois cabinet, however, was reserved, a sign of the shopkeeper movement's diminished confidence in Radicalism: "We await the economic initiatives of the new ministry, and despite out sympathy for some of its members, we believe it prudent to look at the results before making a commitment."[26] The Radical government acted to restore shopkeeper trust. A watered-down version of the Berry bill was appended to the 1896 budget in the form of an amendment. The Chamber, however, refused to cooperate. It voted to disjoin the amendment and banished the Berry bill to committee.[27] The Radicals had failed, and dismally; they would not again stand in the vanguard of business-tax reform.

The issue of *patente* revision was revived once again in 1898 but ex-Boulangists were now very much in control. The *patente* commission to which the Chamber had bequeathed the Berry amendment went through the prescribed motions. The

[24] For the terms of the Berry bill, see Duclos, *La Transformation du commerce de détail*, pp. 65–69.
[25] "Partie officielle," *La Revendication*, 31 April 1896.
[26] "Le nouveau ministère," *La Revendication*, 30 September 1895.
[27] On the fate of *patente* reform in 1895–1896, see Daugan, pp. 166–168; Sénat, *Gauthier report*, pp. 2–3.

Ligue syndicale testified in the amendment's favor as did Marguery's *Comité de l'alimentation*. A bill was at last reported out in November 1897 but failed to pass. Berry immediately moved to attach the bill to the budget of 1898 as an amendment, and this time the maneuver worked. In March, on the eve of the '98 elections, the Chamber passed the budget bill, including the Berry amendment. The Senate, however, balked and voted to disjoin the amendment. The *Ligue* was enraged and suspected the measure had been sabotaged by the Méline government at the behest of the *Chambre syndicale de la nouveauté* and the powerful *Association générale du commerce et de l'industrie des tissus et des matières textiles*. As in 1896, the Berry amendment was shunted to committee. The chairman of the Senate *patente* commission, however, was Gauthier de Clagny, an ex-Boulangist not unsympathetic to the *Ligue*'s cause. Ex-Boulangists, it appeared, were the shopkeeper's surest allies, in the breach when former friends had apparently abandoned the fight.[28]

As the century drew to a close, the *Ligue syndicale* had reason to be discouraged. A decade of intensive interest-group activity had produced meager results. In the aftermath of the Boulanger Affair, Radicals and revisionists had bid furiously for shopkeeper support, and *patente* reform was made the focus of a national political debate. By 1898, however, it seemed Radicals had lost interest. Mesureur was still active, but the *Ligue* cultivated supporters—Georges Berry, Gauthier de Clagny—outside the Radical camp.

A Georges Berry, however, did not have the influence of a Gustave Mesureur, and *patente* reform no longer commanded the attention of parliament. The Berry bill was treated with cavalier unconcern, bottled up in committee, watered down

[28] On the progress of *patente* reform in the late nineties, see Daugan, pp. 176–180; also "La Ligue à la chambre," *La Revendication*, 15 March 1896; H. Destréguil, "Banquet de vautours," *Affiches tourangelles*, 16 June 1898.

and shunted back and forth between the Chamber and Senate. The shopkeeper movement, in a position to shape events in 1890, had been banished to the political wilderness by the end of the decade. But why did the regime, allegedly so sympathetic to the little man, turn its back on the *petit commerçant?*

The explanation is to be sought in part in the business establishment's power and ability to exploit parliamentary institutions to its advantage. It was after all a formidable coalition of commercial interests that thwarted a radical revision of the *patente* in 1893. The small-owner class was clearly not the only or even the most important constituency in a position to make demands on the government of the Republic. One historian has characterized the social base of the regime as "an alliance of capitalists and petty producers."[29] The first and most eloquent exponent of this view was Daniel Halévy. Halévy recognized the Third Republic's small-owner base, but he was also sensitive to the preponderant influence exerted by business interests in government circles. "[T]he Republic which triumphed in 1878," he concluded, "was the Republic of Schneider, Dubouchet and Boucicaut."[30] The fate of *patente* reform in the nineties made plain that in the event of conflict within the republican alliance, it was the *petit indépendant* who was sacrificed in preference to big business; it was the small shopkeeper who was sacrificed in preference to the Schneiders, Dubouchets and, above all, Boucicauts.

THE ECLIPSE OF THE QUESTION OF COMMERCIAL DEFENSE

The frustration of the shopkeeper movement's political aspirations, however, had roots deeper still than the entrenched

[29] Elwitt, *The Making of the Third Republic,* p. 1.
[30] Halévy, *La République des ducs,* p. 316.

power of big business. The shopkeeper movement in the nineties was overshadowed by the rise of labor. The elections of '93 quadrupled socialist representation in parliament from roughly ten to forty deputies. The number of unionized workers in France tripled from 140,000 in 1890, the year May Day was first celebrated, to upwards of 420,000 in 1895, the date of the CGT's founding.[31] No less significant than the numerical expansion of the labor left was the increasingly militant tone of its public rhetoric. The trade-union and socialist movements, as they grew in strength, came to embrace with a new and exclusive fervor the cause of the class struggle. The answer to exploitation and class oppression lay not in popular protest against a privileged oligarchy but in collectivism. The mounting socialist threat moved conservative politicians, both Catholic and nonconfessional, to set aside differences over the religious question in the interests of anti-socialist solidarity. The business community, so divided over tariff policy in the 1880s, rallied as one man in the nineties to defense of the status quo. An obsession with the "social question" drove the issue of commercial defense out of the arena of party politics. Otherwise preoccupied, socialists, conservatives and organized business, all dismissed the shopkeeper movement's concerns as insignificant and anachronistic.

Socialists in the 1880s, it is true, had shown an interest in the shopkeeper cause, but in the ensuing decade this interest turned to cold indifference if not outright hostility. Collectivist discourse at the end of the century abounded in predictions of the small shopkeeper's imminent demise. Jules Guesde, Jean Jaurès, Edouard Vaillant, whatever the political differences that divided them, were agreed that *petit commerce* was doomed to expropriation by the inexorable laws of capitalist concentration.[32] *Ligueurs* naturally objected to prognostica-

[31] See Appendix IV in Watson, *Georges Clemenceau*, pp. 422–423; Sorlin, *Waldeck-Rousseau*, p. 356.

[32] Guesde, *Collectivisme et révolution*, p. 26; Jaurès wrote a series of articles on *petit commerce* which appeared in the *Dépêche de Toulouse* from October to

tions of a shopkeeperless future. The evident determination
of socialists to apply collectivism in practice only made matters worse. In 1893, Vaillant proposed to the Paris city government formation of a municipal *boucherie*.[33] Guesdists on the
Roubaix municipal council in fact organized a city-run phar-
macy in 1894.[34] And then there was the question of socialist
support for the consumer cooperative, an institution feared and
reviled by *petits commerçants*.[35] Collectivists, it appeared, had
a penchant for social experiments ruinous to the retail trade.
The *Ligue syndicale* found the increasing militancy of the trade-
union movement no less unsettling. The *Chambre syndicale des
employés* had testified on behalf of *patente* reform in 1892; by
decade's end, it refused even to consider endorsement of the
Berry amendment. The CSE had come to regard the small
shopkeeper as an employer no less exploitative than the *grand
magasin*. The *petit commerçant* like the department store owner
refused to pay a minimum wage. He too imposed disciplinary
fines and made use of placement bureaux.[36] The position of
the *Chambre syndicale de l'alimentation* (the food-workers' union)
was yet more belligerent. As early as 1893, the organization
had demanded the out-and-out suppression of the employer
class. Anarchist agitators in 1892–1893 and then Alleman-
ists in 1896–1897 propagandized the *Chambre syndicale* on
behalf of the general strike with great success. The food-
workers' union embraced Allemanist theories with some enthusiasm and via Allemanism made its way eventually into
the ranks of revolutionary syndicalism. In the eighties, the

December 1897. They are reprinted in *Oeuvre de Jean Jaurès*, vol. VI, pp.
37–61; "Elections du 3 septembre 1893," *La Revendication*, 31 August 1893.

[33] "Comité de centralisation," *La Revendication*, 31 July 1893.

[34] L. Mazand, "Collectivisme et liberté," *La Revendication*, 15 December
1894.

[35] L. Christophe, "A. M. Jean Jaurès, député," *La Revendication*, 15 May
1894.

[36] APP B/a 153, brochure distributed at meeting of 10 February 1899,
"A propos de la révision des patentes."

main target of food-worker militancy had been the *placeur*. In the nineties, it was the arch-capitalist Alphonse Marguery, the *Ligue syndicale*'s most reliable friend in the business establishment.[37] *Ligueurs* had at first welcomed working-class syndicalism, but at the end of the century the trade-union movement took an ugly turn, or so it seemed to shopkeeper militants.

The working-class left in the nineties began to reconcile itself to the prospect of an organized France, a France governed by functionaries and/or *chambres syndicales* and denuded of parasitical intermediaries. The collectivist/syndicalist vision of a future without *petit commerce* revolted the *Ligue syndicale,* which came to look upon organized labor as an enemy no less formidable than the department store. *"Petit commerce,"* wrote *La Revendication* in 1896, "is our last rampart against the invasion of socialism."[38]

A similar mistrust prevailed in the *Ligue*'s relations with the conservative right. The rise of socialism generated a reflexive movement of social defense. The conservative mobilization of the nineties culminated in 1896 with the formation of the Méline government, a ministry of antisocialist combat based in the Chamber on a coalition of Catholic *ralliés* and Opportunists and buttressed outside of parliament by the support a unified business community. The motives and aims of this conservative alliance were shaped by the urgent need to find an adequate response to pressure from the new labor left.

Two Catholic constituencies in particular were drawn to the Mélinist coalition: liberal Catholics of the Le Playian school and Social Catholics in the tradition of comte Albert de Mun and the marquis de la Tour du Pin. Liberal and Social Cath-

---

[37] On the evolution of the *Chambre syndicale de l'alimentation*, see APP B/a 1408 bis, 4 November 1892; 19 May 1893; 19 June 1896; 13 and 25 March 1897; 18 October 1898.

[38] "Le petit commerce," *La Revendication*, 15 June 1896.

olics alike deplored the decadence of contemporary France. Class conflict, it was agreed, was at the origin of the decline, and the "false principles of 1789" in turn were at the root of class conflict. The Revolution had abandoned France to the destructive power of an individualism untempered by religious faith or moral scruple. France's moral regeneration depended on a restoration of "the social peace," but here liberal and Social Catholics parted company.

Le Playians rejected state intervention as a corrective to the vagaries of the marketplace. The true solution lay in a reestablishment of contact between social classes, and a voluntary show of paternalism on the part of the nation's elite was judged sufficient to that purpose. Social Catholics on the other hand condemned the free-market system out of hand; they were unanimous in advocating construction of an alternative, corporatist economy. The term corporatism conjures up feudal images of seigneurs and peasants, journeymen and masters. A medieval restoration was precisely the vision that had inspired the founders of the Social Catholic movement, de Mun and de la Tour du Pin, but in the 1890s, the movement underwent a transformation. A new generation of theorists— Georges Goyau, Henri Lorin, Henri Savatier—confronted with persistent economic stagnation and an emerging socialist movement, placed a heightened emphasis on the corporation's welfare functions and began to explore the institution's potential as an instrument of economic stabilization. The new corporatism was inspired not so much by legitimist longings for a medieval past as by a desire to restore order to a depressed economy, resolve the social question and thereby conjure away the twin dangers of collectivism and militant trade unionism.[39]

[39] Lorin, "Etudes sur les principes de l'organisation professionnelle," pp. 3–23; Raoul Jay, "L'organisation du travail par les syndicats professionnels," pp. 299–338; Henri Savatier, *La Concurrence déloyale*, pp. 12–14.

Liberal and Social Catholics were committed to defend the principles of hierarchy and property. Le Playians placed their confidence in paternalist policies, corporatists in the order and stability of professional organizations. The papal encyclical *Au Milieu des Solicitudes,* promulgated in 1893, had called on French Catholics to rally to the Republic, to accept the legitimacy of republican institutions. The *ralliement* made possible Catholic participation in the Mélinist majority, but it was Méline's stature as an antisocialist and champion of social defense which attracted the votes of Catholic deputies, whether liberals like the Lyon banker Edouard Aynard or ex-legitimists like Jacques Piou. A segment of Catholic opinion in the nineties moved in the direction of an alliance with Opportunism. Opportunism responded with a decided turn to the right.

In the elections of '93, Opportunist candidates found it expedient to invent a new party label: Progressist. The switch in name coincided with the emergence of a new generation of centrist politician. In the 1890s, the old guard of Opportunism—Ferry, Spuller, Allain-Targé—faded from prominence to be replaced by newcomers like Poincaré, Deschanel and Barthou. The rising generation embraced a new set of priorities. The religious question had preoccupied politicians of Ferry's vintage. The slump of the eighties, the slowness of recovery and, above all, the rise of socialism convinced the new generation that economic, not religious, questions deserved the most urgent attention. Progressists shied away from attacks on the Church and turned their efforts instead to the defense of big business.[40] Paul Deschanel in a speech before a major employers' association sketched in the contours of the nonsectarian, pro-business Republic that Progressists envisioned. He warned his audience of the dangers of foreign

---

[40] For the development of the Progressist outlook, see Sorlin, *op. cit.,* pp. 355–372.

competition. It was necessary to place French industry on a combat footing, to rebuild the merchant marine, to mobilize colonial resources. Educational reform, moreover, was essential to train a new breed of aggressive, practical-minded businessmen and colonists. And in the same breath, Deschanel spoke of the need to reduce competition among businessmen through association: "Yes, we want to increase the industrial and commercial capacities of professional associations so that they may serve as the germ cells of an organization of labor from which will be born, from which is being born even now, a new world of credit, savings, insurance, pensions, conciliation and arbitration."[41] France's future lay not in the traditional Radical/moderate front against the Church, but in an alliance of all conservative social forces to relaunch the economy and counter the socialist threat.[42]

Such a program was tailor-made to France's business elite, and businessmen responded with a solid and appreciative show of support for the Mélinist majority in parliament. The rapprochement between Progressists and *ralliés* was paralleled by a strengthening of ties between organized business and the nation's conservative political establishment, and the motive was much the same in both cases. The short-lived Radical government of Léon Bourgeois attempted in 1896 to legislate an income tax, an effort that failed but which threw a scare into France's fiscally conservative business community.[43] Three years earlier, a bill had been submitted to parliament providing for obligatory employer participation in a state-run accident insurance program. Alexis Muzet of the *Syndicat général*

[41]Comité national républicain du commerce et de l'industrie, *Discours Deschanel*, pp. 24–25; see also p. 23.

[42]*La République française*: "Discours de M. Deschanel," 4 March 1898; Colson, "La politique," 4 March 1898. For the Radical viewpoint, see G. Mesureur, "Un nouveau comité," *Le Voltaire*, 28 January 1898.

[43]AN 27 AS 1, AIAF, *Assemblée générale*, 11 March 1896, p. 20; see also APP B/a 40, press clipping from *Le Petit Parisien*, 25 October 1896.

condemned the measure as an unwarranted and unacceptable invasion of property rights.[44] Businessmen were not prepared to stand idly by while "demagogues" and "doctrinaires," insensitive to the needs of commerce and industry took over the affairs of state.[45] A national congress of *chambres syndicales* was organized in October 1896, the first such assembly in seven years.[46] The congress declared its opposition to tax reform and the accident insurance proposal and appointed a permanent delegation to communicate its views to the government. Muzet acted as president, Mascuraud as treasurer. A half-dozen vice-presidents were elected, representing the organizations which had participated most actively in the congress' proceedings: Marguery, Alfred Pinard (president of the *Alliance syndicale du commerce et de l'industrie*), Frédéric Bertrand (president of the *Chambre syndicale du bâtiment*), Charles Expert-Bezançon (a chemical manufacturer and president of the *Comité central des chambres syndicales*), Ancelot (president of the *Association générale des tissus*), and Larcher (president of the *Syndicat du commerce en gros des vins*). The government, since April of 1896 under the ministry of Jules Méline, accorded the permanent delegation a respectful and sympathetic hearing.

Organized business expressed its gratitude in a most practical manner. In April of 1897, members of the permanent delegation—Expert-Bezançon, Muzet, Marguery, Bertrand—

---

[44] *L'Union des syndicats de France*: A. Muzet, "La prévoyance," 1 May 1897; "Syndicat général. Comité de direction," 2 November 1897; "Syndicat général. Comité de direction," 1 December 1897.

[45] *L'Union des syndicats de France*: A Jolly, "Justes revendications," 1 April 1898; "Chambre syndicale des bois de sciage et de l'industrie," 15 January 1898.

[46] On the proceedings of the Congress, see APP B/a 40, 19–24 October 1896, and clipping from *Le Petit Parisien*, 25 October 1896. See also "Délégation permanente des chambres syndicales de France," *L'Union des syndicats de France*, 15 April 1897.

constituted a *Comite national républicain du commerce et de l'industrie* (CNRCI) to campaign on Méline's behalf in the upcoming '98 elections. A spokesman summed up the CNCRI's program to a reporter from *La Croix:* "The unrelenting war waged against us by the socialists, the dangerous orientation of most trade unions, have imposed on us the obligation to organize for social defense."[47] Socialism and collectivism, declared CNRCI president Expert-Bezançon in a letter to *L'Eclair,* threatened "the "principles of social organization bequeathed to us by the French Revolution: industrial liberty, individual property, free labor."[48] The Méline cabinet was pledged to these principles, and so deserved the unswerving support of commerce and industry.

A preoccupation with a faltering economy and a looming socialist menace set the tone of conservative rhetoric in the 1890s. Defenders of the social order joined forces and cast about for reassuring alternatives to the collectivist vision of the future: paternalism, corporatism, association, employer syndicalism. But whatever the alternative, conservative attentions were fixed on the challenge from the left. The new structure of politics which had begun to emerge at the end of the century turned on the issue of social reform vs. social defense. As for the shopkeeper, he was from the conservative point of view a distracting and minor nuisance, an irrelevancy in a new political world dominated by class issues. Conservatives, and socialists alike made this point with crystal clarity, and the message was not lost on the shopkeeper movement.

Progressists stood in the forefront of opposition to the Berry amendment. Poincaré, Aynard, Charles Jonnart, Henri Boucher—all Progressists—voted against the measure.[49] Mé-

---

[47] "Le comité du commerce et de l'industrie," *La Croix,* 8 October 1897.

[48] Cited in "Comité national républicain du commerce et de l'industrie," *La République française,* 28 January 1898.

[49] "Un document suggestif," *Affiches tourangelles,* 2 June 1898.

line was on record in support of "the suppression of intermediaries." Le Playians were scarcely more sympathetic. Edmond Demolins of the Le Playian journal *Science sociale* dismissed
the shopkeeper movement as "confused" and retrograde,
hopelessly out of touch with the modern world and doomed
to extinction by the laws of the marketplace.[50] *La Réforme sociale,* founded by Le Play himself, published an antishopkeeper diatribe in 1893 blaming working-class misery on the
petit commerçant: "It is he who has provoked cooperative organization by false weighting, adulteration of merchandise,
overcharging and abominable credit practices which reduce
workers to debt bondage, servitude and misery."[51] Similar
suspicions colored Social Catholic attitudes vis-à-vis shopkeepers. The peasant, in need of supplies, was all too often
the victim of unscrupulous retailers who overcharged, falsi-
fied weights and adulterated merchandise. In Brittany, Catholic aristocrats, inspired by de la Tour du Pin's corporatist
doctrines, sponsored organization of peasant purchasing cooperatives to by-pass urban middlemen.[52] In a letter to *La
Croix* published in 1897, Louis Durand, president of the Social Catholic *Union des caisses rurales,* attributed the retail crisis to a surplus of intermediaries. Shopkeepers were too numerous relative to the market; they inflated prices to maintain
income, and consumers had no choice but to defend themselves through cooperation.[53]

The identical criticisms were leveled against shopkeepers
by the business establishment. A speaker at the 1894 annual
banquet of the influential *Association de l'industrie et de l'agriculture française* (AIAF) blamed the high cost of living on intermediaries: "there are so many small shopkeepers, each one

[50] Demolins, *La Question des grands magasins,* pp. 1–4.

[51] A. Fougerousse, "Chronique du mouvement social," p. 798.

[52] Berger, *Peasants against Politics,* pp. 59–65.

[53] "Les coopératives. Lettre de M. Louis Durand," *La Croix,* 21 April
1897.

with a clientele too small to earn a livelihood by selling at a natural price, that prices have been forced up progressively out of all proportion to the real value of the merchandise being retailed."[54] On the issue of business-tax reform, major business associations were in the majority unsympathetic. The Paris Chamber of Commerce, the *Association générale des tissus,* and the *Alliance syndicale* lobbied actively in opposition to the Berry amendment.[55] The 1896 congress of *chambres syndicales* declared its opposition to specialization, indeed to *patente* revision in any form if intended "to regulate the conditions of commercial and industrial competition."[56]

The Mélinist bloc cold-shouldered the shopkeeper movement, and shopkeeper militants responded in kind. *L'Epicerie française* mocked the CNRCI as a "nobility in the new style, which wants to ape the old one."[57] The membership of the *Comité,* a *Ligue syndicale* member explained to *La Croix,* consisted "above all of large-scale merchants and manufacturers," of "Jews and those whom we would label without hesitation monopolists."[58] It was antisocialism, it was preservation of a pro-business government that preoccupied the *Comité national républicain,* not the shopkeeper's fate. *L'Epicerie française* observed of a banquet sponsored by the CNRCI in March 1898:

> We noted the presence of many speculators and swaggering industrialists, of numerous lawyers, doctors, deputies and would-be deputies, but of our own, of the modest and the humble, of the great commercial major-

[54] AN 27 AS 1, AIAF, *Assemblée générale,* 28 February 1894, p. 114.

[55] *Affiches tourangelles*: A. Trépreau, "La Chambre de commerce de Paris, l'Alliance syndicale et l'amendement Berry," 8 August 1898; "Banquet de vautours," 16 June 1898.

[56] "Syndicat général. 11 novembre 1896," *L'Union nationale,* 19 December 1896.

[57] "Chronique," *L'Epicerie française,* 8 May 1898.

[58] "Banquet de dimanche," *La Croix,* 9 October 1897.

ity, of the Third Estate which still exists whatever people say, not a single one.[59]

The conservative mobilization of the nineties made little attempt to accommodate the *Ligue syndicale*. The *Ligue* in turn did not stint in its denunciations of Opportunism, big business and Mélinist notables like Waldeck-Rousseau.

The political prospects of the shopkeeper movement were dismal indeed in the 1890s. The Mesureur bill was a failure and the possibility of a second reform dim. The shopkeeper/Radical alliance had not been a success, defeated in parliament by the determined efforts of France's commercial establishment. By decade's end, moreover, there seemed to be hardly a republican politician still around who took a serious interest in the once critical question of commercial defense. The political context in which the retailer movement operated was changing, and changing in a direction unfavorable to shopkeeper concerns. The *Ligue syndicale*'s capacity to influence events diminished commensurately. It found itself frozen out of the mainstream, marginalized. The margin of politics, however, proved by no means inhospitable to the shopkeeper movement. In contrast to the parties of the mainstream, fringe movements like anti-Semitism and Christian Democracy courted retailer support, and the effort paid off. By the turn of the century, the *Ligue syndicale,* at one time the focus of left-wing attentions and sympathies, had established a tentative alliance with men of the far right.

THE SHOPKEEPER MOVEMENT AND MARGINAL POLITICS AT CENTURY'S END: ANTI-SEMITISM

On the margin of politics in the early nineties, momentum passed from Boulangism to a new and ominous fringe move-

---

[59]L. Mazand, "Commerce et politique," *L'Epicerie française*, 6 March 1898.

ment: anti-Semitism. Anti-Semitism bore a striking but deceptive resemblance to Boulangist revisionism. Anti-Semites like Drumont, the marquis de Morès and Jules Guérin shared in the revisionist critique of new Paris and the *révolution du bon marché;* they exalted the small-owner utopianism of republican tradition but radically altered its political significance. Democracy, whether parliamentary or direct, was anathema to anti-Semites. They reworded the traditonal republican dichotomy of people vs. aristocracy to read people vs. Freemasons, Jews and Protestants. The titled nobility, indeed, even monarchical government, were too highly regarded to be made objects of execration. As for the Church, anti-Semitic leaders, if not declared Catholics like Drumont and Morès, were prepared like Guérin to strike a bargain with the forces of traditionalism. The anti-Semitic movement undertook to reconcile the revolutionary heritage of *morcellement* with the rule of traditional elites—church, landed aristocracy, and monarchy. It pieced together a political program, reactionary in content and design, that was at the same time geared to an audience by tradition impervious to far right appeals: the urban petite bourgeoisie. The shopkeeper movement, frustrated and outcast, responded with interest if not always enthusiasm and via anti-Semitism got its first taste of radical right politics.

The cast of characters who organized and led the anti-Semitic movement were a familiar breed, men of the boulevards all and dedicated cultural reactionaires. Like Déroulède and Rochefort, Drumont was Parisian-born (he was raised in the Ist arrondissement), and like them too, he began his career as an aspiring littérateur, determined to make his mark in the world of journalism and theater centered on the boulevards.[60] As a

---

[60] On Drumont's early career, see Byrnes, *Antisemitism in Modern France*, pp. 140ff.; Mme. Alphonse Daudet, *Souvenirs*, p. 68; Gendrot, *Drumont*, p. 24; Pierrard, *Juifs et catholiques français*, pp. 31ff.; Talmeyr, *Souvenirs de la comédie humaine*, pp. 67–72.

young man, Drumont wrote criticism for *La France théâtrale* and for a brief period held down a full-time position as *chroniqueur* at de Girardin's *La Liberté*. He even made a stab at playwriting, co-authoring a one-act drama produced with the assistance of Dumas fils. Nor did Drumont lack influential connections in the literary world. In the 1870s, he frequented Victor Hugo's salon on the avenue de Clichy and was no less welcome at Alphonse Daudet's. Indeed, it was Daudet who interceded with the Maison Marpon in 1886 to arrange publication of Drumont's massive Jew-baiting diatribe *La France juive*.

The book's publication altered the direction of Drumont's career. A chronicler of second-rate talents, he was transformed overnight into the nation's most notorious and most formidable anti-Semite. Drumont followed up his initial success with a barrage of anti-Semitic polemics: *La Fin d'un monde* (1889), *La Dernière bataille* (1890), *Le Téstament d'un anti-sémite* (1891). In 1889, he organized the short-lived *Ligue antisémitique* and in 1892 founded an anti-Semitic newspaper *La Libre Parole*. In the process, Drumont assembled a hard core of anti-Semitic disciples, litterateurs very much like himself who exploited anti-Semitism to relaunch flagging careers. Jacques de Biez, vice-president of the *Ligue antisémitique,* was a failed art critic, author of a treatise on Manet and resident of the Butte Montmartre. The post of editorial secretary at *La Libre Parole* went to Georges Duval, "an old-timer of boulevard journalism," who sported the "obligatory monocle" of his journalistic mentor Aurélien Scholl. Gaston Méry, an aficionado of palmistry and the Chat Noir, served as the paper's city editor. Second-hand dandies, veterans of the boulevard press, nightclub habitués, the whole rag-tag bunch which rallied to Drumont were in one way or another connected to the boulevard demimonde.[61] And indeed, the paper

[61] Byrnes, pp. 273–279; Gendrot, pp. 37, 84, 90–91, 146.

on which they worked, *La Libre Parole,* occupied premises on the boulevard Montmartre, directly adjacent to Arthur Meyer's *Le Gaulois.* Drumont abandoned a career in letters in 1886, but he never abandoned the boulevard.

Jules Guérin was cast in much the same mold as Drumont and his cohort of down-at-the-heels litterateurs. He was a smart dresser and inveterate café-goer, a permanent fixture at the Brasserie de la Grande Maxéville located just next door to Drumont's newspaper offices. Guérin, the fledgling boulevardier, had once tried his hand at the theater, failed, and only then turned to business as a second career. A series of bankruptcies, broken partnerships and shady transactions landed him in trouble with the law. The anti-Semitic movement offered Guérin a safe haven and fresh field of opportunity as it had other no-talents and *ratés.*[62]

The marquis de Morès was by contrast the perfect clubman, the genuine article of which Guérin was but a second-rate edition.[63] Morès was born into high society, the son of Geneviève de Pérusse des Cars and the Spanish duc de Vallombrosa; and he received an education befitting a young man of aristocratic lineage, sent first to a Jesuit *collège* in Poitiers and then in 1877 to Saint-Cyr. On graduation, Morès moved to Paris, was elected to the Jockey Club and proceeded to squander the family fortune in a life of dissipation. Marriage to Medora Hoffman, daughter of a German-American banker, shored up his shaky financial position. A wealthy man once again, Morès quit the army and in 1883, wife in tow, departed for the badlands of North Dakota to start a cattle ranch. The enterprise ended in bankruptcy, and Morès returned to

[62] On Guérin's early career, see Byrnes, p. 324; Rutkoff, *Revanche and Revision*, p. 74; APP B/a 1104, "Note," undated.

[63] For details of Morès' early career, see APP B/a 1193, 22 May 1890; B/a 1194, clipping from *La Libre Parole,* 25 June 1896 and undated biographical pamphlet, "Un paladin en redingote," by J. Silve de Ventavon. See also Schwarzschild, "The Marquis de Morès," pp. 3–26.

France in 1886, a business failure but ever the bon vivant and clubman. He ran as an anti-Semite in the 1890 Paris municipal elections. The police set a plainclothesman to follow his activities during the campaign. In the space of a week, Morès scarcely stepped off the boulevards. He purchased pastries at Julien's, boulevard des Italiens, and dined at the Café de la Paix. A dozen clubs, from the rue Royale to the rue Scribe, were fitted into his itinerary, including an evening's detour to the Moulin Rouge.[64]

Morès, Guérin, and Drumont were all boulevard types, and the movement of cultural reaction, so powerful in the boulevard milieu of the 1880s, left an unmistakeable imprint on the anti-Semitism they espoused. Drumont may be taken as an example. He mourned the passing of *vieux Paris*. The "Paris of our fathers," he wrote, had been charming and intimate; every *quartier* had had a character of its own. But *vieux Paris* was no more: "without having reached Methusaleh's age, we have witnessed in our lifetime places of elegance, pleasure and conversation lose little by little the physiognomy they once had when we were young."[65] The Palais-Royal had faded into obscurity. The boulevards, once the glory of Paris, were become the playground of patricians and courtesans, a modern-day via appia worthy of Rome in its decadence.[66] In Drumont's first book, appropriately entitled *Mon Vieux Paris,* blame for the city's decline was laid on France's great railroad companies. The Compagnie d'Orléans had vandalized the VIth to construct the Luxembourg railway station. The Gare d'Orsay, which serviced the Compagnie de l'Ouest, hideously disfigured the Esplanade des Invalides.[67] The "financial feudality," in pursuit of profit, leveled entire *quartiers*. The railway boom

[64] APP B/a 1193, 4–10 September 1890.

[65] Drumont, *Mon Vieux Paris*, vol. II, p. vi.

[66] Drumont, *Mon Vieux Paris*, vol. I, pp. 134–135; *idem, La France juive,* vol. II, p. 558.

[67] Drumont, *Mon Vieux Paris*, vol. I, p. 175, and vol. II, p. vii.

had eviscerated the city and opened it to hordes of pleasure-seeking outsiders.[68]

Drumont's hatred of the railroad was matched by an equal and no less savage hatred of the department store. He compared *grands magasins* to the poisonous manchineel. They sucked the life out of entire neighborhoods. The florist, the carpenter, "the humble folk," were driven into bankruptcy.[69] The Boucicaut fortune, Drumont raged, had been "erected on the ruin of myriad local shopkeepers."[70] The big stores were "barracks" which brutalized employees, and yet the press, bought off by department store advertising revenues, maintained a bribed silence.[71]

More than a nostalgia for the pre-Haussmannic city he had known as a boy underlay Drumont's tirades against the railroad and department store. The Compagnie d'Orléans and Bon Marché were singled out as symbols, as manifestations of a larger phenomenon: "the industrial feudality," as Drumont called it. This great feudality threatened the extinction not just of *quartier* life but of all beauty, all culture. It exercised its occult power through the *société anonyme* and factory system whose machine-made manufactures were driving the exquisite handicrafts of the Parisian artisan out of the market.[72] It foisted the new merchandise on an unsuspecting public through vulgar advertising and the ubiquitous poster. The "cosmopolitan orgy" of the World's Fairs were celebrations of its power, the Eiffel Tower, a hideous monument to its triumph.[73]

---

[68] *Ibid.*, vol. I, pp. 170, 181, and vol. II, p. vii.

[69] Drumont, *La France juive*, vol. II, p. 518.

[70] Drumont, *La Fin d'un monde*, p. 105. See also pp. 40–42, 81–82.

[71] *Ibid.*, p. 99. See also, Drumont "Une victime des grands magasins," *La Libre Parole*, 19 May 1894.

[72] Drumont, *La Fin d'un monde*, pp. 81, 125; *idem, La France juive*, vol. II, p. 262.

[73] Drumont, *La Fin d'un monde*, p. iv; *idem, La France juive*, vol. II, p. 262.

The cluster of phenomena—*sociétés anonymes,* poster art, the Eiffel Tower—which Drumont associated with the new feudality is not hard to identify. The "industrialized France" he rejected was a France remade by the *révolution du bon marché.*

The themes that recur persistently in Drumont's work—old vs. new Paris, the humble folk vs. the industrial feudality—transpose in a minor key the struggle he believed dominated modern life, France vs. the Jew. Haussmannization and the depression of the eighties were manifestly the source and inspiration of Drumont's jeremiads, but he was satisfied to attack symptoms and symbols. In lieu of an explanation, Drumont foamed against the Jew, accused of plotting and executing France's decline. If luxury production and aesthetic standards were in decline, Jewish influence was responsible. It was the Jew who had invented collectivism and the *société anonyme.* An entire generation's obsession with atavism, anemia and neuraesthenia was blamed on the Jew. Jews "without scruples" victimized the shopkeeper; the Jewish Péreire brothers were responsible for the destruction of *vieux Paris.*[74]

Drumont's cultural criticism contained an implicit social message that is not difficult to decipher. The cozy *quartiers* he defended were populated by *petits commerçants* and employees. The handcrafted goods whose beauty and tastefulness he extolled were manufactured by artisans and journeymen laboring in modest ateliers. Drumont embraced the cause of an embattled *menu peuple* besieged by a vast array of opposing powers. He styled himself a knight errant of the humble folk against the life-threatening forces of large-scale organization: collectivism, corporate capitalism and "the Jewish International." Drumont in short was a confirmed small-owner utopian who viewed the end-of-century social crisis as a decisive battle in the bitter and eternal struggle of *petits* contra *gros.* Nor was Drumont unique among anti-Semites in his espousal

---

[74] See *La France juive*, vol. I, pp. 108, 122; *La France juive*, vol. II, pp. 283, 291; *La Fin d'un monde*, p. 166.

of the small-owner vision. Morès and Guérin looked on the world in identical terms.

Morès rejected large-scale organization in whatever form. He demanded the suppression of *sociétés anonymes*. The railroad industry stood accused as an Anglo-Jewish monopoly. So, too, the banking business. Rothschild and Company diverted millions into foreign investment while at home a credit shortage throttled French industry. The department store, of course, was not overlooked in Morès' indictment of organized capitalism. He summed up the program of anti-Semitism to Louis Bréhant and two *Ligue syndicale* militants in these terms:

> There is one last goal I am pursuing . . . that's to rid France of the *phylloxera* known as the *kike* who starts out on the boulevard as a peddlar of 'handy liddle oberaglasses' and winds up, rue Laffitte, with a corner on the copper market.
>
> But these aren't the only Jews, and I embrace in one and the same hatred all the Schneiders of Creuzot, the Rothschilds of the Bank, and the Ruels of the Bazar de l'Hôtel de Ville.[75]

The anti-Semitic appeal was pitched to a popular audience of artisanal workers and petits bourgeois, and Morès harbored no illusions on this score. He stood in the '90 municipal elections as a candidate in the "popular" Epinettes ward (XVIIth). He had chosen the district, as he explained to an electoral rally, "because *there* are to be found the workers and petty rentiers who are most interested in my theories."[76]

Guérin's vision of anti-Semitism's potential constituency was

[75] APP B/a 1193, clipping from *L'Assaut*, 27 April 1890. For evidence of Morès' hostility to large-scale organization, see: B/a 1193, *profession de foi*, quartier des Epinettes, 1890, and pamphlet "Rothschild, Ravachol et Cie par Morès et ses amis," 1892, pp. 20–34. B/a 1194, 29 December 1894; clipping from *La Terre de France*, 29 December 1894; and "lettre au peuple," 4 December 1895.

[76] APP B/a 1193, *Profession de foi*, quartier des Epinettes, 1890.

no different. In 1897, he launched the *Ligue antisémitique française* (LAF), the first anti-Semitic organization to attract a significant membership; it counted upwards of 8,000 adherents within the first year of its existence.[77] The LAF presented itself as a "socialist" and even "revolutionary" organization,[78] but the brand of socialism it advocated amounted to little more than a rehash of small-owner utopianism laced with a powerful admixture of anti-Semitic venom. A discriminatory tax on foreign workers, denaturalization and eventual deportation of France's Jewish community, *patente* revision, railroad nationalization and democratization of the Bank of France, such were the principal planks of the league's platform.[79] It was a program aimed not against private property but against "cosmopolitan elements" and the power of monopoly. Guérin in fact rejected collectivism out of hand as the invention of "*arrivistes* and egotists."[80] He championed the cause not of the proletariat but of "the people"—"the worker, the producer, the exploited."[81] France was indeed a nation divided, but the lines of battle were not drawn on the basis of property ownership. In Guérin's vision, "*bourgeoisisme*," government regulation, *sociétés anonymes*, and "cosmopolitan Jewish speculators" were drawn up on the one side; *petits commerçants*, employees, traveling salesmen and wage earners stood on the other. Guérin campaigned under the slogan: "Defend all the workers. Fight all the speculators." "His aim," a police informant reported, "is to constitute a vast organization intended to protect the interests of small commerce, employees and workers."[82]

[77] Sternhell, *La Droite révolutionnaire*, p. 221.
[78] Cited in Wilson, "The Ligue Antisémitique Française," pp. 33, 35.
[79] See Wilson, "The Ligue Antisémitique Française," pp. 34–35; APP B/a 1107, 20 July 1898.
[80] APP B/a 1104, 30 March 1897.
[81] APP B/a 1104, 29 August 1897, 14 August 1896.
[82] APP B/a 1104, 24 August 1898.

Guérin, Morès, and Drumont looked to a "humble folk" of shopkeepers and wage earners as anti-Semitism's natural clientele. It was one thing, of course, to rhapsodize about the unity of the oppressed in the face of the Jewish conspiracy; it was quite another to realize this unity in practice, to build an anti-Semitic movement with a genuine popular following. Drumont was a newspaperman and polemicist, too much a man of words for the job. The task of organization fell by default to Morès and Guérin.

Morès schemed with aggressive and spendthrift zeal to bring working-class organizations into the anti-Semitic camp. In 1892, he disbursed 5,000 francs to finance formation of an anarchist counter-police.[83] The same year, he funneled in excess of 3,000 francs to striking coachmen.[84] The Paris police identified a half-dozen syndical organizations which at one time or another cooperated with Morès or accepted Morès subsidies: ditch diggers, masons, food workers, *loueurs de voitures*.[85] But the militant proletariat was not the sole target of Morès' blandishments.

On the eve of the '90 elections, an article entitled "Les Grands Magasins et le Marquis de Morès" appeared in *L'Assaut*, a Morès-financed newspaper. The author, Louis Bréhant, identified Morès as "the adversary of the Vampire-Department Store" and recounted an interview between Morès and representatives of the *Ligue syndicale*. The marquis expressed a warm interest in the shopkeeper movement:

> The idea is wonderful! Your perseverance magnificent! I will look into the question; leave me some copies of the *Crise commerciale* and of *La Revendication*, but I assure you in advance of my support.[86]

[83] APP B/a 1193, 10 August 1892; see also B/a 1194, 23 January 1893.

[84] APP B/a 1193, 27 January 1892; 2, 9, 16, 25 February 1893.

[85] APP B/a 1193, 20 July 1892; 17 August 1892; 14 and 20 October 1892; 18 November 1892.

[86] APP B/a 1193, clipping from *L'Assaut*, 27 April 1890.

Morès maneuvered skillfully to attract and exploit a small-business constituency. In April 1892, he published an article in *Gil Blas* which accused Dreyfus frères, an important meat supply firm owned by Jews, of selling rotten meat to the army. He was taken to court on libel charges and found guilty. Butchers at the La Villette slaughterhouse, however, welcomed the discomfiture of a powerful business competitor. They organized a series of anti-Semitic conferences in the XIXth (where La Villette was located), and in September, an association of slaughterhouse butchers presented Morès a "saber of honor."[87] Morès acted to capitalize on his popularity in the XIXth. He organized a personal bodyguard, largely composed of La Villette butchers; and he financed publication of a XIXth arrondissement newspaper, *Le Réveil social*, edited by Jules Guérin.[88] Guérin in fact made the organization and manipulation of retailer support something of a personal specialty.

From its inception, Guérin's LAF hammered on the theme that Jews, department stores and cooperatives were indistinguishable. In 1895, he put in an appearance at a *Ligue syndicale* meeting to denounce the iniquities of the department store. "Settle the Jewish question," he harangued the shopkeeping audience, "and all such iniquities will disappear."[89] Adrien Poccaton, vice-president of the LAF's XVIIIth arrondissement committee, pursued a parallel line of attack. "Most department stores and big factories," he told an anti-Semitic rally, "are subsidized only by Jews."[90] Jews were no less the inspiration of cooperative societies: "All these societies . . .

[87] On this and similar incidents, see APP B/a 1193, flier dated March 1892; police reports of 31 March 1892 and 5 September 1892. B/a 1194, clipping from *La Libre Parole*, 1 March 1893, and reports dated 2 and 22 February 1893.

[88] APP B/a 1194, 24 April 1893; B/a 1104, 13 November 1893.

[89] A. Tolleire, "Ligue syndicale," *La France*, 29 November 1898.

[90] APP B/a 1107, 31 March 1898.

are in cahoots with German collectivism which is dominated by Jews scheming to gain control of our commerce."[91] The LAF dreamed of a vast commercial purge to reverse the Jewish invasion. Guérin proposed a boycott of Jewish-owned shops and prepared a list of targeted stores.[92] Poccaton's XVIIIth arrondissement section formed a "committee to fight against department stores and cooperatives." The LAF sponsored a *Groupe des voyageurs de commerce et représentants antisémites.*"[93] And finally, it was the LAF that masterminded the anti-Semitic riots of January–February 1898. Anti-Semitic crowds, not only in Paris but in Marseilles, Nantes, etc., took to the streets attacking Jews and Jewish property. Jewish stores, Jewish-owned department stores in particular, were the anti-Semites' targets of choice.[94] The riots were but the most violent manifestation of a broad-gauged LAF offensive to enlist the shopkeeper movement as a subordinate ally in Guérin's war against the Jews.

Anti-Semitism's small-owner vision, its passionate assault on new Paris and the *révolution du bon marché*, played on themes well suited to a shopkeeper audience. But shopkeepers were republicans, and the anti-Semites repudiated the nation's democratic inheritance. Drumont, for one, held republican democracy in abhorrence. The path to national regeneration, he argued, lay not in popular sovereignty but in a revival of traditional authority. Movements of renewal within the Church and titled nobility excited Drumont's enthusiasm. He was warmly sympathetic to Christian paternalists like the Social Catholic Albert de Mun.[95] In 1896, a Christian Democratic congress was convened in Lyon. Drumont consented to pre-

[91] APP B/a 1107, 31 March 1898.

[92] APP B/a 1104, 1 April 1898.

[93] APP B/a 1107, 31 March 1898.

[94] Wilson, "The Ligue Antisémitique Française," p.35; see also Wilson, "The Antisemitic Riots of 1898 in France," pp. 198–802.

[95] Drumont, *La Fin d'un monde*, pp. 210–212.

side at the closing-night banquet.[96] *Noblesse oblige* and religious zeal, these were Drumont's solutions to the end-of-century crisis. The "Catholic socialism"[97] he espoused, however, was utterly alien to the republican tradition. In the republican vision, a people of shopkeepers and artisans was beset on two fronts, by an old and new feudality. Drumont reordered the balance of forces. The people and the ancien régime, in his scheme, were aligned in a common front against the combined forces of the Red and Gold internationals.

Morès too envisioned an alliance of the people and titled aristocracy. "[T]he aristocracy," he proclaimed, "in revolt against a corrupt government, offers its hand to the petite bourgeoisie, to small industry crushed by syndicates of monopolists."[98] The Church, of course, stood shoulder to shoulder with the petite bourgeoisie and insurgent aristocracy. Morès was a militant Catholic, sympathetic to corporatist doctrine.[99] He reportedly took funds from the Society of Jesus.[100] The Social Catholic movement of de Mun and de la Tour du Pin furnished him with bodyguards and claqueurs, and Social Catholic militants acted as the marquis' go-betweens in negotiations with working-class organizations.[101] Morès preached an alliance of nobility, Church and nation against the Jew. The ultimate goal of such an alliance for Morès, if not for Drumont, was a reinstitution of monarchical authority, a cause which he championed with both vigor and discretion. In April 1890, Morès laid plans with the duc de

---

[96] Pierrard, p. 123.

[97] Drumont, *La Fin d'un monde*, p. 187.

[98] APP B/a 1194, cited from an 1890 conference in "Les Obsèques de Morès," *La Libre Parole*, 19 July 1896.

[99] APP B/a 1194, cited in clipping from *La Libre Parole*, 7 January 1893.

[100] APP B/a 1194, 23 July 1893.

[101] On Morès' relations with the Social Catholic movement, see APP B/a 1193, 20 July 1892, 23 August 1892, 31 December 1892; B/a 1194, 13 January 1893.

Luynes and duc d'Uzès to restore the house of Orléans to the throne of France.[102] The duc and duchesse d'Uzès poured substantial sums into Morès' '90 election campaign and continued to fund the anti-Semitic movement into 1892.[103] The police in April 1893 reported Morès still "in close correspondence with the young duc d'Orléans."[104]

Guérin, on the other hand, was neither a royalist nor a Catholic by conviction. Yet, much as Morès, he was able to count on the support of Orleanists and militant Catholics. The butchers of La Villette contributed important sums to Guérin's anti-Semitic campaign, but the bulk of LAF funds were furnished by the royalist party. Guérin met with the duc d'Orléans at Marienbad in the summer of 1898. A police informant commented on the state of royalist/anti-Semitic relations: "we know from a very good source that the royalist party is making a serious effort to win over Guérin and that the duc d'Orléans has urged that Guérin be 'looked after' [sic] with particular care."[105] Catholic support was expressed not in the form of money but of militants and sympathetic audiences. In March 1898, the police singled out seven arrondissements in which the LAF was active: IV, IX–XI, XVI–XVIII. LAF committees in the IVth, Xth and XVIIth were headed by militants whom the police characterized as "ardent" or "fanatic" Catholics. The vice-president of the XVIth was "an *intransigent* Catholic anti-Semite," and the XIth arrondissement section, police alleged, was composed "for the most part . . . of young people belonging to Catholic youth groups."[106] Guérin played down the religious question, but he did not shun religious audiences. He spoke time and again

[102] APP B/a 1193, 25 April 1890.
[103] APP B/a 1193, 2 March 1890; 29 April 1890; 5 May 1890; 27 June 1892.
[104] APP B/a 1194, 25 April 1893.
[105] APP B/a 1104, 22 July and 13 August 1898.
[106] APP B/a 1107, 28 March 1898.

at meetings of the abbé Garnier's Christian Democratic *Union nationale*. And indeed, in the '98 elections, *Union nationale* voters were expected to provide LAF candidates "a solid bloc of votes."[107]

Drumont, Morès and Guérin seized on the patriotic and small-owner kernel of republican discourse and refashioned it into a shape serviceable to the Church and titled nobility. Even the organizational forms of middle-class radicalism, e.g. the league, were adapted and impressed into the service of throne and altar. The appeals and relentless solicitations of the anti-Semitic movement were bound to strike resonant chords in a shopkeeping audience. But could retailer militants, however isolated and discouraged, bring themselves to renege on their republican loyalties and embrace the cause of anti-Semitic reaction?

In Drumont's case, the answer appears to be a yes, albeit a qualified one. The *Ligue syndicale* held France's leading anti-Semite in the highest esteem. It was in May 1892 that the *Ligue* first made contact with Drumont. *La Libre Parole* was planning a series on *grands magasins*, and the *Ligue* sent over A. Hugonet, a *négociant* and one-time *Ligue* vice-president, to act as consultant. Drumont met with Hugonet and expressed "a lively interest" in the *Ligue syndicale*'s antidepartment-store campaign. *La Libre Parole* subsequently dispatched a representative to meet with Léopold Christophe. The exchange of ambassadors was concluded with a public pledge of mutual support. Drumont promised "to take up defense of the interests that the *Ligue* represents."[108] the *Ligue* reciprocated with a hearty endorsement of Drumont's economic program (fully aware that association with Drumont might cost the Mesureur bill votes).

In the summer of 1892, Drumont was brought to trial on

---

[107] APP B/a 1107, 6 April 1898. See also B/a 1104, 14 August 1896, 30 March 1897, 6 April 1897, 14 April 1897.

[108] "Comité de centralisation," *La Revendication*, 12 June 1892.

a libel charge. He had accused a popular republican deputy, Alphonse Burdeau, of taking a bribe from Rothschild to pass legislation advantageous to the Banque de France. The *Ligue syndicale* sprang to Drumont's defense. The scandals which afflict "our bourgeois republic," *La Revendication* argued, were not of Drumont's invention. Who could doubt "the indisputable good faith of the anti-Semitic polemicist?"[109] Christophe sent a letter of encouragement to Drumont which expressed the *Ligue*'s "sentiments of profound esteem": "Alone in the midst of the Parisian press' pregnant silence, you have had the courage to raise your voice on behalf of small and middle-size shopkeepers."[110] Warm relations between the *Ligue* and Drumont were maintained throughout the nineties. In 1894, Christophe ran for a Senate seat in the department of the Seine. *La Libre Parole* was unreserved in its support. The candidate, wrote Drumont, "represents a very popular cause in Paris: the cause of the small shop crushed by those colossi known as the Louvre and the Bon Marché."[111] The *Ligue* in gratitude voted Drumont a special thanks.[112] But shopkeeper support for Drumont was not untempered. Drumont invited the *Ligue syndicale* to endorse anti-Semitic candidates in the '93 elections. The managing editor of *La Libre Parole* sweetened the invitation with an offer of free publicity in Drumont's newspaper. Christophe accepted the offer of publicity but declined to engage the *Ligue* in an electoral entente with the anti-Semitic movement. Individual *ligueurs* were free to vote as they pleased, but the organization refused to compromise its nonpartisan stance.[113] The *Ligue*'s prickly jealousy of its independence, however, should not obscure its general

[109] E. Rabasse, "M. Drumont," *La Revendication*, 26 June 1892.

[110] "Avis très important," *La Revendication*, 26 June 1892.

[111] *La Libre Parole*: E. Drumont, "La candidature Floquet," 29 December 1893; Ad. Papillard, "L'élection sénatoriale," 7 January 1894.

[112] "La Ligue syndicale," *La Libre Parole*, 5 June 1894; "Comité de centralisation," *La Revendication*, 15 June 1894.

[113] "Comité de centralisation," *La Revendication*, 24 July 1892.

sympathy for Drumont who was looked upon appreciatively as a kindred spirit pursuing parallel aims.

Morès on the other hand failed to take advantage of the shopkeeper movement's anti-Semitic bias. On the eve of the '90 elections, he met with representatives of the *Ligue syndicale*, but relations developed no further. This is not to say that Morès lacked support in the commercial sector, but unlike Drumont he recruited outside the shopkeeper movement, above all among the butchers of La Villette. The slaughterhouse at La Villette was organized along lines to rejoice the most fanatic small-owner utopian. Here was a milieu perfectly constructed to respond to the anti-Semitic appeal, and respond it did.

La Villette was opened New Year's Day 1867. It was intended to provide retail butchers a sanitary location to slaughter animals, but operation of the slaughterhouse quickly passed into the hands of wholesalers. Access to the killing pens was governed by a strictly enforced code. A wholesaler or *chevillard* purchased a right to use of the pens. There were restrictions, however, on the exercise of pen rights. No wholesale enterprise, no matter how large, was allowed ownership of more than two pens. Pen ownership might be subdivided, but no more than three *chevillards* to a pen were permitted. The aim was to encourage middle-sized enterprises, neither too large nor too small.[114]

Observers—du Maroussem, Talmeyr, Coffignon—liked to describe the slaughterhouses as an "island," "a city apart," a "corporation."[115] And, indeed, the denizens of La Villette prided themselves on their corporate solidarity. Employer and employee, it was claimed, worked together in social har-

[114] On the slaughterhouse at La Villette, see Office du travail, *L'Alimentation à Paris*, pp. 202ff.; and "Les taxes nouvelles de l'abattoir," *Journal de la Chambre syndicale de la boucherie*, 7 January 1894.

[115] Office du travail, *L'Alimentation à Paris*, p. 207; Talmeyr, *La Cité du sang*, p. 96; Coffignon, *L'Estomac de Paris*, p. 83.

mony. A wholesaler might turn over twenty thousand francs per week, but he earned the money knife in hand. A manly camaraderie prevailed in the killing pen. Every *tueur* was privileged with a nickname—Caboche, l'Araignée. And the community of work was not dissolved at day's end. Master and man frequented the same neighborhood taverns. The bloody apron, the wooden *sabots* and peculiar gait of the slaughterhouse butcher distinguished him instantly from workers in other trades.[116]

The most serious threat to the corporation came not from internal division but from the outside. In 1891, the municipal government lifted restrictions on the sale of killing pens. *Chevillards* were adamant in opposition and organized a massive protest meeting attended by representatives of Paris' principal butchers' associations, elected officials of the XIXth, Alphonse Marguery and Jules Guérin. Guérin summed up the butchers' position:

> Among the trades which have escaped the pressure of capital, butchering must be counted because all of you— wholesale butchers, laborers that you are—you own the tools you use with your own hands. You have avoided until now the application of mass-producing machines, and for this reason, you have been spared the manipulations of Capital.[117]

It was the speculator and capitalist, not the hard-working independent, who stood to profit from a free-market in pen rights. Guérin called on the city to resist the forces of monopoly, and in fact, the municipal authorities eventually backed down.

State intervention, of course, was not the only threat to corporate solidarity. The fraternity of *chevillards*, du Marous-

---

[116] Coffignon, *op. cit.*, pp. 60–61.

[117] APP B/a 1105, clipping from *Le Réveil du XIXe*, 1 June 1892.

Politics of Shopkeeper Protest

sem claimed, was "more and more" infiltrated by Germans in the form of Alsatians.[118] Kosher butchers, whether Alsatian or not, were regarded with suspicion as outsiders whose alien and distasteful habits disturbed the reassuring uniformity of slaughterhouse life. Cattle, slaughtered in conformity with kosher law, were bled to death. La Villette butchers, it was reported, were revolted by the spectacle, and on occasion took it upon themselves to finish off a dying animal.[119] The *Chambre syndicale de la boucherie*, in 1894, called on municipal authorities to outlaw kosher slaughter.[120]

The character of the La Villette community, its corporate outlook and distrust of outsiders, prepared it to embrace the small-owner utopianism and malignant xenophobia preached by anti-Semites like Morès. It was a rare occasion that Morès made contact with the *Ligue syndicale*, but he was revered by the butchers of La Villette, who served him with a militant and dogged devotion.

Guérin inherited Morès' popularity in the XIXth. Muscular butcher boys stood arm in arm with Catholic youth in the ranks of the LAF's streetfighters. In contrast to Morès, however, Guérin had some success in establishing ties with the *Ligue syndicale*. In 1895, Guérin addressed a joint session of the *Ligue*'s XIth and XXth arrondissement sections. Berry and Christophe were present. Guérin denounced "money-grubbing fat cats," praised small shopkeepers and made a convert in the person of *Ligue* vice-president Louis Gazon.[121] In June 1897, Gazon volunteered to serve on a committee chaired by Guérin to organize ceremonies in commemoration of Morès' death (he had died in 1896).[122] And in March of the follow-

[118] Office du travail, *L'Alimentation à Paris*, p. 203.

[119] Coffignon, *op. cit.*, p. 65.

[120] "Chambre syndicale de la boucherie de la Seine, 8 novembre 1894," *Journal de la Chambre syndicale de la boucherie*, 11 November 1894.

[121] "Comité de centralisation," *La Revendication*, 31 December 1895; A. Tolleire, "Ligue syndicale," *La France*, 29 November 1895.

[122] APP B/a 1194, clipping from *La Libre Parole*, 12 July 1897.

ing year, Gazon joined the LAF, one of the first to do so.[123] It does not appear, however, that the overlap in *Ligue syndicale* and LAF membership was extensive. To be sure, Guérin's organization recruited men in commerce and industry with considerable success. Stephen Wilson has identified ninety-nine LAF members by profession. Over one-third, thirty-six in all, made a living as businessmen. But Guérin's business support was not rooted in the merchant community of central Paris. The *Ligue syndicale* was most active in the Ist, IInd and IXth, the LAF in the Xth, XIth, XVIIIth and XIXth. Christophe's *ligueurs* and Guérin's were not, with the exception of Gazon, the same men.[124]

One is struck by the *Ligue syndicale*'s standoffishness vis-à-vis organized anti-Semitism. But if retailer response was lukewarm, it was not insignificant. Drumont was unmistakeably popular among *Ligue syndicale* militants. *Ligueurs* paid respectful attention to the preachings and posturings of Guérin and Morès. And certain sections of the commercial community—slaughterhouse butchers, traveling salesmen—were even prepared to take out membership in anti-Semitic organizations like the LAF. The anti-Semitic movement was frankly reactionary, its spokesmen a dubious collection of adventurers and failures utterly lacking in republican convictions. That retailer militants entertained amicable relations with the anti-Semites attests to the erosion of radical republican sentiment among shopkeepers. What if the anti-Semitic movement had not been compromised by obvious royalist connections? What if its leaders had not been violent and suspicious characters like Guérin and Morès? Would shopkeeper response then have been so lukewarm? These questions are not entirely hypothetical. Christian Democracy at its origins in the last decades of the century was a movement but marginally less re-

[123] APP B/a 1092, 2 March 1898.
[124] For details on LAF membership, see Wilson, "The Ligue Antisémitique Francaise," pp. 36–38.

actionary than anti-Semitism. It venerated the old regime—the Church and corporations in particular—with a fervor equal to that of any anti-Semite. Yet Christian Democracy was ostensibly reconciled to the Republic, and its founding fathers were reasonable men of substance, like Léon Harmel. Here was a movement that resembled anti-Semitism but without its compromising connections and personalities. And indeed, Christian Democracy exercised a powerful attraction on the *Ligue syndicale* in the 1890s. Anti-Semitism introduced the shopkeeper movement to political reaction, but it was Christian Democracy that brought the relationship to consummation.

CHRISTIAN DEMOCRACY AND THE SHOPKEEPER MOVEMENT

The abbé Garnier was the first to attract the *Ligue syndicale*'s attention. Garnier was a Breton priest come to Paris in 1888 to work on the Assumptionist daily *La Croix*. In 1891, he left the newspaper and founded *L'Action sociale catholique* (ASC), a Church-based pressure group with close ties to de Mun's Social Catholic movement. Garnier's early acceptance of the Republic, however, his rough-and-ready manner and taste for popular politics, set him apart from first generation Social Catholics, men, in the main, of aristocratic background and legitimist inclinations. Differences within the ASC between Catholics of Garnier's "democratic" stamp and traditionalists like de Mun paralyzed the organization. Garnier soon abandoned it, struck out on his own, and in 1893 founded *L'Union nationale*, a Christian Democratic organization unencumbered by ties to Social Catholicism.[125]

[125] On Garnier's *Action sociale catholique*, see APP B/a 1537, 23 June 1892, 5 and 14 December 1892. On Garnier, see Wilson, "Catholic Populism in France," pp. 667–705.

Garnier's break with traditionalism, to be sure, was not complete, particularly on matters of ideology. He remained loyal to de la Tour du Pin's vision of a hierarchical, corporatist society presided over by the Church; but he broadened the application of corporatist doctrine. Organization, he argued, promised relief not only to the working man but to the overburdened *petit commerçant* as well.

Garnier took up defense of the small shopkeeper at an early date. An ASC brochure entitled *Petit commerce et grands magasins* appeared in 1891 calling on Pope Leo to issue an encyclical, a second *Rerum Novarum*, to address the grievances of *petit commerce*.[126] And the grievances, it was acknowledged, were numerous: unfair department store competition, a ruinous tax burden, the erosion of shopkeeper family life under the pressure of economic hardship. Garnier predictably supported *patente* revision; he appeared time and again at *Ligue syndicale* reunions and with equal frequency endorsed the *Ligue*'s program.[127] He did not, however, share the *Ligue syndicale*'s faith in tax reform as a cure-all for shopkeeper problems. The state was not judged an appropriate instrument for the solution of social questions.[128] Garnier rather pinned his hopes on private sector organization: on mixed trade unions, cooperatives and the like. On occasion, he even managed a comment favorable to department stores. *Grands magasins* had after all pioneered commercial techniques beneficial to the consumer. As editor of the *Union nationale*'s press organ *Le Peuple français*, Garnier accepted advertisements from the Bon

[126] APP B/a 1537, "Petit commerce et grands magasins. Conférence de M. l'abbé Garnier," 7 July 1891.

[127] See *La Ravendication*: "Elections du 20 août 1893," 15 August 1893; "Comité de centralisation," 15 September 1893; "Comité de centralisation," 15 October 1893.

[128] On Garnier's antipathy to government interventionism, see Wilson, "Catholic Populism in France," pp. 675–676, and APP B/a 1537, "Le programme social de M. l'abbé Garnier," 18 August 1892.

Marché and Louvre. Indeed, he urged *petits commerçants* to adopt department store merchandising practices, to pool market information and organize purchasing cooperatives. Alone, the independent retailer was outmatched by the *grand magasin*. The survival of *petit commerce* dictated the sacrifice of anarchic individualism and an acceptance of organization.[129]

Garnier appealed to both worker and retailer but not in the name of small-owner utopianism. He promised a corporate future in which small property was guaranteed a niche, but in which organization, not smallness, was the paramount virtue. The *Union nationale* aimed to reconstitute the Boulangist coalition of workers and shopkeepers but in the service of Catholic corporatism, not republican democracy.

Garnier's project met with a modest success. The *Union nationale* attracted a membership of 12,500 in the nineties. Recruitment was concentrated in working-class arrondissements, in the IVth, XIth, and XVIIIth. But shopkeepers, too, showed an interest. Stephen Wilson has remarked on the striking "preponderance of traders and mainly small traders" among the supporters of the *Union nationale*.[130] The *Ligue syndicale* certainly took notice of Garnier's pro-shopkeeper campaign and expressed its appreciation: "It's a funny thing if, in a democratic state, the Church were the only force that dared to attack the financial feudality."[131] The Catholic party's "spirit of decision," *La Revendication* pointedly observed, put to shame the republican establishment, "those on whom the democratic people ought to have been able to count."

[129] APP B/a 1537, 9 March 1894; "Elections du 20 août 1893," *La Revendication*, 15 August 1893; Wilson, "Catholic Populism in France," p. 676; abbé Garnier, "Petit commerce et grands magasins," *Le Peuple français*, 30–31 May 1898.

[130] On *Union nationale* recruitment, see Wilson, "Catholic Populism in France," p. 672.

[131] E. Rabasse, "L'Eglise et la question des grands magasins," *La Revendication*, 28 June 1891.

Garnier's petition on behalf of *petit commerce* was welcomed with enthusiasm by a *Ligue* official, Ernest Ratel, who was moved to join the ASC and rose to a position on its central committee.[132] On the other hand, Garnier's publication of department store ads in *Le Peuple français* exasperated shopkeeper militants.[133] The *Union nationale*'s endorsement of cooperatives was a source of additional strain.[134] And finally, the organization's recruitment in Paris' core arrondissements was lackluster. The *Union nationale*, much as Guérin's LAF, failed to penetrate the downtown stronghold of the shopkeeper movement. Garnier patched together a coalition of workers and shopkeepers, but it was a coalition which did not include the *Ligue syndicale.*

The *Union nationale*, however, was not the only Christian Democratic organization to solicit shopkeeper support. In 1891, a cotton spinner from the Marne, Léon Harmel, launched the *Union fraternelle du commerce et de l'industrie* (UFCI), a non-profit association of Catholic businessmen. Though founded in 1891, the UFCI had its origins in the 1880s. In 1887, the Assumptionist Reverend Father Alet invited fifteen Catholic employers on retreat at the Villa Manrèse in the Paris suburb of Clamart. The group met again the next year at Sacré Coeur and in 1889 made a pilgrimage to Rome. Harmel was persuaded to take part and subsequently assumed direction of the group, christened the UFCI in 1891. At its inception, the organization counted 100 members, but Harmel was an energetic and tireless organizer. In 1896, a membership of 4,000 was reported, and in 1904, the UFCI claimed upwards of 5,000 adherents. The *Union*'s activities were a combination of the devotional and the worldly. Monthly retreats were organized

---

[132] APP B/a 1537, "Petit commerce et grands magasins. Conférence de M. l'abbé Garnier," 7 July 1891; 14 December 1892.

[133] APP B/a 1537, 9 March 1894.

[134] "Elections de 20 août 1893," *La Revendication*, 15 August 1893.

at Sacré Coeur; annual assemblies and local section meetings discussed ways and means to promote business interests and Christianize commercial practice.[135]

The UFCI inscribed "protection of *petit commerce*" at the top of its program.[136] The organization's 1897 congress was given over in its entirety to the problems of small business. Harmel went so far as to promise a pilgrimage to Rome on behalf of "the humble folk":

> . . . we are going to Leo XIII, to the source of all truth, to Him who will be the justiciar and liberator of commerce as he has been of industry.[137]

Harmel was followed by Alphonse Trépreau, a stationer in Paris' Ist arrondissement, who harangued the conference at great length on the urgency of tax relief for the *petit commerçant*. Trépreau insisted on immediate passage of the Berry bill with a strict "specialization" clause. On the question of co-operatives, he hesitated to demand outright abolition but wanted membership restricted to *petits salariés*, to wage earners who paid less than 30F per annum in property taxes. The congress endorsed Trépreau's theses without reservation.[138] The abbé Garnier had stood by the consumer cooperative as an institution beneficial to the working class. The UFCI knew no such scruples. It placed the interests of the *petit commerçant*

---

[135] For details on the *Union fraternelle's* origins, see Rollet, *L'Action sociale des catholiques*, pp. 556–558; "L'Union fraternelle," *La Croix*, 9 September 1896; "Les origines de l'Union fraternelle," *Bulletin de l'Union fraternelle du commerce et de l'industrie* (hereinafter referred to as *BUFCI*), February 1896; "Chronique," *BUFCI*, April 1904.

[136] "Congrès de l'Union fraternelle," *BUFCI*, May 1897.

[137] Discours de M. Léon Harmel," *BUFCI*, July 1897.

[138] For Trépreau's speech and the congress' response, see the series of articles published by Trépreau, under the title, "Rapport," *BUFCI*, August, September, October 1897; also, "Voeux émis au congrès de 1897," *BUFCI*, June 1898.

first. But why this intense interest in the fate of the small shopkeeper?

It was the small owner, the UFCI claimed, who vouchsafed the nation's moral and social equilibrium. The *petit patronat* was a repository of the most sacrosanct virtues: "dignity, individual initiative and family feeling." It was no less the keystone of France's class structure. Harmel spoke of the *petit partronat* as a "buffer class between men of order and the worst revolutionaries."[139] Terrible disasters awaited France if middle-class decline was not checked: "social anemia," "loss of liberty" and revolution.[140] A new regime would emerge on the rubble of the old, yet more oppressive than financial feudalism. Harmel feared the advent of "state communism" above all.[141] The modern state had already arrogated to itself the power to educate, to regulate, to tax. It aspired to omnipotence, to the status of divinity. Worship of the state was bound to be the only form of worship permitted under communism. In the name of freedom, family and Christianity, preservation of a healthy, vigorous *petit patronat* was of the utmost urgency.

The task, however, was no easy one. Laissez-faire capitalism had unleashed a Darwinian struggle in which only the strong survived, and who were the strong? The list was long—usurers, speculators, Freemasons and, above all, Jews. They were an unscrupulous lot, savage egotists prepared to destroy in the pursuit of profit "the bases of our society: religion, family, fatherland, labor, property." "[T]hey are," Harmel proclaimed, "the determined enemies of Jesus Christ."[142]

The enemies of Jesus had prevailed thanks to superior organization. They had devised terrible engines of destruction

[139] "Mémoire à l'épiscopat français," *BUFCI*, June 1897.

[140] Trépreau, "Rapport," *BUFCI*, October 1897.

[141] "Discours de M. Léon Harmel," *BUFCI*, December 1897; "Discours de M. Léon Harmel, *La Croix*, 29 June 1897.

[142] Léon Harmel, "Montmartre," *BUFCI*, March 1898.

with which to subdue the weak—*sociétés anonymes* (a "Jewish invention"), department stores and cooperatives.[143] An oligarchy of monopolists and cosmopolitans, a new financial feudality, had imposed itself on the nation, threatening the extinction of France's small-owner class.

Harmel's organization, of course, repudiated state intervention as a solution to the crisis of small business. "[O]nly a corporatist regime," the UFCI bulletin wrote, "can resolve the social conflicts which endanger and disturb our nation so profoundly."[144] Parliament was impotent, incompetent, the privileged preserve of politicians and demagogues. France's salvation lay in the self-organization of the private sector, in shopkeeper associations, trade unions and employer organizations. Trépreau interpreted the outburst of syndical activity at the end of the century as the opening phase of a corporatist renaissance. The *syndicat* represented a corporation in embryo.[145] In time, it would develop the force and organization to replace the free market as a regulator of economic activity.[146] The modern corporation had political as well as economic virtues. The power of corporate France, the combined weight of the nation's myriad unions, syndicates and professional associations, more than sufficed to smash the oligarchy of speculators and politicians that had monopolized public life in the era of laissez-faire capitalism.[147] The oligarchy had maintained its monopoly through two institutions: parliament and the bureaucracy. Functionaries had robbed the region, the commune, of vitality, to the advantage of central-

---

[143] Harmel, "Montmartre," *BUFCI*, March 1898; "Mémoire pour la défense du petit commerce et de l'industrie privée," *La Croix*, 30 December 1896; "Discours de M. Léon Harmel," *La Croix*, 29 June 1897.

[144] "La loi sur les accidents de travail," *BUFCI*, September 1898.

[145] Trépreau, "Rapport," *BUFCI*, September 1900.

[146] "Discours de M. Léon Harmel," *BUFCI*, July 1897.

[147] "Congrès de l'Union fraternelle," *BUFCI*, May 1897; Trépreau, "Rapport," *BUFCI*, September 1900.

ized institutions, political no less than economic. Special interests had taken over the Chamber of Deputies.[148] The corporate regime promised to restore power to the people, not as participants in a direct democracy, but as members in professional associations. The UFCI aimed to dismantle France's vast bureaucratic apparatus: "decentralization will introduce into communal life the balancing influence of organized social bodies [corps sociaux] and will destroy the pernicious oppression of a system that is now purely administrative." As for parliament, the UFCI envisaged establishment of a corporate Senate, elected by the professions, to counterbalance the oligarchical tendencies of the Chamber.[149]

Retailers, the UFCI firmly believed, had every reason to embrace the new corporatism. The small-business sector was guaranteed representation in the corporate Senate. On the local level, corporatism was certain to strengthen the position of *petit commerce*. In a decentralized France, the UFCI program read, "local commerce, protected by its organizations, will know how to maintain standards of probity and protect local interests against street peddlars, phony debt settlements and Jewish cheating schemes."[150] Even the department store would bend before the power of *petit commerce*—if organized.[151]

The UFCI, like the *Union nationale*, decked out corporatist doctrine in the trappings of small-owner utopianism, but the social vision of the two organizations was not identical. Garnier's group, oriented to a wage earning constituency, had been hesitant in its denunciations of the consumer cooperative and department store. Harmel's, by contrast, gave first priority to retailer interests. If the *Union nationale* had made little headway with the *Ligue syndicale*, the UFCI was much better sit-

---

[148] Trépreau, "Rapport," *BUFCI*, September 1900.

[149] "Congrès de l'Union fraternelle," *BUFCI*, May 1897.

[150] "Congres de l'Union fraternelle," *BUFCI*, May 1897.

[151] "Congrès parisien de 'La Croix,'" *La Croix*, 2 December 1896.

Politics of Shopkeeper Protest

uated to win retailer support. Not the least of the *Union fraternelle*'s advantages lay in its distinctive pattern of recuitment. In composition and geographical distribution, the UFCI membership bore a striking if not exact resemblance to that of the *Ligue syndicale*. The UFCI styled itself an "organization of small commerce and small industry."[152] Hyacinthe Lefranc, a charter member, spoke of the organization as the "*Union fraternelle* of *petit commerce.*"[153] UFCI membership was admittedly more bourgeois in character than Lefranc pretended. Harmel and the UFCI's honorary president Ernest Lefébure were both factory owners. Victor Lecoffre, editor of the *Union fraternelle* bulletin, owned a prosperous and reputable printing business in the VIth. The professions of fifth-five additional UFCI militants are known and may be broken down as follows:[154]

Liberal Professions	5
Rentier/*Propriétaire*	2
Manufacturer/Wholesaler	4
Middleman	3
Luxury Trades	3
Clothing Trades	10
Notions	1
Toilette	1
Household Goods	1
Home Furnishings	4
Printing	1

[152] "L'Union fraternelle à Montmartre et à Reims," *BUFCI*, May 1896.
[153] "Congrès parisien de '*La Croix*,' " *La Croix*, 2 December 1896.
[154] Data taken from *BUFCI*: "Chronique," May 1904; "Chronique," June 1904; "Réunion des Batignolles-Montmartre," January 1905; "Comités de Paris," January 1907.

Books, Photography, etc.	2
Food	3
Building	4
Other	<u>11</u>
TOTAL	55

It is not unreasonable to classify rentiers, manufacturers, and men in the liberal professions as bourgeois. Eleven militants, one fifth of the total, fall into these categories. Just the same, the commercial sector provided the bulk of the UFCI's recruits. Food-and-drink men, clothiers, luxury retailers and middlemen alone constituted 34.6 percent of the *Union fraternelle*'s known membership. *Ligue syndicale* membership, it will be recalled, was concentrated in precisely these four occupational categories. Jewelers, on the other hand, so numerous in the *Ligue syndicale*, were largely absent from UFCI ranks. The *Union fraternelle*, moreover, managed to attract manufacturers and *propriétaires*, categories not at all represented in the *Ligue*. The *Ligue syndicale* and UFCI were alike, but not identical, in social profile. The geographical distribution of membership points to a similar conclusion.

The addresses of fifty-six UFCI militants are known. Mapped by arrondissement (see figure 10), the addresses indicate three concentrations of UFCI recruitment: central paris (Ist, IInd, IXth), the recently built-up XVIIth, and in the east, the manufacturing and commercial zones of the Xth and XIth. Thirty-six militants, 64 percent of the sample, were resident in these six arrondissements. The overlap in *Ligue* and UFCI recruitment was not complete. The *Ligue* was strong in the VIIth; Harmel's organization was not. Conversely, the UFCI was well-represented in the Xth, XIth and XVIIth arrondissements in which *Ligue* recruitment was not extensive. There was, however, one constituency from which both organiza-

FIGURE 10: The Recruitment of UFCI Militants by Arrondissement, 1891-1907

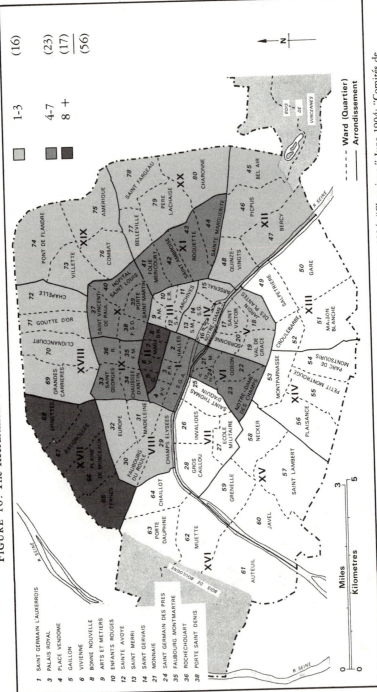

SOURCE: *BUFCI:* "Comité de la Porte Saint-Martin," February 1904; "Chronique," May 1904; "Chronique," June 1904; "Comités de Paris," January 1907.

tions recruited with considerable success, the commercial community of downtown Paris.

Given the UFCI's strength among center-city retailers, given its ingenious adaptation of small-owner themes and commitment to shopkeeper interests, it is little wonder that the *Ligue syndicale*, driven to the margin of politics in search of political allies, should have settled on Harmel's organization as the most congenial alternative available. It was in May 1896 that the *Ligue* first took cognizance of the *Union fraternelle*, in the words of *Ligue* secretary Plista, "a group desirous of discovering the causes of shopkeeper misery."[155] The *Ligue syndicale* central committee appointed an observer to investigate. In June, Christophe consented to publish an extract of the UFCI's program, but the breakthrough came in July.[156] The UFCI held a conference at Landerneau in Brittany. Trépreau addressed the congress on the subject of *petit commerce* and spoke of the *Ligue syndicale* in terms of highest praise. The *Ligue* and *Union*, he declared, were "in absolute agreement from an economic standpoint. From their alliance, a powerful fighting force could be forged."[157] Trépreau's words carried special weight. He was a *Union fraternelle* spokesman, but also a vice-president of the *Ligue syndicale*. Encouraged by Trépreau's remarks at Landerneau, the *Ligue* sent an official representative to the UFCI's next congress in 1897.[158] In March of 1898, the UFCI *Bulletin* published the *Ligue*'s election manifesto,[159] and, to cement relations, the *Union fraternelle* invited Christophe to address a UFCI meeting. Christophe agreed to come, spoke in defense of specialization, and left the impression that he sym-

[155] "Comité de centralisation," *La Revendication*, 31 May 1896.

[156] "Comité de centralisation," *La Revendication*, 15 June 1896.

[157] "Un nouveau groupe de défenseurs," *La Revendication*, 31 July 1896; "Congrès de l'Union fraternelle," 15 October 1896.

[158] "Comité de centralisation," *La Revendication*, 31 October 1896.

[159] "Manifeste de la Ligue de défense du petit commerce," *BUFCI*, March 1898.

pathized with corporatist aspirations. The UFCI *Bulletin* commented on audience reaction: "people remarked to each other on the way home that they had never heard a more eloquent or livelier disquisition on the necessity of a corporatist restoration."[160]

The *Ligue syndicale*'s rapprochement with Harmel's organization proved an astute political maneuver. The UFCI was not in itself a powerful organization, but Harmel had great personal influence. His defense of the *petit commerçant* lent legitimacy to the shopkeeper movement as a cause worthy of Christian concern. Indeed, as the *Ligue* and *Union* drew together in alliance, Catholic interest in the small shopkeeper quickened perceptibly.

The Assumptionist order founded *La Croix* in 1880. The paper was funded by Philibert Vrau and his nephew Paul Féron-Vrau, both Lille textile manufacturers. Féron-Vrau ran a spinning mill, organized much on the model of Harmel's factory in the Val des Bois.[161] Harmel, moreover, maintained friendly relations with the Assumptionist order.[162] The UFCI had every reason to expect a sympathetic press from *La Croix*, and indeed the paper demonstrated a keen interest in the plight of the shopkeeper. *La Croix* published regular accounts of UFCI activities. A page of the paper's weekly supplement was set aside for discussion of commercial questions. And the shopkeeper movement was appreciative. "[I]t's not our fault," *La Revendication* observed ruefully in 1891, "if the newspaper *La Croix* is perhaps the only one to have fought for us in the campaign we have undertaken."[163]

[160] "La conférence de M. Christophe," *BUFCI*, December 1898.

[161] Dansette, *Histoire religieuse,* p. 500.

[162] Sorlin, *La Croix et les juifs,* p. 33.

[163] E. Rabasse, "L'Eglise et la question des grands magasins," *La Revendication,* 28 June 1891. See also *La Revendication*: "Comité de centralisation," 15 April 1893; H. Destréguil, "A propos de la création d'un nouveau journal," 30 November 1896.

La Croix stepped up its pro-shopkeeper campaign in 1896. In September, the paper sponsored a "regional congress" in Brittany at which the crisis of small business was discussed in some detail. A second regional congress met in Paris in December.[164] The agenda was organized by the Reverend Father Bailly, editor of *La Croix*, in conjunction with Harmel, Lefranc and Trépreau. The UFCI predictably dominated the proceedings. The meeting wound up with a decision to contact Georges Berry in support of *patente* reform, and plans were made to organize "the defense of *petit commerce* . . . in conjunction with the small shopkeepers' league."[165] There was, however, one obstacle to a Catholic alliance with the *Ligue syndicale*. The shopkeeper movement's adamant opposition to cooperatives was unacceptable to Catholics like Garnier, for example, who were sensitive to peasant and working-class interests.

La Croix was anxious to reconcile differences and in the spring of 1897 opened its pages to a dialogue between shopkeeper militants and Catholic advocates of cooperation. The *Ligue* gave ground in the debate, accepting the legitimacy of agricultural syndicates and of consumer cooperatives that retailed staple goods to a membership composed exclusively of *petits salariés*.[166] Its conciliatory posture prompted an immediate and sympathetic response from elements of the Catholic right. *La Croix* agreed to publish the *Ligue syndicale*'s election manifesto on the eve of the '98 elections;[167] nor was the paper alone in its expressions of support for the shopkeeper cause.

---

[164] For details of the two congresses, see *La Croix*: "Le congrès de Landerneau," 16 September 1896; "Congrès parisien de '*La Croix*,' " 17 November 1896.

[165] "Congrès parisien de '*La Croix*,' " *La Croix*, 2 December 1896.

[166] *La Croix*: "Les caisses rurales et ouvrières," 13 July 1897; "Caisses rurales et sociétés coopératives," 18 August 1897.

[167] "Manifeste de la Ligue de défense du petit commerce," *La Croix*, 4 May 1896.

A National Catholic Congress was convened in Paris in December 1897, bringing together right-wing Catholics of every persuasion—Christian Democrats, Assumptionists, Social Catholics. Just how the shopkeeper question found its way onto the Paris agenda is not clear, but Trépreau, as representative of the UFCI, presented a lengthy report on department stores and cooperatives. The congress adopted the principle of specialization, backed the Berry bill, and voted a compromise resolution on the issue of cooperatives:

> cooperatives exempted from the *patente* may only enroll members who are wage earners and workers; rural cooperatives are to be exempted altogether. Other cooperative societies must be subject to commercial taxes as any other commercial enterprise.[168]

While lacking in precision, the resolution represented a step in the direction of the *Ligue syndicale*'s revised position on the co-op issue. The congress, Trépreau exalted, had endorsed the *Ligue*'s program in all essentials.[169] The *Ligue syndicale* in the late nineties had drawn closer to the UFCI. The association brought the shopkeeper movement support from unexpected quarters, from Christian Democrats, Assumptionists and now even some Social Catholics. The right wing of the Catholic movement had begun to mobilize itself in the service of *petit commerce*.

CONCLUSION

The shopkeeper movement was frozen out of the political mainstream in the 1890s. The power of big business frus-

---

[168] "Congrès national catholique," *Affiches tourangelles*, 9 December 1897; "Congrès national catholique," *La Croix*, 5–6 December 1897.

[169] Trépreau, "La loi des patentes," *BUFCI*, May 1898; G. Chartrain, "Un succès," *Affiches tourangelles*; 9 December 1897.

trated *Ligue* hopes for a satisfactory business-tax reform. The rise of socialism preoccupied public opinion, eclipsing the question of commercial defense. Where were shopkeepers to turn for support?

The 1890s witnessed the emergence of new movements, anti-Semitism and Christian Democracy, adept at the manipulation of small-owner themes. In the hands of a Drumont or an Harmel, however, small-owner rhetoric was drained of its radical republican content and refashioned in the interest of a monarchical or corporatist restoration. Anti-Semites and Christian Democrats preyed upon the little man's cultural anxieties, on his fears of collectivist expropriation and socialist revolution. The democratic thrust of the small-owner vision was blunted and the accent placed instead on the xenophobic and antimonopolist strains of popular radical thought. The adaptation of the small-owner tradition to reactionary ends represented a remarkable innovation. Anti-Semites and Christian Democrats innovated as well in their skillful use of mass mobilization techniques. Press campaigns, street demonstrations and an endless round of conferences and congresses barraged popular audiences with the simple claim: the little man's interests were best served by the right, not by Opportunists, socialists or Radicals. And shopkeepers, desperate and vulnerable, responded with interest and even some warmth. The indifference of the republican mainstream pushed the retailers' movement to the right. But, as the evolving character and content of the right's appeal indicate, the movement was pulled as much as pushed.

The inventiveness of Christian Democracy and anti-Semitism, the ability of the two movements to apply radical rhetoric and the techniques of mass politics to reactionary ends, has justly earned them the appellation—new right. It was then to this new right that the shopkeeper movement began to turn in the 1890s. The *Ligue syndicale* maintained cordial relations with anti-Semites like Drumont and Guérin, but with Christian Democracy relations developed on a more intimate basis. The UFCI, an organization similar to the *Ligue* in ideology and composition, was the vehicle of shopkeeper rapprochement with militant Catholicism. From 1890 to 1893, Radicals had acted as the *petit commerçant*'s broker in the arena of national politics. By the late nineties, the privilege of representing *petit commerce* had passed to the far right. The shift in the shopkeeper movement's political allegiances was not widely recognized. It was the Dreyfus Affair that made public just how far the movement had evolved from its Radical past.

9

· · ·

The Politics of Economic
and Cultural Despair

THE DREYFUS AFFAIR brought to the surface the
shopkeeper movement's alignment with the radical right.
Organized *petit commerce* sided publicly with anti-Dreyfusard
Nationalism and enlisted in the Nationalist movement's campaign to arrest France's decline into a decadent cosmopolitanism. The Nationalist movement in turn took up the cause of
commercial defense, advertising itself as an embattled defender of small-owner values. Shopkeeper politics in late
nineteenth-century Germany have been characterized as the
"politics of economic despair."[1] The characterization is of course
an adaptation of Fritz Stern's phrase the "politics of cultural
despair," coined to describe the cultural pessimism of three
German critics whose careers spanned the years 1850–1930.[2]
In France, the politics of economic and cultural despair con-
verged at the time of the Dreyfus Affair. How and why did
this convergence occur? Was it a matter of simple, mutual
self-interest or did a more profound commonality of experience and outlook underlay the shopkeeper/Nationalist alliance?

[1] Gellately, *The Politics of Economic Despair*.
[2] Stern, *The Politics of Cultural Despair*.

THE DREYFUS AFFAIR

Alfred Dreyfus, a Jewish captain attached to the army General Staff, was convicted in 1894 of passing military secrets to the Germans. The unfortunate Captain Dreyfus was packed off to Devil's Island, and the case appeared to be closed. In November 1897, however, new evidence emerged incriminating a certain Commandant Esterhazy, a well-bred but dissolute officer who had for a brief period served in military intelligence. The military was obliged to file charges of espionage against Esterhazy. But the army had little incentive to press for a conviction which would have called the Dreyfus verdict into question and embarrassed high-ranking officers who had staked their reputations on Dreyfus' guilt. Esterhazy was brought to trial in January 1898 and duly acquitted. The decision outraged Emile Zola who published a broadside in Clemenceau's *L'Aurore* under the title *J'accuse*, charging the army with a willful miscarriage of justice. The government acted expeditiously to silence pro-Dreyfusard critics like Zola and Clemenceau. It undertook to prosecute Zola for libel and at the same time publicly ordered a review of the evidence in the Affair, fully confident such an inquiry would establish Dreyfus' culpability once and for all. The maneuver backfired, for it was soon discovered that much of the evidence in the case had been forged by an over-zealous intelligence officer, Colonel Henry. Henry was confronted with the forgeries, confessed and subsequently committed suicide. The case against Dreyfus, it appeared, had collapsed. He was brought back from Devil's Island in August 1899 to face a second court martial. To the astonishment of friends and sympathizers, he was convicted a second time. The civil authorities refused to allow the verdict to stand. A presidential pardon was hastily arranged in September, but it was not until 1906 that the courts officially exonerated Dreyfus and instructed that he be reinstated in the army.

Dreyfus' vindication was not achieved without vigorous opposition, from the army and its allies, but also from powerful and popular extraparliamentary leagues. The publication of *J'accuse* was the occasion of explosive anti-Semitic riots organized by Jules Guérin's *Ligue antisémitique*. The climate of unrest and uncertainty heightened over the subsequent summer months. Henry committed suicide in August. In September, news reached France of a tense confrontation between French and British military units in the Sudan. French troops under the command of Captain Marchand had occupied the town of Fachoda on the Nile but were forced to withdraw in the face of British threats and a show of superior military force. The Fachoda incident coincided with a surge of labor unrest. In September and October, Paris railwaymen and ditch diggers went on strike. Troops were called in to maintain order. There was talk of a general strike and rumors of a preemptive military coup. The regime appeared at the point of dissolution. Guérin's anti-Semites, joined by Paul Déroulède and a reconstituted *Ligue des patriotes*, were determined to administer the coup de grâce. Riotous antigovernment demonstrations were mounted in late October as parliament reconvened after the summer recess. In February 1899, the president of the Republic, Félix Faure, died and was replaced by Emile Loubet, a provincial lawyer known to favor a revision of the Dreyfus case. Street demonstrations greeted Loubet's election and on the 23rd, the day of Faure's funeral, Déroulède staged a coup d'état which ended in dismal failure. Another coup attempt was planned to coincide with the opening of Dreyfus' retrial at Rennes in August, but the government learned of the scheme and acted to arrest the ringleaders.

The high tide of extraparliamentary agitation had been reached. The leagues continued to oppose any move to rehabilitate Dreyfus but resorted with less frequency to street actions. Electoral politics was now the chosen terrain, and the Nationalists, as league candidates styled themselves, won stunning victories in Paris, first in the municipal elections of 1900 and then in the national elections of 1902. But the leagues failed to attract substantial provincial support. Unable to topple the regime or defeat it through the ballot (save in Paris), the leagues had reached an impasse. Nationalism began to wither as a political movement, but it had left its mark on the structure of politics in France.[3]

Firstly, the emergence of Nationalism altered the balance of power on the margin of politics. The movement's dynamism attracted militant Catholics who had in the nineties formed the constituency of Christian Democracy.[4] The hopes, moreover, of a Drumont or a Guérin to dominate the extra-parliamentary right faded with the revival of Déroulède's *Ligue des patriotes* and the formation in January 1899 of the powerful and well-connected *Ligue de la patrie française* (LPF). Secondly, the Nationalist surge radically transformed the political complexion of Paris politics. In 1900–1902, the Paris municipal council and parliamentary delegation, for decades dominated by Radicals, passed into the hands of Nationalists aligned with elements of the traditional right. Paris, once the city of revolution par excellence, became in the twentieth century the city of Nationalism, the Stavisky riots and the ultrapatriotic leagues of the 1930s.[5] And finally, the Nationalist outburst destroyed the alliance of *ralliés* and Progressists which had sustained Méline in power for over two years.

The street demonstrations of 1898–1899 stirred the regime's defenders to organize a government of republican defense. Waldeck-Rousseau took office in June 1899 at the head of an anti-Nationalist coalition which included Radicals, left-

---

[3] On the Nationalist leagues, see Sternhell, *La Droite révolutionnaire*; Watson discusses Nationalism's electoral successes in "The Nationalist Movement in Paris, 1900–1906," pp. 49–84.

[4] Rollet, *L'Action sociale des catholiques*, pp. 443–444.

[5] On Paris' swing to the right, see Watson, "The Nationalist Movement in Paris."

leaning Progressists and even Jaurèsian socialists. Piou's *ralliés* predictably swung into oppposition, as did a fraction of the Progressist party. Barthou and Poincaré followed Waldeck-Rousseau, but Méline and Deschanel refused to support the new administration. A parallel realignment occurred in the business world. Like the Progressist party, Expert-Bezançon's CNRCI split down the middle. In March 1899, Alfred Mascuraud formed the *Comité républicain du commerce et de l'industrie* (CRCI), an association of pro-republican businessmen which became one of the mainstays of the Waldeckist administration. The CRCI fancied itself the sole legitimate heir of the CNRCI. Mascuraud referred to the new organization as a "reconstitution" of the old *Comité Expert-Bezançon*.[6] He was careful, of course, to substract the adjective "national" from the CNRCI's title, but otherwise the *Comité Mascuraud* and *Comité Expert-Bezançon* bore the same name. There was, moreover, an overlap in membership between the two organizations. Marguery joined the CRCI as did a half-dozen officials of Alexis Muzet's *Syndicat général*.[7] Not everyone, however, was prepared to follow Mascuraud into the camp of republican defense. Muzet himself, for example, sided with the opponents of the Waldeck-Rousseau government. He ran in the elections of 1902 as an "antiministerial." "I reject with all my heart," a Muzet poster proclaimed, "that sectarian Republic which tolerates internationalism, the red flag and sows hatred and division among the best sons of France.[8] Expert-Bezançon was described in *Le Siècle* as "a ferocious nationalist."[9] Conservative CNRCI businessmen, unable to stomach

---

[6]"Le banquet du Comité républicain du commerce et de l'industrie," *Bulletin officiel du Comité républicain du commerce et de l'industrie*, December 1901.

[7]See the CRCI poster in support of F. Faure, APP B/a 206, 1902 elections, Ist arrondissement.

[8]APP B/a 206, Muzet poster, 1902 elections, Ist arrondissement.

[9]APP B/a 695, clipping from *Le Siècle*, 8 May 1900.

Waldeckist policies, took refuge in the Catholic-inspired *Union du commerce et de l'industrie pour la défense sociale* or in the Mélinist *Fédération des industriels et des commerçants français*.[10]

The political impact of Nationalism was immediate and devastating. Whence came the movement's explosive power?

Shopkeeper Nationalism

Historians have identified the "lower middle class," "*la petite et moyenne bourgeoisie*," as Nationalism's principal constituency.[11] *Petits commerçants* above all, it is claimed, were susceptible to the appeal to the new right. Nationalist candidates campaigned with greatest success in "areas of moderate income, where there were large numbers of small shopkeepers and businessmen and white-collar workers."[12] The rank and file of the Nationalist leagues, moreover, was recruited from very much the same milieu.[13]

Turn-of-the-century observers, from *La Petite République* to *Le Temps*, from the *Comité Mascuraud* to the LPF made an identical observation: shopkeepers were Nationalists; *petits commerçants* constituted "the better part of Nationalism's clientele."[14] Anatole France's *M. Bergeret à Paris* contains a fictionalized account of the 1900 municipal elections. Two

[10] "Le congrès du parti radical et radical socialiste," *Bulletin mensuel du commerce et de l'industrie*, July 1905; BCC I 8–63, *Fédération des industriels et des commerçants français*, flier, March 1903.

[11] See, for example, Raoul Girardet, "Pour une introduction à l'histoire du nationalisme français," p. 522; Rutkoff, *Revanche and Revision*, p. 263.

[12] Watson, "The Nationalist Movement in Paris," p. 80.

[13] Rebérioux, *La République radicale?* p. 160.

[14] The citation is from a Nationalist campaign poster, APP B/a 208, Dausset poster, 1902 elections, IIIrd arrondissement; see also Gérault-Richard, "Le petit commerce," *La Petite République*, 9 May 1902; "Chronique," *Bulletin mensuel du commerce et de l'industrie*, May 1902; APP B/a 944, 29 October 1901; *Le Temps*, 12 May 1902.

imaginary candidates—one Radical, the other Nationalist—
confront one another in a hotly contested campaign. The Nationalist Lacrisse wins and attributes his victory to the votes
of republicans fed up with the Republic: "It's a cast of mind
that is not rare in Paris among small businessmen." The defeated Radical, Anselme Raimondin, arrives at much the same
conclusion: "My defeat has but one cause: the discontent of
petty *boutiquiers* crushed between department stores and cooperatives."[15] But just how accurate were such assessments?
Did the organized shopkeeper movement enlist in the service
of Nationalism as it had on behalf of Boulanger a decade earlier?

The shopkeeper movement entered a period of flux and reorganization at the turn of the century. The *Ligue syndicale*
fell on hard times.[16] *La Revendication* no longer appeared regularly. *Ligue* morale sagged and membership declined. Financial problems developed, and the *Ligue syndicale* found itself
obliged to solicit funds, with little success, from fraternal organizations like the *Comité de l'alimentation*. Léopold Christophe's retirement in 1901 aggravated the *Ligue's* difficulties,
depriving the organization of its ablest orator and most reliable source of financial support. Leadership of the shopkeeper
movement passed from the *Ligue syndicale* to a new body, the
Parti commercial et industriel (PCI).

The PCI's origins date from 1900. Georges Berry's *patente*
reform, holed up in Senate commission for two years, was about
to be reported out. The *Ligue syndicale*, on Berry's urging, called
an extraordinary reunion of retailer associations. The meet-

[15] France, *M. Bergeret à Paris*, pp. 201, 213.
[16] For evidence of the *Ligue's* difficulties, see: "Comité de l'alimentation.
Séance du 22 juillet 1898," *Journal de l'alimentation*, 28 October 1898; "La
Ligue n'a rien fait?" reprinted from *La Revendication* in *Affiches tourangelles*,
21 February 1901: "Avis aux présidents des groupes de défense commerciale," *Affiches tourangelles*, 4 July 1901; "Pas d'argent, pas de Suisse," *La
Défense commerciale et industrielle*, 28 September 1902.

ing, held in February 1900, plotted strategy to force passage of the Berry bill and made plans to convene a formal National Congress of Leagues and Commercial Groups in the fall to review the bill's progress. The National Congress met in September. Christophe presided, assisted by Trépreau, but the *Ligue* did not dominate the proceedings as in February. Provincial organizations were well represented. Of the 139 retailer associations which participated, 100 were based in the departments. The provincials challenged the Paris *Ligue*'s right to speak for the entire shopkeeper movement and insisted on formation of a national commercial federation superior to the *Ligue syndicale* and with a substantial provincial representation. The Congress appointed a commission of six to organize the proposed federation, and for the moment, the *Ligue syndicale* went along. Trépreau for the *Ligue* took part, as did Jumin of the *Chambre syndicale de la charcuterie*. The commission completed its work in June 1901. A meeting was held to launch the new federation, christened the *Parti commercial et industriel*. Once again, provincials controlled the majority. The PCI's steering committee of twenty-one included four *ligueurs*, three officials of Paris-based *chambres syndicales*, but all the rest were non-Parisians, including the president, two vice-presidents and a secretary general.[17]

The *Ligue syndicale*'s subordinate status in the new organization nettled its leadership, which broke with the PCI in November. Trépreau, however, remained with the PCI as did a substantial percentage of the *Ligue*'s rank and file. Twenty-four *chambres syndicales* formerly affiliated to the *Ligue syndicale*

[17] For details of the PCI's pre-history, see *Affiches tourangelles*: "Convocation des présidents des ligues et groupes commerciaux," 18 January 1900; "L'assemblée des groupes industriels et commerciaux de France," 1 March 1900; "Troisième congrès des ligues et groupes commerciaux et industriels français," 4 October 1900; "Organisation du petit commerce en formation," 6 June 1901. See also Joseph Bernard, *Du Mouvement d'organisation et de défense du petit commerce français*, p. 86.

switched allegiance to the *Parti commercial.* The PCI formed local sections in Paris in the Ist, XIIIth, XVth and XIXth, effectively stripping the *Ligue* of its membership in these arrondissements. The PCI attempted with some success to supplant the *Ligue syndicale* in Paris. The shopkeeper movement had become national and, in the process, leadership of the movement shifted from Paris to the provinces. In 1895, the *Ligue* had claimed 150,000 adherents. In 1902, it was the PCI's turn to boast of its mass membership. Eight hundred retailer organizations representing an alleged 200,000 members took part in the PCI's first National Congress in October 1902.[18]

The shopkeeper movement, divided and in transition at the time of the Dreyfus Affair, was, however, almost unanimous in its support of the Nationalist cause. This was most certainly true of the *Parti commercial*'s leadership. The PCI's two general secretaries, Auguste Demeuré and Alphonse Trépreau, were both on record in opposition to a revision of the Dreyfus case. In July 1902, Demeuré and Trépreau organized a PCI section in Paris' Ist arrondissement. The section's membership included three of the arrondissement's four municipal councillors: Pierre Levée, a Nationalist Catholic, and Maurice Quentin and Ferdinand Le Menuet, both officials of the *Ligue des patriotes.*[19] Demeuré, president of a retailer organization in the Paris suburbs, repented of his anti-Dreyfusism in 1906.[20] Trépreau's commitment to Nationalism, however,

[18] On the competition between the *Ligue* and the PCI, see, once again, *Affiches tournagelles*: "Parti commercial et industriel," 7 November 1901; Auguste Marcoux, "Simple réponse," 28 November 1901; "Réponse de M. Trépreau," 13 December 1901; "Communications du PCI," 24 April 1902 and supplement; "Nécessité de la création d'un journal du Parti commercial," 11 October 1902.

[19] "Communications officielles du PCIF," *Affiches tourangelles*; 17 July 1902.

[20] Demeuré, "Emile Zola et M. Charles conseiller municipal," *Fédération de la Seine*, 4 August 1906.

was more thoroughgoing. He praised Déroulède as "the valiant of the valiant," "the chivalrous champion of patriotism."[21] It was on Trépreau's suggestion that the *Union fraternelle* contributed money to *La Libre Parole*'s fund to raise a monument in memory of Colonel Henry.[22]

The PCI's vice-president, Henri Destréguil, was also a convinced anti-Dreyfusard. Destréguil, owner of a Tours newspaper, professed himself an acolyte of Drumont's Catholic socialism. Destréguil's paper reprinted in May 1898 a diatribe against Jewish department stores originally published in *La Libre Parole,* and Destréguil himself wrote approvingly of Drumont's attacks on the 1900 exposition.[23] In 1898, Destréguil had sponsored formation of a regional retailers' association, the *Ligue du parti commercial des départements du Centre*, a direct antecedent of the PCI. Given Destréguil's Nationalist leanings, it comes as no surprise that the *Ligue du parti commercial* selected Georges Berry and Lucien Millevoye as principal speakers at its annual conference held in June 1900. Both were ex-Boulangists; both were Nationalists.[24] Their participation in the conference persuaded Henry Maret of *Le Radical* that the *Ligue du parti commercial* was a "Nationalist auxiliary," a view shared by Paul d'Estournelles, a center-left deputy from Mamers.[25]

Christophe, it might be added, also participated in the proceedings, which raises the question of the *Ligue syndicale*'s

---

[21] Trépreau, "Les proscrits et les assomptionnistes," *Bulletin de l'Union fraternelle du commerce et de l'industrie*, February 1900.

[22] "Souscription pour Mme. Henry," *Bulletin de l'Union fraternelle du commerce et de l'industrie*, January 1899.

[23] Albert Monniot, "Bazars juifs," reprint from *La Libre Parole* in *Affiches tourangelles*, 19 May 1898; H. Destréguil, "Prochain congrès des ligues commerciales de France à Paris ou à Tours," *Affiches tourangelles*, 11 January 1900.

[24] "Conférence et banquet," *Affiches tourangelles*, 7 June 1900.

[25] *Affiches tourangelles*: "Protestation," 24 May 1900; "Une lettre de M. d'Estournelles," 17 May 1900.

stance vis-à-vis Nationalism. The problem is not easily resolved because issues of *La Revendication,* the major source for *Ligue* activities, have not been conserved after 1896. On balance, however, the evidence suggests that *ligueurs* were hostile to the Dreyfusard cause, if not in fact favorable to Nationalism.

The *Union syndicale des tailleurs,* for example, a *Ligue* affiliate since the early nineties, utterly rejected the possibility of Dreyfus' innocence. The *Union syndicale* was anticlerical in its sympathies; indeed, it judged the Combes government's militant anticlericalism with approval. And yet it was outraged when Dreyfus was exculpated in 1906:

> You can say whatever you want. No matter what a defendant's religion or political opinions may be, we just can't believe that judges (even military judges!) would condemn a man twice if they didn't believe he was guilty.[26]

There were, of course, *Ligue* militants who were more extreme in their anti-Dreyfusard commitments.

Louis Gazon, as one might expect, believed fervently in Dreyfus' guilt. At a meeting of Republican Socialist Patriots in February 1898, he accused Zola, then on trial, of taking bribes from the "Jewish syndicate."[27] The *Ligue syndicale*'s one-time secretary, Plista, was known to attend *Patrie française* reunions.[28] But by far the most active *ligueur* in the Nationalist cause was Digard, a former *Ligue* section president and president of the *Chambre syndicale des marchands de chaussures en détail.* Digard ran in 1904 as a Nationalist candidate in the Archives ward of the IVth arrondissement. According to a police report, the LPF contributed 15,000F to his unsuccessful

---

[26]Sylviano, "Simple note," *L'Idéal,* 3 June 1906.
[27]APP B/a 1092, 22 February 1898.
[28]APP B/a 1334, 16 June 1900.

campaign.[29] But it was not as a candidate that Digard made his most important contribution to the Nationalist movement.

In April 1899, prefect of the Seine de Selves ordered that all exterior shop displays *(étalages)* be removed from sidewalks after noontime on Sundays and after 8:00 p.m. the rest of the week. The prefect acted on the recommendation of the Paris municipal council which in turn had taken up the issue at the instigation of councillor Arthur Rozier. Rozier, a socialist and official of the *Chambre syndicale des employés,* had proposed the measure as a means to shorten the shop employee's work day. Storeowners formed an ad hoc association—the *Chambre syndicale des étalagistes*—to protest the new regulations which, it was felt, gave an unfair competitive advantage to businesses, *grands magasins* in particular, with display windows. Digard took the initiative in organizing the *étalagistes'* association and acted as its first president.[30]

In the 1900 elections, the *Chambre syndicale des étalagistes* campaigned against incumbents who had voted in favor of Rozier's proposal. Nationalist candidates, as newcomers, benefited from the *étalagistes'* strategy, a fact which Digard was determined to impress on the municipal council's newly elected right-wing majority. He called a meeting in May at the Hôtel Moderne "to which all the Nationalist councillors were invited." The police made a report of Digard's remarks at the session: "He made clear that it was thanks to the *étalagistes'* intervention in the recent elections that the old majority had been swept out of the Hôtel de Ville. It was to *petit commerce,* in short, that the new men owed their election."[31] The Na-

[29] AN F⁷ 13230, 6 May 1904.

[30] On the formation of the *Chambre syndicale des étalagistes,* see APP B/a 153, 11 February and 26 May 1899; "Les étalages," *L'Epicerie française,* 3 June 1900; "Chambre syndicale des marchands de chaussures en détail du département de la Seine," *L'Union des syndicats de France,* 1 January 1899.

[31] APP B/a 153, 27 May 1900; AN F⁷ 12458, 26 May 1900.

tionalists were quick to express their gratitude. At its first post-election session, the municipal council voted on a motion by Gabriel Bertrou, Nationalist councillor from the Gaillon ward (IInd), to suppress the new *étalages* regulations. Prefect de Selves promptly issued the appropriate decrees.[32]

Militants like Digard, Gazon and Plista earned the *Ligue syndicale* a reputation as a "league of reactionaries." The *Ligue* made little effort to dispel such suspicions. Five elected officials were invited to the *Ligue syndicale*'s extraordinary reunion in February 1900. Four were Nationalists: Berry, Millevoye, Georges Girou and Stanislas Ferrand.[33] Anti-Nationalists, of course, criticized the *Ligue syndicale*'s weakness for right-wing politicians, to which the *Ligue* unashamedly replied: "We take our friends where we find them."[34]

Of Paris' principal retailer associations, only the *Comité de l'alimentation* appeared immune to the temptation of Nationalism. Marguery, after all, had aligned himself with the pro-Dreyfusard *Comité Mascuraud*. But the appearance was deceiving. A Nationalist groundswell in the food-and-drink trades almost brought Marguery's career as president of the *Comité de l'alimentation* to a premature end. The first signs of trouble appeared in the grocers' journal, *L'Epicerie française*. In March 1898, the paper's editor-in-chief, L. Mazand, expressed satisfaction with the guilty verdict delivered at Zola's libel trial: "the nation has pulled itself together: with an energetic shrug of the shoulders and a vigorous kick, it has put everything back in order."[35] In the spring of 1899, Déroulède and his lieutenant, Marcel Habert, were brought to trial on charges

[32] "Les étalages," *L'Epicerie française*, 3 June 1900.

[33] "L'assemblée des groupes industriels et commerciaux de France," *Affiches tourangelles*, 1 March 1900.

[34] "Une déclaration de la Ligue syndicale de Paris," *Affiches tourangelles*, 15 August 1901.

[35] L. Mazand, "Ceux qui ont jugé Zola," reprinted from *L'Epicerie française* in *Affiches tourangelles*, 10 March 1898.

of sedition in connection with the failed February coup attempted by the *Ligue des patriotes* (LDP). The accused were acquitted to the delight of *L'Epicerie française*, which applauded the "audacity of these two brave men." The president of the jury, moreover, had been a grocer which moved the paper to exult: "From now on, people will associate with our profession the epithet: Patriotic like a grocer."[36] *Marchands de vins*, it appears, were no less susceptible to the Nationalist appeal. The PCI's Ist arrondissement section was organized by Trépreau, Demeuré, the Déroulèdists Quentin and Le Menuet and not least of all Charles Girardin, president of the *Chambre syndicale des débitants de vins*.[37] Wineshopkeepers, as a police report of 1903 acknowledged, were "well disposed toward the government's adversaries; they proved it during the last municipal elections, which swept the Nationalists into the Hôtel de Ville."[38]

Nationalism's strength in the food-and-drink trades undermined Marguery's control of the *Comité de l'alimentation*. In the 1900 elections, Marguery weighed in at the last minute against two Nationalist candidates, Gaston Méry in the Faubourg Montmartre (IXth) and Alfred Houdé in the Porte Saint-Martin (Xth). The maneuver did not succeed, and both wards voted Nationalist. Jules Guérin's newspaper, *L'Antijuif*, credited the victories to dissidents in the *Comité de l'alimentation* who had refused to follow Marguery's instructions:

> We call to mind the last minute maneuver by the Paris *Comité de l'alimentation* to throw its support on election eve behind a few more or less shame-faced Dreyfusards who counted on the surprise to win the election for them. Our comrades in *l'Alimentation* . . . threw them-

[36] G. Vidal, "Bravo, l'épicerie," *L'Epicerie française*, 4 June 1899.
[37] "Communications officielles du PCIF," *Affiches tourangelles*, 17 July 1902.
[38] AN F^7 12458, 20 February 1903.

selves into the campaign with their accustomed dedication and energy, and the scheme failed.[39]

Marguery confronted a yet more serious challenge in 1902. In April, the *Comité* met to parcel out endorsements to meritorious candidates in the upcoming elections. Marguery, over opposition, pushed through an endorsement of Mesureur, but he could not persuade committee members to back other well-known Dreyfusards: Henri Brisson, Gustave Rouanet and especially Alexandre Millerand. Marguery resigned, and the *Comité* proceeded to vote endorsements of fifteen antigovernment candidates, of whom nine were Nationalists.[40] *Le Radical* protested that the *Comité* had been seized in a Nationalist coup—"invaded by Nationalist agents and converted into an instrument of [Nationalist] propaganda."[41] *L'Ami des petits commerçants* attributed Marguery's defeat to a small shopkeeper revolt: "This Committee, presided over by M. Marguery, has served as an intermediary between big and little commerce. People reproached it, however, for submitting all too easily to the orders of the Paris commercial establishment to which it sometimes sacrificed the little man's interests."[42]

Historians and contemporaries were right to situate *petit commerce*, at least organized *petit commerce*, on the Nationalist right. The PCI, *Ligue syndicale* and *Comité de l'alimentation*, all, to varying degrees, were implicated in the Nationalist explosion of 1898–1902. But why did the shopkeeper movement,

[39] APP B/a 695, clipping from *L'Antijuif*, 11 May 1900.

[40] The nine Nationalists were Auffray, Berry, Bonvalot, Holtz, Humbert, Massard, Millevoye, Paulin-Méry and Spronck. APP B/a 1408 bis, clipping form *La Liberté*, 23 April 1902; P. Vinay, "Dissolution du Comité de l'alimentation," *Journal de l'alimentation*, 20 May 1902; "La démission de M. Marguery," *L'Ami des petits commerçants*, 5 May 1902.

[41] "Les Nationalistes et le petit commerce," *Le Radical*, 25 April 1902.

[42] "La démission de M. Marguery," *L'Ami des petits commerçants*, 5 May 1902. Tempers cooled in the aftermath of the elections, and Marguery returned as the *Comité*'s president.

ostensibly committed to a nonpartisan stance, involve itself so actively in right-wing politics? What motivated militant shopkeepers to embrace Nationalism?

SHOPKEEPER MOTIVES

Two varieties of motive have been isolated to account for shopkeeper involvement in the Nationalist explosion. Some historians have attributed Nationalism's "evident success among the lower middle class of Paris" to a morbid fear of working-class socialism, to a deep-seated "yearning for conservatism."[43] Shopkeepers were determined to protect private property against a hydra-headed movement of social reform led by trade unionists, collectivists and Radical Solidarists. The regime was lacking in antibureaucratic, antisocialist zeal, but not the Nationalist leagues to which shopkeepers turned in desperation. Charles Seignobos, on the other hand, has written of turn-of-the-century Nationalism: "The nationalist, militarist and anti-Semitic tendency springs from the Parisian lower middle class of radical origins, but, above all, of rebellious tradition."[44] Radicalism and frustration, impotence and rebelliousness, these were the sentiments which moved *petits commerçants* to enlist in support of political reaction. Historians have assigned radical or conservative motives to *petits commerçants* on the basis of educated guesswork. An examination of the shopkeeper movement's response to Nationalism will show that the motives of retailer militants were in fact more complicated than a straightforward middle-class conservatism or radical plebeian fractiousness.

The interpretation of retailer Nationalism as an antileft

[43] Watson, "The Nationalist Movement in Paris," p. 62; Rebérioux, *op. cit.*, pp. 36–37.

[44] Cited in Weber, *The Nationalist Revival*, pp. 25–26.

conservative reflex has much to recommend it. The specter of collectivism did indeed haunt *petits commerçants* and for good reason. In the election years 1900 and 1902, socialists all too frequently took the opportunity to denounce, threaten and insult shopkeepers. Even the occasional Radical was persuaded to join in the attack. *L'Aurore* and the socialist *La Petite République* blamed the Nationalist victory in the 1900 elections on the shopkeeper vote. The laws of economic development, the papers agreed, doomed the shopkeeper to extinction, but "a crippled *petit commerce*" had pigheadedly refused to accept its fate. Shopkeepers looked to political reaction as an instrument to arrest the progress of economic concentration.[45] *L'Aurore* and *La Petite République* debated strategies to punish *petit commerce* for failing to recognize the inevitability of its demise. Jean Jaurès wrote of the necessity "to organize, to discipline the immense commercial anarchy of Paris."[46] The consumer's cooperative was settled on as the most potent weapon against the small business sector. Francis de Pressensé in *L'Aurore* commented on the election results: "wherever working-class emancipation has been carried forward by cooperatives with a socialist character, wherever the yoke of *petit commerce* has been broken or at least alleviated, we have been spared the scandal of a Nationalist invasion."[47] *La Petite République* made the identical observation and concluded: "The petty merchant detests us; he's made that perfectly clear. Let's eliminate him and form cooperatives."[48]

Again in 1902, small shopkeepers were singled out for abuse by the republican left. This time, however, it was the Radical press which took the lead. *Le Radical* was moved to fury

[45] F. de Pressensé, "Les amis du peuple," *L'Aurore*, 10 May 1900; E. Charnay, "Les petits commerçants," *La Petite République*, 26 May 1900.

[46] J. Jaurès, "Décision," *La Petite République*, 19 May 1900.

[47] F. de Pressensé, "Lendemain de la défaite," *L'Aurore*, 16 May 1900.

[48] M. Charsay, "Le rôle des coopératives dans les élections," *La Petite République*, 16 May 1900.

by the Nationalist takeover of the *Comité de l'alimentation* and proposed to take reprisals: "It's a question of organizing co-operative associations wherever the Paris *Syndicat de l'alimentation* has endorsed Nationalist candidates."[49] The Nationalists fared well in the first round of voting in the 1902 elections, stirring an angry counterattack in *L'Aurore,* aimed at *petits commerçants:*

> Can you hear them exulting? All the false-weighting merchants, all the adulterators, all the debasers of money, all the pimping hotel keepers fighting over the patronage of prostitutes, all the milkmen who poison newborns, the whole band of grocers, bakers, butchers, pothouse keepers, *charcutiers,* . . . that whole thieving bunch waiting in ambush to fleece the passerby is overjoyed.[50]

And lest *petits commerçants* failed to get the left's message, socialist hecklers appeared at shopkeeper meetings to make their views known. A "socialist squad" showed up at the *Ligue du parti commercial*'s conference in June 1900. Berry's speech was interrupted with cries of "You're a Nationalist!" "*Vive la Sociale!*" and "No more *petit commerce!*" while an antishopkeeper crowd outside sang the Internationale and the Carmagnole. Such demonstrations enraged shopkeeper militants who responded with a declaration of war.[51]

The PCI conceived itself as "a powerful dike against collectivism."[52] The party's program was devised as a counterfoil "to the collectivists' utopias."[53] Even its name, the *Parti commercial*, had been chosen "in opposition to the *Parti ouvrier* of M. Guesde."[54] The *Chambre syndicale des étalagistes* was no

---

[49] "Le Nationalisme et le petit commerce," *Le Radical,* 25 April 1902.

[50] A. Goullé, "Le petit commerce," *L'Aurore,* 29 April 1902.

[51] "Conférence et banquet," *Affiches tourangelles,* 7 and 14 June 1900.

[52] "Aux commerçants, aux industriels!" *La Défense commerciale et industrielle,* 21 September 1902.

[53] "Le Parti commercial," *Affiches tourangelles,* 27 June 1901.

[54] Bernard, p. 86.

less adamant in its anticollectivism. The *Aurore* article of 1902 prompted the *étalagistes* to publish a pro-Nationalist declaration which was postered all over Paris:

> For the second time, in 1900 as again today, we believe it our right and our duty . . . to rally the army of small commerce. . . . We see on one side the collectivists, the adversaries of *petit commerce*. On the other, the anticollectivists and therefore the defenders of small commerce and small industry.[55]

Whether by revolution or by cooperation, *L'Epicerie française* had remarked in 1898, socialists meant to dispose of the shopkeeper. Had *petits commerçants* any choice but to return evil for evil.[56]

The shopkeeper movement's opposition to collectivism was not, of course, a new phenomenon. Indeed, the anticollectivist polemics of 1900–1902 recall the anticollectivist polemics of the nineties. Retailer militants, in 1900 as in 1890, applauded "patriotic" socialists who railed against the forces of monopoly—bankers, mine owners and railway magnates.[57] But socialists went too far who preached the vicious and mistaken doctrine of class struggle, who incited dissension between *patrons* and workers. In commerce, an *étalagiste* poster claimed, employer and employee were not divided but "intimately linked" in a community of shared labor.[58] The beneficent concord of the small shop was France's surest guarantee of social peace. *Petit commerce,* moreover, was the cradle of virtues

[55] APP B/a 209, *étalagiste* poster in support of Cloutier, 1902 elections, IVth arrondissement.

[56] L. Mazand, "Le congrès socialiste," *L'Epicerie française*, 14 October 1900.

[57] "Les théories collectivistes sur la suppression du commerce," *L'Ami des petits commerçants*, 20 June 1902.

[58] APP B/a 209, *étalagiste* poster in support of Cloutier, 1902 elections, IVth arrondissement; see also B/a 696, poster signed by Gabriel Garreau, secretary general of the *Chambre syndicale des étalagistes*, 1903 by-election, Xth arrondissement.

cherished by all Frenchmen—thrift, family-mindedness and independence. Maurice Talmeyr singled out the *marchand de vins* as the epitome of "the old-style French shopkeeper" up in arms against socialist "speculations."

> He raises with fervor the flag of personal democracy against an anonymous democracy, without soul or justice. . . . He too has come—precisely because he has his honor to maintain, a family, a plot of land, a shop— to mourn for the old world and to seek its resurrection.[59]

Collectivist socialism, shopkeeper activists argued, aimed to destroy the virtuous harmony of this "old world" and in its stead to erect a hateful, bureaucratic tyranny. The triumph of collectivism, *L'Ami des petits commerçants* warned, meant a "recrudescence of *fonctionnarisme*," "the odious dictatorship of lawyers and doctors."[60] An anonymous bureaucracy, a mandarinate of professionals—these were the institutions destined to replace *petit commerce* in the socialist vision of the future.

The left's antishopkeeper polemics did indeed goad organized *petit commerce* into an outburst of antisocialist reaction. This formula, however, does not fully capture the complexity of motive underlying shopkeeper Nationalism. Collectivism, *L'Ami des petits commerçants* insisted, was the stalking horse of a cabal "of millionaire monopolists."[61] If collectivism triumphed, prophesied Demeuré of the PCI, "big capital too would triumph, inaugurating a century of lucre on a foundation of proletarian errors."[62] Big capital—the "financial oligarchy," "cosmopolitan financiers," "the aristocracy of

[59] Talmeyr, "Le marchand de vins," in *La Cité du sang*, pp. 164-165.

[60] Sylvain, "Le petit commerce injurié par Albert Goullée," cited in *Affiches tourangelles*, 15 May 1902.

[61] Sylvain, "Le petit commerce injurié par Albert Goullée," cited in *Affiches tourangelles*, 15 May 1902.

[62] "Le Parti commercial," *Affiches tourangelles*, 27 June 1901.

money"—posed a threat to shopkeepers no less serious than socialism.[63]

In the United States, shopkeeper militants claimed, capital exercised its domination through the trust. Department store tycoons like Jaluzot and Dufayel, the "big business interests" of the *Comité Mascuraud*, were France's counterparts to the *"trusteurs"* Gould, Rockefeller and Vanderbilt.[64] What made this "capitalist feudality" so dangerous was its corrupting influence, its power to subvert and manipulate the political process. It was the *Comité Mascuraud*'s millions which had brought the Waldeckist administration into office.[65] Indeed, was not Waldeck himself a paid agent of the money power? He drove in Dufayel's car and vacationed on Dufayel's yacht. He was a corporate lawyer who counted wheeler-dealers like Gustave Eiffel among his clients.[66] Parliament, *La Revendication* charged, had become the plaything of millionaire speculators utterly indifferent to the people's welfare.[67] The entire regime had fallen captive to big business. What better proof than the fate of the Berry bill, batted back and forth between the Chamber and the Senate. And what of the government's handling of the Dreyfus Affair?

The violent agitation stirred up by "that stupid business Dreyfus and Cie." was ruinous to trade, but the government

[63] "Rapport général du 3e congrès des ligues et des groupes," *Affiches tourangelles*, 17 January 1901; APP B/a 209, *étalagiste* poster in support of Cloutier, 1902 elections, IVth arrondissement; "Sur le yacht de Mémer," *L'Ami des petits commerçants*, 1 August 1902.

[64] *L'Ami des petits commerçants*: "L'homme aux cinq millions d'appointement," 1 October 1902; "Un rapport officiel sur les Trusts," 15 July 1902.

[65] APP B/a 209, *étalagiste* poster in support of Cloutier, 1902 elections, IVth arrondissement; "Le banquet de commerce et la presse," *L'Ami des petits commercants*, 1 November 1902.

[66] "Sur le yacht de Mémer," *L'Ami des petits commerçants*, 1 August 1902.

[67] L. Christophe, "Ligueurs, allons au Sénat," cited in *Affiches tourangelles*, 26 January 1899.

appeared unable or unwilling to resolve the crisis.[68] The construction workers' strike of 1898 was devastating to *petit commerce*, and yet the Brisson ministry hesitated to act. Shopkeeper militants interpreted the government's hesitations as a sign of complicity. Pro-Dreyfusard disturbances and the regime's reluctance to restore order were two sides of a single conspiracy, concocted and covertly managed by "agents of the Syndicate of treason," by "men of the cosmopolitan bank" who reaped enormous profits from France's economic disarray.[69]

By all rights, the republican press ought to have protested the regime's corruption, but the journalists who ran Paris' big dailies were "professionals of politics" no less than the deputies in parliament. The "intellectuals of the venal press" were as much in the pay of big capital as the "intellectuals" who ran the government.[70] The entire enterprise was rotten, from the office of Prime Minister, to the houses of Parliament, to the so-called free press. The regime's indifference obliged the shopkeeper to reflect to himself:

> . . . if the Republic does not conduct itself with respect toward *petit commerce*, to which it owes so much, then probity and justice are no longer on its side. Little matter if it is overturned.[71]

The Republic's decadence, *L'Ami des petits commerçants* diagnosed, had but one cause—the concentration of wealth. The remedy was no less straightforward—a revolt of "the humble

---

[68] L. Mazand, "Chronique," *L'Epicerie française*, 11 September 1898.

[69] A. Vervoort, "Le commerce et l'Affaire Dreyfus," *Le Jour*, 24 September 1898; "Union fraternelle," *La Croix*, 20 December 1898; see also APP B/a 1032, 11 October 1898.

[70] "Ligueurs! Unionistes! Syndiqués!" *La Défense commerciale et industrielle*, 28 September 1902.

[71] *L'Ami des petits commerçants*: "Aux railleurs," 1 September 1902; P. Sylvain, "La République et le petit commerce," 15 February 1902; Sylvain, "Les petits commerçants et la République," 5 June 1902.

folk" against "capitalist monopolies and trusts."[72] The salvation of the Republic and the cause of commercial defense were bound up one with the other. "To defend *petit commerce,*" *L'Ami* summed up, "is to defend the Fatherland itself."[73] Parisian shopkeepers voted Nationalist in 1900 and 1902 because they feared collectivism but also to rescue the Republic from monopoly capital and its allies in government and the press. The shopkeeper vote, however, was not solely inspired by the negative motives of fear and resentment.

Retailer activists attacked bureaucracy, monopolies, intellectuals and cosmopolitans, but shopkeeper vocabulary included as well a set of code words charged with positive connotations: independence, the people, "the humble folk," and the Fatherland. The language of shopkeeper Nationalism contained all the antinomies characteristic of small-owner utopianism. A Republic of *petits commerçants* and wage earners, this was the vision which underlay the shopkeeper movement's two-front attack on cooperatives and department stores, on collectivism and the money power at the time of the Dreyfus Affair.

The vision then which moved shopkeeper militants to embrace Nationalism was much the same as that which had inspired shopkeeper Boulangism. But two critical differences must be pointed out. The call for direct democracy which had figured so prominently in shopkeeper rhetoric of the 1880s was almost entirely absent in 1900. Secondly, in the Boulangist period, the shopkeeper movement had not shied away from the socialist label; militants in fact had sought out ties to socialist organizations like the *Chambre syndicale des em-*

---

[72] "Rivaux des rois," *L'Ami des petits commerçants,* 1 September 1902; Sylvain, "Pourquoi les grands magasins ne triompheront pas," *L'Ami des petits commerçants,* cited in *Affiches tourangelles,* 12 June 1902; and "Le petit commerce et le prolétariat," *L'Idéal social,* 16 August 1903.

[73] Sylvain, "Pourquoi les grands magasins ne triompheront pas," *L'Ami des petits commerçants,* 1 April 1902.

ployés. At the turn of the century, however, socialism had become a term of abuse in shopkeeper vocabulary, and the only working-class organization with which the movement maintained relations was the *Fédération nationale du travail*, a federation of yellow trade unionists.[74]

The small-owner utopianism of the 1880s with its radical democratic overtones and socialist associations is rightly understood as an offshoot of radical republicanism. It contained, of course, powerful conservative elements: a deeply felt suspicion of the new world of progress and industry, a xenophobic parochialism, and an attachment to the old-fashioned values of thrift, work and family. The new structure of politics which emerged in the nineties, the sure-footed advance of the small owner's twin enemies—big business and collectivist socialism—magnified the reactionary potential of small-owner doctrine. The revised version which gained currency at the turn of the century—devoid of democratic fervor and twisted by an obsessive antisocialism—was stripped of the qualities which had justified its classification as an ideology of the left. And yet, in its continued scorn for big business and the "sham" of parliamentary government, it retained the appearance of its one-time radicalism. A balance of radical and conservative impulses was always a feature of small-owner utopianism. The balance, at the turn of the century, was distinctly weighted to the conservative side. The radical republicanism of the 1880s had given way to the radical Nationalism of the Dreyfus Affair.

A combination of radical and conservative motives then turned shopkeeper militants to the Nationalist cause. *Petits commerçants* looked to Nationalism as a weapon to strike at a status quo administered by men like Waldeck-Rousseau and Alexandre Millerand; but shopkeepers also looked on Nationalism as a rampart against undesired change, as the salvation

[74]"Le petit commerce et le prolétariat," *L'Idéal social*, 16 August 1903.

of an old world on the verge of extinction. Did Nationalism live up to expectations? Was it the radical/conservative champion of small-owner utopianism sought after by a desperate shopkeeper movement?

THE PLEBEIAN LEAGUES AND SMALL-OWNER UTOPIANISM

Historians have distinguished two varieties of Nationalism: "the Nationalism of the faubourgs, that of Barrès, Rochefort Déroulède, Drumont" and the bourgeois Nationalism of the *Ligue de la patrie française.*[75] The former—plebeian, violent and antiliberal—foreshadowed the fascist movements of the 1930s; the latter—middle-class and conservative—prefigured, not fascism, but Poincarism and the politics of the *Bloc national.*[76] This schema, however, glosses over the shared origins and core of common beliefs which united the two wings of the Nationalist movement. The *Patrie française* militant—like Déroulède, Drumont and Rochefort—sprang from the boulevard milieu. Plebeian and bourgeois Nationalist alike embraced the small-owner vision, arrived at via a reaction against Haussmannization and the end-of-century *révolution du bon marché.* Both varieties of Nationalism boasted a similar combination of boulevard fractiousness and small-owner enthusiasm, a combination which had won shopkeeper support in the eighties and nineties and which did so again at the turn of the century.

Plebeian Nationalism lends itself most readily to such an analysis. The great street demonstrations with which the

[75] Sternhell, *Maurice Barrès*, p. 344.

[76] On Nationalism as a radical, plebeian movement, see also Rutkoff, p. 265; and Rémond, *The Right Wing in France*, p. 216. On Nationalism as a precursor of Poincarism, see Rioux, *Nationalisme et conservatisme*, p. 117.

memory of the plebeian leagues is so intimately linked, were all played out on the boulevards. Publication of Zola's *J'accuse* triggered the first Nationalist *journée*. The demonstration began in the Latin Quarter. Four to five hundred students assembled at the boulavard Saint-Michel and rue Gay-Lussac and then headed for the Right Bank. The demonstrators crossed the Seine at the Pont Royal and made their way up the avenue de l'Opéra en route to the boulevard Montmartre. "Café customers along the way," a police observer reported, "on hearing shouts of: 'Down with Zola!' 'Death to the Jews,' joined [the demonstration] and added considerably to its numbers."[77] The police acted promptly to disperse the crowd, and the demonstration which had begun at 4:00 was over by 4:30. In October 1898, the Chamber reconvened after its summer recess, an event which provoked a second round of boulevard demonstrations. A vast anti-Dreyfusard crowd filled the streets from the rue Royale to the Opera House. Dreyfusard papers were burned, and demonstrators assaulted "a band of cosmopolitans and intellectuals" that had stationed itself in front of Durand's. A police cordon at the intersection of the rue Royale and Place de la Concorde blocked the path to the Chamber. A crowd of three thousand, egged on by Déroulède, Habert and Paulin-Méry, broke through the cordon but were driven back by police at the Pont de la Concorde. A brigade chief was beaten up in the melee; police arrested Jules Guérin who was on the scene and charged him with the offense. Crowds continued to gather into the evening hours, but there was no further danger to the Chamber of Deputies.[78]

The most serious demonstration of the Affair, the most threatening to the regime, occurred in February 1899, and

[77] APP B/a 1043, 15 January 1898.

[78] For details, see APP B/a 1105, clippings from *Le Radical*, 26 October 1898 and *La Libre Parole*, 26 October 1898; B/a 1032, clippings from *L'Intransigeant*, 27 October 1898, and *Le Jour*, 27 October 1898.

once again the boulevards provided the *mise en scène*. In the wake of Faure's death, parliament voted Loubet president of the Republic. Paris learned of Loubet's election at 4:30 p.m. on February 19. A police observer commented on the city's response: "as always happens on such troubled occasions, a great excitement reigned in front of the newspaper offices in and around the boulevard, rue and faubourg Montmartre."[79] By 10 o'clock, an estimated 20,000 persons had taken to the streets, and the crowd was thickest in front of *La Libre Parole*'s offices at the boulevard Montmartre. Cafés in the vicinity were jammed with excited patriots, shouting, "Down with Loubet!" "Dump Him!" "Long Live The Army!" Police arrested 150 demonstrators before order was restored.[80] It was less than one week later that the LDP attempted its coup d'état. Faure's funeral provided the occasion. A column of troops which had participated in the funeral cortège returned to barracks via the Place de la Nation. Déroulède intercepted the column as it crossed the square and attempted to persuade the commanding officer, General Roget, to march on the Elysée Palace. LDP militants, joined by royalists and anti-Semites, were already in place along the route "to whip up the crowd, take control of it if necessary, and lead it behind the troops who were expected to march on the Elysée via the boulevards."[81] A rising on the boulevards, backed by the military, this was the combination with which Déroulède planned to topple the regime. Roget, as we know, refused to cooperate in the scheme, the coup fizzled, and the February days came to an end.

Déroulède was ready to try his luck a second time in August 1899. The coup, as in February, was to be launched from

[79] APP B/a 905, report dated September 1899.

[80] APP B/a 905, report dated September 1899; see also clippings from *Le Petit Bleu*, 19 February 1899, and *Le Gaulois*, 19 February 1899, and *L'Eclair*, 19 February 1899.

[81] APP B/a 1104, 25 February 1899.

the boulevards. Dreyfus' retrial opened at Rennes on August 7; the LDP planned to strike on the 12th. According to Déroulède's plan, *ligueurs*, joined by military men in mufti, were to be stationed on the Left Bank at the boulevard Saint-Michel and boulevard Saint-Germain, and on the Right Bank at the boulevards from the rue Royale to the Place de la République. "[I]t is said," a police informant reported, "that General Négrier will be stationed on the boulevards between the Madeleine and the boulevard Montmartre and that at a given moment he will make himself known to the crowd and lead it in a march on the Elysée."[82] Déroulède decided to bring Guérin's anti-Semitic league into the plot at the last minute. The government, however, learned of the coup plans and made preemptive arrests. Police picked up Déroulède without difficulty, but Guérin barricaded himself in the LAF's fortified headquarters on the rue Chabrol. The headquarters, nicknamed Fort Chabrol, remained under police siege for forty days before Guèrin surrendered.

When Nationalists descended into the streets, they made straight for the boulevards. The plebeian Nationalists have a reputation as gutter roughnecks, a reputation richly deserved. Guérin's butcher boys did not hesitate to break heads or smash shop windows. LDP militants went armed with leaded canes. The butcher Ernest Barillier, one of Déroulède's close associates, was known to carry a pistol. The street tough, however, represented but one side of the plebeian Nationalist persona. The well-dressed boulevardier, with a taste for theater and the races, represented another. The example of Rochefort comes to mind, as does that of Simone de Beauvoir's father, a Déroulèdist and ardent Nationalist. She provides an ambivalent portrait of him in her *Memoirs of a Dutiful Daughter*.

M. de Beauvoir came of a good family which had come down in the world. He styled himself an aristocrat and held

[82] APP B/a 1104, 6 August 1899.

in highest esteem the graces of the well-born—wit, charm and good breeding. As a young man, he was an elegant dresser, a dandy, an Epicurean who took his pleasure at the theater, café and racetrack. The young de Beauvoir longed for a career on the stage but settled down to become a lawyer. He remained an avid theater-goer, however, finding in the theater a welcome respite from the boredom of middle-class respectability. The Republic, as the embodiment of bourgeois philistinism, disgusted him, and it was in disgust that he turned to Nationalism.[83] Déroulèdism, as the theater, offered release from the disappointments and pettiness of an unwanted middle-class existence.

Plebeian Nationalism, like Boulangism, was bred in the spirit of boulevard revolt, and, like Boulangism, it was firmly planted in the traditions of small-owner utopianism. Déroulèdist and anti-Semitic candidates in the elections of 1900–1902 pressed a relentless attack on collectivism. The attack, however, was not premised on the sanctity of private property, but on the virtues of smallness. The triumph of socialism, Nationalists charged, meant the "annihilation of small business."[84] Had not the left made its antishopkeeper bias clear? Were not the socialists the most ardent exponents of cooperation? Nationalist candidates quoted ad nauseum from *L'Aurore* and *La Petite République* to make their point.[85] A France without shopkeepers was unimaginable. Power would pass to an irresponsible and spendthrift bureaucracy. A life of servitude awaited workers and employees denied all possibility of access to the ranks of the propertied. Dr. Péchin, anti-Semitic candidate in the XIIth against the incumbent Miller-

[83] De Beauvoir, *Memoirs of a Dutiful Daughter*, pp. 32–36.

[84] See remarks by Lucien Millevoye, cited in "Conférence et banquet," *Affiches tourangelles*, 7 June 1900.

[85] See, for example, APP B/a 209, Cloutier posters, 1902 elections, IVth arrondissement; B/a 218, Barillier poster, 1902 elections, XIXth arrondissement.

and, summed up the horrors of socialism in a poster addressed "*Commerçants et Consommateurs de Gaz*": "collectivism represents for us the negation of all individual liberty; society will be transformed into a vast prison, where the jailers will be foremen, more or less irresponsible and themselves dependent on higher-ups, such that we will all be subjected to a military discipline of a new kind."[86]

To block the progress of economic and political concentration, Nationalists urged employers and employees to make common cause. Socialists preached collectivism and the doctrine of class struggle. Nationalists replied with a program of reforms to rally the shopkeeper and worker alike: *patente* legislation for the *petit commerçant* and a pension scheme funded by a tax on foreign labor for the wage earner.[87] Cloutier, the Déroulèdist candidate in the IVth, stated the alternatives succinctly:

> On the one side, the candidate for defense of the small shopkeeper whose interests are tied to those of the laborer. On the other, the candidate of the Saint-Mandé . . . program which calls for the suppression of individual property and consequently the ruin of French commerce.[88]

Anticollectivism, of course, was not the sole theme of the Nationalist campaigns.

Plebeian Nationalist discourse abounded in abusive characterizations of big business, all borrowed from the stock of

[86] APP B/a 211 Péchin poster, 1902 elections, XIIth arrondissement.

[87] For Nationalist statements in support of *petit commerce* against the socialist threat, see: APP B/a 944, E. Ballière, 19 April 1900; B/a 935, E. Archdeacon, 19 April 1902; B/a 213, Congy poster, 1902 elections, XIth arrondissement; B/a 1334, Barillier, 16 December 1900; B/a 216, Lepelletier poster, 1902 elections, XVIIth arrondissement; B/a 211, Meiss poster, 1902 elections, XIIth arrondissement.

[88] APP B/a 209, Cloutier poster, 1902 elections, IVth arrondissement.

small-owner doctrine: "the big cosmopolitan banks," "the Jewish plutocracy," "vast anonymous and foreign enterprises."[89] Jews, plutocrats and foreigners, the litany went, stole and speculated at the expense of "*les humbles.*" And who were the humble? Cloutier denounced the socialist candidate in the IVth, Gabriel Deville, as an agent of "Jewish high finance which creates misery by shamelessly exploiting workers and *petit commerce.*"[90] Congy, who ran as a Republican Socialist Patriot in the XIth, attacked Dreyfusards in almost identical terms: "They are on the side of the big banks, of cosmopolitan agitators and monopolists who starve the worker and ruin small commerce."[91] International capital victimized the people—the shopkeeper, the worker—and, Nationalists argued, no redress was to be had from parliament.

The Berry bill, the Déroulèdist Gauthier de Clagny told a Nationalist rally, had been delayed three years "because of the opposition of big financiers well connected in government circles."[92] Parliament's irresponsible conduct was easy to explain. Speculators and foreigners, the "godfathers" of the "parliamentary oligarchy," were making enormous sums on the people's misfortunes.[93] A vast conspiracy, concocted by millionaire Jews and their henchmen in parliament, had been mounted against the French nation. LDP militant E. A. Ballière prophesied a slide into anarchy, if the humble failed to

[89] APP B/a 212, Houdé poster, 1902 elections, Xth arrondissement; B/a 944, Ballière, 19 April 1900; B/a 209, Cogrel poster, 1902 elections, IVth arrondissement; B/a 213, Congy poster, 1902 elections, XIth arrondissement; Millevoye cited in "Conférence et banquet," *Affiches tourangelles,* 7 June 1900.
[90] APP B/a 209, Cloutier poster, 1902 elections, IVth arrondissement.
[91] APP B/a 213, Congy poster, 1902 elections, XIth arrondissement.
[92] APP B/a 935, 21 March 1902.
[93] APP B/a 213, Congy poster, 1902 elections, XIth arrondissement; B/a 944, Ballière, 19 April and 3 March 1900; Millevoye, " 'L'Affaire' et les affaires," *La Patrie,* 27 May 1900; B/a 209, Cogrel poster, 1902 elections, IVth arrondissement.

resist: "the parliamentary regime will break all moral bonds, will undermine national activity by strikes fomented abroad [and] will deliver the country into the hands of cosmopolitan monopolists."[94]

A single, unifying vision underlay the two principal themes—opposition to monopoly and anticollectivism—of the plebeian Nationalist campaigns. A people of shopkeepers and wage earners was besieged by an alarming array of hostile forces: Jews, foreigners, collectivists, politicians, financiers. The people's enemies, however diverse, shared a common set of traits in the Nationalist scheme of things. They were parasites who jabbered or speculated but did not engage in productive work; they were partisans of large-scale organization indifferent to the values of independence and personal responsibility; they were outsiders with no sense of local solidarity. Nationalists, of course, made every effort to identify themselves as insiders, home-grown members of the small-owner community. A Barillier poster opened with the declaration: "I am not a politician. Parisian shopkeeper."[95] Déroulèdist and anti-Semitic candidates made a point of claiming modest origins; "son of the *quartier*," "child of the people," "son of the people" and like phrases crop up time and again in Nationalist campaign literature.[96]

A well-publicized devotion to the city of Paris helped establish a candidate's parochial sympathies. Gabriel Bonvalot, an explorer and Déroulèdist deputy of the Xth, was founder of the *Comité pour la défense des espaces libres*, an association of civic-minded Parisians to preserve and expand the city's park system.[97] Paul Escudier, municipal councillor of the Saint-

---

[94] APP B/a 944, undated electoral bulletin.

[95] APP B/a 947, Barillier poster, 1900 elections, Rochechouart ward.

[96] APP B/a 209, Failliot poster, 1902 elections, IVth arrondissement; B/a 211, Meiss poster, 1902 elections, XIIth arrondissement; B/a 211, Péchin poster, 1902 elections, XIIth arrondissement.

[97] Eugène Hénard, *Etudes sur les transformations de Paris*, vol. III, p. 83.

Georges ward, specialized in studies of "the history and mores of *vieux Paris*."[98] Quentin, Déroulède's lawyer and municipal councillor of les Halles, claimed to have been born "in the *quartier* which he represents and which he has never abandoned."[99]

It was precisely Nationalism's localist, small-owner vision that motivated its furious Anglophobia. England—the imperial state par excellence, the financial capital of the world—represented the antithesis of the self-sufficient community. It was, in Nationalist eyes, an oligarchical octopus determined to extinguish small-owner values. How else was England's savage attack on the Boer Republic to be explained? The Boers, after all, were a nation of farmers, "a little people" in the words of one Nationalist.[100] Georges Berry saluted the Boer leader Kruger as "the representative incarnate of a republic of the people and of patriotism."[101] The conflict of Boer vs. Englishman, declared the Déroulèdist Henri Galli, recapitulated Nationalism's struggle against the "Dreyfus syndicate."[102] When the Nationalist-controlled Paris municipal council welcomed Kruger at the Hôtel de Ville in December 1900, it was to strike a blow in the name of small-owner values against the combined forces of Anglo-Jewish finance.

Plebeian Nationalism, with its boulevard bravado and small-owner commitments, calls to mind the Boulangist movement. But there are differences. Boulangists had prescribed direct democracy as the cure for excessive concentration of power. Nationalists looked to more authoritarian government. They advocated a revision of the constitution with a president elected by the people, a cabinet chosen by and responsible to the executive, and a parliament with limited ini-

[98] Gay, *Nos Ediles*, pp. 161–162.
[99] *Ibid.*, p. 37.
[100] AN F⁷ 12458, 24 January 1900.
[101] APP B/a 1334, 16 December 1900.
[102] APP B/a 1336, 28 March 1900.

tiative in fiscal matters.[103] Barillier spoke of a "Republic of the people, for and by the people"; Ballière invoked the "principles of 1789."[104] The republican flourishes of Nationalist rhetoric, however, lacked the democratic commitment which had distinguished militant Boulangism. Citizens, the Nationalists explained, had a duty to boycott Jewish stores. A police informant jotted down Barillier's remarks to an audience of supporters: "He proclaimed himself an anti-Jew, enemy of the department store and added that, at his house, no one bought a thing from Jewish businesses."[105] Such was the nature and extent of public participation envisioned by the Nationalists.

Secondly, plebeian Nationalism in contrast to Boulangism, failed to attract a working-class constituency. The LDP, for example, had been able in the eighties to establish sizeable local organizations in Paris's peripheral arrondissements. The situation was much changed at the turn of the century. Galli reported on the state of league organization in 1902. In the XVth, once an LDP stronghold, Galli conceded: "There is much to do." Reorganization had salvaged weakened committees in the XIIth and XIVth, but divisions still paralyzed activity in the XVIIIth and XIXth. Galli characterized league organization in the XXth as "embryonic."[106] Plebeian Nationalism was not only less democratic than Boulangism but less proletarian as well.

These changes, of course, did not diminish Nationalism's

[103] APP B/a 209, Cogrel poster, 1902 elections, IVth arrondissement; B/a 1033, clipping from L'Eclair, 1 January 1900, entitled "Déclaration de M. Paul Déroulède"; B/a 947, Barillier poster, 1900 elections, Rochechouart ward.

[104] APP B/a 947, Barillier poster, 1900 elections, Rochechouart ward; B/a 944, Ballière, electoral bulletin, 1900.

[105] APP B/a 947, 21 June 1901; see also B/a 212, Houdé poster, 1902 elections, Xth arrondissement.

[106] See Galli reports of 9 December 1902 and 7 July 1903, AN F⁷ 12870.

appeal to the militant *petit commerçant*. On the contrary, the shopkeeper too had lost interest in direct democracy; he, too, found the working class uncompromising and hostile. Indeed, there was scarcely an issue on which shopkeeper and Nationalist disagreed, from *patente* revision, to gas prices, to *étalages* regulations. A fundamental congruence of perspective underlay this agreement on questions of immediate policy. The Déroulèdist *ligueur*, no less than the shopkeeper militant, was a small-owner utopian, determined to purge France of large-scale organization, foreign influence and moral decay so that the nation's healthy core—a people of independent proprietors and upwardly mobile wage earners—might be preserved.

Given the shared small-owner vision of plebeian Nationalist and shopkeeper militant, it comes as no surprise that maps of shopkeeper militancy and plebeian Nationalist strength overlap extensively. The LDP's best organized local committees were located in Paris's central arrondissements: the Ist, IInd, IVth and IXth.[107] These arrondissements, moreover, voted overwhelmingly Nationalist in the 1900 municipal elections. Of the sixteen municipal councillors elected, ten were Nationalists, including a half dozen of the movement's leading personalities: Quentin, Le Menuet, Gabriel Bertrou, Galli, Barillier and Gaston Méry. Three Radicals, a Bonapartist, one Nationalist Catholic and one "anti-ministry" Radical filled the remaining six seats. In 1902, as in 1900, electoral politics were dominated by Nationalists, and Nationalists for the most part of the plebeian variety. Nationalists won five of the six seats at issue. Archdeacon edged out Muzet in the Ist. Cloutier was elected in the IVth and Berry in the IXth. The sixth seat went to a conservative, Georges Berger. The electoral base of plebeian Nationalism included strongholds in the artisanal Xth and newly constructed XVIIth, but the movement's center of gravity may fairly be located in Paris' commercial core,

[107] AN F⁷ 12870, 7 July 1903.

in precisely the arrondissements that had launched the shopkeeper movement.

Plebeian Nationalism was perfectly suited to a shopkeeper constituency, and center-city *petits commerçants* responded with a vote of confidence. But what of that other species of Nationalism, the stuffy, conservative Nationalism of the *Patrie française* (LPF)? At first glance, the LPF appears an organization most uncongenial to the small-owner aspirations of shopkeeper militants.

THE *Patrie Française* AND SMALL-OWNER UTOPIANISM

Jean-Pierre Rioux, historian of the LPF, has emphasized the organization's bourgeois, conservative character, and not without cause. [108] University and lycée professors, members of France's various academies, well-known and established professionals in medicine and law, flocked to the league when it was formed in January 1899. The salons of the faubourg Saint-Germain lent moral and financial support. The business community, above all, lavished funds on it. The Catholic-leaning *Union du commerce et de l'industrie pour la défense sociale*, it was reported, provided one million francs in subsidies to the LPF's 1902 electoral campaign. [109] On the local level, it was the middle class, more than big business, which provided the bulk of *Patrie française* officials. The LPF's extensive network of ward and arrondissement committees in Paris was

[108] Rioux, pp. 65–66.

[109] Bader, *The Nationalist Leagues*, p. 186; see also APP B/a 693, 11 May 1900; B/a 1420, 24 September 1902; AN F⁷ 12870, 10 December 1903; and BHVP, Actualités, série 119, Commerce et Industrie, *Union* pamphlet dated 1903.

manned in large part by manufacturers, wholesalers and above all members of the liberal professions.[110]

On first inspection, LPF ideology appears to corroborate the thesis of the organization's bourgeois, conservative origins. It deplored state interference in the citizen's private affairs, whether in matters of religion or public welfare. And it repudiated socialism as the ultimate expression of bureaucratic, interventionist thinking. *Patrie française* militants, in reaction against the "wastefulness" and "chaos" of parliamentary government, proposed to limit the Chamber's initiative in fiscal matters and to strengthen the executive branch through popular election of the president. The *Patrie française* posed as the bulwark of freedom and "social peace" against a host of ideologues and outsiders—internationalist socialists, political placemen, Jacobin centralizers, anticlerical sectarians and so forth. These were themes with an appeal to middle-of-the-road voters, and some historians have identified precisely this group as Nationalism's principal electoral clientele. The LPF drew its strength in Rioux's phrase from "the conservative republican tradition."[111]

A final argument may be adduced in support of this thesis. The *Patrie française* was closely connected to conservative

[110] APP B/a 1334: 10 June 1901, Gaillon; 11 May 1903, Archives; 3 August 1900, Arts-et-Métiers; 11 May 1903, St.-Gervais-Arsenal; 21 March 1900, VIth arrondissement; 13 June 1903, St.-Germain des Près; 22 May 1900, St.-Thomas d'Aquin; 18 February 1900, Faubourg Montmartre; 14 March 1900, IXth arrondissement; 8 March 1902, Hôpital Saint-Louis; 12 March 1903, XIth arrondissement; 25 June 1903, Folie-Méricourt; 15 February 1903, XIIth arrondissement; 26 May 1900, Montparnasse; 24 April 1900, Plaisance. See also Rioux, p. 29.

[111] On the conservative dimension of the *Patrie française* program, see Sternhell, *La Droite révolutionnaire*, p. 136, and *Maurice Barrès*, p. 344; Rioux, pp. 40ff.; Bader, pp. 62ff. On the *Patrie française's* bourgeois electoral clientele, see Bader, p. 219, and Louis Giard, *Les Elections à Paris sous la IIIe République*, vol. I, pp. 89, 129, and vol. II, pp. 308–310.

groups—to Mélinists and Pioutists. Its leadership was well stocked with right Progressist sympathizers, including Jules Domergue, editor of the Mélinist journal, *La Réforme économique*. Marcel Dubois, "M. Méline's alter-ego" according to a police informant, lectured on a regular basis for the league.[112] And league president Jules Lemaître was known to favor an alliance with the Mélinist wing of the Progressist party.[113] The LPF's relations with the *rallié* Jacques Piou were yet more intimate. In 1901, Piou founded an all-Catholic party, the *Action libérale* (re-christened the *Action libérale populaire* in 1902). The ALP was exceedingly well funded. Ten million francs on one estimate were contributed to its 1902 election campaign.[114] Piou used the party's millions to control, indeed, to buy up the LPF. The *Patrie française* suffered a serious setback in the 1902 elections despite a strong showing in Paris. Lemaître's irresolute leadership and the authoritarianism of the *Patrie française*'s general secretary, Gabriel Syveton, demoralized a discouraged rank and file. The *Patrie française* disintegrated and its membership in large part passed over to Piou's ALP.[115] The LPF rump, short of militants and funds, became dependent on the *Action libérale* for periodic injections of financial support. Piou, as the *Patrie française*'s de facto treasurer, gained enormous influence in the organization. Indeed, by 1905, he was in a position to determine the election of Lemaître's successor as LPF president, the Catholic conservative Henri de Marcère.[116]

Still, the conservative propensities and bourgeois stuffiness

[112] APP B/a 1336, 9 July 1900.
[113] APP B/a 1336, 2 January 1900 and 21 February 1902; see also Bader, p. 225.
[114] Bader, pp. 192–195.
[115] APP B/a 1276, 30 July 1903; see also Fatoux, *Les Coulisses du nationalisme*, pp. 18, 29; B/a 1336, 13 March 1903; Bader, p. 268.
[116] APP B/a 1150, 18 April 1905; B/a 1137, 4 April 1904, 28 May and 19 April 1905.

of the LPF can be overestimated. Just as there were two sides to the plebeian Nationalist persona—rough-neck and boulevardier—so there were two sides to the *Patrie française* militant. The LPF, however *bien-pensant* at first glance, contained its share of boulevard types: disgruntled men about town, dandified littérateurs and *vieux parisiens*. The list of contributors to the LPF's house organ, *Les Annales de la Patrie française* contains a roster of familiar names: Lemaître, Maurice Donnay, Georges Montorgueil, Maurice Talmeyr, Maurice Barrès, Léon Daudet, Etienne Grosclaude, and so on.[117] All were afficionados of boulevard life, historians of its mores, men of the theater, of the press and of the café. Textile magnates financed the *Patrie française*, but so did Boni de Castellane and the comtesse de Janville (Gyp).[118] In December 1898, the LPF *en formation* published a patriotic appeal signed by a score of academicians, but also by the likes of Forain, Caran d'Ache and Edmond Benjamin, caricaturists and critics of the new boulevards.[119] Even the LPF's academicians and lycée professors smacked of the boulevards or of its Montmartre outpost. Comte Albert Vandal—historian, *immortel* and signatory of the *Patrie française* appeal—enjoyed the reputation of a "man of the world" and was admired for his fashionable dress.[120] The novelist cum Nationalist Paul Bourget liked to play the dandy's part, complete with monocle, filtered linen and gold-pommeled cane.[121] *Gil Blas* compared Henri Lavedan, another Academician and *Patrie française* recruit, to Henry Meilhac "from whom he inherited his Parisianism and stinging wit."[122]

[117] See, for example, the title page of the 15 May 1900 edition of the *Annales de la Patrie française*.
[118] Rioux, p. 53; Missoffe, *Gyp et ses amis*, p. 166.
[119] Rioux, p. 11fn.
[120] Louis Madelin, "Albert Vandal," *La République française*, 5 September 1910.
[121] Ponton, "Naissance du roman psychologique," p. 75.
[122] "Henri Lavedan," *Gil Blas*, 2 June 1892.

The Academician most prominent in the league hierarchy was, of course, Jules Lemaître, a Chat Noir habitué and hardly the model of bourgeois conservatism. He was a supreme ironist, a *feuilletonniste* and *chroniqueur* of sparkling talent, renowned for the playful skepticism and finesse of his prose. Even Syveton, a lowly lycée professor from Reims, affected the monocle and mannered theatricality of a Parisian man about town. [123]

If *Patrie française* littérateurs cultivated the boulevard style, it was because the boulevard, its cafés, pressrooms and theaters, was their stamping ground. The salons of the faubourg Saint-Germain, above all the salon of Lemaître's paramour, the comtesse de Loynes, offered a welcome hospitality to the upper-crust of Nationalism. *Patrie française* stalwarts like Léon Daudet, however, unabashedly preferred the headier stimulus of the café. "Real wit," he wrote, "is called for in the café and recompensed on the spot with sound and weighty laughter, whereas all too often, the wit of the salons is but counterfeit coin, worn-out junk, approved, propagated, stretched out by constrained and polite smiles." [124] Indeed, it was at the Café de la Paix that Daudet, in the company of Lemaître and Ernest Judet (editor of *L'Eclair*) awaited the outcome of the 1902 elections, much as Boulanger had awaited the outcome of the '89 elections at Durand's. The boulevards, of course, were ruled from the newspaper office no less than from the coffeehouses, and *Patrie française* littérateurs were no strangers to the world of journalism. Louis Dausset, a lycée professor and one-time LPF secretary general, wrote for *L'Echo de Paris*, as did at one time or another, Syveton and Lemaître. Talmeyr in the nineties had done crime reporting for *Gil Blas*. The staff at the *Journal des débats* included a sizeable contingent from the *Patrie française*: Lemaître, Emile Faguet, René Doumic

[123] Benoist, *Souvenirs*, vol. III p. 71.
[124] Léon Daudet, *Salons et journaux*, p. 297.

and Maurice Spronck, Nationalist deputy of the VIIth. But no journal was more hospitable to LPF litterateurs than Arthur Meyer's *Le Gaulois*. Meyer characterized *Le Gaulois* as "a branch office of the Academy," and indeed, the newspaper's payroll was studded with *Patrie française* Academicians: Barrès, Bourget, Vandal, Doumic, Faguet, Henry Houssaye, Costa de Beauregard.[125] These men, of course, practiced a brand of journalism that has vanished with the nineteenth century. At great boulevard newspapers like *Le Gaulois* or *Le Figaro*, the line between journalism and *belles lettres* was not sharply drawn. The newspaper personalities of the eighties and nineties were not reporters or muckrakers but critics and *feuilletonnistes*.[126] The LPF dominated this world of literary journalism. Nor did it fail to attract recruits from that third pillar of boulevard life, the theater. The dean of theater critics at the turn of the century was Jules Lemaître. Francisque Sarcey, a critic of lesser stature, signed the LPF appeal, as did playwrights Lavedan and Pailleron.[127] Maurice Donnay collaborated on the *Annales de la Patrie française* and caused a sensation on the boulevards with an anti-Semitic play, *Retour de Jérusalem*, first staged in 1903. Donnay began his career, as we have seen, at the Chat Noir, descended to the boulevards where he made a reputation as an author of light comedies and ended an honored member of the Académie française. Nationalists from Lemaître to Simone de Beauvoir's father adored Donnay plays, perhaps because the typical Donnay hero—an aging boulevardier, debonair, experienced, gray at the temples but still handsome—represented a flattering portrait of themselves.[128] In 1903, Léon Fatoux, a disillusioned LPF militant, published a "behind the scenes" exposé of the LPF which bore

[125] Billy, *L'Epoque 1900*, p. 364; Meyer, *Ce que mes yeux ont vu*, pp. 360–361.

[126] Billy, p. 368.

[127] Charle, "Champ littéraire et champ du pouvoir," pp. 248–249.

[128] Bertaut, *Le Paris d'avant guerre*, pp. 136–138.

the title *Les Coulisses du nationalisme*. Fatoux's book, much as Mermeix's *Coulisses du boulangisme* in 1890, marked the close of a movement which had played itself out on the boulevards.

The leadership of the *Patrie française* as of the plebeian leagues was recruited from the same boulevard milieu. The *Ligue des patriotes*, to be sure, showed a greater aptitude for street action, for rough-and-tumble militancy than the *Patrie française*. Lemaître's crowd preferred the more civilized surroundings of the café and pressroom. The gulf between the two, however, should not be exaggerated.

Bourgeois and plebeian Nationalists shared not only a common origin but a similar set of cultural preoccupations. The men of the LPF longed not only for social peace, but for a resurrection of *vieux Paris* with its boulevards uncorrupted by commercialism, with its cozy *quartiers* unviolated by the pickaxe of Haussmannization. François Coppée, Parnassian poet and one-time co-president of the *Patrie française*, may be taken as an example. Coppée turned his back on *Paris nouveau* to celebrate the little pleasures of *quartier* life. When he died in 1909, he was eulogized by Jean Richepin as a "local poet, a regional and parish-pump poet who embodied and celebrated his *petit pays*, his nook, his village."[129] The *petit pays* Coppée incarnated was, of course, Paris, not the Haussmannized city with its "monumental solitudes," but Paris of the faubourgs populated by honest citizens of modest means, by butchers, fruit sellers, grocers and blacksmiths.[130] Coppée styled himself a "Nationalist gavroche," a "*gamin de Paris*"; Dickens, Balzac and Hugo were his heroes, and Coppée, like them, was a passionate *flâneur*.[131] His evocations of popular life, however, scarcely rose above the bathetic. He specialized in

[129] APP B/a 910, clipping from *La Libre Parole*, 6 June 1910.
[130] Coppée, *Souvenirs*, p. 238.
[131] For Coppée's tastes, see APP B/a 910, clippings from *L'Echo de Paris*, 8 February 1892 and 21 March 1900.

genre scenes, portraits of Sunday crowds and July 14th street balls.[132] Coppée cherished the vision of an older and smaller Paris, "where reigned the gentle peace and poetry of a province." "Paris," Coppée wrote, "is to me such a hell at times / That I dream of a city very calm and without rails."[133]

Coppée's nostalgia for a picturesque, pre-industrial Paris was not uncharacteristic of bourgeois Nationalists. In 1897, the Paris municipal council organized a *Commission du vieux Paris*, charged with preservation of the city's architectural patrimony. Adrien Lamouroux, municipal councillor of les Halles, had sponsored the idea and served as the Commission's first president. Lamouroux, a Radical, ran with *Patrie française* backing in the 1900 elections and was slated to be chosen council president by the new Nationalist majority had he not died prematurely.[134] In 1902, the municipal council voted 10,000F as prize money for a *concours d'enseignes* organized by the ex-Déroulèdist and LPF member, Edouard Détaille, in conjunction with John Grand-Carteret, a dedicated preservationist and historian of old Paris. The competition was intended to stimulate public interest in Paris' stock of old and picturesque signs, vestiges of a commercial culture less crass than the loud advertising of modern Paris.[135]

Preservationism was indeed a favored field of Nationalist activity. When land speculators put together a plan to parcel out the Champ de Mars for real-estate development, the opposition was led by Maurice Spronck of the LPF and Gabriel Bonvalot of the LDP. It was, once again a Nationalist, the

---

[132] For a sample of Coppée's work, see his collection, *Les Humbles,* in *Oeuvres de François Coppée*, vol. II, *Poésies 1869–1874* (Paris, n.d.).

[133] Coppée, *Souvenirs*, p. 260; *Oeuvres de François Coppée,* vol. II, p. 118.

[134] See the obituary of Lamouroux in *Annales de la Patrie française,* 15 September 1900; APP B/a 1150, 14 May 1900. For the origins of the *Commission du vieux Paris*, see Sutcliffe, *The Autumn of Central Paris*, p. 208.

[135] Baudin, *L'Enseigne et l'affiche*, p. 85; Détaille wrote an introductory letter to John Grand-Carteret's *L'Enseigne*.

poet and LPF militant, Jean Lahor, who launched the *Société pour la protection des paysages de France*.[136] During the 1904 municipal elections, the *Annales de la Patrie française* published an "appeal to electoral committees and to Parisian voters for conservation of open spaces," signed by Lahor's group, Bonvalot's *Comité pour la défense des espaces libres* and the *Amis des monuments parisiens*.[137]

Nationalists saw themselves as defenders of the picturesque against the encroachments of the machine age. And as might be expected, no symbol of the machine age more infuriated Nationalists than the Eiffel Tower. "The Eiffel Tower," commented the *Annales de la Patrie française* in 1900, stands over on the Champ de Mars like "some foreigner."[138] Coppée wondered at the uselessness of "that crazy pyramid."[139] And Lavedan dismissed the tower in an outburst of contemptuous epithets. "It has always represented for me," he wrote in *Le Gaulois*, "the basilica of Syndicalism and the column of Riot, Our Lady of the Strike."[140]

Patrie française littérateurs were no more generous in their reactions to the new, mass culture born of the crisis of the eighties. Lemaître railed against the "false luxury" that had corrupted France's bourgeoisie.[141] Lahor decried the junk goods "sold in the bazaars of our cities . . . that trash (*camelote*) manufactured and distributed to the profit of a few and to the detriment of the buyer, small industry and *petit commerce*."[142] Nor could Lahor endure the "brutal" advertising that defaced

[136] Charles-Brun, *Le Régionalisme*, p. 195. Baudin (p. 83), on the other hand, gives the credit to Robert de Souza.
[137] "Le mouvement nationaliste," *Annales de la Patrie française*, 1 May 1904.
[138] "Le génie national à l'Exposition," *Annales de la Patrie française*, 1 June 1900.
[139] Cited in de Foville, *La Tour Eiffel*, p. 15.
[140] H. Lavedan, "La Tour Eiffel," *Le Gaulois*, 19 December 1910.
[141] J. Lemaître, "Quelques opinions salutaires," *Annales de la Patrie française*, 15 October 1900.
[142] Lahor, *L'Art pour le peuple*, p. 6.

the streets of his beloved *"Ville-lumière."* The vulgar commercialization of street life, he wrote, blinded the eye and perverted the public taste. Indeed, highbrow Nationalists time and again returned to the theme of a decline in public standards. The decline was apparent in the gross banality of café-concert songs, in the cosmopolitanism of furniture styles.[143] The press, Arthur Meyer lamented, had become a machine.[144] And then there was Zola—"the brutal and sad poet of blind passion" in Lemaître's phrase, "a vigorous but trivial personality" in Doumic's.[145] Hugo was Coppée's favorite; the *Annales de la Patrie française* found in Alphonse Daudet's sentimental portraits of *quartier* life a commendable "love of the parish pump";[146] but Zola revolted the Nationalist critics. He was too ambitious, too "scientific." He wrote of a world in which sexuality and the crowd, in which animal passions and mass institutions reigned to the detriment of sentiment and high culture.

The predilections and resentments of cultural reaction shaped the LPF's social vision. The new world of culture placed a premium on professionalism and mass appeal, on standardization and large-scale production. The LPF accordingly assailed all that was standardized and large scale: big government, corporate industry and, of course, the department store. Zola and the "intellectuals" of the university were plotting the destruction of French culture in collusion with panbureaucrats like Jaurès, plutocrats like Mascuraud, and the agents of Jewish high finance led by Alfred Dreyfus himself.[147] Who stood

[143] "Causerie des comités de la Patrie française," *Annales de la Patrie française*, 1 May 1901; Lahor, *L'Art nouveau*, p. 34.

[144] Meyer, p. 369.

[145] Lemaître, *Les Contemporains*, p. 255; Doumic, *Portraits d'écrivains*, p. 222.

[146] G. Aubray, "Les écrivains et la nation," *Annales de la Patrie française*, 1 May 1900.

[147] J. Lemaître, "Le collectivisme," *Annales de la Patrie française*, 1 March 1902. On Mascuraud, see the *Patrie française* brochure, "Le Bloc et son

with France against such a formidable coalition of enemies? The people of the faubourgs celebrated by Coppée, artisans and shopkeepers still loyal to the aesthetic and commercial standards of a passing era. Nationalist defense of the *quartier* and of craftsmanship was easily translated into a passionate small-owner utopianism.

The struggle between anti-Dreyfusards and Dreyfusards pitted the *quartier* against the metropolis, taste against mediocrity, but above all, the people against its oppressors—foreigners, *accapareurs*, and collectivists. *Patrie française* propaganda contrasted "Coppée, risen from the people, Lemaître, son of a provincial schoolmaster" with "Reinach whose father lived in the Frankfurt ghetto, Zola whose father was a retired Italian officer . . . , [and] Rothschild the first stone of whose fortune was laid on the Waterloo battlefield."[148] Lemaître denounced Waldeck-Rousseau as a "miserly bourgeois" and "capitalist lawyer."[149] The Nationalist press reviled socialist doctrine in the name of "freedom of labor, *petit commerce* and small property."[150]

The LPF, however highbrow its leadership, however bourgeois its local cadres, made every effort to cultivate a popular clientele. The working man was promised a "national fund for sickness and unemployment insurance." Syveton advocated a special tax on foreign labor and proposed to use the revenue to fund a pension scheme for French workers.[151] But

---

oeuvre," in APP B/a 1337; also L. Dausset, "Le discours de M.Combes," *Annales de la Patrie française*, 15 October 1902. The LPF's anti-Semitism was not as fanatical as that of a Guérin or Drumont, but was nonetheless pervasive and determined. See, for example, the articles by Jean Forcade in the *Annales de la Patrie française*: "La question juive," 15 February 1901; "L'esprit juif," 15 July 1901.

[148] APP B/a 1334, 14 March 1901.

[149] APP B/a 1334, 4 May 1900.

[150] APP B/a 942, clipping from the pro-Nationalist *La Liberté*, 4 May 1902.

[151] APP B/a 1276, 18 April 1902; see also Watson, "The Nationalist Movement in Paris," p. 63.

Nationalists reserved the greatest solicitude for *petits commerçants*. Here was the victim par excellence of the Dreyfusard syndicate's machinations. The shopkeeper paid the heaviest taxes; he was fleeced by *sociétés anonymes*, threatened with extinction by "the department store feudality" and abused by socialists.[152] The antinational cabal had chosen its target with diabolical perspicacity. The shopkeeper embodied the solid virtues that had made France strong and stable. Georges Thiébaud, ex-Boulangist and Nationalist candidate in the 1902 elections (XVth), pledged himself to defense of "that valiant commercial democracy which has made a little place for itself through hard work, thrift and probity."[153] Destruction of *petit commerce* threatened the very life of the nation. *Patrie française* candidates, of course, backed the Berry bill, an extension of the *patente* to cooperatives, a legislated reduction in gas prices—the whole range of protective measures demanded by shopkeepers since the 1880s.[154] And the LPF went beyond verbal appeals in its effort to enlist small-owner support.

The LPF recognized early on that it had to shed the image of a narrowly middle-class organization.[155] Local meetings were organized in the IInd, Vth, and VIIth, aimed specifically at a shopkeeper clientele.[156] "The committees of the *Patrie française*," a police spy reported on Bastille Day 1901, "are organizing in their respective *quartiers* public ceremonies to convince people of their republicanism and also to win over

[152] Jules Domergue, *Comment et pourquoi les affaires vont mal en France*; see also APP B/a 942, Auffray, 22 April 1902; B/a 215, Thiébaud poster, 1902 elections, XVth arrondissement; AN F^7 12458, Barrès, 9 March 1903.

[153] APP B/a 215, Thiébaud poster, 1902 elections, XVth arrondissement.

[154] AN F^7 12458, Barrès, 9 March 1903; APP B/a 942, Auffray, 25 April 1902 and Auffray poster, 1902 elections, Vth arrondissement.

[155] APP B/a 1336, 20 February 1900.

[156] APP B/a 1276, Syveton, 24 April 1902; B/a 942, Auffray, 8 May 1902; B/a 1334, Spronck, 24 April 1901.

wineshopkeepers and café owners who are, in Lemaître's words, 'the great electors of Paris.' "[157]

The LPF's Academicians and lycée professors did not hesitate to immerse themselves in the petty details of small-owner politics, and the politicking paid off. The bulk of the LPF's grass-roots supporters, according to *Patrie française* official, A. Delsol, was made up of "employees, small shopkeepers and laborers in modest circumstances."[158] In the elections of 1902, Syveton won a seat in Paris' IInd arrondissement; Dausset lost a closely fought contest in the IIIrd. Both candidates, over the course of the campaign, published posters with long lists of local backers, identified by name and profession. These lists corroborate Delsol's testimony as to the popular character of the LPF rank-and-file membership (see Tables 20 and 21). It was, moreover, in Paris' "popular" wards and arrondissements that the LPF scored its most impressive electoral successes. In 1900, *Patrie française* candidates won contests in the Enfants-Rouges ward (IIIrd), the Sorbonne (Vth), and the Porte Saint-Denis (Xth). To be sure, seats in the well-to-do VIIth and parvenu XVIIth also went to the LPF, but the *quartiers* involved—the Gros-Caillou and Batignolles—were essentially lower middle class, populated by a mixture of rentiers, employees and shopkeepers. The league placed two candidates in 1902, Syveton in the IInd and Spronck in the VIIth (Gros-Caillou and Ecole Militaire). Dausset, in the IIIrd, just lost to Louis Puech, an anti-Dreyfusard Radical who made an energetic and successful bid for the shopkeeper vote.[159] The league enjoyed one last electoral victory in 1905. Archdeacon, deputy of the Ist, died unexpectedly, and a by-election was held

[157] APP B/a 1150, 14 July 1901.

[158] "Le mouvement nationaliste," *Annales de la Patrie française*, 1 September 1901.

[159] See APP B/a 208, Puech poster, 1902 elections, IIIrd arrondissement. *La Petite République* ("M. Puech," 26 May 1900) charged that Puech had passed over to the Nationalists.

Cultural Despair

TABLE 20. Professions of Syveton Backers in the 1902 Elections

BOURGEOISIE

Liberal profs.	Rentier/ proprietor	Merchant	Middleman	Wholesaler	SUBTOTAL
7	0	16	4	2	29

LOWER MIDDLE CLASS

Employee	Other white-collar	Concierge	SUBTOTAL
47	0	0	47

TRADES

Luxury	Clothing	Food	Other	SUBTOTAL
0	7	6	7	20

WORKING CLASS

Boy labor	Day labor	Skilled labor	SUBTOTAL
1	22	0	23

MARGINALS

Soldier	Student	Retired	Misc.	SUBTOTAL	TOTAL
0	1	1	1	3	122

SOURCE: APP B/a 207, Syveton poster, 1902 elections, IInd arrondissement

TABLE 21. Professions of Dausset Backers in
the 1902 Elections

BOURGEOISIE					
Liberal profs.	Rentier/ proprietor	Manufacturer	Middleman	Wholesaler	SUBTOTAL
25	8	22	25	9	89

LOWER MIDDLE CLASS			
Employee	Other white-collar	Concierge	SUBTOTAL
95	1	3	99

TRADES				
Luxury	Clothing	Food	Other	SUBTOTAL
64	16	27	26	133

WORKING CLASS			
Boy labor	Day labor	Skilled labor	SUBTOTAL
25	5	23	53

MARGINALS					
Soldier	Student	Retired	Misc.	SUBTOTAL	TOTAL
3	4	3	16	26	400

SOURCE: APP B/a 210, Dausset poster, 1902 elections, IIIrd arrondissement

to fill the vacant post. The contest went to one of the LPF's charter members, a long-time small-owner utopian, Maurice Barrès. The LDP and LPF then shared a similar clientele. It was middle and lower middle-class constituencies, concentrated above all in the city's commercial center, that made the electoral fortunes of the *Patrie française* as of the plebeian leagues.

CONCLUSION

A community of origins, a common commitment to *quartier* life and aesthetic standards, and a shared social vision united the leadership of the Nationalist movement's two wings. This conclusion clarifies two problems: the intellectual origins of the anti-Dreyfusard leagues and the motivations of shopkeeper support for Nationalism.

On the issue of intellectual origins, one school of interpretation has linked the emergence of the Nationalist right to a crisis of overproduction in the book and newspaper trades.[160] Between 1840 and 1875, the publishing industry turned out on the average 218 new novels per year. In the period 1886–1890, per annum production of new titles shot up to 653, and then the market collapsed. Book prices tumbled, and *maisons d'éditions* struggled to maintain profits through expanded production. Houses that published best-selling authors like Zola were able to make mass production pay, but for the rest, stepped-up output simply meant increased quantities of unsold books. Publishing houses closed down, and the average number of new titles per year dropped in the nineties to 402. From the writer's point of view, the crisis meant less opportunity to publish, smaller advances and diminishing royalties. Alternative employment was to be had in news-

[160] Byrnes, *Antisemitism in Modern France*, pp. 280–290.

paper offices, but journalism, too, was soon overcrowded. The publishing crisis thwarted the literary and intellectual ambitions of an entire generation of educated youth. It was among the denizens of this new Grub Street, of this *"prolétariat de bacheliers"* in Barrès' phrase, that the Nationalist leagues recruited.[161]

It has rightly been pointed out, however, that a substantial percentage of Nationalist "intellectuals" were not failures at all, but men of established reputation entrenched in France's Academies and university. Nationalism, Christophe Charle has argued, recruited among a literary elite that felt threatened by an invasion of parvenus, of professional journalists and upwardly mobile *universitaires* who did not share in the old guard's aesthetic preoccupations.[162] The press did indeed undergo a radical transformation at the turn of the century. In the old days, journalists had been semibohemians who divided their time "between the newspaper office, the theater and the club"; an interview, in André Billy's phrase, "was still called a conversation."[163] Zola noted in 1894, however, that "[i]nformation has changed journalism, killing off *les grands articles*, claiming more space every day for dispatches, for news. . . ."[164] Sports, politics and interviews finished off the *chronique*; the *feuilletonniste* gave way to the star reporter. Papers which traded in the facts, however highly colored, developed a mass readership. The old press, unable to withstand competition, either adapted or went out of business. A parallel

---

[161] *Ibid.*, p. 290. Christophe Charle has examined the crisis of overproduction in literature in an article of considerable interest: "L'expansion et la crise de la production littéraire," pp. 44–65. The statistics cited on book output are drawn from the Charle article.

[162] Charle, "Champ littéraire et champ du pouvoir," pp. 240–264.

[163] Capus, *Boulevard et coulisses*, p. 21; Billy, p. 360. See also Duvernois, *Apprentissages*, p. 204.

[164] Cited in Claude Bellanger et al., *Histoire générale de la presse française*, vol. III, p. 278.

complex of changes has been observed in the university world. The academic establishment—professors of letters like Faguet, historians like Vandal—found itself under challenge from upstarts who practiced new disciplines or practiced old disciplines in new ways. Sociology, the newest discipline, with its stress on method and empirical research, represented a total negation of the literary culture in which old-line professors were steeped. Even in an established field like History, the new generation—men like Lavisse, Mathiez, and Monod —evinced a diminished interest in artistry or readability, touting instead German methods of fact-finding and textual verification.[165] The arrival of the new model academic, moreover, coincided with a rapid expansion of the student body. The number of students enrolled in the Paris Faculty of Letters nearly doubled in the first decade of the century, rising from 3,476 in 1900 to 6,363 in 1910.[166] The old guard with its literary bent found itself swamped by new colleagues and new students untutored in the gentlemanly ways of the old university. The trained reporter and positivist academic, the mass-circulation daily and expanded university revolutionized cultural life. The man of letters, a dilettante and amateur, was displaced by the intellectual, a by-product of mass culture who compensated for a certain lack of style or personality with a hard-nosed professionalism. Nationalism, some have claimed, fed on the resentments of established academics and journalists, men who had not failed so much as lost out.

One line of argument views the Nationalist man of letters as a frustrated failure, another as a besieged establishmentar-

---

[165] A point that has been made by: Rémond, "Les intellectuels et la politique," p. 869; Rebérioux, "Histoire, historiens et dreyfusisme," pp. 412–414.

[166] Zeldin, *France 1848–1945*, vol. II, p. 330. See also Charle, "L'expansion et la crise de la production littéraire," pp. 56ff.; Clark, *Prophets and Patrons*, pp. 29–33, and Weisz, *The Emergence of Modern Universities in France*, pp. 225ff.

ian. The two interpretations, however, can be reconciled. The green-clad Academic and the demimondain journalist represented the twin poles of boulevard life. The *cursus honorum* of the old boulevards ran from the newspaper office, however lowly, to the Institute. An aspiring man of letters began his career as a journalist. If a critic, he haunted the pressrooms in an attempt to place reviews, articles and *pièces d'occasion.* Writers, too, were obliged to publish first in the press. Zola's novels were regularly serialized in boulevard newspapers, and of course it was as a short-story writer for *Gil Blas* that de Maupassant made his reputation. Most would-be littérateurs never made it beyond the dingy offices of second-rate journals. But if successful, the rising man of letters could hope to win appointment as *chroniqueur*-in-chief at one of the more prestigious newspapers; and if extraordinarily able and well connected, a university chair or even elevation to the Academy awaited him.

But boulevard culture came under intense external pressure. The commercializing impact of Haussmannization had eroded the exclusive and closed character of the boulevard milieu. The triumph of mass consumerism consequent upon the downturn of the 1880s brought the process to completion. The coffeehouses, highbrow entertainments and literary newspapers of an older cultural community were submerged in a flood of brasseries, cafés-concerts and advertising. The crisis of overproduction in literature, the emergence of a mass press and the transformation of the university may be seen as so many additional ramifications of the economic slump of the eighties. The Great Depression brought ruin to old-line shops which serviced an elite clientele in the city's old neighborhoods; commercial enterprises like department stores, with access to a mass market, survived and prospered. So in literature, best-selling novelists like Zola prospered in spite of the *crise du livre*, while writers with too select an audience felt the pinch of hard times. In the business world, the *révolution du bon marché* undercut the lower reaches of the luxury trade and opened the marketplace—once an elite preserve—to a new generation of consumers. So in the press and the university, mass-circulation dailies and the social sciences outbid *belles lettres* for an emergent mass public.

The eclipse of boulevard culture brought disappointment to journalists and littérateurs whatever their position on the old hierarchy of success. The marginals could never hope to rise in a world of shrinking opportunities. As for the successful, the emergence of new cultural hierarchies devalued their achievement. The marginals and the successful, the frustrated and besieged had reason to make common cause. They were equally victims of a profound cultural change. The old world, of course, did not vanish noiselessly but made a supreme effort in anti-Dreyfusard Nationalism to postpone defeat. But why should the shopkeeper movement have lent itself to this enterprise?

Nationalism won the support of organized *petit commerce* for a multiplicity of reasons—because it underwrote the shopkeeper program of anticooperative legislation and *patente* reform, because it exploited shopkeeper fears of encirclement by the combined forces of corporate capital and organized labor. But shopkeeper militants were also drawn to Nationalism because the anti-Dreyfusard movement spoke a language they understood, a hybrid tongue of cultural reaction and small-owner utopianism. The similarities in shopkeeper and Nationalist rhetoric were not accidental. Shopkeeper and Nationalist both were responding to identical experiences of disruption, disruption brought on by urban change and economic transformation. The once prosperous shopping district of *vieux Paris,* the old boulevards that in by-gone days had been the privileged stamping ground of France's cultural elite, both were victims of Haussmannization and the *révolution du bon marché.* Shopkeeper activists endorsed Nationalism at the turn of the century out of self-interest, out of fear and frustration, but also because they recognized in Nationalism an ideology that reflected an experience kindred to their own. The struggle of shopkeeper against department store, of littérateur against intellectual, constituted parallel reflexes of revolt, bound by like origins, a shared commitment to cultural and commercial hierarchies in retreat and a common set of enemies. The Dreyfusard cause indeed represented the very antithesis of the vision of France that shopkeeper and Nationalist militants clung to. Who after all were Dreyfus' supporters: Mascuraud, Zola, Jaurès? This unholy trinity stood for all that shopkeepers and Nationalists feared most, big business, mass culture and organized labor. The struggle against Dreyfusism fused the twin movements of commercial and cultural reaction in a single, united front to defend a dying small-owner world against the forces and institutions destined to inherit power in the emergent corporate world of the twentieth century.

10

. . .

Epilogue: In the Aftermath
of the Dreyfus Affair

THE FOCUS of Part II has been the politics of retailer activism in Paris. It ends, appropriately I think, with the conclusion of the shopkeeper/Nationalist alliance at the turn of
the century. Even in the less agitated post-Dreyfus years, Paris's
core arrondissements—the breeding grounds of shopkeeper
militancy—continued to return Nationalist veterans to public
office, men like Barrès, Berry, Bienaimé, Dausset and Galli.
To this extent, the entente between center-city retailers and
the anti-Dreyfusard right was enduring. In the aftermath of
the Affair, moreover, Paris-based organizations, whether the
shopkeepers' *Ligue* or the Nationalist leagues, faded from
prominence. The principal scene of action, both in retailer
and right-wing politics, shifted to a broader plane. The *Ligue
syndicale* lost its ascendancy within the shopkeeper movement
as provincial-dominated groups like the *Parti commercial et industriel* assumed the mantle of leadership. The anti-Dreyfusard
leagues were similarly eclipsed. In the Belle Epoque years,
the far right's pretensions to a monopoly on the rhetoric of
nationalism were successfully contested by a rising generation
of establishment conservatives. The privilege of "speaking for
the nation" increasingly passed from league agitators whose
activities were largely confined to the capital to politicians—
Barthou, Deschanel and, above all, Raymond Poincaré—with

national reputations and constituencies. Indeed, as one historian has remarked, with the succession of national revival ministries that took office after 1910, "it was the government itself which became nationalist."[1] For two reasons then, the turn of the century marks a convenient stopping point for a Paris-centered study. Political alignments had hardened in Paris, and local Parisian politics had lost their centrality as the focal point of retailer and nationalist agitation.

There is just the same good cause to undertake a brief review of events in the post-Dreyfus era. Parisian right radicalism was not so much by-passed in the Belle Epoque as subsumed into wider currents, more temperate in political orientation. The PCI, for all its anti-Dreyfusard sympathies, acted expeditiously to extricate itself from far right entanglements. Its leaders, provincials unmarked by the plebeian radicalism of the Paris retail community, were not fully comfortable with extremist tactics which, in any event, had produced little in the way of concrete results. The PCI never amounted to much as an electoral organization and, admitting defeat, beat a retreat to the more familiar terrain of "nonpartisan" pressure-group politics. It signaled its change of course with a change of name. In 1903, the PCI gave way to the *Fédération*, later *Confédération des groupes commerciaux et industriels* (CGCI).[2] The CGCI's shift to moderation cost it retailer support. Its membership declined sharply to an estimated 25,000 in 1904, but then rose again to a peak of roughly 80,000 on the war's eve.[3] The *Confédération*'s continuing, if reduced, strength ultimately persuaded the vestiges of the Parisian shopkeeper movement to acknowledge its preeminence. The *Ligue syndicale* rump affiliated to the CGCI

[1] Guillemin, *Nationalistes et "nationaux,"* p. 90.

[2] Nord, "Le mouvement des petits commerçants," pp. 46–47.

[3] *Bulletin officiel de la Fédération des groupes commerciaux et industriels,* January 1904, p. 1; Martin Saint-Léon, *Le Petit Commerce français,* p. 108.

in 1906. And by 1913, the *Union fraternelle* had become a regular participant in *Confédération* congresses.[4]

The Nationalist leagues evolved along parallel lines. A sober appraisal of Nationalism's failures as well as a venal opportunism prompted anti-Dreyfusard veterans to abandon radical agitation. To be sure, many one-time *ligueurs* emigrated to the *Action française*, but Maurrasism was not the only or even the principal heir to end-of-the-century Nationalism. The parties of the parliamentary right, the *Action libérale populaire* (ALP) in particular, absorbed much of the old leagues' leadership and clientele. The ALP deployed its considerable financial resources to gain a controlling influence over the remains of the Nationalist movement. The Christian Democratic *Union nationale* had by the turn of the century become an ALP affiliate, and Piou bought out Garnier's organ *Le Peuple français* in 1909. *La Libre Parole* was purchased in 1910, and direction of the paper passed to a Piou lieutenant, Joseph Denais.[5] Christian Democrats and anti-Semites were not the only objects of Piou's machinations. By 1909, the ALP, with the assistance of Paul Féron-Vrau of *La Croix*, had acquired the major Nationalist newspapers: *La Patrie, La Presse* and *L'Eclair*. The *Ligue de la patrie française* too, as we have seen, had fallen under Piou's dominance by this time. Even the *Ligue des patriotes* was targeted. Déroulède's growing religious sympathies and the ALP's astute financial manipulations combined to reduce

---

[4] "Réunion des délégations de la Fédération des groupes commerciaux et industriels de France et de la Ligue syndicale," *Bulletin officiel de la Fédération des groupes commerciaux et industriels*, October 1906, p. 33. The *Ligue* broke once again with the CGCI in 1910, but applied for readmission shortly thereafter. On the *Union fraternelle*, see *Bulletin officiel de la Confédération des groupes commerciaux et industriels*: "Assemblée générale du 6 mars 1913," March 1913, p. 35; and "Assemblée générale statuaire du 9 février 1914," February 1914, p. 20.

[5] APP B/a 1537, 17 June 1902; AN F[7] 12878, 9 January 1909; Weber, *The Nationalist Revival*, p. 76.

the *Ligue*, according to a police report of 1904, to "an auxiliary of the *Action libérale*."[6] Not all of Déroulède's colleagues, however, were prepared to follow him into the Catholic camp. Galli, Le Menuet and Dausset broke with Déroulède
to align themselves with the moderate *Alliance républicaine démocratique* (ARD).[7] The move proved enormously advantageous, to Galli at least, who was elected president of the Paris
municipal council on the eve of the war thanks to centrist
votes. Galli used his political influence in Paris to muster
support for Poincaré's presidential bid in 1913 and, in February of that year, organized a "sensational reception" at the
Hôtel de Ville to celebrate Poincaré's victory. The new president attended the ceremonies and at a discreetly later date
rewarded the ex-Boulangist, ex-Nationalist Galli with the
Legion of Honor. "Since our arrival on the scene in 1900,"
Galli was reported to have said, "we have turned our backs
on the Elysée and the government; we are now on the most
excellent terms with them both."[8] The parties and politicians
of the national revival, from the ALP to the ARD, from Piou
to Poincaré were perhaps the greatest beneficiaries of the break-
up of the Nationalist movement.

Parisian right radicalism then was reintegrated into the
conservative mainstream, the *Ligue syndicale* into the CGCI,
the Nationalist leagues into the national revival. As this process unfolded, the local entente between center-city Parisian
retailers and anti-Dreyfusards gave way to a national alliance
encompassing *Confédération* militants and Poincarists. The
CGCI's shift to moderation predisposed it to the conservative
and antisocialist policies of the Poincarist coalition. The es-

[6] APP B/a 1340, 9 October 1904. See also AN F[7] 12878, 20 October
and 31 October 1905; F[7] 12719, 14 June 1909.

[7] AN F[7] 12873, 27 November 1912; APP B/a 1660, Dausset, report
dated November 1919.

[8] APP B/a 1088, 10 March 1913; see also the report of 11 April 1913;
and BN NAF 16024, *Poincaré Papers, Notes journalières*, 24 January 1913.

tablishment right's eagerness to rally all the healthy forces of the nation against France's enemies at home and abroad awakened conservative interest in organized *petit commerce* as a potential ally. By 1910 in fact, as I will show, the small business movement and the mainstream right had drawn together in formal alliance.

Events in Paris lose their specificity after the turn of the century. For this reason, I have not accorded them fuller treatment. But an epilogistic excursus into the Belle Epoque years may be justified on two counts. It will demonstrate firstly that retailer militancy can take other forms than a far right extremism, and secondly, that the republican synthesis, however much under pressure, still retained a remarkable capacity to assimilate challenges to its legitimacy.

THE RAPPROCHEMENT OF
Petit commerce AND
THE CONSERVATIVE ESTABLISHMENT

The emergence of the CGCI heralded the rise of a new generation of retailer militants, conservatively inclined businessmen who were profoundly and preeminently antisocialist.[9] The secretary general of the *Confédération* in the decade before World War I was E. Bellamy, a stationer of some means and president of the *Chambre syndicale des papetiers*. Through Bellamy, the CGCI was linked to the most conservative wing of France's business establishment. Bellamy was well-connected in the big business world and indeed served as an officer on Expert-Bezançon's *Comité central des chambres syndicales*. Through E. de Paloméra, elected CGCI president in 1910, the *Confédération* was linked as well to Social Catholic circles. A busi-

[9] For the discussion that follows, see Nord, "Le mouvement des petits commerçants" pp. 47–54, unless otherwise noted.

nessman from the Charente, de Paloméra headed the Cognac
local of the *Action libérale populaire*. He exercised sufficient influence within the party to arrange a sympathetic discussion
of the shopkeeper question at the ALP congress of 1908.

The growing influence of conservative antisocialists like de
Paloméra and Bellamy signaled a new receptivity to Catholic
corporatist doctrine and a softening of the shopkeeper movement's traditional antipathy toward big business. A *Confédération* spokesman wrote in 1906:

> . . . insensibly, without being aware of it, by the force
> of events, we are returning to the *maitrîses* and corporate
> juries of yesteryear to which every apprentice had had to
> submit a chef d'oeuvre before being admitted to the sta-
> tus of worker."[10]

The *Confédération* interpreted the rise of the *syndicat*, of
professional organization, as a prefiguration of an emergent
new corporatism. Shopkeeper syndicalism had a double role
to play in this process. To it, first and foremost, fell the responsibility of resolving the crisis of small business. From the
Confédération's point of view, this crisis was not solely the
consequence of department store competition. One "must not
condemn large-scale industry, large-scale commerce nor attempt to do them injury."[11] Small shopkeepers themselves were
in no small part to blame for their economic predicament; it
was incumbent upon them to modernize, to abandon routine
and to recognize that their salvation lay in collective action
under the auspices of trade associations. The duty of shopkeeper *syndicats* accordingly was "to make small and medium-
sized businesses stronger" by organizing purchasing cooperatives and by improving credit facilities and professional edu-

[10] "Congrès de la pâtisserie française," *Bulletin officiel de la Fédération des
groupes commerciaux et industriels*, March 1906, p. 4.

[11] AR, "Les économistes politiques et la classe moyenne," *Bulletin officiel
de la Fédération des groupes commerciaux et industriels*, December 1905, p. 12.

cation.[12] Secondly, shopkeeper associations were looked to as instruments of combat against the enemies of private property. It was up to the trade association to lead the fight against bureaucracy and the interventionist state. But the most fearful enemy confronting men of property was the workers' movement. The *syndicat*, it was hoped, would serve as a rallying point for all the friends of order. Against an emerging working-class bloc, it could mobilize a bloc of the middle classes (*classes moyennes*).[13] And CGCI militants conceived the notion of *"classes moyennes"* in the broadest terms to encompass all productive forces that made a genuine contribution to the national economy. On this definition, the term middle class embraced large-scale commerce and industry as well as *petit commerce* and the *petit artisanat*. Only cosmopolitan finance, judged to be parasitical and unpatriotic, was explicitly excluded.[14] Middle-class ideology did not obliterate deep-seated

[12] AR, "Les économistes politiques et la classe moyenne," *Bulletin officiel de la Fédération des groupes commerciaux et industriels*, December 1905, p. 12; see also, "Les achats en commun," *Bulletin officiel de la Fédération des groupes commerciaux et industriels*, December 1904; A Robiquet, "L'enseignement commercial et industriel," *Bulletin officiel de la Fédération des groupes commerciaux et industriels*, December 1904; L. Gauss, "Rôle de la banque populaire," *Bulletin officiel de la Confédération des groupes commerciaux et industriels*, August–September 1907.

[13] The *Confédération* very early on referred to itself as "the most important organization of the middle classes": "Rapport," *Bulletin officiel de la Fédération des groupes commerciaux et industriels*, October 1905, p. 11. In 1908, the *Confédération* organized a special "Comité d'études pour l'organisation des classes moyennes": Alfred Aunis, "Organisation économique des classes moyennes," *Bulletin officiel de la Confédération des groupes commerciaux et industriels*, September 1908, p. 78. For the *Confédération*'s aggressive intentions vis-à-vis the labor movement, see A. Trépreau, "Nécessité et urgence d'un programme général économique," *Bulletin officiel de la Confédération des groupes commerciaux et industriels*, April 1907, p. 12.

[14] *Bulletin officiel de la Confédération des groupes commerciaux et industriels*: Alfred Aunis, "Organisation économique des classes moyennes," September 1908, p. 75; "Défense du commerce français contre l'invasion des produits étran-

shopkeeper suspicions of *les gros* but focused them on a narrower spectrum of interests.

The CGCI's conversion to a politics of middle-class defense opened up the possibility of a rapprochement with the Progressist and *rallié* right, and the right seized the opportunity. It discarded its lofty disdain for the *petit commerçant* and reoriented its thinking to accommodate shopkeeper interests.

To be sure, Catholic involvement in retailer politics was not a new phenomenon. Christian Democrats had cultivated close ties with the shopkeeper movement in the 1890s. But after the turn of the century, they were joined and their influence eventually supplanted by Social Catholics like Pierre du Maroussem, Etienne Martin Saint-Léon and Frantz Funck-Brentano. The praise that retailer militants had once reserved for Léon Harmel was now bestowed on a Martin Saint-Léon who rendered welcome and invaluable service to the CGCI as a publicist and organizer.

It was the notion of middle-class defense that fired Social Catholicism's mounting zeal for the shopkeeper cause. The idea had filtered into French Social Catholic circles via Belgium. In 1899 and again in 1901, Belgian Social Catholics had hosted "International Congresses of the Petite Bourgeoisie," attracting the attention and participation of French intellectuals, in particular Georges Blondel and Funck-Brentano, both followers of Le Play. The world-wide enthusiasm sparked by these congresses generated interest in the formation of a permanent body to study the problems of the petite bourgeoisie. In 1904, the *Institut international pour l'étude du problème des classes moyennes* was founded, with its headquarters in Brussels. French Social Catholics such as Victor de Clercq, an ALP militant

gers. Rapport de M. Maurice Patriarche," January–February 1913 (annexe), pp. 14–17; "Compte-rendu du lle Congrès national. Séances du congrès," April–May 1913, pp. 59ff. See also Henri Duflos, "Les grands bazars financiers," *L'Idéal*, 7 February 1909.

and veteran of the *Union fraternelle*, and Martin Saint-Léon, affiliated with the *Institut* and undertook to propagate the *classes moyennes* point of view at home.

The attractiveness of middle-class defense lay in its promise of a third way between the twin evils of collectivism and laissez-faire individualism. Social Catholics embraced shopkeeper syndicalism as a counterweight to an expansive and threatening labor insurgency and as a node of order in an anarchical free-market economy. Indeed, might not the example of a successful middle-class syndicalism inspire emulation, converting doubters to the virtues of professional association and preparing the way for the emergence of an alternative, organized economic system neither collectivist nor plutocratic? Social Catholics looked to middle-class syndicalism not only as a stabilizing influence in a socially divided France but also as the driving wedge of a long hoped-for corporatist renaissance.

Far more remarkable than pro-shopkeeper stirrings on the Catholic right was the new-found interest of secular conservatives in retailer militancy. In the 1880s and 1890s, business interests and Progressist politicians had dismissed the shopkeeper as an unworthy parasite. It could still be hoped at the end of the century that a free-market based economic recovery would solve the material problems of the working class. A dose of paternalism, some conceded, might be salutary. The more pessimistic demanded protectionist policies to guarantee French business privileged access to local markets, arguing that prosperity for the businessman meant prosperity for his workers. But all agreed that business, whether through the free play of market forces, a show of good will, or an exercise of regulatory power could, acting alone or with minimal assistance from the state, resolve the social question. The unbroken progress of the socialist and trade-union movements, however, undercut such fond hopes. A good many conservatives providentially discovered the virtues of the little man. His sober and regular habits raised hopes of a more stable world. But he was to be valued most for his strategic location at the juncture where capital and labor met. The small shopkeeper, by virtue of his middling rank, blurred the lines of social cleavage and tempered the shock of the class struggle. A diminished confidence in the ability of business to solve the social question spawned in establishment circles a militant *Mittelstandspolitik*, and a *Mittelstandspolitik* expressed in an unmistakeably nationalist idiom. The maintenance of France's position as a ranking world power depended on preservation of the social peace at home. As a force for order and stability, the middle classes had a critical role to play in the defense of France's greatness as a nation. Not only the defense but also the reassertion of French grandeur was at stake. The middle classes, conservatives had come to believe, were an untapped reservoir of vital entrepreneurial energies. Release these energies and France would reemerge as a first-rate economic power, rolling back its continental rivals, the Germans above all. A *réveil des classes moyennes* portended a national awakening that would rout France's adversaries on both the domestic and international fronts.[15]

CONSERVATIVE REINTEGRATION

As the CGCI moved away from the far right, Social Catholics and Progressists anxious to exploit the conservative potential of organized *petit commerce* developed an opportune sympathy

[15] APP B/a 1658, clipping from *Le Temps*, 29 June 1907, "M. Poincaré chez les commerçants détaillants"; Maurice Colrat's and Emile Loubet's speeches to the *Association de défense des classes moyennes*, "Congrès des classes moyennes," *Les Etudes fiscales et sociales*, November–December 1909, pp. 66–67 and 168–172; Colrat's remarks in "Le rôle social des classes moyennes," pp. 27–28; and "Réunion du 4e Conseil général de l'Union des intérêts économiques," *Le Réveil économique*, 12 March 1913.

for the shopkeeper cause. This rapprochement blossomed into a full-fledged alliance thanks in large part to the perseverance and imagination of Maurice Colrat, marquis de Montrozier. Colrat was particularly well equipped for the task. He was welcome in establishment political circles and had important connections in the business world. Colrat had begun his career as a secretary in Raymond Poincaré's law office and later did election work for Poincaré and Eugène Motte, both Progressists. While campaigning for Motte, scion of a wealthy textile family, Colrat met his future wife, Anne Delaune, daughter of a Roubaix textile magnate and Progressist deputy from the Nord.

Colrat took advantage of his connections to assemble a grand coalition of conservative interests, and the theme of middle-class defense provided the essential ideological cohesive. In 1907, Colrat founded the *Association de défense des classes moyennes*. The *Association* mobilized the combined support of Social Catholics like Martin Saint-Léon, of Progressists and of conservative business interests, notably R. S. Carmichael's *Union des syndicats patronaux des industries textiles* (a spinoff of the AIAF). But its influence extended as well into the shopkeeper community. All major retailer defense organizations belonged, foremost among them the CGCI but also the *Ligue syndicale*. There can be, moreover, no doubt as to the conservative thrust of the middle-class mobilization orchestrated by Colrat.

On the eve of the national elections of 1910, the *Association* in conjunction with the CGCI drew up an "economic charter" which was circulated among prospective candidates. Endorsed by the nation's most important business associations, from pressure groups representing heavy industry (the *Comité des forges*, the *Comité des houillères*, the *Union des industries métallurgiques et minières*, etc.) to the Paris-based *chambre syndicale* organizations headed by Pinard, Muzet, Marguery and others, the charter made plain a united business community's

Epilogue

determination to preserve the sanctity of private property, to combat *étatisme*, and to resist social reform. In the fall of the same year, the *Comité d'études et de défense fiscale*, an offshoot of the *Association* chaired by Carmichael (a former president of the CGCI also served as first vice-president), organized an impressive meeting at the Salle Wagram attended by more than 3,500 businessmen. The meeting's keynote speaker was Raymond Poincaré who, to frenetic applause, summed up the assembly's spirit in these terms:

> Yes *messieurs*, it pleases me to repeat what the preceding speakers have said: we demand respect for private property, liberty for the private household, the right to secrecy for businessmen; we insist upon the regular operation of public services and the freedom of labor. But in so doing, it is not our intention to advance the cause of reaction, to oppose fiscal and financial reform with a preconceived hostility. But we do say no to the principles of inquisition and tyranny which, under the guise of progress, are being insinuated hypocritically into our laws. . . .[16]

At a second mass meeting of businessmen, held in 1913, the assembly repeated the same antisocialist sentiments expressed in 1910; but it also proclaimed its staunch support for the three-year military service law. An impressive array of business interests, ranging from groups defending the small shopkeeper to those defending big business, lined up solidly to support the legislative centerpiece of Poincaré's *réveil national*.[17]

An alliance of center-city shopkeepers and anti-Dreyfusards

[16] "Salle Wagram," *L'Union des syndicats patronaux des industries textiles de France*, November–December 1913 (annexe), p. 265.

[17] "La situation financière de la France," *L'Union des syndicats patronaux des industries textiles de France*, November–December 1913 (annexe), pp. 403–404.

had swung Paris to the far right in 1900. Opposition to the nation's political establishment eased, however, as the remnants of Parisian right radicalism were incorporated into mainstream movements that transcended the local Parisian scene. Extremist protest gave way to conservative reintegration. The double challenge from retailer and Nationalist militants had been parried and turned to the advantage of the Poincarist right. But how firm was the establishment's grip on the forces of discontent it had for the moment apparently mastered? Was it sufficiently firm to withstand the shocks of war and depression? These questions, however, are perhaps better left to historians of the inter-war years.

Conclusion

THE END OF THE CENTURY was midwife to a new age. Contemporaries wrote of a *crise des métiers* and the triumph of mass production. Paris' old downtown area skidded into decline; *petit commerce*, it was said, was a relic of the past, a troubled and troublesome hold-over in an age of department stores and cooperatives. In politics, public debate turned from the time-honored conflict of notables and democrats to the social question. Mass organizations—parties, trade unions and pressure groups—threatened to eclipse the clubs and committees of a passing era. The transformation in cultural life was no less remarkable. New men, *universitaires* and intellectuals, unceremoniously elbowed aside the boulevardiers and men of letters who had presided over public taste for nearly a century.

It is easy to exaggerate the extent and impact of this complex of changes. Paris certainly experienced a decisive break with its nineteenth-century past. Once a radical republican city, divided between *menu peuple* and a dominant, albeit beleaguered, bourgeoisie, it became a right-wing stronghold, a citadel of the middle classes besieged by left intellectuals and proletarian *banlieusards*. Elsewhere in France, however, the rhythms and struggles of nineteenth-century life continued much as before, undisturbed by economic concentration and consumerism, by the heady stimulants of mass politics and mass culture. Paris, all the same, was a harbinger of things to come; the *massif central* and Brittany, too, were destined to bear the full weight of these changes, though perhaps not until the 1950s.

Conclusion

The temptation is strong to view the transformation I have outlined in terms of a shift from the traditional to the modern. The various shorthands devised to summarize the change—from boutique to department store, from atelier to factory—point strongly toward such an interpretation. But what after all is tradition? A premarket economy, the ancien régime in politics and a culture based on patronage? In that case, it is mistaken to label as traditional the "world we have lost" of the late nineteenth century. The nineteenth-century economic nexus of artisan-manufacturer/commissionnaire/shopkeeper was indeed under pressure in the eighties and nineties but precisely because it was market-oriented, because its market share was reduced by depression and competition from the more dynamic combination of mass producer and mass retailer. The club and committee may appear rudimentary forms of political organization, but they thrive only on the ruins of old regime government, where representative institutions and the electoral process, however circumscribed in practice, have set limits on the absolutist ambitions of king, clergy and nobility. As for boulevard culture, with its newspapers, theaters and cafés, it is "public opinion" which reigns here, not the court or some well-heeled Maecenate. Indeed, the market and its values penetrated every sphere of life, certainly in nineteenth-century Paris. Politicians bargained for votes, boulevardiers trafficked in *belles lettres*; and businessmen made fortunes in hair oil and textiles. Balzac's France was hardly traditional, archaic or backward-looking. How then is the transition from Balzac's world to the world of the twentieth century to be characterized?

The end of the century witnessed a crisis of liberalism and the emergence of a new "age of organization."[1] Adolphe Thiers

---

[1] The "crisis of liberalism" theme has been explored by a number of historians but by none with more subtlety than Carl E. Schorske. See Schorske's *Fin de Siècle Vienna*, pp. 5–10. For the concept of an "age of organization," see Wolin, *Politics and Vision*, pp. 352–434.

may be taken as a symbol of the passing liberal era: a man of great personal culture, suspicious of democracy and sympathetic to an aggressive entrepreneurialism. The era which he embodied, from the July Monarchy to the first years of the Third Republic, placed the highest premium on the individual of outstanding ability: the genius, the notable, the captain of industry. But liberal individualism was under siege at the end of the century. *Sociétés anonymes*, department stores, an expanded university, nascent mass parties—bureaucracies of every variety, whether private or state-run—cast a lengthening shadow over public life. Little wonder that corporatist thinking enjoyed a revival in the nineties, a revival that presaged the corporatist policies of Vichy and even the *planisme* of the Liberation era.

The push toward organization was in large part a response to economic depression. The slump began with a series of major bank failures, the collapse of Jay Cooke and Co. in 1873 and the *krach* of the Union Générale in 1882. A sudden contraction of affairs followed in the wake of the financial crisis as wary investors withheld capital. But the crisis was more thoroughgoing than a momentary loss of investor confidence. The emergence of new, industrial economies since mid-century—Germany and the United States are the prime examples—had intensified international competition for markets. The newcomers, employing the most up-to-date equipment and technology, challenged not only English supremacy in the heavy industrial sector but also French dominance in the area of luxury manufactures. As the marketplace grew more crowded, production outstripped effective demand, prices tumbled, and profits fell.

Several courses of action lay open to the hard pressed businessman. Exclusion of foreign manufactures from the domestic market offered short-term relief from unwelcome competition, and most industrial economies experimented with protectionism. Germany passed protectionist legislation in 1879 and the United States in 1890; France voted the Méline tariff in 1892. An alternative lay in the capture and exploitation of untapped foreign markets; and mindful of such possibilities, interested businessmen underwrote the imperial designs of their respective national governments. A final possibility was to gird for the struggle and beat out the competition, an option that entailed rationalization and a brutal reduction of production costs. And businessmen did not hesitate. The late nineteenth century is famous for its mergers and monopolies, for sweated labor and mammoth factories—and with good reason. Businessmen under pressure exploited and mass produced; they expanded and devoured rivals in a frantic effort to stay afloat in a fiercely competitive market. Darwinian theory did indeed seem to describe with uncanny accuracy the world in which the late nineteenth-century entrepreneur operated. The economic struggle for life, however, had the most unexpected consequences.

Victory went not to individuals so much as to organizations: trusts, corporations and department stores. The push toward mass production fed expansion of an industrial proletariat. It promoted, moreover, development of new product lines, of mass-produced goods, cheap enough to make consumers of people at one time excluded from the marketplace. A corporate economy, organized socialism, an emergent mass culture, these were the consequences of the end-of-the-century slump.

THE ORIGINS OF THE *Ligue syndicale*

Not everyone welcomed such changes. Public discussion was filled with talk of invasion: the invasion of junk goods, of *faubouriens*, of cosmopolitanism. And no one was more vociferous in opposition to the new age than the center-city Parisian shopkeeper. Why did *commerçants* mobilize in protest? Why was the *Ligue syndicale* formed?

The process, I have argued, is to be looked at from a long-term perspective. The boom decades of mid-century set the stage for a shopkeeper *prise de conscience* in two respects. Firstly, the commercialization of central Paris isolated commerce as a particular function and made it possible for retailers to conceive of themselves as a distinct social group and not just as members of a particular profession or of some larger unit, such as "the people" or "*les classes laborieuses.*" The expansion of Paris, however, was uneven. The city's old shopping district did not profit from growth to the same degree as the retailers—small and large—situated on the avenues and boulevards of new Paris. The retail community created by uneven development contained two competing commercial centers, one expansive and flush, the other prosperous still but in eclipse. It was the latter that provided the initial impulse to form the *Ligue syndicale.* But it required first a rude shock to wake old Paris merchants from the morbid lethargy of slow decline.

The onset of the Great Depression gave the needed jolt. The sudden contraction of business placed extraordinary pressure on second-rank businesses. Moreover, the structural crisis brought on by the slump, the *révolution du bon marché* in Néré's phrase, was crushing to merchants who served the lower reaches of the luxury market. Tailors and jewelers who sold quality goods but not top quality found themselves undersold by retailers of "*la camelote,*" cheaply produced luxury items from ready-to-wear clothing to costume jewelry. Not all retailers were hard hit by the crisis, not the department stores that purveyed the new merchandise, nor the Boucherons and Laliques who maintained a tight grip on the top of the market. The selective impact of the depression had a geographical dimension as well. The city's fanciest retailers clustered on the brilliant new streets created or refurbished by Haussmannization. Large-scale retailers showed a preference no less marked for new Paris sites that provided access to a mass market. Paris' new shopping district survived, even prospered, through the slump. Not so the merchants of old Paris—

second-rank retailers left behind in the Palais-Royal and passage Choiseul, unable to afford a more advantageous location. Here the depression brought ruin, and decline turned into collapse. Local businessmen mobilized in a desperate and ultimately futile effort to recover the prosperity they had once known. But the streets and arcades of old Paris never fully revived from the crisis, and they remain today the commercial backwater they became at the end of the century.

This account of shopkeeper mobilization has several virtues. Firstly, it shifts the weight of interpretation away from the *grand magasin* toward transformations in the shape and structure of the urban retail market. The department store thesis leaves unexplained the *Ligue syndicale*'s peculiar pattern of recruitment, its strength in certain trades and in certain neighborhoods. An analysis of *Ligue* ideology, moreover, reveals a set of retailer preoccupations—with changes in the character of city life and in patterns of production and consumption—that too narrow a focus on the department store cannot account for. The alternative interpretation I have proposed, however, does suggest reasons why the department store was singled out as the principal target of retailer resentment. The *grand magasin* profited enormously from baron Haussmann's redesign of the Parisian cityscape; it was the major beneficiary of the consumer revolution spurred on by foreign competition and French industry's drive to cut production costs. As a symbol of *Paris nouveau* and as a major merchandiser of the new goods, the department store drew the fire of embittered retailers the real source of whose problems lay in the larger forces that determined the character and direction of department-store growth. From this perspective, the rise of the *grand magasin* ceases to be the most critical feature of commercial change in the last decades of the century, and attention is shifted instead to the long-term consequences of Haussmannization and the immediate impact of the *révolution du bon marché*.

Finally, the account I have offered tallies with what is known about other movements of small-owner protest. The artisan movement in Germany, according to Volkov, was strongest in regions that had undergone a rapid, but uneven development, followed by a prolonged experience of economic depression.[2] Farmer protest in late nineteenth-century America was concentrated in the South and Great Plains, regions which in the aftermath of the Civil War had experienced a remarkable surge of commercial development. The railroad boom in the post-bellum era had opened the West to agricultural settlement, and homesteaders came by the thousands to take advantage of the new opportunities. In the South, yeoman farmers increasingly turned to cotton production for the market to maintain a precarious independence. The extension of the market, however, also fostered the growth of new economic organisms—banks, railroads, general stores—which, because of the scale of their operations and their considerable capital resources, took the largest portion of the profits from commercial expansion. The collapse of agricultural prices in the 1870s and 1880s brought the simmering tensions between independents and the forces of monopoly to the surface. The onset of rural depression demolished the small-owner aspirations of Western and Southern farmers, fueling their anger against the "money power." And it was these men who spearheaded the rural radicalism of the 1880s.[3] Non-French examples sustain the argument that a sequence of rapid, uneven expansion and abrupt collapse is the motor force behind small-owner protest.

Whatever the virtues of such a schema, how does it reflect on the general theories of petit-bourgeois mobilization out-

[2] Volkov, *The Rise of Popular Anti-Modernism in Germany*, pp. 32–46, 61–94, 329.

[3] See, for example, Hicks, *The Populist Revolt*, pp. 1–95; Hofstadter, *The Age of Reform*, pp. 46–59; and most recently, Hahn, *The Roots of Southern Populism*.

lined in the introduction to this study? The status anxiety thesis has a certain *prima facie* plausibility. *Ligue syndicale* militants did in fact feel disadvantaged and abused in a world that apparently set greater store by fast talk and sales gimmickry than the old-fashioned values of thrift, hard work and self-reliance. But the status argument has weaknesses. It claims that small businessmen, squeezed between big labor and big capital, mobilized against a world that no longer accorded *"les petits"* the recognition they deserved. Parisian shopkeepers in the 1880s, however, were not hostile to trade unionism, which on the contrary was viewed as a potential ally in the battle against monopoly. The status loss thesis is also too crude to account for the *Ligue syndicale*'s selective recruitment. If anger against bigness was the major cause of shopkeeper mobilization, why did some *petits commerçants* and not others rally to the *Ligue*? Had not all independent entrepreneurs lost status in the new world of large-scale organization? As a final point, the concept of status anxiety is inadequate to describe the crisis that ravaged the shopping district of old Paris in the latter part of the century. Contrast Walter Benjamin's evocation of Paris' arcades at mid-century with Céline's sketch of the passage Choiseul in 1900.[4] In the one, all is brilliance and prosperity; in the other, gloom and stagnation. The transition from Benjamin's arcades to Céline's was abrupt and devastating, compressed into a twenty-year period at the end of the century. A commercial community was shattered in the process, morally but also materially. The phrase "status anxiety" conjures up images of backbiting envy and wounded pride, of a small-minded craving for prestige and petty jealousies. Do these images convey the feelings of bitter defeat that old Paris retailers felt as the world they had known was demolished by urban change and economic depression?

[4] Walter Benjamin, *Charles Baudelaire*, pp. 36–37, 157–160; and interview with Céline in the introduction to Céline, *Castle to Castle*, p. x.

No, it was an experience of real decline, and not relative deprivation or status loss, that launched the shopkeeper movement. Two clarifications, however, need to be made in this connection. Firstly, the decline in question does not necessarily imply proletarianization. The shopping district of old Paris, despite the end-of-century crisis, retained its commercial identity. Local retailers, however depressed, were not converted en masse into dispossessed wage earners. Secondly, the experience of decline generates an impetus toward mobilization, but only within a context of social polarization. Haussmannization created dual commercial districts in downtown Paris, and the depression meted out widely divergent fates to the two. One flourished, the other collapsed. To the retailers who lost out, the prosperity so near at hand, the very proximity of success was infuriating; the unfairness, the arbitrariness of it all spurred them to action and provided a focus for their hostilities. They detested all that was associated with the affluent world just next door, from its department stores and banks, to its rectilinear boulevards and cosmopolitan atmosphere. The downwardly mobile do not always mobilize in resistance. But when a neighbor, with no particular claim to virtue, is thriving amidst the general misfortune, it is hard to contain one's anger. Decline *and* polarization were the twin conditions that bred lower middle-class resentment.

THE POLITICS OF LOWER MIDDLE-CLASS MOBILIZATION

Discussion of lower middle-class resentment raises the second issue touched on in the introduction: the political significance of petit-bourgeois mobilization. The shopkeeper movement in fin-de-siècle Paris made a pilgrimage from left to right. *Ligue syndicale* ideology to be sure contained a potent dose of cultural and economic reaction—of antimodernism in Volkov's phrase—and it is tempting to categorize the *Ligue* as reactionary *ab initio*. No doubt *ligueurs* reviled the modern metropolis and the *révolution du bon marché*. And then there is the small-owner ideology which shopkeeper militants espoused with such fervor. The radical republican tradition since Rousseau had cherished a vision of community based on small property, but was not such a vision outmoded, indeed nostalgic and backward-looking in the new age of organization? But this image of the reactionary shopkeeper is too one-sided. *Ligueurs* did not balk at an alliance with the working-class left. Nor in the 1880s did shopkeepers abandon themselves to authoritarianism. Militants who became involved in partisan politics sided with Radical-Socialism, a movement of undisputed left-wing pedigree. Or they rallied to Boulangism, and Boulangism, too, at least in its popular Parisian incarnation, was a movement of the left, social and democratic in its concerns.

The shopkeeper movement did in fact begin on the left and moved right in the 1890s, an evolution that seems to confirm the thesis of a liberal to fascist switch advanced by Lipset and like-minded social scientists.[5] But I would like to take issue with the sociological school on three points.

(1) Firstly, the shopkeeper movement's political antecedents were radical republican, not liberal. The *Ligue syndicale* was a partisan of the omnicompetent, unicameral legislature, undaunted by liberal second thoughts about the tyranny of the majority. There is a Jacobin ring to this position, but not to the *Ligue*'s advocacy of direct democracy. If a revolutionary tradition must be found in which to situate the shopkeeper movement, the republican socialism of the 1830s or the democratic socialism of the Second Republic would appear the likeliest choices with their triple commitment to radical democracy, public virtue and the *peuple*. Liberals of Thiers' persuasion—constitutionalist, latitudinarian and deeply distrust-

[5] See Introduction, pp. 11–12.

ful of the "vile multitude"—were bound to regard all these commitments with serious misgivings.

The odd mix of qualities that constituted the retailer movement at its origins calls to mind, not liberalism or even the antimodernism of Volkov's master artisans, so much as the Populism of American farmers.[6] The farmers' movement in the United States, like the *Ligue syndicale*, was rooted in a constituency of independent proprietors, men and women committed to small-owner values and suspicious of the new corporatism. Populists divided the world into producers and parasites, into the people and the trusts. A rising aristocracy of wealth, they claimed, was threatening the common folk with a new form of slavery. The money power imposed its rule through corruption, bribing politicians and promoting vice to demoralize the people. And Populist attacks on the money power, like those of the *Ligue syndicale*, were tinged with a corrosive xenophobia and anti-Semitism. "The Rothschilds," one Alabama Populist declared, "are the head and front of the greatest financial conspiracy ever attempted in the history of the world."[7] To the parasitism, corruption and cosmopolitanism of corporate America, the Populists opposed the traditionalist trinity of labor, virtue and country, values cherished by all Americans but which found their most perfect expression in the family farm. Historians like Richard Hofstadter have pointed out the reactionary potential of Populist ideology, but recent work has challenged this interpretation, underlining Populism's democratic aspirations and its pursuit of a farmer/labor alliance against corporate capital.[8] American

[6] For the following discussion, see the works cited above by Hicks and Hofstadter; also, Goodwyn, *Democratic Promise*; Green, *Grass-Roots Socialism*; Hackney, *Populism to Progressivism in Alabama*; Wright, *The Politics of Populism*.

[7] Cited in Hackney, p. 82.

[8] Hofstadter, pp. 60–93. Goodwyn's work, cited above, represents a thoroughgoing refutation of Hofstadter's thesis. See also Pollack, *The Populist Response*, pp. 43–67.

Populists combined moral conservatism and a faith in small ownership with a genuine radicalism that focused on citizen participation and issues of social welfare. The same can be said of the *Ligue syndicale*, and it is possible to recognize in the *Ligue* the embryo of a French populism.

However the *Ligue*'s politics are to be characterized—radical republican, populist, Radical-Socialist or Boulangist—they were left-wing, but not liberal, or even pseudo-liberal. On this point, the French case deviates from the "liberal to fascist" schema. Just the same, the shopkeeper movement still ended up on the right, as predicted by the sociological school. But what prompted the movement's abandonment of the left? Was it the experience of depression that drove the petite bourgeoisie to extremist politics, as Lipset has argued? I have stressed instead political variables. Economic crisis launched the *Ligue syndicale*, but it was politics that shaped its rightward trajectory. On this point, too, the French case deviates from the sociological model.

(2) The *Ligue syndicale*'s relations with the left soured in the 1890s. The socialist movement's evolution toward militant collectivism alienated *ligueurs*, and the *Ligue* in turn alienated labor with its campaign against consumer cooperatives. Shopkeeper militants now found themselves under assault from below and above, from collectivists no less than from department store apologists. Available avenues of political redress offered besieged shopkeepers little hope of relief. Organized business and its allies in parliament emasculated the business-tax bill of 1893 and obstructed further reform. The entire political system, it appeared, was determined to sidestep the shopkeeper question. The left debated collectivism and Solidarism; the political establishment worried about social defense and class reconciliation. Encircled, frustrated and excluded, the shopkeeper movement cast about for new allies.

The radical right offered the best alternative. Anti-Semites, Christian Democrats and Nationalists made a concerted effort to court the shopkeeper. The anti-Semitic movement, tainted with old-regime connections, had a limited appeal to *ligueurs*, although Drumont as an individual was held in high esteem. The Christian Democratic *Union fraternelle*, however, managed to strike up an alliance with the *Ligue*. The UFCI was serious and accepted the Republic; not least of all, its social and geographical profile closely resembled that of the *Ligue syndicale*. But it was anti-Dreyfusard Nationalism that held the greatest attraction for shopkeeper militants. Nationalist littérateurs spoke the same language as shopkeeper militants—the language of small-owner utopianism and cultural reaction. The *petit commerçant* recognized in the man of letters a common defender of a commercial and cultural milieu threatened with extinction. It was not just demagoguery and manipulation that drew the shopkeeper movement to Nationalism, but a shared perspective based, as I have tried to show, on a shared experience of disruption.

In view of the Parisian shopkeeper movement's shifting pattern of alliances in the nineties, it might well be argued that retailer militancy was essentially unstable in character, lacking a coherent core of beliefs to shape its political choices. To be sure, there were changes in the movement's outlook. Novel and disturbing themes crept into shopkeeper vocabulary or were accorded a new importance: authoritarianism, hostility to working-class organization, and cultural reaction. But amidst all these changes, elements of continuity can be discerned. The Parisian *petit commerçant*, whether as Radical or Nationalist, conceived social life as a three-tiered structure with the independent slotted in between labor at the bottom and *grand commerce* at the top. In the perfectly ordered social system envisioned by shopkeepers, workers aspired to small-owner status and posed no threat. Retailer militants recognized the existence of social injustice, but it was a manageable problem to be handled with timely doses of social reform. The oppressive power of big business was of course a looming danger, but one that could be countered by restrictive legislation

limiting the growth of large-scale enterprise. The maintenance of the social equilibrium was thus premised on an ongoing state commitment to dampen labor discontent and
control monopoly. Vigilance was essential to insure that the
government met its obligations, and this required in turn the
active and direct participation of shopkeepers in public affairs. Shopkeepers did not see their vision of a balanced social
order as a selfish one. The system they imagined guaranteed
the integrity of the neighborhood, the workshop, and above
all the family. And these communities were the breeding
ground of values held sacred by all Frenchmen: independence, thrift, hard work and paternal authority. To be French
implied, even demanded, a devotion to the virtues of smallness. It was this conviction that underlay the shopkeeper militant's determined and unflagging patriotism. Whatever his
political commitments then, the shopkeeper remained a patriot, localist in his sympathies, obstinate in his demand for
a more active and direct role in government affairs, and firm
in his belief that small property was the *sine qua non* of a har-
monious social order.

What changed in the late nineteenth century was not retailer ideology, which, despite important modifications, remained remarkably consistent throughout, but the political
context in which Parisian shopkeepers operated. In the nineteenth century, the small-owner creed had been very much at
home on the left and, indeed, constituted a major current of
radical republican thought. But in Paris in the 1890s, the
left ceased to be, as it had once been, hospitable to the shopkeeper vision. Radical-Socialist politicians were unable or unwilling to deliver fully on promises to protect the little man.
The emergence of the social question and the rise of collectivist socialism in particular turned the left's attention away
from the once critical issue of commercial defense. The small-
owner faith as a consequence was dislodged from its left-wing
anchorage and became free floating. To the extent that Na-

Conclusion

tionalists made a bid to adapt the small-owner vision into a doctrine of the right, they succeeded in attracting the support of small-owner proponents and of shopkeepers above all. Retailer militants moved from left to right, but they did not radically alter their belief structure in the process. It was not so much that shopkeepers had changed as that the left and right had changed, the left proving itself increasingly unreceptive and the right increasingly sympathetic to small-owner politics.

This explanation of the shopkeeper movement's "turn to the right" raises several points of interest not only about petit-bourgeois politics but also about the nature of the far right in the late nineteenth century. Historians have traced the roots of fascism to the pre-World War I era.[9] Attention has focused on the radical right as a precursor of fascism, and the radical right's origins in turn have been attributed to a breakdown of liberalism. The breakdown was real enough, but in Paris, it was not liberal collapse that gave birth to the new right so much as a crisis in the radical republican tradition, politically marginalized and increasingly at odds with an emergent corporate capitalist order. Mussolinian fascism, Renzo de Felice has argued, had its origins in Italy's republican tradition.[10] The fascis, after all, was a symbol of republican justice. The Parisian shopkeeper movement's volte-face in the 1890s suggests that de Felice's argument has application in France as well.

Historians have stressed and rightly so the "newness" of the radical right.[11] This is not to say that there was no relationship between the old right and the new. Christian Democracy was an offshoot of de la Tour du Pin's Catholic traditionalism. Royalist interests maneuvered with considerable

[9] See Noakes' review of Robert Gellately's *The Politics of Economic Despair*, in the *Times Literary Supplement*, 30 May 1975.
[10] De Felice, *Fascism, An Informal Introduction*, pp. 102–106.
[11] Sternhell, *La Droite révolutionnaire*, pp. 24–28.

success to gain control of the anti-Semitic movement. Nor was Nationalism immune to the manipulative intrigues of *ralliés* and secular conservatives like Piou and Méline. The new right's establishment and old regime connections, however, should not obscure the novelty of the phenomenon. But wherein lies this novelty? Nationalism, it is recognized, owed much to nineteenth-century radicalism. The league form of organization, so characteristic of the old popular radicalism, was appropriated by the new right and applied to a new purpose: mass mobilization for antiparliamentary street action. The leagues of the turn of the century borrowed the theme of "*la patrie en danger*" from the old republican left, but they infused traditional patriotic appeals with a xenophobic and anti-Semitic rhetoric geared to a defensive-minded popular audience, fearful of foreign invasion whether military, cultural or commercial.[12] But the new right's greatest ideological coup was to contest the left's control of small-owner doctrine. In Paris, the Nationalist movement won the contest and into the bargain a definite edge in the competition for small-owner support. The new right's newness—and the source of its appeal to an urban petit-bourgeois constituency hitherto resistant to a reactionary politics—lay in its skillful assimilation of radical organizational and ideological forms.

Such a conclusion presupposes, of course, that politics and ideology were crucial determinants of the shopkeeper movement's political about-face. The point bears repeating, given the sociological school's supposition that petit-bourgeois protest translates directly and without political mediation into a fascist or protofascist politics. The fact remains, however, that the shopkeeper movement did execute a "turn to the right" in the 1890s. Does this not suggest that there is some inherent connection between lower middle-class mobilization and right-wing extremism, whether that connection is mediated

---

[12] Rémond, *The Right Wing in France*, p. 208.

Conclusion

by politics or not? I would argue on the contrary that the political thrust of petit-bourgeois protest is an open-ended question, and here I take issue for the third time with the sociological model.

(3) For example, in the United States the disintegration of the Populist movement in the mid-nineties profited Bryanite Democrats and later Progressive Republicans, but only an occasional Populist—a Tom Watson or Milford Howard—ended a jingo, xenophobe, or racist.[13] German artisan and shopkeeper associations did indeed manifest a keen interest in the anti-Semitic right, but after the turn of the century, they retreated into a more conservative politics of middle-class defense. Indeed, an alliance with big business organizations was actively pursued, which culminated in 1911 in the formation of the *Kartell der Schaffenden Stände*, a united front of pressure groups representing small owners, heavy industry and agricultural interests.[14]

A parallel evolution has been observed in France. In the aftermath of the Dreyfus Affair, retailer militancy settled into a course of relative political moderation. Organized *petit commerce* in 1900 had stood in opposition to the nation's political establishment. By 1914, it had become enmeshed in an antisocialist business coalition committed to Poincarist policies. The political reorientation of retailer militancy is to be explained in part by a shift in the balance of power within the shopkeeper movement itself as the weight of influence passed from the radical, Paris-based *Ligue syndicale* to conservative

[13] On Populism's successors, see Goodwyn, pp. 426–514; Hicks, p. 421; Hofstadter, pp. 132–133; Mowry, *Theodore Roosevelt*, p. 11. On Watson and Howard, see Woodward, *Tom Watson*, pp. 370ff.; and Hackney, p. 117.

[14] Blackbourn, *Class, Religion and Local Politics in Wilhelmine Germany*, pp. 196–230; Eley, *Reshaping the German Right*, pp. 316–334; Gellately, *The Politics of Economic Despair*, pp. 181–189; Winkler, "From Social Protectionism to National Socialism," pp. 14–16.

· 494 ·

national organizations like the *Confédération des groupes commerciaux et industriels.* But it is also to be explained by a change in the political strategy of establishment elites. Belatedly awakened to the conservative potential of *petit commerce,* the parliamentary right maneuvered astutely to patronize and exploit the retailer movement's tendencies toward moderation. The retailer movement's turn to conservatism did betoken a shift in shopkeeper ideology. Militant *petits commerçants* tempered their long-standing animosity toward big business. The traditional stress on the integrity of the neighborhood gave way to a heightened emphasis on the *syndicat* as the instrument of the petty retailer's salvation. The notion of the shopkeeper as a man of the people was eclipsed by a new self-referent, the shopkeeper as a member of the *classes moyennes.* But the extent of the transformation in retailer world-view can be exaggerated. The CGCI militant, like his *Ligue syndicale* forebears, proclaimed the virtues of smallness, independence and family life. He was still an ardent patriot and still particularist in his loyalties, if now to the *syndicat* rather than to the neighborhood. And he remained convinced that the *petit commerçant* was a man in between. At the turn of the century, the retailer movement had seen itself hemmed in between a hostile labor movement and an indifferent big business elite. In 1914, it was labor and cosmopolitan finance that squeezed the small businessman. If the notion of middle-class defense permitted a rapprochement with elements of the business community, it did not signify a total renunciation of the shopkeeper militant's deep-rooted conception of society as a three-tiered structure.

But whether it is most appropriate to stress change or continuity, the essential point to be retained is that the shopkeeper movement in the 1900–1914 period altered its political stance from radical reaction to conservative accommodation. Specialists of petit-bourgeois protest in twentieth-century France have noted an oscillation between periods of antiestablishment radicalism and of sober-minded conservatism. Evidence for this observation has largely been drawn from the Poujadist movement of the mid-1950s. Poujadism began as a taxpayers' revolt with demagogic and nationalist overtones. The movement's activist elan, however, soon dissipated, and its lower middle-class following subsided into a more traditional conservatism that profited political moderates like Antoine Pinay and Charles de Gaulle. Poujadism unfolded in a sequence of radical mobilization and conservative reintegration,[15] but this pattern of development was not unique to the 1950s. In the pre-World War I era, too, organized *petit commerce* abandoned extremist politics for a more centrist position. Retailer militants aligned themselves with the far right in 1900 as again in the mid-fifties, but the commitment in each case proved neither irreversible nor permanent.

The trajectory from radical republicanism to Nationalism traced by the Parisian shopkeeper movement in the 1890s fits in with a certain panoramic vision that classifies the nineteenth-century petite bourgeoisie as *quarante-huitard* and the twentieth-century as National Socialist.[16] In light of the French case, however, certain revisions are in order. The lower middle class began its political pilgrimage on the left, but not necessarily on the liberal left; it journeyed to the far right, but its journey did not necessarily end there. But most importantly, I have wanted to argue that the petite bourgeoisie's notorious turn to the right was by no means a foregone conclusion. Politics and ideology made a difference. It is this point that should be kept in mind as we enter a new era of lower middle-class mobilization.

[15] G. E. Lavau, "Classes moyennes et leur comportement politique," p. 60.
[16] See, for example, Volkov, pp. 5–6. Arno Mayer has advanced a similar thesis: "The Lower Middle Class as Historical Problem," esp. p. 416. See also Wiener's reply: "Marxism and the Lower Middle Class," pp. 666–671.

Bibliography

I. Unpublished Sources

A. ARCHIVES NATIONALES, PARIS (AN)

27 AS 1–2, Association de l'industrie et de l'agriculture française.

C 5498–5499, Mesureur Commission.

C 5607, Patentes.

C 7467, Enquête sur la situation du commerce en France, 1914.

F^7 12445–12448, Agissements boulangistes.

F^7 12454–12458, Surveillance des nationalistes.

F^7 12717–12721, Patrie française, Nationalistes, Action libérale.

F^7 12870–12877, Ligue des patriotes.

F^7 12878, Action libérale.

F^7 12882–12883, Antisémites.

F^7 13229–13230, Ligue de la patrie française.

B. ARCHIVES DE LA PRÉFECTURE DE POLICE, PARIS (APP)

B/a 40, Congrès national des chambres syndicales patronales.

B/a 119, Exposition universelle de Paris, 1889.

B/a 153, Chambre syndicale des employés.

B/a 203–218, Legislative Elections, 1902.

B/a 485, Pétitions addressées à Monsieur le Maréchal, Président.

B/a 485, 503–504, Situation commerciale et industrielle, 1886–1890.

B/a 497, L'Affaire boulangiste.

B/a 693–696, Municipal Elections, 1900.

B/a 901, Action libérale.

B/a 905, Demonstration, 23 February 1899.

B/a 910, François Coppée.

B/a 935, E. Archdeacon.

B/a 942, Jules Auffray.

B/a 944, E. A. Ballière.

B/a 947, Ernest Barillier.

B/a 963, Louis Boeuf.

B/a 1032–1034, Paul Déroulède.

B/a 1043, Demonstration, January 1898.

B/a 1092, Louis Gazon.

B/a 1104–1106, Jules Guérin.

B/a 1107–1108, Ligue antisémitique.

B/a 1137, Eugène de Ménorval.

B/a 1150, Jules Lemaître.

B/a 1172, Alphonse Marguery.

B/a 1193–1194, Marquis de Morès.

B/a 1250, Henri Rochefort.

B/a 1276, Gabriel Syveton.

B/a 1292, Maurice Vergoin.

B/a 1334–1337, Ligue de la patrie française.

B/a 1337–1340, Ligue des patriotes.

B/a 1408 bis, Chambre syndicale de l'alimentation.

B/a 1420, Syndicat général du commerce et de l'industrie.

B/a 1465–1469, Comité républicain national.

B/a 1517–1519, Comités boulangistes.

B/a 1537, Action catholique.

B/a 1658, Raymond Poincaré.

B/a 1660, Louis Dausset.

B/a 1668, Henri Gallichet.

C. ARCHIVES DE LA SEINE, PARIS (AS)
D_1M^2, Premier arrondissement, Listes électorales, 1875, 1885, 1895.
D^9P^2, Palais-Royal, Patente registers, 1885, 1890, 1895, 1900.

D. BIBLIOTHÈQUE DE LA CHAMBRE DE COMMERCE, PARIS (BCC)
I 8–63, Fédérations, Confédérations.

E. BIBLIOTHÈQUE HISTORIQUE DE LA VILLE DE PARIS (BHVP)
Actualités, Au Bon Marché.

Bibliography

Actualités, Magasins du Louvre.

Actualités, série 119, Commerce et Industrie.

CP 3430, Palais-Royal, Pièces diverses.

F. BIBLIOTHÈQUE NATIONALE, PARIS (BN)

Nouvelles Acquisitions Françaises 10278, Emile Zola, notes for *Au Bonheur des Dames* (cited throughout as BN NAF 10278, Zola).

Nouvelles Acquisitions Françaises 16024–16027, *Poincaré Papers, Notes journalières* (1912–1914).

II. PUBLISHED SOURCES

A. NEWSPAPERS AND PERIODICALS

L'Action libérale populaire, 1904–1908.

Affiches tourangelles, 1897–1902.

L'Ami des petits commerçants, 1902.

Annales de la Patrie française, 1900–1905.

L'Aurore, 1900–1902.

La Bijouterie, 1888.

Bulletin de l'Union fraternelle du commerce et de l'industrie, 1895–1910.

Bulletin du Syndicat du Palais-Royal, 1882–1883.

Bulletin mensuel du commerce et de l'industrie, 1901–1910.

Bulletin officiel de la (Con)fédération des groupes commerciaux et industriels, 1904–1914.

Bulletin officiel de l'Union syndicale, 1902.

Bulletin officiel du Comité républicain du commerce et de l'industrie, 1900–1901.

Le Commerçant, 1882.

La Crise commerciale, 1887–1891.

La Croix, 1896–1900.

La Défense commerciale et industrielle, 1902.

Le Démocrate, 1890.

Les Droits du peuple, 1890.

L'Economiste français, 1882–1884.

L'Epicerie française, 1898–1900.

Les Etudes fiscales et sociales, 1908–1910.

Fédération de la Seine, 1904–1906.

La France, 1893–1895.

Le Gaulois, 1910.

Gil Blas, 1892.

L'Idéal, 1905–1909.

L'Idéal social, 1903–1905.

Le Jour, 1898.

Journal de la Chambre syndicale de la boucherie, 1894–1899.

Journal de l'alimentation, 1898–1902.

La Libre Parole, 1893–1895.

La Nation, 1889.

L'Opinion, 1910–1914.

Le Parti ouvrier, 1889.

La Patrie, 1900.

La Petite République, 1900–1902.

Le Peuple français, 1894–1898.

La Plaine Monceau, 1890.

Le Premier Arrondissement, 1889–1894.

Le Radical, 1902.

La Réforme sociale, 1881–1914.

La République, 1889.

La République française, 1898–1910.

La République illustrée, 1889.

Le Réveil économique, 1910–1914.

La Revendication, 1888–1896.

La Revue des deux mondes, 1881–1914.

Le Socialiste, 1888–1890.

Le Temps, 1902.

L'Union démocratique, 1887–1889.

L'Union des syndicats de France, 1897–1902.

L'Union des syndicats patronaux des industries textiles de france, 1913.

L'Union nationale du commerce et de l'industrie, 1884–1909.

Le Voltaire, 1898.

B. GOVERNMENT PUBLICATIONS

Annuaire statistique de la Ville de Paris, 1881–1902.

Atlas administratif des 20 arrondissements de la Ville de Paris, pub-

lié d'après les ordres de M. le baron G. E. Haussman, Sénateur, Préfet de la Seine. Paris, 1868.

Atlas municipal des vingt arrondissements de la Ville de Paris dressé sous l'administration de M. E. Poubelle, Préfet, sous la direction de M. Alphand, Inspecteur Général. Paris, 1895.

Chambre des Députés. *Procès-verbaux de la commission chargée de faire une enquête sur la situation des ouvriers de l'industrie et de l'agriculture en France.* Paris, 1884. (Cited throughout as Chambre des Députés, Spuller Commission.)

Chambre des Députés. *Rapport fait au nom de la commission chargée d'examiner les propositions de loi: 1 de M. Mesureur et plusieurs de ses collègues; 2 de M. du Saussay; 3 de M. Le Veillée relatives à la réforme de la législation des patentes, par M. Terrier. Annexe au procès-verbal du 12 juillet 1892.* Paris, 1892. (Cited throughout as Chambre des Députés, *Terrier Report.*)

Journal officiel de la République française: débats parlementaires, Chambre des Députés. 1893.

Office du travail. *La Petite Industrie (salaires et durée de travail):* Vol. I, *L'Alimentation à Paris.* Paris, 1894. (Cited throughout as Office du travail, *L'Alimentation à Paris.*) Vol. II, *Le Vêtement à Paris.* Paris, 1896. (Cited throughout as Office du travail, *Le Vêtement à Paris.*)

Préfecture de la Seine. *Secrétariat général, Service de la statistique municipale, résultats statistiques du dénombrement de 1881 pour la Ville de Paris.* Paris, 1884.

Préfecture du département de la Seine. *Commission d'extension de Paris. Aperçu historique et considérations techniques préliminaires (circulation, espaces libres),* vol. I. Paris, 1913.

Préfecture du département de la Seine. *Direction des finances. Commission des contributions directes de la Ville de Paris. Les Propriétés bâties de la Ville de Paris en 1889 et en 1890.* Paris, 1890.

Préfecture du département de la Seine. *Direction municipale des travaux du cadastre de Paris (Albert Fontaine, directeur). Commission des contributions directes, Ville de Paris. Le Livre foncier de 1911.* Paris, 1911.

Sénat. *Rapport fait au nom de la commission des patentes, par M.*

Gauthier. Annexe au procès-verbal de la séance du 4 avril 1900. Paris, 1900. (Cited throughout as Sénat, *Gauthier report.*)

C. BOOKS, DISSERTATIONS, PAMPHLETS

Adorno, Theodore, *et al. The Authoritarian Personality.* New York, 1950.

Aftalion, Albert. *Le Développement de la fabrique et le travail à domicile dans les industries de l'habillement.* Paris, 1906.

Ambrière, Francis. *La Vie secrète des grands magasins.* Paris, 1938.

Arbellot, Simon. *La Fin du boulevard.* Paris, 1965.

Artley, Alexandra. *The Golden Age of Shop Design: European Shop Interiors, 1880–1939.* London, 1975.

Audiganne, Armand. *Mémoires d'un ouvrier de Paris, 1871–1872.* Paris, 1873.

Augé de Lassus, L. *La Vie au Palais-Royal.* Paris, 1904.

Bader, Jeffrey. *The Nationalist Leagues in France after Dreyfus, 1898–1906.* Doctoral dissertation, Columbia University, 1975.

Baedeker, K. *Paris and Its Environs.* London, 1891.

Balzac, Honoré de. *Lost Illusions.* Tr. Kathleen Raine. New York: Modern Library, 1967.

Barberet, Joseph. *Monographies professionnelles.* 7 vols. Paris, 1889.

Barbier, P., and F. Vernillot. *Histoire de France par les chansons.* Vol. VIII: *La IIIe République de 1871 à 1918.* Paris, 1961.

Barrès, Maurice. *Scènes et doctrines du nationalisme.* 2 vols. Paris, n.d.

Bastié, Jean. *La Croissance de la banlieue parisienne.* Paris, 1964.

Baudin, Henry. *L'Enseigne et l'affiche.* Geneva, 1905.

Beau de Loménie, E. *Les Responsabilités des dynasties bourgeoises.* Vol. II: *De MacMahon à Poincaré.* Paris, 1977.

Bellanger, Claude, *et al. Histoire générale de la presse française.* Vol. III: *De 1871 à 1940.* Paris, 1972.

Benjamin, Edmond, and Paul Desachy. *Le Boulevard, croquis parisiens.* Paris, 1893.

Benjamin, Walter. *Charles Baudelaire. A Lyric Poet in the Era of High Capitalism.* London, 1973.

Benoist, Charles. *Souvenirs.* Vol. III. Paris, 1934.

Berger, Suzanne. *Peasants against Politics: Rural Organization in Britanny, 1911–1967.* Cambridge, Mass., 1972.

Bibliography

Bernard, Joseph. *Du Mouvement d'organisation et de défense du petit commerce français.* Doctoral dissertation, University of Paris, 1906.

Bertaut, Jules. *Le Boulevard.* Paris, 1924.

————. *Les Dessous de la "Troisième."* Paris, 1959.

————. *Le Paris d'avant guerre.* Paris, n.d.

Billy, André. *L'Epoque 1900.* Paris, 1951.

Blackbourn, David. *Class, Religion and Local Politics in Wilhelmine Germany: The Centre Party in Württemberg before 1914.* New Haven, Conn., 1980.

Bloch, Ferdinand. *Types du boulevard.* Paris, n.d.

Boucard, Max. *La Vie de Paris.* Paris, 1892.

Les Boulevards. L'Avenue de l'Opéra et la rue de la Paix. Illustrés. Paris, n.d. [1880s].

Les Boulevards de Paris. Paris, 1877.

Braibant, Charles. *Histoire de la Tour Eiffel.* Paris, 1964.

Brants, Victor. *La Petite Industrie contemporaine.* Paris, 1902.

Byrnes, Robert. *Antisemitism in Modern France.* New Brunswick, N. J., 1950.

Capus, Alfred. *Boulevard et coulisses.* Paris, 1914.

Caron, François. *An Economic History of Modern France.* New York, 1979.

Castelnau, Jacques. *Belle Epoque.* Paris, 1962.

————. *En remontant les grands boulevards.* Paris, 1960.

Céline, Ferdinand. *Castle to Castle.* Tr. Ralph Mannheim. New York, 1968.

Chambre de Commerce de Paris. *Enquête sur les conditions du travail en France pendant l'année 1872.* Paris, 1875.

Chambre syndicale des tissus et nouveautés de France. *Discours prononcés au banquet du 7 février 1895.* Paris, 1895.

Champier, Victor, and G.-Roger Sandoz. *Le Palais-Royal.* Vol. II. Paris, 1900.

Charles-Brun, J. *Le Régionalisme.* Paris, 1911.

Chevalier, Louis. *La Formation de la population parisienne au XIXe siècle.* Paris, 1950.

Clark, Terry. *Prophets and Patrons: The French University and the Emergence of the Social Sciences.* Cambridge, Mass., 1973.

Claudin, Gustave. *Mes Souvenirs, les boulevards de 1840–1870.* Paris, 1884.

————. *Paris*. Paris, 1867.

Clément de Ris, comte L. *Les Enseignes de Paris*. Paris, 1877.

Cochin, Augustin. *Paris, sa population, son industrie*. Paris, 1864.

Coffignon, A. *Les Coulisses de la mode*. Paris, n.d. [1880s].

————. *L'Estomac de Paris*. Paris, n.d.

————. *Le Pavé parisien*. Paris, n.d.

Comité national républicain du commerce et de l'industrie. *Discours prononcé par M. Paul Deschanel, 2 mars 1898*. Paris, 1898.

[Coppée] *Oeuvres de François Coppée*. Vol. II: *Poésies 1869–1874*. Paris, n.d.

Coppée, François. *Souvenirs d'un parisien*. Paris, 1910.

Cornu, Marcel. *La Conquête de Paris*. Paris, 1972.

Cucheval-Clarigny, A., and E. Flavien. *Etude sur le Bon Marché*. Paris, n.d.

Dansette, Adrien. *Le Boulangisme*. Paris, 1946.

————. *Histoire religieuse de la France contemporaine*. Paris, 1965.

D'Ariste, Paul. *La Vie et le monde du boulevard (1830–1870)*. Paris, 1930.

Dasquet, Marc. *Le Bon Marché*. Paris, 1955.

Daudet, Alphonse. *Trente ans de Paris*. Paris, 1889.

Daudet, Mme. Alphonse. *Souvenirs autour d'un groupe littéraire*. Paris, 1910.

Daudet, Léon. *Paris vécu*. Paris, 1969. [Repr. 1928 ed.]

————. *Salons et journaux*. Paris, 1917.

Daugan, J. *Histoire et législation des patentes des grands magasins*. Paris, 1902.

Daumard, Adeline. *Maisons de Paris et propriétaires parisiens au XIXe siècle*. Paris, 1965.

D'Avenel, vicomte G. *Le Mécanisme de la vie moderne*. 4 vols. Paris, 1902–1904.

De Beauvoir, Simone. *Memoirs of a Dutiful Daughter*. Tr. J. Kirkup. Harmondsworth: Penguin, 1974.

De Felice, Renzo. *Fascism, An Informal Introduction to its Theory and Practice*. New Brunswick, N. J., 1977.

De Foville, Alfred. *La Tour Eiffel*. Paris, 1888.

————. *La Transformation des moyens de transport et ses conséquences économiques et sociales*. Paris, 1880.

Bibliography

De Lannoy, A.-P. (A. Pawlowski). *Les Plaisirs et la vie de Paris (guide du flâneur)*. Paris, 1900.

De Maupassant, Guy. *Bel-Ami*. Tr. Douglas Parmée. Harmondsworth: Penguin, 1975.

Demolins, Edmond. *A quoi tient la supériorité des Anglo-Saxons*. Paris, 1896.

————. *La Question des grands magasins*. Paris, 1890.

De Seilhac, Léon. *L'Industrie de la couture et de la confection*, Paris, 1897.

Destréguil, Henri, *La Crise commerciale et industrielle, ses causes—ses faits—ses remèdes*. Tours, 1902.

Deverin, Henri. *La Résurrection du Palais-Royal*. Paris, 1905.

Domergue, Jules. *Commment et pourquoi les affaires vont mal en France*. Paris, 1905.

Donnay, Maurice. *Autour du Chat Noir*. Paris, 1926.

————. *J'ai vécu 1900*. Paris, 1950.

————. *Mes Débuts à Paris*. Paris, 1937.

Doumic, René. *Portraits d'écrivains*. Paris, 1892.

Drumont, Edouard. *La Fin d'un monde*. Paris, 1889.

————. *La France juive*. 2nd ed. Vol. I. Paris, n.d.

————. *La France juive*. 43nd ed. Vol. II. Paris, n.d.

————, *Mon Vieux Paris*, 2nd ed. 2 vols. Paris, 1896.

Dubuisson, Dr. Paul. *Les Voleuses de grands magasins*. Paris, 1902.

Du Camp, Maxime. *Paris et ses organes*. Vol. VI. Paris, 1875.

Duclos, Léon. *La Transformation du commerce de détail*. *Thèse de droit*, University of Paris, 1902.

Ducray, Camille, *Paul Déroulède, 1846–1914*. Paris, 1914.

Du Maroussem, Pierre. *Les Enquêtes, pratique et théorie*. Paris, 1900.

————. *La Question ouvrière*. 4 vols. Paris, 1891–1894. I: *Charpentiers de Paris, compagnons et indépendants* (1891); II: *Ebénistes du faubourg Saint-Antoine* (1892); III: *Le Jouet parisien* (1894); IV: *Halles centrales de Paris* (1894).

Duverger, Maurice. *Political Parties*. Tr. B. and R. North. London, 1964.

Duvernois, Henri. *Apprentissages. Souvenirs des années 1885–1900*. Paris, 1930.

————. *Le Boulevard*. Paris, 1927.

Bibliography

D'Ydewalle, Charles. *Au Bon Marché, de la boutique au grand magasin.* Paris, 1965.

Eley, Geoff. *Reshaping the German Right, Radical Nationalism and Political Change after Bismarck.* New Haven, Conn., 1980.

Elwitt, Sanford. *The Making of the Third Republic, Class and Politics in France, 1868–1884.* Baton Rouge, La., 1975.

Englund, Steven. *The Origins of Oppositional Nationalism in France (1881–1889).* Doctoral dissertation, Princeton University, 1981.

L'Esprit montmartois. Interviews et souvenirs par Maurice Donnay, Dominique Bonnaud, Vincent Hyspa. Paris, 1938.

Evenson, Norma. *Paris: A Century of Change, 1878–1978.* New Haven, Conn., 1979.

Fatoux, Léon. *Les Coulisses du nationalisme.* Paris, 1903.

Fegdal, Charles. *Les Vieilles Enseignes de Paris.* Paris, 1913.

Fohlen, Claude. *L'Industrie textile au temps du Second Empire.* Paris, 1956.

Forestier, J. C. N. *Grandes Villes et système de parcs.* Paris, 1906.

Fournier, Edouard. *Histoire des enseignes de Paris.* Paris, 1884.

France, Anatole. *M. Bergeret à Paris.* Paris: Livre de Poche, n.d.

————. *Penguin Island.* Tr. Belle Notkin Burke. New York: Signet, 1968.

Fridenson, Patrick. *Histoire des usines Renault.* Vol. I: *Naissance de la grande entreprise.* Paris, 1972.

Fromm, Erich. *Escape from Freedom.* New York, 1971.

Funck-Brentano, Frantz. *Grandeur et décadence des classes moyennes.* Paris, 1903.

Gaillard, Jeanne. *Paris, la ville 1852–1870.* Paris, 1977.

Garrigues, Henri. *Les Grands Magasins de nouveautés et le petit commerce de détail.* Paris, 1898.

Gay, Ernest. *Nos Ediles, 1904–1908.* Paris, n.d.

Gay, Peter. *The Dilemma of Democratic Socialism, Eduard Bernstein's Challenge to Marx.* New York, 1952.

Gellately, Robert. *The Politics of Economic Despair, Shopkeepers and German Politics, 1890–1914.* London, 1974.

Gendrot, Alfred (Jean Drault). *Drumont, la France juive et la Libre Parole.* Paris, 1935.

Giard, Louis. *Les Elections à Paris sous la IIIe République*. 3 vols. Doctoral dissertation, University of Dakar, 1966–1968.

Gide, Charles. *Les Sociétés coopératives de consommation*. Paris, 1910.

Giedion, Siegfried. *Space, Time and Architecture*. Cambridge, Mass., 1954.

Giffard, Pierre. *Paris sous la Troisième République, les grands bazars*. Paris, 1882.

Ginisty, Paul. *Les Anciens Boulevards*. Paris, 1925.

Goodwyn, Lawrence. *Democratic Promise, The Populist Moment in America*. New York, 1976.

Gouault, Jacques. *Comment la France est devenue républicaine, 1870–1875*. Paris, 1954.

Goudeau, Emile. *Dix ans de bohême*. Paris, 1888.

―――. *Paysages parisiens, heures et saisons*. Paris, 1892.

Grand-Carteret, John. *L'Enseigne, son histoire, sa philosophie, ses particularités*. Grenoble, 1902.

Green, James R. *Grass-Roots Socialism, Radical Movements in the Southwest, 1895–1943*. Baton Rouge, La., 1978.

Greenberg, Louis. *Sisters of Liberty, Marseille, Lyon, Paris and the Reaction against the Centralized State, 1868–1871*. Cambridge, Mass., 1971.

Grosclaude. *Exposition comique*. Paris, 1889.

Guérin, Daniel. *Fascism and Big Business*. Tr. F. and M. Merrill. New York, 1973.

Guérin, Urbain. *L'Evolution sociale*. Paris, 1891.

Guerrand, Roger-H. *L'Art nouveau en Europe*. Paris, 1965.

Guesde, Jules. *Collectivisme et révolution*. Paris, 1904.

Guide de l'étranger à Montmartre. Paris, 1900.

Guillemin, Henri. *Nationalistes et "nationaux" (1870–1914)*. Paris, 1974.

Gyp (comtesse Martel de Janville). *Bob à l'exposition*. Paris, 1889.

Hackney, Sheldon. *Populism to Progressivism in Alabama*. Princeton, N. J., 1969.

Hahn, Steven. *The Roots of Southern Populism, Yeoman Farmers and the Transformation of the Georgia Upcountry, 1850–1890*. New York, 1983.

Halévy, Daniel. *The End of the Notables*. Tr. Alain Silvera. Middletown, Conn., 1974.

Bibliography

―――――. *La République des ducs*. Paris, 1937.

Hanagan, Michael. *The Logic of Solidarity, Artisans and Industrial Workers in Three French Towns, 1871–1914*. Urbana, Ill., 1980.

Hauser, Arnold. *The Social History of Art*. Vol. IV: *Naturalism, Impressionism, The Film Age*. New York, n.d.

Haussmann, G. E. *Mémoires du baron Haussmann*. 3 vols. Paris, 1890–1893.

Hénard, Eugène. *Etudes sur les transformations de Paris*. 8 vols. Paris, 1903–1909.

Hénard, Robert. *La Rue Saint-Honoré*. 2 vols. Paris, 1909.

Hicks, John D. *The Populist Revolt, A History of the Farmers' Alliance and the People's Party*. Lincoln, Neb., 1961.

Hoffmann, Stanley. *Le Mouvement Poujade*. Paris, 1956.

Hofstadter, Richard. *The Age of Reform*. New York, 1955.

Hugo, Victor. *Notre-Dame de Paris*. Paris: Flammarion, n.d.

Hutton, Patrick. *The Cult of the Revolutionary Tradition, The Blanquists in French Politics, 1864–1893*. Berkeley and Los Angeles, Calif., 1981.

Huysmans, J.-K. *Croquis parisiens*. Paris, 1886.

James, Henry. *The Princess Casamassima*. New York: Penguin, 1977.

Jarry, Paul. *Les Magasins de nouveautés*. Paris, 1948.

[Jaurès] *Oeuvre de Jean Jaurès*. Vol. VI. Paris, 1933.

Johnson, Douglas, *France and the Dreyfus Affair*. London, 1966.

Judt, Tony. *Socialism in Provence, 1871–1914, A Study in the Origins of the Modern French Left*. Cambridge, Mass. 1979.

Kahn, Gustave. *L'Esthétique de la rue*. Paris, 1901.

Kayser, Jacques. *Les Grandes Batailles du Radicalisme, des origines aux portes du pouvoir, 1820–1901*. Paris, 1962.

Labrousse, E. and F. Braudel, eds. *Histoire économique et sociale de la France*. Vol. IV, pt. 1. Paris, 1979.

Lahor, Jean (Dr. Cazalis). *L'Art nouveau*. Paris, 1901.

―――――. *L'Art pour le peuple à défaut de l'art par le peuple*. Paris, 1902.

Landes, David. *The Unbound Prometheus*. Cambridge, Mass. 1969.

Laudet, F. *La Samaritaine*. Paris, 1933.

Lavedan, Pierre. *Histoire de l'urbanisme à Paris*. Paris, 1975.

Bibliography

Lazare, Louis. *Les Quartiers pauvres de Paris*. Paris, 1868.

Lemaître, Jules. *Les Contemporains. Première série*. Paris, 1886.

Leroy-Beaulieu, Paul. *L'Art de placer et de gérer sa fortune*. Paris, 1906.

Levallois, Ernest. *Une France nouvelle*. Paris, 1907.

————. *Paris propre*. Paris, 1910.

Levillain, Philippe. *Boulanger, fossoyeur de la monarchie*. Paris, 1982.

Lipset, Seymour Martin. *Political Man, The Social Bases of Politics*. New York, 1963.

Lottin, E., *Conséquences du percement de l'avenue de l'Opéra au point de vue commercial*. Paris, 1877.

Loua, Toussaint. *Atlas statistique de la population de Paris*. Paris, 1873.

Le Louvre. Grand hôtel et grands magasins. Paris, n.d. [late 1870s].

Macé, Gustave. *Un Joli Monde*. Paris, 1887.

Malet, Henri. *Le Baron Haussmann et la rénovation de Paris*. Paris, 1973.

Mannheim, Karl. *Man and Society in an Age of Reconstruction*. New York, n.d.

Martin Saint-Léon, Etienne. *Le Petit Commerce français, sa lutte pour la vie*. Paris, 1911.

Masters of the Poster, 1896–1900. Tr. Bernard Jacobson. New York, 1977.

Mayer, Arno J. *Dynamics of Counterrevolution in Europe, 1870–1956*. New York, 1971.

————. *The Persistence of the Old Regime*. New York, 1981.

Mayeur, Jean-Marie. *Les Débuts de la IIIe République, 1871–1898*. Paris, 1973.

————. *Un Prêtre démocrate, l'abbé Lemire, 1853–1928*. Tournai, 1968.

Mény, Georges. *Le Travail à domicile, ses misères, les remèdes*. Paris, 1910.

Meuriot, Paul. *Les Agglomérations urbaines dans l'Europe contemporaine*. Paris, 1897.

Meyer, Arthur. *Ce que mes yeux ont vu*. Paris, 1911.

Miller, Michael. *The Bon Marché, Bourgeois Culture and the Department Store, 1869–1920*. Princeton, N. J., 1981.

Millot, Maurice. *La Comédie boulangiste, chansons et satires*. Paris, 1891.

Missoffe, Michel. *Gyp et ses amis*. Paris, 1932.

Montorgueil, Georges. *Paris au hasard*. Paris, 1895.

————. *La Vie des boulevards, Madeleine-Bastille*. Paris, 1896.

————. *Le Vieux Montmartre*. Paris, 1925.

Moss, Bernard H. *The Origins of the French Labor Movement, 1830–1914*. Berkeley, Calif., 1976.

Moulin, Tony. *Paris en l'an 2000*. Paris, 1869.

Moura, Doctor. *La Butte des Moulins*. Paris, n.d.

Mowry, George. *Theodore Roosevelt and the Progressive Movement*. Reprint edition. New York, 1960.

Mumford, Lewis. *The Culture of Cities*. New York, 1970.

Néré, Jacques. *Le Boulangisme et la presse*. Paris, 1964.

————. *La Crise industrielle de 1882 et le mouvement boulangiste*. 2 vols. Doctoral thesis, University of Paris, 1959.

Neumann, Franz. *The Democratic and the Authoritarian State: Essays in Political and Legal Theory*. Glencoe, Ill., 1957.

Nicolet, Claude. *L'Idée républicaine en France, essai d'histoire critique*. Paris, 1982.

————. *Le Radicalisme*. Paris, 1967.

Pagèze, Louis. *La Ruine de Paris par le métropolitain*. Paris, 1894.

Paris 1900. Masterworks of French Poster Art. Ed. Herman Schardt. Stuttgart, 1970.

Le Parisien chez lui au XIXe siècle, 1814–1914. Exposition Catalogue. Paris, November–February 1977.

Pasdermadjian, H. *The Department Store*. London, 1949.

Paxton, Robert O. *Vichy France, Old Guard and New Order, 1940–1944*. New York, 1972.

Perrot, Michelle. *Les Ouvriers en grève, France, 1871–1890*. 2 vols. Paris, 1974.

Pierrard, Pierre, *Juifs et catholiques français*. Paris, 1970.

Pinkney, David. *Napoleon III and the Rebuilding of Paris*. Princeton, N. J., 1972.

Pollack, Norman. *The Populist Response to Industrial America*. New York, 1966.

Poulantzas, Nicos. *Fascisme et dictature*. Paris, 1974.

Printania, cent ans de jeunesse. Paris, 1965.

Bibliography

Raison-Jourde, Françoise. *La Colonie auvergnate de Paris*. Paris, 1976.

Ranulf, Svend. *Moral Indignation and Middle Class Psychology*. New York, 1962 [originally published 1938].

Raymond, M.-G. *La Politique pavillonnaire*. Paris, 1966.

Rebérioux, Madeleine. *La République radicale? 1898–1914*. Paris, 1975.

Reboux, Paul. *Histoire et les dessous de Paris. Les grands boulevards*. Paris, 1946.

———. *La Rue de la Paix*. Paris, 1927.

Reich, Wilhelm. *The Mass Psychology of Fascism*. New York, 1971.

Reinharez, Claudine, and J. Chamarat. *Boutiques du temps passé*. Paris, 1977.

Rémond, René. *The Right Wing in France from 1815 to de Gaulle*. Tr. James Laux. 2nd ed. Philadelphia, 1969.

Rioux, Jean-Pierre. *Nationalisme et conservatisme, la Ligue de la patrie française, 1899–1904*. Paris, 1977.

Rochefort, Henri. *La Grande Bohême*. Paris, 1868.

Rogin, Michael. *The Intellectuals and McCarthy, The Radical Specter*. Cambridge, Mass., 1968.

Rollet, Henri. *L'Action sociale des catholiques en France, 1871–1901*. Paris, 1947.

Roman, Jules. *Paris Fin de Siècle*. New York, 1960.

Rudelle, Odile. *La République absolue*. Paris, 1982.

Rutkoff, Paul. *Revanche and Revision: Paul Déroulède and the Ligue des Patriotes, 1897–1900*. Doctoral dissertation, University of Pennsylvania, 1971.

Saalman, Howard. *Haussmann: Paris Transformed*. New York, 1971.

Saarinen, Elias. *The City: Its Growth, Its Decay, Its Future*. New York, 1943.

Saint-Martin, André. *Les Grands Magasins. Thèse de droit*, University of Paris, 1900.

Sarrazin, Jehan. *Souvenirs de Montmartre et du quartier latin*. Paris, 1895.

Savatier, Henri. *La Concurrence déloyale, l'accaparement et l'organisation moderne du commerce et de l'industrie*. Paris, 1896.

Scholl, Aurélien. *L'Esprit du boulevard*. Paris, 1886.

Bibliography

Schorske, Carl. *Fin de Siècle Vienna, Politics and Culture.* New York, 1980.

―――. *German Social Democracy, 1905–1917, The Development of the Great Schism.* New York, 1955.

Seager, Frederic. *The Boulanger Affair, Political Crossroad of France, 1886–1889.* Ithaca, N. Y., 1969.

Sorlin, Pierre. *La Croix et les juifs.* Paris, 1967.

―――. *Waldeck-Rousseau.* Paris, 1966.

Stern, Fritz. *The Politics of Cultural Despair, A Study in the Rise of the Germanic Ideology.* Garden City, N. Y., 1965.

Sternhell, Zeev. *La Droite révolutionnaire, 1885–1914.* Paris, 1978.

―――. *Maurice Barrès et la nationalisme français.* Paris, 1972.

―――. *Ni droite, ni gauche, l'idéologie fasciste en France.* Paris, 1983.

Sutcliffe, Anthony. *The Autumn of Central Paris, The Defeat of Town Planning, 1850–1970.* London, 1970.

Talmeyr, Maurice. *La Cité du sang.* Paris, 1901.

―――. *Souvenirs d'avant le déluge.* Paris. 1927.

―――. *Souvenirs de la comédie humaine.* Paris, 1929.

Tharaud, Jean and Jérôme. *La Vie et la mort de Déroulède.* Paris, 1925.

Thomson, David. *Democracy in France Since 1870.* 5th ed. New York, 1969.

[Trotsky] *The Basic Writings of Trotsky.* Ed. Irving Howe. New York, 1963.

Vachon, Marius. *La Crise industrielle et artistique en France et en Europe.* Paris, 1886.

Vaillat, Léandre. *En écoutant Forain.* Paris, 1931.

Vallès, Jules. *Le Tableau de Paris.* Ed. Lucien Scheler. Paris, 1971.

Valmy-Baisse, J. *Les Grands Magasins.* Paris, 1927.

Vanier, Henriette. *La Mode et ses métiers, frivolités et lutte des classes.* Paris, 1960.

Verhaeren, Emile. *Les Villes tentaculaires.* Paris, 1895.

Veuillot, Louis. *Les Odeurs de Paris.* Paris, 1867.

Vibert, Paul. *Mon Berceau.* Paris, 1893.

La Vie d'une grande industrie moderne dans un vieux quartier de Paris, offert par la Belle Jardinière. Paris, 1930.

Bibliography

Volkov, Shulamit. *The Rise of Popular Anti-Modernism in Germany, The Urban Master Artisans, 1873–1896*. Princeton, N. J., 1978.

Vouters, Henri. *Le Petit Commerce contre les grands magasins et les coopératives de consommation*. Paris, 1910.

Warnod, André. *Ceux de la Butte*. Paris, 1947.

———. *Fils de Montmartre*. Paris, 1955.

Watson, D. R. *Georges Clemenceau*. London, 1974.

Weber, Eugen. *The Nationalist Revival in France, 1905–1914*. Berkeley, Calif., 1968.

Weisz, George. *The Emergence of Modern Universities in France, 1863–1914*. Princeton, N. J., 1983.

Willette, Léon-Adolphe. *Feu Pierrot 1857–19?*. Paris, 1919.

Williams Roger L. *Henri Rochefort, Prince of the Gutter Press*. New York, 1966.

Williams, Rosalind. *Dream Worlds. Mass Consumption in Late Nineteenth Century France*. Berkeley and Los Angeles, Calif., 1982.

Wolin, Sheldon S. *Politics and Vision, Continunity and Innovation in Western Political Thought*. Boston, 1960.

Woodward, C. Vann. *Tom Watson, Agrarian Rebel*. Repr. ed. New York, 1975.

Worth, Gaston. *La Couture et la confection des vêtements de femme*. Paris, 1895.

Wright, James E. *The Politics of Populism, Dissent in Colorado*. New Haven, Conn., 1974.

Zeldin, Theodore. *France, 1848–1945*. Vol. II: *Intellect, Taste and Anxiety*, Oxford, 1977.

Zola, Emile. *Au Bonheur des Dames*. Paris, Livre de Poche, n.d.

———. *La Curée*. Pais: Livre de Poche, n.d.

———. *Pot-Bouille*. Paris: Livre de Poche, 1957.

D. ARTICLES

Abercrombie, Patrick. "The Many-Tentacled Town. The Vision of Emile Verhaeren." *Town Planning Review*, 3 (July 1912), pp. 133–149.

Angot des Retours, J. "Les Grands Magasins du Louvre." *La Réforme sociale*, 22 (1891), pp. 95–99.

Bibliography

Audiganne, A. "Industrie et commerce." *Paris dans sa splendeur*, vol. II (Paris, 1861), pp. 1–24.

Bechhofer, Frank, and Brian Elliot. "An approach to a Study of Small Shopkeepers and the Class Structure." *Archives européennes de sociologie*, 9 (1968), pp. 180–202.

Bernard, Joseph, and Louis Hoffman, "Le petit commerce et les grands magasins." *La Réforme sociale*, 61 (1911), pp. 293–303.

Beurdeley, P., and G. Drucker. "Les grands magasins et la liberté commerciale." *Annales économiques*, 5 May 1890, pp. 569–586.

Bonnet, Henri. "La carte des pauvres à Paris." *La Revue des deux mondes, 5e période*, 35 (1906), pp. 381–420.

Cahen, Léon. "L'enrichissment de la France sous la Restauration." *Revue d'histoire moderne*, 5 (May–June 1930), pp. 178–207.

"C'était hier le boulevard." *Vrai*, December–January, n.d., pp. 5–31. [This article is listed in the BHVP subject catalogue under the rubric "Boulevards."]

Charle, Christophe. "Champ littéraire et champ du pouvoir: les écrivains et l'Affaire Dreyfus." *Annales ESC*, 32 (March–April 1977), pp. 240–264.

———. "L'expansion et la crise de la production littéraire." *Actes de la recherche en science sociale*, 4 (July 1975), pp. 44–65.

Cognacq, Gabriel. "Causerie sur les grands magasins." *L'Echo des Roches*, no. *hors série* (Summer 1973).

Colrat, Maurice. "Le rôle social des classes moyennes." *La Réforme sociale*, 60 (1910), pp. 27–28.

Cottereau, Alain. "Le métro et les mouvements municipaux." *Colloque de Dieppe*, 8–9–10 April 1974, *Politiques urbaines et planification des villes*, pp. 776–786.

Crouzet, François. "Encore la croissance économique française au XIXe siècle." *Revue du Nord*, 54 (1972), pp. 271–288.

Daumard, Adeline. "L'avenue de l'Opéra de ses origines à la guerre de 1914." *Bulletin de la société de l'histoire de Paris et de l'Ile-de-France*, 1967, pp. 157–195.

Dausset, Louis. "Paris et les transports en commun." *La Revue*, 15 January 1913, pp. 170–185.

Bibliography

D'Avenel, vte. G. "Le mécanisme de la vie moderne. Les grands magasins." *La Revue des deux mondes*, 4e période, 124 (1894), pp. 329–369.

———. "Le mécanisme de la vie moderne. Les magasins de l'alimentation." *La Revue des deux mondes*, 4e période, 129 (1895), pp. 806–836.

D'Azambuja, G. "Les grands magasins doivent-ils tuer les petits?" *Science sociale*, 32 (October 1901), pp. 277–294.

Delcourt, André. "Les associations parisiennes de propagande en faveur de l'enseignement populaire dans les premières années de la Troisième République." *L'Actualité de l'histoire*, 4 (April 1953), pp. 8–20.

Deverin, Henri, "La résurrection du Palais-Royal." *L'Architecture*, 14 October 1905, pp. 387–388.

Dolléans, Edouard. "Les temps héroiques du syndicalisme." *L'Homme réel*, May 1937, pp. 7–23.

Doty, C. Stewart. "Parliamentary Boulangism after 1889." *The Historian*, 32 (February 1970), pp. 250–269.

Du Maroussem, Pierre. "Les grands magasins tels qu'ils sont." *Revue d'économie politique*, 7 (November 1893), pp. 922–962.

Feyeux, A. "La question des grands et des petits magasins." *La Réforme sociale*, 5 (1883), pp. 358–364.

Fougerousse, A. "Chronique du mouvement social." *La Réforme sociale*, 25 (1893), pp. 797–799.

Fouillé, Alfred. "Dégénérescence? Le passé et le présent de notre race." *La Revue des deux mondes*, 4e période, 131 (1895), pp. 793–824.

Fournier, E. "Promenade dans Paris." *Paris dans sa splendeur*, vol. II (Paris, 1861), pp. 1–76.

Funck-Brentano, Frantz. "Les causes et les conséquences de l'affaiblissement des classes moyennes en France." *La Réforme sociale*, 38 (1899), pp. 549–574.

Girardet, Raoul. "Pour une introduction à l'histoire du nationalisme français." *Revue française de science politique*, 8 (September 1958), pp. 505–528.

Hautecoeur, Louis. "De l'échoppe aux grands magasins." *Revue de Paris*, 54 (August 1933), pp. 811–841.

Hoffmann, Stanley. "Paradoxes of the French Political Com-

Bibliography

munity." In *In Search of France*, ed. Stanley Hoffmann, pp. 1–117. New York, 1965.

Honoré, Frédéric. "Les employés de commerce à Paris." *La Réforme sociale*, 30 (1895), pp. 277–289.

Hutton, Patrick, H. "Popular Boulangism and the Advent of Mass Politics in France, 1886–1890." *Journal of Contemporary History*, 11 (January 1976), pp. 85–106.

Janneau, Guillaume. "De l'échoppe au 'shopping center.' " *L'Oeil*, February 1957, pp. 4–17.

Jay, Raoul. "L'organisation du travail par les syndicats professionnels." *Revue d'économie politique*, 8 (April 1894), pp. 299–338.

Lasswell, Harold. "The Psychology of Hitlerism," *The Political Quarterly*, 4 (1933), pp. 373–384.

Laut, J. M. "Le boulevard d'aujourd'hui." *Le Figaro illustré*, April 1910.

Lavau, G. E. "Classes moyennes et leur comportement politique." In *Partis politiques et classes sociales*, ed. M. Duverger (Paris, 1955), pp. 49–84.

Lévy-Leboyer, Maurice. "La croissance économique en France au XIXe siècle." *Annales ESC*, 23 (July–August 1968), pp. 788–807.

———. "La décélération de l'économie française dans la seconde moitié du XIXe siècle." *Revue d'histoire économique et sociale*, 49 (1971), pp. 485–507.

———. "Les processus d'industrialisation: le cas de l'Angleterre et de la France." *Revue historique*, 239 (April–June 1968), pp. 281–298.

Lorin, Henri. "Etudes sur les principes de l'organisation professionnelle." *L'Association catholique*, 15 July 1892, pp. 3–23.

Martin, Benjamin. "The Creation of the Action Libérale Populaire, An Example of Party Formation in Third Republic France." *French Historical Studies*, 9 (Fall 1976), pp. 660–689.

Mataja, Victor. "Le grand magasin et le petit commerce." *Revue d'économie politique*, 5 (May–June 1891), pp. 451–479.

Mayer, Arno J. "The Lower Middle Class as Historical Problem." *Journal of Modern History*, 47 (September 1975), pp. 409–436.

McBride, Theresa. "A Woman's World: Department Stores and the Evolution of Women's Employment, 1870–1920," *French Historical Studies*, 10 (Fall 1978), pp. 664–683.

Noakes, Jeremy. "The Politics of Economic Despair." *Times Literary Supplement*, 30 May 1975, p. 587.

Nord, Philip. "Le mouvement des petits commerçants et la politique en France de 1888 à 1914." *Le Mouvement social*, 114 (January–March 1981), pp. 35–55.

Parsons, Talcott. "Some Sociological Aspects of the Fascist Movements." In *Essays in Sociological Theory*. Glencoe, Ill., 1963.

Poète, Marcel. "Les idées bergsonniennes et l'urbanisme." In *Mélanges Paul Neguelsco* (Paris, 1935), pp. 575–585.

Ponton, Rémy. "Naissance du roman psychologique." *Actes de la recherche en science sociale*, 4 (July 1975), pp. 66–81.

Rebérioux, Madeleine. "Histoire, historiens et dreyfusisme." *Revue historique*, 255 (April–June 1976), pp. 407–432.

Rémond, René. "Les intellectuels et la politique." *Revue française de science politique*, 9 (December 1959), pp. 860–880.

Richardson, A. E. "Visage du magasin de détail à travers les âges." *Le Commerce moderne* (August–September 1954), pp. 23–27.

Rougerie, Jacques. "Remarques sur l'histoire des salaires à Paris au XIXe siècle." *Le Mouvement social*, 63 (April–June 1968), pp. 71–108.

Saposs, David. "The Role of the Middle Class in Social Development: Fascism, Populism, Communism, Socialism." In *Economic Essays in Honor of Wesley Clair Mitchell* (New York, 1935), pp. 393–424.

Schwarzschild, Steven S. "The Marquis de Morès, The Story of a Failure (1858–1896)." *Jewish Social Studies*, 22 (January 1960), pp. 3–26.

Silverman, Debora. "The 1889 Exhibition: The Crisis of Bourgeois Individualism." *Oppositions*, 8 (Spring 1977), pp. 71–91.

Bibliography

Talmeyr, Maurice. "Cafés-concerts et music-halls." *La Revue des deux mondes, 5e période,* 10 (1902), pp. 159–184.

Tomel, Guy. "Le Palais-Royal." *Monde moderne,* 1899.

Watson, D. R. "The Nationalist Movement in Paris, 1900–1906." In *The Right in France,* edited by David Shapiro, pp. 43–84. London, 1962.

Weber, Eugen. "The Right in France: A Working Hypothesis." *American Historical Review,* 65 (April 1960), pp. 554–568.

Wehler, Hans-Ulrich. "Bismarck's Imperialism 1862–1890." *Past and Present,* 48 (August 1970), pp. 119–155.

————. "Industrial Growth and Early German Imperialism." In *Studies in the Theory of Imperialism,* ed. R. Owen and B. Sutcliffe (London, 1972), pp. 71–90.

Wiener, Jonathan. "Marxism and the Lower Middle Class: A Response to Arno Mayer," *Journal of Modern History,* 48 (December 1976), pp. 666–671.

Wilson, Stephen. "The Antisemitic Riots of 1898 in France." *The Historical Journal,* 16 (December 1973), pp. 789–806.

————. "Catholic Populism in France at the Time of the Dreyfus Affair: The *Union Nationale.*" *Journal of Contemporary History,* 10 (October 1975), pp. 667–705.

————. "The Ligue Antisémitique Française, 1897." *Wiener Library Bulletin,* 25 (1972), pp. 33–38.

Winkler, Heinrich. "From Social Protectionism to National Socialism, The German Small-Business Movement in Comparative Perspective." *Journal of Modern History,* 48 (March 1976), pp. 1–18.

Index

Index

Index

and cultural reaction, 329–46, 349; and the Eiffel Tower, 344; and exposition of 1889, 344; and the French revolutionary tradition, 324–25; and the Métropolitain, 345; and Montmartre, 341–43; as a movement of the far right, 303–304, 349; as a movement of the left, 304–307, 348–49; and municipal liberties, 343; and Nationalism, 349; and *patente* reform, 326, 327, 347–48, 353, 357, 358–59, 360; and the press, 338; and Radicalism, 305–306, 317, 321, 347–48; as a republican movement, 321n, 321–25; and the shopkeeper movement, 301, 307–15, 317–21, 346–50, 487, 489; and socialism, 306–307; and the working class, 304, 305–306, 325–26; and xenophobia, 325–26, 328, 349

boulevards, 87, 91; and anti-Semitism, 373–76; and Boulangism, 335–41; and the boulevard press, 329–31; and *camelots*, 171, 174, 340, 341; and the commission trade, 169; and cultural reaction, 328–31; democratization of, 174–75, 176; and department stores, 133, 135, 180–81; and eclipse of boulevard culture, 463, 479; and the end-of-century slump, 181–82; growing business presence on in the fin de siècle, 170; and Haussmannization, 125; under the July Monarchy, 91, 122; as luxury thoroughfare, 127; and Nationalism, 433, 436–37, 447–50, 462–63; and popular entertainments, 177–79; and prostitution, 171; reaction against commercialization of, 174–76; and the *révolution du bon marché*, 150; under the Second Empire, 93–94, 138–40; shops on, 91–94, 110, 169–170; as site of Christmas street markets, 197; as site of Nationalist *journées*, 433–36; as theater district, 132–33

Bourgeois, Léon, 359, 367

Bourget, Paul, 447, 449

Bourse, 103, 104, 110, 121, 171, 284, 331, 333–34, 338

Bréhant, Louis (shopkeeper militant), 309, 379

Brelay, Ernest, 271, 271n

Brisson, Henri, 28, 37, 38, 316, 347, 423, 430

Brousse, Paul, 40, 43

Bruant, Aristide, 334, 342

business tax. See *patente*

Butte des Moulins, 215–18; contrasted with avenue de l'Opéra, 224, 237; depopulation of, 225; as slum, 220; as victim of Haussmannization, 231; as working-class *quartier*, 218, 231

cabarets, 332–35, 341

Café Anglais, 138, 178, 178n, 329

Café de la Paix, 376, 448

Café de Madrid, 177

Café de Paris, 92, 138, 177

Café des Variétés, 123

Café Riche, 93, 138, 338, 341

cafés: on the boulevards, 122–23;

Index

Index

49; undermechanization of, 145
Funck-Brentano, Frantz, 169, 472
Furniture trade, and the end-of-
century slump, 148, 155, 156,
168, 191, 193–94

Gagne-Petit, 96, 130–31, 166,
205, 211, 214, 254, 296
Gaillard, Jeanne, 82
Gaillon ward, 124
Galérie Colbert, 122, 139, 188
Galérie des Machines, 103, 132,
330
Galérie Vivienne. *See* passage Vi-
vienne
Galéries Lafayette, 169, 296
Galli, Henri, 312, 441, 442, 468
Gambetta, Léon, 3, 163, 177,
306, 313, 321, 349
Garnier, abbé Théodore, 386,
392–95, 396, 399, 405, 467
Garnier, Charles, 92, 224, 329
Gauthier de Clagny, 360, 439
Gazon, Louis (shopkeeper mili-
tant), 45, 58, 263, 271n, 281,
289, 290, 312, 390, 391, 419,
421
Gide, Charles, 199
Gil Blas, 329, 330, 382, 447,
448, 462
Girard, A. (shopkeeper militant),
25, 28, 31, 45, 292, 294,
309–310, 311–12, 346
Girard, E. (shopkeeper militant),
316
Girou, Georges, 319, 421
Goodwyn, Lawrence, 15
Gounod, Charles, 329, 337
Goyau, Georges, 365
Grand-Carteret, John, 75, 451
grands magasins. See department
stores

Great Depression, 4, 10, 13, 24–
25, 480–81; and decline of artisanal sector, 152–53; impact
of on commercial geography of
Paris, 182–91, 200, 482–83,
486; impact of on the Palais-
Royal ward, 240–54, 258; impact of on Paris trades, 191–
200, 202–203, 482; and *Ligue
syndicale* ideology, 282–91, 296,
298; and shopkeeper mobiliza-
tion, 142, 153, 204
Grébeauval, Armand, 345
Green, James, 15, 16
Grenelle ward, 108
Gros-Caillou ward, 50, 456
Grosclaude, Etienne, 330, 447
Guérin, Daniel, 10, 10n
Guérin, Jules, 373; as boulevar-
dier, 375; and the *Ligue syndi-
cale*, 382, 391, 395, 407; and
Nationalism, 411, 412, 422,
434, 436; and the old right,
385, 386; and small-business
organization, 382–83
Guérin, Urbain, 160–61
Guesde, Jules, 362, 363, 426
Guilbert, Yvette, 334
Guyot, Yves, 271, 357
Gyp (comtesse Martel de Janville),
344, 447

Habert, Marcel, 421, 434
Halévy, Daniel, 361
Halévy, Ludovic, 336, 337
Helles, les, 78, 103, 110, 113,
130, 132, 198
Halles ward, 312, 441, 451
Hamel, Alfred (shopkeeper mili-
tant), 45, 196, 256, 257, 257n,
258

Index

Harmel, Léon, 392, 395–405,
407, 472
hat industry, 145
hat trade, 185; in the Palais-Royal
ward, 247; and unemployment,
155
Hauser, Arnold, 106
Haussmann, baron Georges, 76,
99, 100, 101, 102, 103, 104,
106, 107, 110, 111, 118, 220,
483
Haussmann, boulevard, 106, 131
Haussmannization, 100–101; and
building design, 105–106, 114,
125, 132; and commercialization of central Paris, 109–12;
and the department store, 127–
37; economic motives of, 101–
104; imagery of, 99, 133; and
impact on commercial geography, 120–27, 138–42, 482,
486; and impact on industry,
107–109; and impact on social
geography, 113–18; and machine architecture, 103; and the
Palais-Royal ward, 214–40,
257–58; and Paris street system, 102–103; political motives
of, 104–105; and rectilineal
street design, 105; shopkeeper
hostility to, 296, 298; and
shopkeeper mobilization, 100–
101, 121, 137–38, 141–42; social motives of, 105–106
Hauteville, rue d', 109
Hénard, Eugène, 190, 238, 255
Henry, Colonel, 410, 411, 418
Hériot, Auguste, 60, 80, 81, 118
Hiélard, L., 34
Hoffman, Stanley, 3
Hofstadter, Richard, 488

Honoré, Frédéric, 354
Hôtel de Ville, 96, 104, 130
Hugo, Victor, 105, 343, 344,
345, 374, 453; admired by
shopkeepers, 276
Hugonet, A. (shopkeeper mili-
tant), 386
Humbert, Alphonse, 345, 423n
Huysmans, J.-K., 178

Institut international pour l'étude du
problème des classes moyennes, 472–
73
Italiens, boulevard des, 93, 170,
171, 172, 173, 186, 338, 376
Ivry, 108, 109

Jacques, Edouard, 302, 310
Jaluzot, Jules, 61, 66, 79, 80, 81,
131, 279, 297, 354, 355, 429
Jamais, Emile, 353, 355–56
Jaurès, Jean, 362, 425, 453, 464
Jay, Louise, 61, 81
jewelry trade: and the end-of-century slump, 155, 195–96; and
Ligue syndicale recruitment, 96;
in the Palais-Royal, 251–54; in
the Palais-Royal ward, 241–44
Jockey Club, 139, 176, 339, 375
journalism: Boulangist attitudes
toward, 322, 322n; and the
Boulangist press, 338; and the
boulevard press, 329–31; and
department store advertising,
69, 165; and Nationalism,
448–49, 453, 459–60; shopkeeper attitudes toward, 293;
transformation of in the fin de
siècle, 460, 461, 463
Judt, Tony, 16

Index

Index

Index

Index

Index

Index

Index

Index

Library of Congress Cataloging-in-Publication Data

Nord, Philip, 1950–
 Paris shopkeepers and the politics of resentment.

 Bibliography: p.
 Includes index.
 1. Merchants—France—Paris—Political activity—
History—19th century. 2. Stores, Retail—France—
Paris—History—19th century. 3. Paris (France)—
Politics and government. I. Title.
HF5429.6.F7N67 1986   322'.3'0944361   85-42695
ISBN 0-691-05454-1